Buddha in Sri Lanka

BUDDHA
IN
SRI LANKA

Remembered Yesterdays

SWARNA WICKREMERATNE

Foreword by

GEORGE D. BOND

STATE UNIVERSITY OF NEW YORK PRESS

Published by
State University of New York Press, Albany

© 2006 State University of New York

For information, address State University of New York Press, Albany, NY
www.sunypress.edu

Production by Christine Hamel
Marketing by Susan M. Petrie

Library of Congress Cataloging-in-Publication Data

Wickremeratne, Swarna, 1939–
    Buddha in Sri Lanka : remembered yesterdays / Swarna Wickremeratne ;
foreword by George D. Bond.
        p. cm.
    Includes bibliographical references and index.
    ISBN: 978-0-7914-6881-4 (hardcover : alk. paper)
    ISBN: 978-0-7914-6882-1 (pbk. : alk. paper)
    1. Theravāda Buddhism—Sri Lanka—Customs and practices. 2. Religious life—
Theravāda Buddhism. 3. Sri Lanka—Religious life and customs. 4. Wickremeratne,
Swarna, 1939–   . I. Title.

BQ356.W56 2006
294.3'91095493—dc22

                                                              2005030808

                    10 9 8 7 6 5 4 3 2 1

In loving memory to my father, who made all things possible.

And to my father-in-law, my other father,
who believed in me and guided me in meaningful ways.

May the good karma in this, my effort, go to
all beings in their search for love and compassion.

All that we are is the result of our thoughts
It is founded on our thoughts
And made up of our thoughts
With our thoughts we make the world

ॐ

Should a person perform a meritorious deed,
He should do it again and again,
He should find pleasure therein;
Blissful is the accumulation of merit

—From the Dhammapada

Contents

Foreword

There is an old debate in the study of religion and culture concerning who understands the subject best: the insider or the outsider. Some have argued that only the insiders can truly understand a religion, for they participate in it and see its inner meanings. Others, however, have argued that the outsider has a distinct advantage. The classic statement of this position was offered by Durkheim, who held that the outside observer had a better opportunity to understand the structure and meaning of religious experience. Durkheim noted, "Merely because there exists a 'religious experience' . . . it by no means follows that the reality which grounds it should conform objectively with the idea the believers have of it" (*The Elementary Forms of Religious Life*, trans. K. Fields [New York: Free Press, 1995, 420]). Thus, the debate between the insiders and outsiders has raged over the years. Historians of religion have tended to gravitate toward a more dialogical position, one that accepts that the truth in this debate lies somewhere in the middle. Wilfred C. Smith in his book, *The Meaning and End of Religion*, suggested that the study of religion should focus not on artifacts or texts but on persons. The outsider should try to understand the viewpoint of the insiders and should dialogue with the insiders to appreciate their perspective on the meaning of the religion. This same wisdom has been given by anthropologists such as Evans-Pritchard and Mary Douglas, who emphasized the need to focus on the people rather than the texts or the beliefs of a religion and culture. The field of Buddhist studies has also stressed the importance of dialogue with the insiders and has urged an appreciation of not only the texts but also the people and their practices. Richard Gombrich's key study, *Precept and Practice: Traditional Buddhism in the Rural Highlands of Ceylon* (1971), made the point that the study of Buddhism should extend beyond texts and traditional academic boundaries.

Since then many books have been written that have attempted to balance the Westerners' outside view of Buddhism with an understanding of the insiders' perspectives and practices. Scholars have come to recognize that this dialogue is necessary in order to understand religion, but the question is always, how can one establish it?

Swarna Wickremeratne's book provides one way, and a very interesting way, of entering into dialogue with Sri Lankan Buddhism. Through her stories and reflections on the practices of Buddhists in her homeland, she offers the reader new insights into the meaning and intention of Theravada Buddhism. This is not a study of Buddhist philosophy or texts, although she has some valuable comments on both, but it is primarily a memoir of her experiences with Buddhists and Buddhism in Sri Lanka. The stories she relates allow the reader to engage with the insiders in the religion. Having been a frequent visitor and sometime resident of Sri Lanka for over three decades, I appreciate the value of these kinds of stories. I know that my own understanding of Buddhism has always been enormously enriched by my contacts with friends in Sri Lanka and by my experiences of living in Buddhist communities where one can share in their lives and viewpoints. Swarna Wickremeratne's stories represent the next best thing to visiting Sri Lanka and establishing a dialogue with the people. Her accounts of monks she has known and of her Buddhist relatives in Sri Lanka provide the kinds of insights that one can only get from those who participate in the culture and the religion. She relates wonderful stories about growing up in Sri Lanka and experiencing Buddhism from the inside. For example, she tells us what it was like to celebrate the Sinhala New Year and to participate in Buddhist devotional practices in her home. She also explains the Sri Lankan attitude toward relic worship, including the belief that if one does not offer devotion to a relic it will disappear. These are the kinds of details that one seldom finds in scholarly works but that are basic for an understanding of the culture of Buddhism in Sri Lanka. Some of her stories provide valuable historical information about figures such as the Venerable Mapalagama Wipulasara and other monastic leaders. She also provides important details about the life of the monks, including the difficulties that they experience in trying to serve the people in the rural areas. Another important theme in the book concerns the lives of women in Sri Lanka and their practice of the religion. Having grown up in the culture, she is able to describe the perspectives of Buddhist women and the ways that women are viewed in that culture. She tells us, for example, about her experiences as a woman traveling to the sacred shrine of Kataragama and how she participated in that great festival.

As an insider to Sri Lankan Buddhism, but also as an outsider who has lived and studied in the West, Swarna Wickremeratne has a good standpoint for fostering a dialogical understanding of Buddhism. She conveys many insights about Buddhism and also much of the joy that Buddhists have in the practice of their religion. Through her stories and accounts the reader/outsider can understand better the symbols of ultimacy in the quest of the Buddhist insiders and can also appreciate the sense in which both insiders and outsiders are engaged in a common quest.

George D. Bond
Northwestern University

Terminology and Related Concepts

The island of Lanka, my birth place and the focus of my book, is named in the Mahabharata but occurs frequently as one would expect, in the great epic of the Ramayana. The word *Lanka* means shining, resplendent, and golden. The Arab term for Lanka was *Serendib*. It has been suggested that this word was itself a derivative of the word *Sinhala-Diwipa* becoming in time *Serendiva*. The land was known as Ceylon during the entire period of British rule and widely known as such. The word *Ceylon* is a derivative of the Dutch word *Zeilan*. The current term *Sri Lanka* is a neologism, coined in recent times.

The terms *Sinhala* and *Sinhalese* are interchangeable in common usage and could mean either the Sinhala language or the Sinhalese as a self-conscious ethnic group.

The majority of the Sinhalese are Buddhists. Due to historical influences arising from the close relationships of Lanka to South India, many Hindu gods and deities have become objects of continued worship by Buddhists. I use the terms *gods, devas, deviyo,* and *deities* to refer to them and to other gods indigenous to Lanka such as the gods Natha and Saman. On the whole, the terms occur interchangeably in the text. Hindu gods are accommodated in devales or kovils.

In a variety of situations I have used the word *dana* (literally "giving") in the text, the meaning is made plain in each instance by the context in which the term occurs. In Buddhist usage in Sri Lanka, the term *dana* is used to mean different types of giving for merit. The term "giving dana" is a common usage for performing a dana ceremony, although it may mean "giving a giving."

Pirit or *paritta* are protective chants recited by Buddhist monks to laypeople. It is referred to as "pirit chanting." When chanting is performed ceremoniously it is referred to as "pirit ceremony" or "pirit chanting ceremony." I use the terms *pirit chanting,* and *pirit ceremony* to mean the same act of reciting pirit.

I use *stupa*, *chetiya*, and *dagaba* interchangeably. They refer to a large bell or mound-shaped edifice in Buddhist temples in Sri Lanka and elsewhere. The structures are a part of the baggage of Buddhism from India. According to Buddhist belief they contain relics of the Buddha.

Where it was appropriate I have used Sinhala verses with translations from many different sources, fourteenth century poems, folklore, and Jataka stories that have come to me transgenerationally and from what I have learned in Sunday school in my youth. They are very much a part of Buddhist lore in Sri Lanka. Some Buddhist terms that I use in the text may not always reflect their meaning literally but resonate in popular Buddhist culture.

Acknowledgments

This book was written in Chicago over a period of two years. In a more meaningful sense, however, its genesis goes back to the significant inspirational springs that were a part of my childhood in Ceylon. I take this opportunity to reverentially pay tribute to my late father, who I remember had faith in me and in my potential and taught me with vintage gravitas the ethics of right and wrong, and the significance of moral choices. I would also pay tribute to my traditional-minded mother, at whose feet early in childhood I learned the ins and outs of Buddhist domestic rituals, the folklore of Buddhism, and the charm of Buddhist temples. Above all, by her example, she showed how meaningful it was to practice the noble Buddhist ethic of *dana* (generosity, giving) and not count the cost. In a sense one remains a child, yearning always to release the best in oneself. In family vein I wish to acknowledge, also, my debt to my brother Bernard and his wife, Sheila, who encouraged and helped me to immigrate to the United States. My brother Henry and his wife, Muriel, deserve mention. Henry's help and encouragement to the family, has been a constant source of strength, especially in my early days in Oxford, and then throughout my life.

In the critical years that mattered, however, the towering presence in my mind is that of Stanley Jayaraj Tambiah who, as a professor of anthropology at Harvard, together with his wonderful wife, Marywinn, took my small family under their wings and helped us in many ways through my two and a half years at Harvard. With their help and inspiration, I made a critical career switch from being an Oxford-trained educationalist to an information specialist in the trendy, fast-moving universe of information retrieval. My heartfelt gratitude and thanks go to Tambiah and Marywinn for a generosity, the like of which I have not encountered since.

My deepest gratitude to George Bond for his kindness and intellectual support. I would like to thank Tracy Pintchman of the Theology Department at Loyola University Chicago who first read my manuscript, encouraged me, and on her own explored the possibilities of getting it published.

In the matter of putting the manuscript together, I was helped by the venerable Deegalle Mahinda of Bath Spa University in England who went through my Pali usage and made insightful observations on my manuscript. He was a continuing source of encouragement. I owe more than a nominal debt to Maduluwave Sobitha, the chief incumbent of the Sri Naga Vihara in Kotte. Our association spans more than two decades. I am grateful for his insights and his willingness to share his ideas. In the same vein I wish to express my gratitude to the venerable Thalangama Devananda of the newly established Indiana Buddhist Institute, in Forte Wayne, Indiana, who kept my spirits up and provided inner-circle input on the working of Buddhist institutions in Sri Lanka. He is the fit *golanama* of his great mentor, the venerable Aluthnuvara Anurudha, the chief incumbent of the Kotte Rajamaha Vihare, who figures in the text and was an invaluable research source. I found the cumulative inputs of a variety of Buddhist monks a rare and invaluable resource. I began to see the world through their eyes and it was enriching.

I owe a great debt of gratitude to my husband Ananda who gave me courage and with unwavering enthusiasm read my manuscript, encouraged me in moments of despair, revised and re-revised it and constantly saw to it that I was doing my work. It is his book as it is mine. I warmly thank my son, Channa, who encouraged me and appreciated feeling the usefulness of the work I was doing. My daughter, Ranmini, was my mentor in critically going through the manuscript and suggesting with insight when changes could be made. Her input was of critical relevance, and I thank her for her encouragement and attending to the task of its scrutiny with charm, grace, and impish humor. My oldest sister, Senelatha, and her husband, Wasantha, my sisters Sudharma and Mallika, my nephew, Kirthi, and his charming wife, Thilani, encouraged me with great affection and pride.

I also take this opportunity to say a big thank you for my dear friend of my youth M. Henry Gunawardane, who encouraged me to go to university and was a strong source of support emotionally and in many other ways at difficult times.

Many loving hands helped me on, and I thank numerous friends in Sri Lanka who would put aside their obvious burdens and travails to listen to me and enhance my insights with unfailing charm. I would also like to thank my colleagues, Sister Rita Stalzer, C.S.J., and Carol Franklin of Loyola University Chicago, for encouragement they gave me. I acknowledge Karan Shah for helping to format the manuscript, and Matt Hohmann for his editorial help.

A special work of thanks to Mohan Wickremersinghe for allowing me to use the photograph on the front cover of the book, and Manjula Peiris for the map.

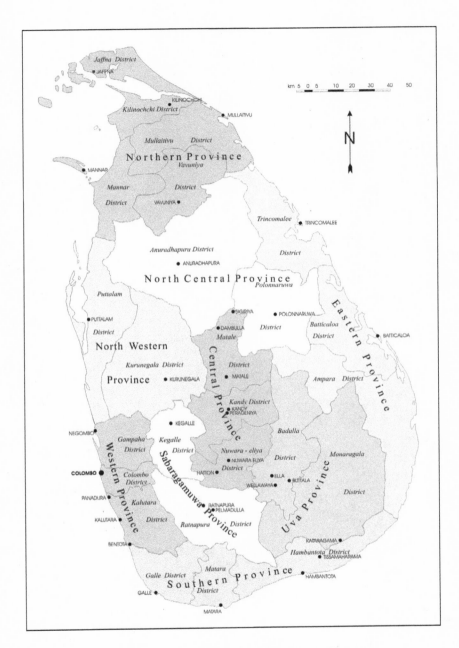

Sri Lanka: Administrative Districts and Main Towns

ONE

Beginnings and Looking Beyond

———————

How does one translate amorphous thoughts into the formal language of reason, to make sense? I do not know. I cannot think of sophisticated academic reasons for writing this book. It was a labor of love. I was moved by the simple notion that what I had to say might be of interest to others. In the pages that follow I explain how I came to be interested in the fascinating study of Buddhism in Sri Lanka, a people I love, and what all that has meant to me.

Born in Sri Lanka, I was exposed to culturally diverse experiences. I grew up in a Buddhist home under the influence of my Buddhist mother and participated in traditional Buddhist rituals. I was also influenced by Catholic relatives, who were our care givers. Becoming a part of my husband Ananda's family exposed me to a host of new cultural experiences, giving me opportunities to interact with Buddhist monks and Buddhist society in general. In a simple and unpretentious way, I thought of sharing my experiences with my friends, colleagues, and others. I am bewildered by the variety of experiences I have encountered in my life: living in three continents, studying (if that is the word) in three universities, being a citizen in three countries, involved in the political process of each, and making warm and enduring friends of different hues, inclinations, and modes of thinking. It was as if I were born and reborn in multiple incarnations, each incarnation bringing with it elements of serendipity and joy. I wonder at each mile I have walked, people I have known, books I have read, places I have worked, trees and flowers I have come to know, and beds on which I have slept. I often wonder who am I, where I belong. I have become in a sense homeless. All these things may appear banal, but they overwhelm me.

I am in many ways bicultural. I live between two worlds. America is my adopted country, the "melting pot," a nation that promises to transform all immigrants into Americans. I wake up to a Starbruck's coffee and a dough-nut, drink Evian water, play with Ipods, exchange text messages, visit crowded super malls, and watch television with its endless array of sports and celebri-ties. *Oprah Winfrey*, *Larry King Live*, the ubiquitous CNN, the spinmeisters of the media, and *Saturday Night Live* are all familiar to me. My other world is very different: the sun rises and sets at the same time every day, with no well-defined climatic variations, the tropical paradise. Buddha is worshipped along with many other gods, and a variety of practices and beliefs, each with their own festivals and holidays. Social inequality is institutionalized in the caste system, authority is respected, cricket is known, loved, and played. This then is the land of my birth, Lanka, a gem in the summer seas. I toggle between the two cultures. I am neither one nor the other. I am both in and in between two contrasting worlds.

Although I have made the United States my home for almost three decades, I have never left Sri Lanka. Some of my family still lives there. I have friends there and a home I visit regularly. I speak the languages of Sri Lanka, and I am much rooted there. My imagination, interests, associations, and thoughts never migrated here.

A young man in London was going through the private papers of his father, a writer, who had recently died. The son had often suggested to his father that he should live elsewhere, in a better place. The father would invari-ably smile and say that he was happy where he was. The son discovered the rea-son after his death. Prominently highlighted on the inner cover of a diary the father had diligently kept were these words ascribed to an unknown Buddhist monk: "Make yourself at home wherever you live, but call no place your home." It is an ideal impossible to live up to. Here in this wintry wasteland, it is with a clutch that I hear far away in Sri Lanka the haunting call of the *koha*, one rarely sees but hears vibrantly heralding the dawn of new things, new hopes.

Mine is a chronicle of personal experiences, intended for the general reader. As the phrase goes in popular Buddhist literature, it is *hudi janayage pahan sanvegaya sandaha*, which, in a loose translation means, for "the edifica-tion, well-being, and enjoyment of the many." I quote and refer to Buddhist texts and the Buddhist dharma, but do not address the doctrinal aspects of Buddhism and its teachings. Nor do I go into the history or origin of the con-cepts and practices that I refer to in this work. You will find merely my obser-vations, encounters, and reminiscences of a layperson, a woman. It is a soft treading of the ground.

LIVING IN KANDY

I consider myself fortunate to have met a number of well-known Buddhist monks distinguished for their scholarship and erudition, as well as traditional monks who in their modest inconspicuous way serve the needs of a large number of Buddhist laypersons, with hardship and sacrifice. I was also fortunate to become connected with Ananda's family in Kandy. That was my good karma. The family was respected and recognized in Kandy for their patronage and support of Buddhist causes. As a member of this household, I was exposed to many interesting experiences, which made deep impressions on me.

When I moved to Kandy, as a young adult, I did not realize, as I do now, that immigration from Colombo to Kandy amounted to something more than a mere change of scene. It was in Kandy, especially in the environment of the Dalada Maligava (Temple of the Tooth Relic) and the lake, that I felt the living presence of Buddhism. There was in the air certain serenity and ancientness as if the past were whispering to me. The muffled sounds of the *hevisi* drums being beaten at the Dalada Maligava and carried across the placid waters of the lake enhanced this feeling. Indeed, the town of Kandy and the surrounding areas abounded in temples and *viharas* remarkably preserving the ambience of the original structures. A breeze stirred, and the rustling leaves in the garden would whisper tales of Kandy long ago in the days of the fabled kings. It was said that if you walked around the lake late at night (a distance of a little over two miles), you would run into the deranged figure of Ahelepola Kumarihamy, asking whether you had seen her children, all of whom were cruelly killed (regardless of age or innocence), victims of the rage of the last king of Kandy.

I had many Catholic relatives whose belief systems were an integral part of my growing up. I attended Catholic schools in Sri Lanka, studied the Bible with Irish nuns, participated in rituals, and learned to pray using a rosary. Working in a Catholic university here in Chicago gave me the opportunity to attend courses relating to biblical studies and the history of religions. My writings reflect these influences. It is as if I had walked under many arches in my life, each one surpassing its predecessor in the impact it made on me. I have come to realize that what is beautiful about life is its subtle, slow unfolding.

In the following chapters I have referred to Buddhist texts I studied, including popular Buddhist literature and Jataka stories. Jataka stories in particular were part of my upbringing, side by side with Grimm's fairy tales. I have also quoted from writers such as Robert Knox, who among others enhanced my knowledge of the social, religious, and political history of Sri Lanka, which I studied as undergraduates in Peradeniya University.

AN ENGLISH CAPTIVE

Robert Knox was taken into captivity in 1659 by the king of Kandy, who was ruling the near-impregnable and powerful kingdom in the highlands of Ceylon (Sri Lanka). The king had effective control over parts of the seacoast, although the maritime regions were technically in the hands of the Dutch, who had wrested these areas from their predecessors, the Portuguese. Knox's father, the captain of an ill-fated frigate, was shipwrecked off the coast of Ceylon along with eighteen of his shipmates and died shortly afterward, an event Knox describes with touching and deep-felt affection. Knox and many of his companions spent twenty years of somewhat lax and privileged captivity. They learned to speak Sinhala, dressed in Kandyan clothing, grew their hair like the Kandyan men, and lived like villagers. Unlike many of his fellow captives, Knox did not marry a Sinhala woman. He traveled around meeting a variety of people so that his impressions of Sinhala culture are considered reliable. He escaped to Dutch territory and finally reached England, where he became a legend, and in the spirit of the age, a heroic Christian, whose faith had survived infinite tribulations. In a celebrated account of this remarkable period of his life, *An Historical Relation of Ceylon*, Knox has written an insightful ethnography of the Sinhalese in the Kandyan kingdom, their customs, language, rituals, religious beliefs, and Buddhism. His observations on the last subject are often vitiated by his unbending fealty to his own faith, often attributing the evidence of ethical and moral behavior, which he found among the Sinhalese, to the influence of Christianity.

Living in America meant the evolution in my mind of new perspectives and images, which enriched my understanding of what is loosely described as Buddhist culture. My professional training in information technology in Simmons College, along with my work in university libraries both at Harvard and in Chicago, gave me unique opportunities for accessing a rich wealth of literature on Buddhism and its culture. I met a variety of graduate students and professors working on Buddhism in Sri Lanka, who wanted assistance in finding difficult-to-access materials. In this way too I became familiar with materials relating to Buddhist literature.

THEY ARE BUDDHISTS

The simple fact of having been born into a Buddhist household meant that I was immersed in the culture of Buddhism and that it was deeply ingrained into my system. Due to other influences and experiences I refer to in the text, I was able to acquire a detached perspective, which in some ways helped me to look at Buddhism from the angle of an outsider. In a way I was discovering Buddhism in my adult life.

A reader unfamiliar with the subject of Buddhism may rightly wonder who a "Buddhist" is. To be a Buddhist one has to take refuge in the Buddha, the dharma, and the Sangha, and take *pansil* (Five Precepts), commit oneself to observe them, thereby becoming a Buddhist layman. Five Precepts should be recited daily and kept always. In addition one takes part in simple ceremonies, goes to the temple on *poya* (full moon) days, and makes ritual offerings of food from time to time to monks, a practice that is called "*dana.*" Above all one lives a spiritual life conscious of the need to be compassionate and generous.

OUR COLONIAL MASTERS

I give a glimpse of the way Buddhists practice their religion, or a lived Buddhism. I have attempted to put together the ancient rituals and practices of Buddhists, their extrareligious belief systems, and how Buddhism influenced these and how these have in turn become part of Buddhist practice. I have tried to show the role of temples and Buddhist monks in Sri Lankan society. Temples in Sri Lanka are not only places of worship but serve multiple purposes. They are also repositories of knowledge, schools imparting knowledge, sanctuaries for the ill, both in mind and body and serve a host of other functions. As in other religions, there is a difference between the precept and the practice of Buddhism. Sri Lankan Buddhism is unique, perhaps because Sri Lanka was occupied and ruled by foreigners for five centuries. The Portuguese made a great effort to convert the natives to Catholicism, especially in the regions bordering the sea, which were dominated by them. The Dutch who followed them were Protestants and in turn carried out their missionary activities of conversion by giving the natives material rewards and positions in the administration, a policy that greatly facilitated their conversion.

The trend continued when the British displaced the Dutch to become the undisputed colonial masters of the island until Sri Lanka became an independent country in 1948. Some Sri Lankans tempted by official favors became Christians, but the vast majority remained Buddhists and maintained connections with the temple and the monks. The first-generation converts were mostly Christian by name, but the missionaries focused on the generation to come, who eventually became faithful Christians. In contrast to the time of the Portuguese when Sri Lankans who were converted to Christianity became Catholics, under the British, the converts became Protestants, Anglicans, Wesleyans, or Baptists. In spite of the bitter sectarian rivalry in England, in the colonies the Christian missionaries made common cause against Buddhism, in what they thought was a benighted heathen land.

TWO CULTURES THEN AND NOW

For centuries Buddhism and the Buddhist monks had received great support from the state. The traditional function of a king in a Buddhist country was to protect Buddhism. He was given the epithet *dharmaraja*, which means "the lord who rules righteously." It was his duty to give patronage to Buddhism and refrain from doing anything that would be detrimental to its interests. However, with foreign rule, Buddhist temples and the monks lost the traditional patronage from the state. Moreover, as an inducement to adopt the new religion—Christianity—natives were given many forms of material incentives. There were many temptations in the form of the granting of honorific titles that appealed to a people, still immersed in the ethos of feudal thinking, inducements of a monetary nature, grants of land, government jobs, tax exemptions, and policies of covert persecution. In spite of all enticements, the majority of the Sinhala people remained Buddhists.

The European presence (from 1505 until 1948) together with Christianity confronted Buddhism with a challenge with far-reaching consequences, which outlasted the periods of foreign domination. The legislative changes brought about by the European rulers had an adverse impact on existing Buddhist institutions (primarily Buddhist monasteries). More far-reaching though less visible were the changes within the Buddhist community. Uneven economic opportunities that arose out of policies of the British led to the rise of an anglicized elite class of Sri Lankans who, though comparatively few in number, wielded enormous influence. They saw themselves as the representatives of the people and were regarded as such by the British rulers. The urban-centered elite could be clearly differentiated from the mass of the Sri Lankans. The British reached out to the latter by reviving traditional institutions of governance such as *gamsabas* (village councils) and by restoring irrigational facilities, the twin institutions on which the rural agrarian system had been based. The well-intended policies had the effect of reinforcing the village ethos and further perpetuating the cultural gap between the two forms of Buddhists, which I have sought to identify.

The duality marked the final emergence of mutually separate Sri Lankan cultures. Some of the elite elements in Sri Lankan society became Christians, a change that clearly enhanced their mobility. The majority remained nominally Buddhists. But in a self-conscious way they distanced themselves (with increased Anglicanization) from the traditional forms and rituals, which were associated with Buddhism. In time they became the progenitors of a new form of urban Buddhism, choosing to relate to Buddhism largely in an intellectual way in terms of its attractive ideology. Pioneer Western books on Buddhism created in their minds, as the ideal norm, a textualist-based vision of what a Buddhist society ought to be. A class divide that originally arose from the impact of economic factors was legitimized by religion and culture. When the dust cleared, in Sri Lanka there were two forms of Buddhism with the potential for future differentiation. Sri Lanka for all the differences that prevail is a mix of things, a pastiche of sorts. The overall phenomenon I have described has the potential to create a sense of unease among Sri Lankan Buddhists as to whom they really are.

A BUDDHIST CULTURAL IDIOM

I have tried in the pages that follow to share with the reader my impressions of Buddhist society as it exists in Sri Lanka today. By interweaving my own personal experiences and impressions with what I describe, I hope that I have succeeded in giving the text authenticity and meaning. I tried to deal with the trends of a culture influenced largely by Buddhism, which has existed in Sri Lanka for well over two thousand years. I am aware that culture is an amorphous term and one hard to define with any degree of precision. It may, however, be sensed or appropriated by its manifestations. I refer to modalities of thinking, idioms of speech, syntaxtical forms of grammar with a partiality for impersonal speech, and preference for the passive voice focusing on action rather than an author. These may be related to the matrix of Buddhism and its weltanschauung, or as the world view was popularly understood at ground level by Sri Lankan Buddhists themselves. I found it fascinating that numerous Catholic friends and relatives in Sri Lanka carry on in their everyday conversations and actions as if they themselves were part of a Buddhist matrix but of course being unaware of it. It was for example not uncommon for Sri Lankan Catholics to refer to bad karma or to see the effects of some situation in terms of not doing the right thing in previous lives, and so on. Even after the lapse of many generations of being Catholic in a predominantly Buddhist country, they have been unable to completely shed cultural affinity to Buddhists and Buddhism.

A WORD ABOUT THE TEXT

To get down to more practical matters, I have divided the text into themes. In the first section I deal with the overall cultural setting of Sri Lankan society, its hierarchical nature based on the structures of caste and underlying ideological assumptions pertaining to caste. I have traced belief systems, trasgenerational modes of thinking, and finally the overall pervasive influence of Buddhism in Sri Lankan culture. Within the cultural dimension I have not neglected the significant role played by indigenous medicine and its therapeutic systems.

In the second section I have concentrated on seminal Buddhist theories pertaining to karma, rebirth, and the significant Buddhist tradition of giving (*dana*) and how Buddhists deal with death. In doing so I have taken care to move away from doctrinal and theological perspectives, focusing instead on these very themes as they are realized in actual religious practice as the reality of living sociological Buddhism in Sri Lanka. I have written about the significance of healing rites, *pirit* (ceremonies), pilgrimages, *bana* preaching, and perennially popular Bodhi *pujas* as part and parcel of the Buddhist popular culture.

Whichever way we look at Buddhist culture, its core integral element in recent times has been the institution of the Sangha (order of monks) in Sri

Lanka. I have treated the order of Buddhist monks in my narration not as it is widely perceived as an undifferentiated monolith but as a vibrant diversity: the traditional monks and a new facet of monks who are sensitive to the changing needs of the Buddhist laity and have creatively adapted strategies and forms of interactivity with the lay community to meet broader social needs. In the process, I have highlighted the personalities of prominent monks who belong to both genres. On the whole, in the narration of my text, I have seen the new developments as evidence of the resilience and dynamism of the monkhood. This sensitivity to change might well be a key principle in understanding the successful survival of the institution of Buddhist monkhood well over two millennia.

Last, as a segment in its own right, I have brought together into a single focus the widely practiced extra-Buddhist religious forms of worship, some traditional, and others innovatively novel, which is a significant feature in the newly emerging topography of Buddhism in Sri Lanka. I have drawn attention to the virtual rejuvenation and resurrection of the traditional pantheon of gods associated with popular Buddhism and newer and innovative forms of worship. As part of my overview I have encompassed the widespread resort to propriation of spirits and godlings, traditionally associated with healing, enmity, and wrecking vengeance on enemies.

Since all of the foregoing is about the structure of the text, in originally conceiving in my mind what should and should not constitute its main themes, I was aware of the feminist dimension or what is colloquially called "feminist issues." It is these days *de riguer* to explicitly touch on feminism in the unraveling of broad sociological issues, so why not in a study such as mine, which purports to be a survey of popular Buddhism in Sri Lanka viewed in the prism of continuing personal recollections and first hand experiences? I was also very much aware that the harp in feminist-biased studies is played primarily on two strings, namely, drawing attention to total negligence of feminist issues and emphasizing discrimination.

Buddhism in Sri Lanka is a mixed bag. First in Buddhist theory, and indeed as it is consciously practiced, there is no gender differentiation when it comes to the overarching schema of the dharma. In the rituals I refer to in the text extensively—namely Buddhist prayer, homage, taking the precepts, lighting lamps at sacred localities, Bodhi *pujas*, pilgrimages, and so on, or in the initiation and execution of each ritual—women are key players, or put in another way, women in Sri Lanka are not ritually excluded as in Hinduism. In a sense one has to scratch hard to see evidence of institutionalized discrimination.

THE PERILS OF A BUDDHIST EVE

Within the Buddhist historical tradition we have Buddha's reluctance, in spite of the importunities of his disciple Ananda, and the dramatic *pada yatra* of

Buddha's foster mother Prajapathi Gotami, to establish a feminist order. We see too the failure of such an order to take root in all Buddhist countries, notwithstanding the moderate success achieved in Sri Lanka by Bhikkhuni Kusuma to establish such an order. Buddhist monks in Sri Lanka are hesitant to give it recognition and accept the Bhikkhuni order as equal in status. Last summer when I was researching in Thailand on popular Buddhism, for a period of several weeks, the Bangkok news media dramatically highlighted the controversies concerning the issue of feminism. In northern Thailand a Buddhist patriarch of a famous monastery excluded women from entering the inner sanctum of his monastery, which hitherto they had freely done, on the grounds of menstruation and pollution. The patriarch of Doi Suthep in Chiang Mai followed suit. All over Thailand educated elitist Buddhist women were in uproar and agitated for the removal of the prohibition. When I left, a sensible compromise, which is the hallmark of Buddhism in Thailand and accounts for its enviable resilience, was being worked out.

Then again, in popular Buddhist belief, women are born to the unfortunate state of being women presumptively because of bad karma from past lives. Its corollary is that in their present lives if they live up to Buddhist standards and consciously do good karma, they will be rewarded by being born as a man in their next life. There is a practice in traditional homes, Buddhist, Hindu, and even converted Christians, of the wife worshipping her spouse. That the husband is the theoretical head of the household is rarely questioned. His authority prevails even where the wife is more educated than the husband. These ideas and practices, among a host of others, have become a part of the Sri Lankan culture and are transmitted to newer generations as an integral part of the Sri Lankan popular culture. It is, however, possible that the old ways of thinking may soon disappear given the catalyst of rapid economic change in Sri Lanka.

In this text a running motif points to the failure of Buddhism in Sri Lanka to undermine, let alone eradicate, the preexistence of male domination and male chauvinism, both derivatives of an older anthropology of things. With all the negative attitudes toward women it is paradoxical that Sri Lanka had the first woman prime minister and then a woman president. All this fit into our complex and cosmopolitan culture. There is a popular saying in Sinhala culture that women possess sixty-four *mayams* (tricks) designed to attract, seduce, deceive, and lead men astray. These *mayams* are hyperbolic and imaginary. They have never been categorized, listed, or defined. They may take the form of laughter, anger, crying, affection, flirting, or any other form of simulated behavior. It is also lyrically expressed in a popular song that Bhrahma— the god of creation, created the woman by mixing together the most venomous poison of every variety of poisonous snake and added honey and milk to it. So beware; the mix may appear sweet as honey, but it may also contains deadly poison!

SIGMUND FREUD DRIVES A THREE WHEELER

Reading the text one may get the idea that the author is foreign to the culture about which she writes. I am much a part of this culture, and I interact with it as a native should. My long years of living abroad have not removed me from being a native in my own land. But evidently I do not pass muster in the eyes of the casual observer, the omniscient three-wheeler driver. Last summer in Colombo, I got into a three wheeler, the "Baja" it is called, the universal, affordable and popular means of transport in modern Sri Lanka and in the East, the local counterpart of a taxicab in Chicago. After the initial protocols of speech with the driver, our conversation flowed freely. It so happened that the Baja driver was a dropout from a prominent local university who announced that he knew psychology and impressively dropped the name of Freud. Much to my private amusement he added that he was a shrewd observer of human behavior and never missed a trick, all the time looking at me in his small rear mirror. He told me during the short ride of his ambitions of collecting money to go to Dubai for a job to earn real money. The Baja was swerving dangerously around other larger vehicles to get to our destination, and I was getting nervous and told the driver that I was in no hurry. I was surprised at how good he was at his job and how he could avoid being run over. He remarked on how fluently I spoke the native language and idiom but also thought I might be living in some other country. He asked me where I was from. I said that I was from Kandy and gave him the local street name. He repeated his question with a ring of irritation, and I repeated my answer. To continue the conversation, I told him that I live in Chicago. At that he exclaimed, "Oh that is where love is." I asked him to explain. He replied, "When young lovers waiting for a bus hold hands, we say it is love like in Chicago."

TWO

Growing Up in Sri Lankan Culture

SOME YEARS AGO, in randomly picking up a copy of the *Times Literary Supplement*, my eye fell on a review of a biography of Evelyn Waugh or Thomas Hardy. I am now unable to say which it was. What I do remember was a remark made by the reviewer that each one of us, despite all our protestations on being our own unique person, is in reality the product of a trinity of forces: parents, teachers, and the church or religion under whose influence we have been nurtured. Few could have survived the triple forces (which hit us at the most vulnerable point of our life, childhood) without the telltale scars molding us for the rest of our lives. Each element in the fateful trinity meant well by us. I see the truth as I look back on my life often bewildered by an inability to know myself. Perhaps the answer lies in a jumble of things. Let me begin with religion.

SRI LANKANS BECOME BUDDHISTS

As in other Theravada Buddhist countries, in Sri Lanka the majority of the people (Sinhala, or Sinhalese), almost 70 percent, are Buddhists. From infancy, people become Buddhists. Rituals and ceremonies are part of the process. The *pansil* (Five Precepts) is taken daily. The Buddha is worshipped with the offering of flowers, lamps, and incense sticks, and *gathas* (stanzas) are recited. In addition, visits are made to the temple on *poya* (full moon) days. Buddhists listen to *bana* (preachings) and Buddhist stories over the radio, on television, or at the temple regularly. These are common practices, all part of the process of becoming Buddhists.

I recall meeting Venerable Havanpola Ratnasara, a well-known Buddhist monk, in front of the British Museum Library when I was a student, and he

11

was doing his Ph.D., in 1966. My first instinct was to go down on my knees and pay my respects in the Buddhist tradition. It was ingrained in me as though I were a preprogrammed robot. The monk was pleased at my Buddhistness and commented that I was well brought up. What I did was rather difficult since I was wearing a short dress (those were the days of mini-skirts). People around (mostly English) were intrigued by what I did.

MY FATHER

I was born in Colombo into a family of mixed ethnic origins and religious beliefs. My father came from an English-speaking, Westernized family in southern Sri Lanka and moved to Colombo. Many of his brothers, six in all, went to England for higher education, which was the practice in those days for middle-class families. Some brought back foreign wives or married into Eurasian (better known as Burgher) families. On the whole my father's family was *sankara* (overly anglicized) and cosmopolitan.

My father was not a Buddhist. Such was the extent of his anglicized upbringing that he did not read or write any of the indigenous languages. This was not uncommon at the time. With nationalistic feelings growing in the country, after independence from British rule in 1948, he felt a certain cultural inadequacy. He believed that one had to be conversant in Latin, which to him was the hallmark of education. He had eleven children. We were in some ways victims of my father's cultural ambivalence. A private tutor was brought to the house during weekends to teach us Sinhala and Buddhists texts. It was not an enjoyable experience. Although we liked Mr. Gunesekara, our pedagogic mentor, we did not welcome him on weekends. There was about Mr. Gunesekara a certain courtly, old-fashioned manner. He was not a traditional Sinhala pedagogue; he was educated in the Western tradition and was quite sophisticated. He taught us Sinhala literature and shared with us a wealth of his *obiter dicta* and his life philosophies. He took us on day excursions to places of educational interest. We visited the museum, the town hall, and the parliament. We rode in the tramcar in Colombo, a mode of transport at the time, which ran on rails in the middle of the streets, ringing of a bell as a warning for pedestrians to step aside. These were fun events.

Mr. Gunesekara, a hard taskmaster, made us learn the Buddhists texts and Sinhala literary works. We were too young to appreciate the value of what he tried to teach us. We memorized the poems and *gathas* and recited them to him like parrots. At this time English was the medium of instruction, and we learned little Sinhala in schools. But for the tutor I would not have had a good knowledge of Sinhala and Buddhist literary sources. Although I resented Mr. Gunesekara's instructions, and blamed my father for the ordeal, now I am grateful. The instruction enriched my education and became a useful tool when I was interacting with a plurality of cultures. I remember the verse that we memorized, that education was a pearl of great price. It was expressed in these terms:

Degurun visin thama daruvanta dena nomada dana nam
viyatun saba meda inta idiriva silpa danumi.

The greatest and most bountiful gift that parents could give a child
to equip him to hold his own even among the fraternities of the
learned.

My father was a strict disciplinarian. He emphasized education and set us strict times for study; the older ones were expected to help the younger siblings. As there were many of us we had the minimum of things. My father made the distinction between need and want. He often quoted an imaginary Chinaman saying, "Good things no cheap, cheap things no good." As young girls we wore Clarke shoes and socks, but our friends chose fashionable, locally made sandals. We had few things, but we had the best.

There was a traveling bookman who came to our house every week, a relict in Sri Lanka in the 50s and 60s. English books were expensive, and the man on the bicycle with loads of paperback books was a welcome sight. He was our traveling library and was received with enthusiasm. He invariably wore an imported, worn out English coat as if to emphasize that he was after all in his own right genteel. We paid two rupees or so a week, and we got three books, which were exchanged the following week. This was a bargain, as we had eleven of us waiting to read. My father encouraged reading and readily provided the money.

As I write I remember with a touch of nostalgia a host of other itinerant personalities like the bookman I have described. They were typical cultural icons who have long since disappeared from the Sri Lankan landscape. There was for example the "Chinaman" who carried at the back of his bicycle layers of beautiful cloth, made in China, embroidered tablecloths, bedspreads, and packets of noodles. I looked forward to his visits since noodles were a comparative novelty. Then there was the man who periodically dropped by to sharpen our household knives and scissors. We would watch him with awe as he deftly held the knife over a rapidly revolving wheel of stone, causing a steady cascade of sparks. I remember the gaunt, stern figure of the man who came to regroove the *mirisgala*, a rectangular slab of stone, which was traditionally used in the kitchen to grind the condiments, used in Sri Lankan curry-style cuisine. The concept of "going shopping" was not known, and the house-to-house vendor was the shopping source.

My father was the only one of his six brothers to marry a Sinhalese Buddhist. My uncles were Christians, and some of their wives belonged to other nationalities. We were exposed from an early age to racial and religious differences. We also had poor Catholic relatives, who worked in our household and took care of us. Their influence on my thinking on religion was profound. Deeply Catholic, they taught us to say the rosary at bedtime, spoke of "God," and read bible stories to us. Some of us found Christianity more interesting than Buddhism. The idea of being forgiven for sins by confessing and the universal love of God was appealing to me. I thought that Buddhism was pessimistic, emphasized suffering, and was not realistic.

THARALA, THE CATHOLIC VILLAGE

During our school holidays we went to our Catholic relatives in the predominantly Catholic village Tharala, about twenty miles from Colombo. Life in this village revolved round the church. There were no telephones, and the method of communication was the ringing of church bells. There was great communal activity in Tharala. The entire village attended the church on Sundays dressed in their best. Our relatives took us to the church regularly, and I saw men, made to wear a crown of thorns in church on Sundays as punishment for not attending regularly. In Tharala religion was a serious matter.

Christmas time was festive, and we all loved going to Tharala then. Everyone in the village rich and poor celebrated Christmas and made fruit cakes, which they called "Christmas cake." They also made wines out of ginger and local fruits such as *lovi*. Pigs and goats were killed for the occasion. Our cousin would kill a pig and share the meat with her neighbors.

One Christmas, a memorable incident took place. My eldest brother, Bertram, was completely shattered by the killing of the pig. As a pointed gesture of protest, that evening, in spite of the lateness of the hour, he (then fourteen years old) left Tharala to return to Colombo. The idea of killing for meat in the household was something he could not tolerate. In our house as in other Buddhist homes animals were not killed for meat. He was a kind, gentle person and showed compassion for all. Bertram leaving by bus alone in the evening caused great concern. On another occasion when we were all visiting some of our relatives in the country where amenities were rather crude, my brother, while in an outhouse toilet, was surprised to see within its narrow confines another occupant, a fairly large snake. He remained calm, sure that the reptile would not harm him because he felt no animosity to the animal. He practiced *maitria* (loving kindness). The rest of us thought that our brother was strange.

I recall a story that I heard from my mother. The Buddha on one occasion was told of a monk who had died by snakebite. Asked why the monk died the Buddha said that the monk had not shown *maitria* toward the four tribes of snakes. Four tribes of snakes in Buddhist lore are classified according to the way they transmit the poison: by stinging, sight, touch, and air. If he had practiced *maitria* to all the snakes, he would not have been harmed.

My mother by contrast came from a traditional, established Sinhala Buddhist family. She was quite the opposite of my father. Even as children we saw the contrast, the disagreements, and wondered why they had ever got together. My mother from our early days was determined to make us all Buddhists, and she worked hard at it.

My grandmother came from Anuradhapura (a city famous for religious worship, also the ancient capital of Ceylon). She was a Buddhist but different from my mother. She was light hearted, fun loving, and unconventional. She taught us to swim in numerous waterways in Anuradhapura and showed us many facets of village culture in the holy city. When our mother was resting in the afternoon, grandmother took us to the jungles near Anuradhapura to show us wild animals. I particularly liked the *vanduru sabha*, assemblies of monkies, which looked like meetings. There was a leader, a big monkey seated on a little rock, or sometimes on a tree stump, and a large number of monkeys gathered around listening or imitating the leader. Monkeys attended in large groups, with mothers carrying the little ones. When they saw us they scattered.

Our grandmother owned a nice house in the sacred city, which she donated to the monks for a monastery. She built a small house for herself because no permanent construction was allowed within the sacred city. The perimeters of the holy city were demarcated, and her property fell within its limits. She was offered land outside of the city as compensation but declined it. We often wondered why she gave away a nice house to live in a little house. When asked about it, she would wryly answer that she could not take it with her when she died, so she gave it away. We could not comprehend the meaning of all this then. She left all her ancestral property to the holy city and did not claim any land in exchange. After her death no one went to claim the land. This attitude was very much against the grain of the general thinking of Sri Lankans, who zealously guard what they earn and leave every bit of property to their kith and kin.

CASTE WAS ALL AROUND

Our society, though primarily Buddhist, was hierarchical and structured. Caste and class distinctions conditioned social interaction. People are born to high or low castes, which determine their importance or the comparable lack of it in society. A person born to a low caste could never leave it. In our homes there were prescribed forms of behavior and conduct for people of lower castes. If one was born into a lower caste and was also poor, one had very little chance in life to better one's condition. Low caste and the poor would enter the house through the back door. There were specially built low seats set aside for them. Special cups and plates were also set aside for their use. Respectful terms of address were used, when addressing the chief of the household. I often wondered how they fit into Buddhist precepts. It troubled me that our playmates of the lower castes and poor when visiting our house could never sit on the normal chairs and eat with us or call us by our names.

Buddhism teaches equality and kindness, but my mother always had an explanation to justify her behavior. There was a *dhoby* family at the edge of our property. The *dhoby*, whose business it was to wash other people's clothes, belonged to the *dhoby* caste. Once a week the female *dhoby, redinanda* (clothes aunt), would collect our dirty clothes and bring them back washed, starched, and ironed. She was a welcome sight. I later learned that there was a host of reciprocal obligations that were not clearly defined but were observed in performing and receiving these services. One such I stumbled on accidentally. Being poor, they did not buy many clothes for themselves. They wore our clothes in the process of servicing them. Once I noticed the *redinanda* wearing my favorite sari, which upset me. When I complained, she humbly explained that it was part of their right to wear the clothes we gave to wash. While they had it, they had a right to it. Later I thought that it was a pretty sari, and she too may have liked wearing it. Was this another rite of exchange in our culture? I had to share my clothes with the *dhoby*, conceding tacitly her right to wear it. Although I was annoyed with her at first, I understood the system. After all, it is Buddhist tradition that we only have the right to use things; nothing really belongs to us. There are also a host of traditions and customs involved in the relationship with the *redinanda*, some of which I have explained in another chapter, dealing with my coming of age ceremonies, where *redinanda* is the chief player.

My mother and her relatives warned us not to be too friendly with boys of lower classes or the ones that were not of the same social status, anticipating future problems. When contracting marriages in Sri Lanka, emphasis is placed on caste. The marriage advertisements in the newspapers, which is a prevalent mode of finding suitable marriage partners, have the acronym *GBS*, Goigama by cast, Buddhist by religion and Sinhala by race or *KBS* for Karava for caste, very like *WASP* (White Anglo-Saxon Protestant) in America. Growing up we did not know what our caste was, and to my brothers and sisters these divisions and distinctions made no sense. My mother and her relatives were devout, practicing Buddhists. My mother believed that high-caste people had good morals.

MY MOTHER

My mother in spite of all her beliefs and practices was kind and generous to all. Her greatest pleasure was to give to the poor and the needy. Many in the community depended on her. The fisherman was a good example. Martin, the fish vendor, brought freshly caught fish from the sea (we lived near the sea) in a basket, which he carried on his head. He went around the neighborhood crying out "*malu, malu*" meaning "fish for sale." Martin was a character. A tall muscular man, he was quick to grin. In every household he was a bit of a heartthrob to the female servants, who gathered round to exchange small talk with "Martin aiya" (brother Martin). He sliced the fish with éclat—a man who clearly enjoyed his job. He was a daily visitor to our house for many years. Whether my mother needed fish or not, Martin made his appearance in our house. When Martin got sick my mother gave him medicine and hot coriander tea. He would leave his basket on the floor and sit on the front step, and a servant would serve him breakfast and hot tea. He brought the best fish for my mother.

Years later when I visited my mother I would take extra tee shirts apart from the gifts I took for our relatives. My mother would give them away. Nice food items from America were shared with neighbors and friends. Martin when he saw me would exclaim, "Oh your daughter has come to see you," meaning, is there a gift for me? Once I saw him selling fish wearing a Chicago Bulls tee shirt. Martin had heard about Chicago and Al Capone, but the Bulls was not a concept he could grasp. My mother had regular visitors who came to see her with various requests. In her simple way she said the more one gave, the more blessings multiplied. She taught us that this was a Buddhist way of accruing good karma.

Those who worked in our household as servants were considered part of the household. My mother took care of their needs even after they had left her service. She found employment for their children and made us use whatever influence we had as adults to assist her in doing this. Some lived in her house while working in a factory or a government office since they could not afford to pay for board and lodging. Once I had an argument with her for giving away one of my favorite saris to a girl to be worn at an interview. When I asked her why she did not give one of my older dresses, she said that the girl needed something nice and that my old clothes were not good enough. Those who had been with her for a long period were married off with dowries of land and money.

Edwin was one such. I knew him practically all my life, and all of us dearly loved him. When my uncle became the first Sri Lankan government printer, Edwin was given employment in the press. He had no formal education and therefore no paper qualifications, but he was quite able and clever. He earned a comfortable salary. Late in life he married a young woman and had a large family. His wife was attractive and flirtatious, this made him angry and jealous. My mother preached to him that it is the Buddha's word in *Parabava Sutta* that one should not marry a young woman when in middle age because it causes destruction. Edwin too had his share of weaknesses. He liked to drink, which caused conflict in the family, and Edwin always came back to us. My parents took care of his needs, and they were kind to his family. We found employment for some of his daughters, and they became fairly successful in life. When he was old he came to stay with my mother, who built a little house for him in her compound and took care of him. My mother made him take *atasil* (Eight Precepts) on *poya* days and taught him Buddhism. Edwin loved liquor, and taking *atasil* did not excite him.

SUNDAY SCHOOL

Growing up we all went to the *dahampasela* (Buddhist Sunday school). My mother was determined in her way to make us good Buddhists. Whatever we did or did not do was forgiven and forgotten if we went to Sunday school. I disliked Sunday school as it was boring and unrelated to our life as children.

Buddhist monks taught us the philosophy as taught by the Buddha. We were required to memorize a popular fifteenth-century poetry book of religious stanzas to imbibe virtue, the *Loveda Sagarava*—an extraordinary, popular collection of stanzas full of moral aphorisms, which were easy to commit to memory. We learned Jataka stories relating to the previous births of the Buddha. The monks taught us central Buddhist concepts such as suffering, its causes, and the need to end suffering. We did not see life as suffering, and all this profound teaching did not make much sense. We thought life was fun. We had not experienced any discomfort or loss in life, and the teachings had neither relevance nor meaning. In disappointment monks often said teaching us was like pouring water on a lotus leaf. They told us that to end suffering we must attain "nirvana" by giving up desire. We loved desire and all that went with it.

We were made to take *atasil* on *poya* days, which we very much disliked. On such occasions we got together and played games with stones. We invented an intricate game using small stones along with its complicated system of rules. Seated on the temple grounds we played stone games all day, and we knew the art of concealing the stones in our *sil* clothes. Our friends were a family of six young boys of our same ages who were made to wear long white dresses as *sil* outfits, quite unsuitable for sitting on the floor. We made fun of them for showing off their male parts.

There was a large mango tree in the temple. We threw stones and sticks at the tree to knock down mangoes, which upset the junior monk. He spent quite a few minutes on the theme of how we gathered bad karma by this act of stealing from the temple property. He added that we would suffer in our next life, perhaps be born with injured arms or be in want. We were too young to think of the next life. Besides, it was quite out of proportion to the act of eating raw mangoes. We were kids, and we loved mangoes. The trees were blessed with an abundance of fruit, enough to go around. The novice monks who played with us would sneak into the temple kitchen and bring salt and pepper, to flavor the fruit, and we would all eat together. The adult monk was young and handsome, and the girls were attracted to him. We wondered if he was also temple property, a "forbidden fruit."

When I was young I wondered why my mother was so attracted to religion. My mother and father had little in common to hold together a marriage. My mother may have in a way of compensation turned to religion. My parents were of different backgrounds spiritually, socially, and educationally. My mother, clearly a martyr, must have prayed for a better and more amicable marriage in her next life. She always told us of the possibility of getting better things in the next birth. She had a small shrine room in the house, which she visited twice a day to offer flowers and perform *pujas*. These were done with piety and devotion. We were coaxed to join her, and we were rewarded. She also forgave any misdeeds. She had the practice of sitting at the dinner table at night after the evening meal to relate Jataka stories from the Buddhist texts. These were stories from the life of the Buddha, and we enjoyed the sessions as a family and looked forward to them as she was great storyteller. All these stories had a moral and an ethical ending, and telling them was her way of teaching us good values and her version of bedtime stories.

Paying respect to parents and elders is a Buddhist custom. We worshipped our parents every morning before we left for school, and they in turn blessed us, a way of showing gratitude and respect. It was not considered proper form to argue openly with parents. If we disagreed we were quiet about it and resolved it privately by discussion. The idea was that parents knew better and had our interests at heart.

UNIVERSITY: THE OTHER EDEN

Our family in a sense was unique. Out of ten children (my youngest brother died at the age of sixteen), nine entered the university, which in the early 1960s was an achievement. The Peradeniya University at this time was exclusive. Out of the five thousand or so that sat the university entrance exam each year, only one hundred and twenty-five were admitted. It was prestigious to be a graduate of Peradeniya.

University was mostly for the urban affluent middle class, and the medium of instruction was English. On my visits to see my sisters in Peradeniya, the beauty of its surroundings and academic reputation enchanted me. I was determined to go there to study. At this time the Peradeniya campus had only arts faculty. My father encouraged me to enter the medical college, which was in Colombo, as I had taken to science and mathematics, along with my brother Bernard, but I quietly switched to arts in order to go to Peradeniya.

I enjoyed attending Peradeniya University. I was known from the first day in residence hall, much to my annoyance, as someone's sister. This was not without its advantages; it was easy to make friends. I was determined to get a degree and also have a good time. Having grown up with many siblings, I was gregarious and ran for many offices. I talked a lot and made friends easily. My popularity on campus helped me to run successfully for the women students' representative in the student council my first year. I was hardly conscious of politics, but I found myself thrown into it. Meeting Sir Nicholas Artygalle (who was a classmate of my father), then the vice chancellor of the university, and sitting for a picture with him was exciting to me as a teenager. Some years later I drew Ananda's attention to the framed picture hanging on the wall of my uncle's house in Ratnapura. It was good karma all the way for a while.

In my second year in Peradeniya, the warden of the residence hall made me a student subwarden when she discovered my mathematical and organizational skills. This gave me some authority and helped financially as several of my siblings were in other faculties of the university, all of which was a burden on my father. My father had a good income, which disqualified us from getting bursaries, which were primarily set aside for poor students. My father was proud that I was active in the university. He always encouraged his daughters to compete with men and instilled in us the confidence that women were as capable or even more so than men if we applied ourselves. This was a rather novel idea at the time.

CITY CROWS AND VILLAGE CROWS

The University of Peradeniya was predominantly middle class and urban. Girls from Colombo, Kandy, and other city schools dominated and formed into cliques. Conformity was the norm in our young days. One had to be "kultur" to be "in" with the crowd. In dress, behavior, and speech "kultur" stood out. It was unnatural and unfair, but this was the society then on the Peradeniya campus. The British had left Ceylon a decade ago, but they seemed to have influence even then.

Siriyawathie, my roommate-to-be, had a village upbringing, and in appearance and behavior looked very different from my city friends. There was nothing wrong with this, but as a young adult from a different background, I was unaccustomed to dealing with so much diversity. However, this alone did not bother me. At first it was a culture shock, but having lived with eleven sisters and brothers I felt I could handle it. Siriyawathie too had problems with me. My mini skirts, numerous friends, effervescent, fleeting ways bothered her from the start. Every male friend I had she classed as my boy friend, and I had many. The problem at first seemed formidable. Hoping to take the easier route, I went to our warden, Mrs. Cooke, and protested. She listened and after a pep talk told me this would be a great educational and social experience for me, and I should give it a try. If after a term I was still unhappy, she would make a change. I agreed and decided to face the challenge.

Kindness and sharing had been instilled into us by our mother. Putting aside my initial sense of unease, with good spirits I began to try to relate to my roommate. I unobtrusively taught her the nuances of the Western culture such as they were understood and interpreted by upper-middle-class anglicized Sri Lankans. The novelty of Peradeniya residential life—the use of forks and spoons, flush toilets, and waitresses—was clearly daunting to someone who came from a strictly rural milieu. Siriyawathie was not alone; over the years the influx of rural undergraduates to Peradeniya had begun to increase. But looking back it is clear that there was a class divide separating two societies compelled to live cheek by jowl with each other. There was mutual—albeit harmless—class warfare between the *kolamba kakas* (the crows from Colombo who were the anglicized elite) and the *game kakas* (the genre of crows who hailed from the rural areas). Often young adults could be cruel in interacting with one another. In the Sinhala culture banter is a remarkably charming form of conversation and social intercourse that accommodates spontaneous wit and liveliness. However, often in our culture banter degenerates into hurtful spite and cruelty. I saw evidence of both in my Peradeniya days. It took me years to realize that what I saw in Peradeniya was evidence of a fractured society, teetering uneasily on a class divide.

I began to see my roommate, Siriyawathie, in a kinder light and was affectionate to her without being patronizing. She seemed to appreciate all this and would often thank me. Although as a student subwarden I was entitled to a room of my own, I continued to share my room with her. When I walk down memory lane, I am not sure whether or not she ended up harboring deep resentment toward me.

I GOT MARRIED

Few months after final exams I found myself married to Ananda. Getting married has its own story. I had a boyfriend, but he belonged to a lower caste, according to my mother, although he was educated and kind. To my mother he was not a suitable marriage partner. However, Ananda was the most appropriate as he came from a respectable family. He was a man of means, well educated, elitist, good looking, and had everybody's dream job. He was a young lecturer recruited to the faculty, all a woman could dream of in getting a husband. The fact that I liked another man at the time did not matter. Ananda was charming and showed great affection for me. My mother and my siblings threatened me that if I did not marry Ananda they would not have anything to do with me, and I would not be considered a member of the family. As a young woman I had no rights to express my opinion or fight for my rights. We women have obligations but few rights. I took the easy way out and married Ananda in a quiet ceremony.

The way we got married did not please my father-in law. He believed in horoscopes and traditional customs. Ananda's older brother intervened, all was reconciled in a short time, and he became the ideal father-in-law. Many months later, while going for a walk in the evening round the Kandy lake, he told me that he had no objection to my marrying Ananda, but the way I did it was very wrong. It was embarrassing to him, and for many months he had to face society in shame. If my caste, my background, and my family were compatible it would have been a marriage to celebrate. This was the only time he referred to my marriage. He accepted me totally as his daughter-in-law. He was a father to me in a unique sense until he passed on. His home was my home in every sense of the word. As a wife I had to make many changes and adapt to fit into Ananda's traditional household.

A few months after our marriage Ananda got a scholarship to Oxford, and we left the comfortable home of my father-in law. I became Ananda's Sri Lankan wife, performing the traditional duties of a wife. I walked a foot behind him, and it was my obligation to cook for him, wash his clothes, and take care of him. I accepted the new role with a host of obligations. In Sri Lankan society women make efforts to become wives. We were happy at Oxford.

MY OTHER FATHER AND MOTHER

On our return to Sri Lanka, we lived many years with Ananda's parents. I came to receive their affection and care. I often thought then I was blessed with good karma. Four years in Oxford gave me extreme confidence bordering on arrogance. I thought I knew everything. My parents-in-law gently showed me that what I knew was little compared to what I did not know, including the virtue of being humble. When we had problems and concerns, we could lay them at their feet, and they treated them as if they were their own. I never felt lonely or abandoned. From my mother-in-law I learned many valuable lessons, which served me throughout my life. I well remember she told me never to react to bad or unpleasant situations but always to sit back and rethink things. She explained that impulsive reaction to situations destroyed relationships. I will always remember a sagacious observation she made: What you feel, what you think is your property. What you say is public property.

We continued to live in Kandy, which was my husband's home. Although I was a young woman who had returned from Oxford, I was the daughter-in-law of a prominent lawyer in the city. According to our culture I had very little individual identity, and I was for the rest of my young adult years known and identified as the daughter-in-law and the wife of someone. I had to fall in line with the prevailing cultural norm, and its involved restraints, which were somewhat rigorous. They were undefined, unwritten customs. To be respected one had to be mindful of prescribed forms of dress, and aware of how one talked and conducted oneself. Discreetly, elders in the household monitored the degrees of conformity and departures from the norm in these and related matters. Whatever my personal beliefs were, to be respected I had to be a Buddhist and act like a Buddhist. I was barred from wearing mini-dresses (a common form of Western dress in the late 60s), and I had to make my skirts long or make new ones. Evidently dresses of the sort I wore were a distraction and an embarrassment in a conservative and traditional household. I was not allowed to wear slacks, which was akin to wearing trousers that middle-class men wore in Sri Lanka. On these matters my father-in-law, a benevolent dictator who dominated a large household, did not mince his words.

Ananda's family had been Buddhist for generations and was one of the affluent families on whom the Malwatta Vihare in Kandy depended for patronage and support. Living in the household I learned to be a traditional Buddhist and about Buddhist rituals. As part of the household, I had the opportunity to participate in temple-related ceremonies, visit many temples for religious activities, and in the process get to know the monks. I accompanied my father-in-law, an active public figure, to numerous social functions. On one such occasion I was amused when wine was served while I was chatting with a well-known doctor, who had known my father-in-law over the years, when out of nowhere he appeared and from the side indicated by gesture that wine was forbidden to me. On such occasions my father-in law would proudly introduce me to his friends as his daughter-in-law, no doubt privately pleased that I was attired in a sari, traditionally worn by women in South Asian countries. I did not wear the sari in the traditional conservative way, but he never criticized me on the shortness of the blouse or the low-rider style in which I wore the sari.

In my teaching days at Dharmaraja College, in Kandy, there were monks on the staff, and we became friends. The association with monks enriched my life and made it less stressful. They were in many ways barefoot psychotherapists, who in their own right gave their time and energies without remuneration to all and sundry. I often discussed my day-to-day stresses of life with them. What I told them was like a safety deposit box in a bank, safe and secure.

During this period, I had minor conflicts with my sisters-in-law. One of them particularly thought that I was fashionable and Westernized and criticized my form of dress regularly. I wore pretty saris low on the hips and short blouses with my midriff exposed. It was the trend then. I was not willing to change my dress style. She believed that young women teaching in schools were a distraction to the boys. Indeed I was only a few years older than many of my students. I did not know how to handle the criticism, and it caused me stress. I loved the boys, the teaching, and the school. I confided in my monk friends, who gave me good advice. The monks cautioned tact, to strike a balance between showing deference to my sister-in-law's viewpoint and at the same time continuing to be my own person. They reminded me about the famous frescoes in Sigiriya where beautiful women of surpassing charm were depicted with little other than scanty cloths to cover their breasts and with their midriffs exposed. What attracted the onlooker was really the charm and refined dignity of the women. I realized that such subtlety would be lost on my overly pragmatic sister-in-law.

VILLAGE MEDICINE MAN

There was a culture of treating disease in our homes. My mother often consulted the local *vedamahattaya* (medicine man) when we had ailments and for preventive medicine generally. The *vedamahattaya* was a male in the traditional setting. He occupied a unique place, being a generalist he treated all ailments of the mind and body. Unlike the university-degreed doctors practicing Western medicine in cities, the *vedamahattaya* claimed no paper qualifications. His knowledge of herbal medicine and traditional remedies for cure had come to him from generations of handing down carefully preserved information, mostly from father to son. He was the service person of medicine in the village. His treatment and payment were connected with the Buddhist idea of good and bad karma, translated as *pin* for good karma and *pau* for bad karma. Attending to the sick and ailing was considered in Buddhist culture a way of acquiring *pin* (merit), and after receiving treatment, the patient would say "*pinsiddaveva*" ("may you acquire good merit"), instead of a "thank you" and make an unspecified monetary payment. One did not have to make appointments to see the village physician but took a few betel leaves with a payment that the patient could afford placed on it. Whether there was money or not, the village physician treated all those who needed his services. Often villagers who had no ready cash paid the *vedamahattaya* with garden produce.

Sri Lanka has its ancient herbal medicine system based on the Ayurvedic tradition. For treatment of disease, various types of herbs, leaves, stems, flowers, and buds of plants are used. Some are prepared for the ailment as it occurs and others ahead of time as oils and mixtures. Villagers possess a good knowledge of various medicinal herbs, plants, and trees. They are carefully tendered and preserved. Medicines prescribed are directly connected to the food one consumes while taking the medicine. Food is basically categorized as foods that cool the body and those that cause heat. Along with the medicine, specific food items good for the condition are prescribed as well as those to avoid. It is a rather involved system of checks and balances, inexpensive, available, and affordable to the villages. In the absence of Western qualified doctors and well-equipped hospital facilities the monk and the *vedamahattaya* serve as physicians and surgeons on the spot.

The Ayurvedic system has a different cartography of the body. Every kind of known illness is treated under this system, the theory being that health is based on vital energies of the body and that when there is an imbalance, illness results. The physical and mental health requires a balanced circulation of three energies—bile, phlegm, and vital wind—which work through the channels, organs, tissues, and coordinating centers of the body. When these energies are out of balance or impeded in their flow, illness results. The cause of the imbalance could be poor diet, emotional shock or trauma, fatigue, tension, overwork, exposure to bad weather, or microorganisms.

PHARMACOLOGY IN A SRI LANKAN HOUSEHOLD

My parents dealt with sickness and the prevention of it in two different ways. My father believed in Western medicine, with its chemically based medicines and scientific proof. The other was the herbal system, in which my mother had faith, the Ayurvedic medicine. We were treated simultaneously under both systems. My mother acquired some of her knowledge by means of transgenerational beliefs and traditions, and some of it simply folklore. She practiced them on us, and it all seemed to work well in the traditional setting.

I remember listening in to a story of a poor woman whose husband was the driver of a bullock cart. They had many children, and she got pregnant every year. She became pregnant for the seventh time, and the villagers were sorry for her. She discreetly made a visit to the *vedamahattaya* for some medicine or advice to end the pregnancy. The *vedamahattaya* was outraged by the suggestion, since his services were performed for good karma, and he believed ending life was bad karma. However, the story continued that she went to the village woman who performed the task secretly with herbal concoctions.

The *vedamahattaya* felt our pulse on the wrist, or did a tongue diagnosis, and with empirical observation assessed the imbalance in our body. As a cure, herbal-mineral supplements were given to correct the imbalance. The herbal supplements were combined according to classical formulas. In order to retain the balance, an herbal soup (*kasaya*), was prescribed. It included leaves, barks, roots, and flowers of creepers, trees, or bushes, familiar to the villagers. Servants in the household gathered the ingredients to make the decoction, prescribed by the *vedamahattaya*. As a young person I had many of these decoctions for ailments. Herbal materials were cut, sliced, or powdered coarsely, and one part of the amalgamation was boiled in four, eight, or sixteen parts of water (usually cups) and finally reduced to a quarter. The system also involved dietary changes. Unlike the Chinese, native medicine in Sri Lanka does not include animal products or insects. Sometimes medicinal *thaila* (oils), which were specially prepared, with intricate combinations of herbs, were recommended for ailments such as arthritis, broken bones, aches, and pains. Whenever we complained of a body ache, hot fermentation was followed by an application of medicinal oil.

For a head cold, my father consulted the doctor and brought a mixture of chemicals along with some tablets to swallow. My mother gave us a drink of a good coriander brew, to which fresh ginger and garlic were added for extra strength and efficacy. It served as a comforting drink, hot and soothing, and seemed to work. I later gave it to my children. For a head cold the sure-fire remedy was steam inhalation. A mixture of coriander and fresh lime leaves were boiled in a clay pot. When it gave out a strong aromatic steam, we sat in front of the pot, head covered with a sheet to prevent the steam from escaping, and inhaled the hot steam until we sweated. The effect of this was remarkable as it soothed the clogged passages of the nostrils and relieved the headaches in a natural way. This was a popular remedy in our household, soothing and comforting.

For a persistent cough we used juice of a lime, with fresh ginger and sugar or honey. A popular decoction for a persistent cough was the *pas panguwa*, five items boiled together: they were coriander with roots, fruits, and leaves of the *katuvelbatu* plant with raisins to drink three times a day for two days. There is now a commercial version of this packeted and sold for foreign consumption. Ananda in his own upbringing is a great believer in this traditional medicinal concoction.

The traditional system of medication had deep roots going back in time. Robert Knox gives us glimpses of a do-it-yourself pharmacology accessible to all:

There are no professional physitians nor chyrurgeons, but all in general have some skill that way, and are physitians and chyrurgeons to themselves. Their medicines they make of leaves that are in the woods, and the barks of trees. With which they purge and vomit themselves, and will do notable cures upon green wounds and also upon sore eyes.

For purging they make use of a tree called Dallugauhah. It bears no leaves, nothing but thorns, and is of a soft substance. Being cut there runs out a white thick milk; in which we soak some whole corns of pepper a whole night. The next day the pepper is taken out and washed clean, and then boyled in fair water with a sower fruit they call Goraka and they drink and it purgth very well.

For drawing and healing of sores, they have a leaf called Mockinacola; it is a very like our tunhoof or ground-ivy, only it is a brighter green. They only take the leaf and clap it upon the sore.

It is a speedy cure of the itch, to take Coudouro giddi, a fruit of a tree in form somewhat like a mussel but bigger. This fruit they cut in slices and fry it in coker-nut oyl. And with this oyl they anoint the body.

For ordinary Caudle for women in child-bed, is goraka boyled in water
with pepper and ginger. Women in that condition use nothing else. (Knox,
1958:181–83)

As kids we often suffered from stomachaches. My mother gave us two
home remedies. One was garlic roasted over hot coals mixed with wild bees'
honey. This simple home remedy has now become a health fad among sophisticated Westerners, interestingly also as a prescription for longevity. Living in
the United States I have long been used to the redoubtable Larry King holding forth on the virtues of garlic. It pays. For more severe aches, there is the
essence of fresh ginger root ground with garlic mixed with wild bees' honey.
My father, unbeknown to my mother, gave us a shot of brandy, and the cure
was instant. The silent war amused us.

There were preventive sides of these cures. Mother believed that our
blood needed purifying once a year to prevent disease. Before the beginning
of the school year, we were all made to drink a decoction made by boiling bitter dried fruit called "*aralu*," in the morning on an empty stomach. It was bitter and unpleasant, and it made us purge all morning. This was for cleansing
of the system and blood to prevent illness. My father preferred to give us cas-
tor oil, which was equally unpleasant and had the same effect.

There was also a substitute for the tetanus injection. When we injured
ourselves we were made to drink a tea made out of a root called "*venivelgata*."
One could not imagine the bitterness of this without experiencing it.

In the tropical climate our houses had their share of insects. For
swellings caused by insect bites, my mother ground red sandalwood into a
paste with lime as a cure. When my sisters had pimples on their faces,
white sandalwood paste ground with lime was used as a cure. For other
types of swelling boiled *margosa* leaves were used as a hot fermentation.

Then there were the folklore type practices. When we had vomiting
the magical cure was to blow over a hot piece of wood from the kitchen
fire. It may well have been a distraction or the force of psychological suggestion, a part of our traditional culture. The pomegranate tree (*delun*) is
used for many ailments in Sri Lanka. We had many *delun* in our garden
grown for medicinal purposes. The buds of the tree were boiled and given
to stop chronic diarrhea, especially in children. The same infusion also
relieved bronchitis. Powdering the flowers of the pomegranate tree and
applying them would check nose bleeds.

Our culture classifies food into categories. Some foods are considered
"heating" and others "cooling." There is no scientific basis for the determina-
tion. If one eats tuna, or other meat, which is considered heating, it must be
balanced with a cooling food such as okra, or cucumber, and the all-popular
sago pudding, which we all loved. Young king coconut water, regarded as cooling, is valued as a health drink for many ailments. However, it is not to be taken

when one is suffering from a cold. Certain foods such as okra and bitter gourd are not eaten at night. It is an involved science with its own regimen.

Mr. Munasinghe, familiar with local traditions, history, and especially herbal medicine, had his story. The locally grown common tree *rukattana* is widely known as a cure for poisonous snakebites. The five ingredients of the tree—the buds, leaves, the flowers, the bark, and the roots—are boiled together to make a decoction to give a patient to extract the poison out of the body. Once a snake bit a village girl, and in spite of treatment she slipped into a coma and died. Villagers bury their dead quickly as they do not go through the process of embalming. She was poor and was buried in a coffin made out of *rukkattna*, an inexpensive wood. In shock they failed to remove the little valuable jewelry she was wearing. A robber noting this visited the cemetery in the night and dug up the grave. At the same time, the buried woman woke up from her coma. The robber, at the sight of the rising dead body, ran away fearing a ghost. The girl made her way home and knocked at the door in the middle of the night. Her pleased relatives reckoned that the poison extracting qualities of the *rukattana* used for the coffin may have saved her.

VIAGRA, THE VILLAGE VERSION

What ails the body may take many forms. Sri Lankans refrain from talking about sex and related matters openly. Sex, like alcoholic drinks, are taboo subjects. Nevertheless, there is a science of herbal medicine known to villagers to improve sexual desires and remedy impotence. I was walking down the main street in Kandy and picked up a few green vegetables I was familiar with from my young days. Mr. Munasinghe, my companion, recognizing one leafy vegetable that I had bought, told me the popular verse relating to the aphrodisiac qualities of this herb known to villagers. He was rather shy about repeating it in my presence, but I insisted. His father was an Aurvedic physician and knew the science of the herbs, which he shared with me.

> *Valpenela saka; Gitelen malavala ka;*
> *Abu notakana eka; Patai siyayak ambun eka*

Val penela is an herb (I do not know the botanical term for this) when tempered in ghee, and eaten, the man who ran away from his wife will seek hundreds of wives.

Locally grown fruit, durian with a foul odor is well known for its aphrodisiac properties. There are many folk tales and songs relating to herbs and fruits considered medicinal remedies for many such ailments and they are familiar to the villagers. We had a fun conversation sharing stories and folklore on the generally taboo subject of male virility, and medicinal remedies in our native culture for sexual inadequacies. I, in turn, graphically described the extravagant claims made on behalf of Viagra by the United States' mass media. My Sri Lankan friends listened with amazement (they may have even thought I was praising the virtues of Viagra) and with concern commented that these new drugs may have side effects.

In my Dharmaraja days in the 70s I wore high-heeled shoes, which were then the fashion. As a result I often suffered from ankle sprains. I continued to wear the same type of shoes and went often for treatment. The orthopedic surgeon's treatment was to wrap my ankle in an elastic bandage for six weeks. I was not happy, and my monk friend suggested an alternative. He knew a young monk in Asgiriya temple who was well known for his skill in treating broken and dislocated bones. I agreed to give it a try, as I was getting tired of the bandage.

I went to the temple at seven in the morning with a bandage as instructed. Eager to help, the monk was ready. He had a certain type of medicinal grass cut fine and ground to a paste with fresh turmeric roasted in mustard oil, and it was wrapped around my ankle with the bandage. I was asked to rest and come again in twenty-four hours. I did as I was told. When the bandage was removed, the swelling was gone, and I had less pain. On my second visit the monk took some medicinal stones and rubbed the injured area saying mantra for a few minutes. He packed the area with warm bags of crushed medicinal seeds tied into cloth bundles. Once this process was over, medicinal oil was applied to the warm ankle. I was a little embarrassed as the monk was young, and he was treating my foot. But the monk was perfectly at ease. He assumed the position of a doctor, a healer, a professional, and treated me with compassion. I have no doubt that his kindness and compassionate thoughts healed me even more than the medicine. He did not take any money, and I got the oil and the herbs to take home and continued the treatment. I was well in seven days as he had promised, and I continued to go there whenever my ankle was sprained. The monks not only were the healers of the mind but also knew the art of healing the total person.

BOOMING HERBAL FARE

The herbal remedies in Sri Lanka have taken a new age trend. In luxury hotels as well as in wayside eateries, they are a breakfast menu item, freshly prepared, steaming hot pots of herbal porridge offered as an alternative to much-advertised oatmeal in the West. They come in many varieties of herbs claiming to cure every conceivable disease. These are popular and much sought after by foreign tourists as well as the locals.

Special herbal formulations prepared from local herbs harvested naturally—"organic," sun dried, or shade dried at room temperature and mixed

according to ancient formulas—are sold everywhere. They claim to possess
therapeutic properties for the cure of numerous ailments, such as kidney problems, diabetes, gastric disorders, hepatitis, rheumatism, impotency, and relief
from menopause, insomnia, common cold, and constipation—the list is endless. The names and remedies are familiar to me as a native. It was exciting
that I could now pick a variety of them for my American friends who are into
alternative medicine. These were originally available only through my
vedamahattaya, with involved ways of preparation, but now straight from the
store shelf, in conveniently packeted form. *Samahan* packets for colds and
influenza are the most common. They are sworn to be effective, convenient to
carry, and universally available. They are a quick and easy alternative to the *pas
panguwa* (five herbs) for cough and colds, which needed to be freshly brewed
and therefore somewhat cumbersome.

A visit to the popular herbal medicine store gave me a variety of options
from which to choose. I picked up a few bags of *karapincha* tea (curry leaf
with which I flavor my curries), said to be endowed with properties to lower
cholesterol. A friend in Chicago had diabetes, and my eye flashed to the
packets of *kotahalahimbutu* tea to get her blood sugar levels down. My father-
in-law had diabetes. He claimed the drink in moderate and regulated quantities kept the disease under control. Then there was *gotukola* and *beli mal* tea
for a golden skin, which I had in the form of hot porridge for breakfast in
Ananda's father's house. *Panela* for heart pain, *iramusu* and *neeramulliya* for
urine problems, in short the whole gamut of native herbs claiming to cure all
diseases, each in instantly dissolvable form for quick consumption, like
instant coffee or instant nirvana.

What was most fascinating was that they cost so little money for the
extravagant claims made. Finally, I had to buy a chew of betel for my friend.
The owner of the store, a pretty woman with a degree in Ayurvedic medicine,
gave me an introduction to the modern version of the village betel chew in
ready-made form. She called it the "medicinal betel chew." I was wondering
what was medicinal in the old chew of the village betel, which was supposed
to cause mouth cancer. Now it comes in a small a packet without chunam and
tobacco. It does not stain the mouth like the original version but makes one
feel drugged. In the locally prepared concoctions, there are only vague requirements to state the contents. After all this is all in the developing world, where
there are no strict approval procedures enforced by health authorities.

THREE

Festival of New Beginnings

The New Year

SRI LANKAN NEW YEAR is a solar festival, which marks the passing of the sun from the zodiac of Pisces to the zodiac of Aries inaugurating the coming of New Year. In the traditional astrological belief system, the sun completes its movement across the twelve segments of the Zodiac in the course of one year, taking one month to travel each constellation. The beginning is determined to be the time the sun enters the Aries zodiac. The period of transition is the period of celebration. It is celebrated in April usually on the thirteenth or the fourteenth day of that month depending on when the auspicious times occur.

The Sinhala and Hindu New Year, which falls in the month of Bak (April) is celebrated both by the Sinhalese and the Tamils. Bak (fortune) coincides with the coming of the paddy harvest, the season for fresh fruits, especially mangoes, the blossoms of spring, blue skies, and the song of the *koha*, all associated with prosperity and abundance. It is a fun and festive time, symbolizing new beginnings. It is time to look forward to what the future has in store instead of looking back on all the hurts and pain of the past. It is a time to heal, a time to forgive, and a time to make a fresh beginning.

CUCKOO ANNOUNCES THE COMING OF THE NEW YEAR

The sound of the *koha* is associated with the advent of the Sinhala and Tamil New Year; the bird is often called the Avurudu *koha*—the New Year Cuckoo.

The *koha* is an early bird, and its call is strident, plaintive, and easy to imitate. The legend has it that the *koha* never makes a nest of its own. It takes a free ride by laying its eggs in the crow's nest. The unsuspecting crow sits on *koha* eggs in addition to her own and not only hatches them but also tends and feeds the fledglings until they begin to sing, a sound markedly different from the crow's calls. At this point the young ones are chased away as unwelcome guests but thanks to nurturing in the nest are able to fly away.

The Sinhalese and the Tamil communities in Sri Lanka celebrate the festival of the New Year separately, with their own customs and traditions. Wherever they live in modern times most Sri Lankans try to observe these customs and traditions, adjusting the time zones. In my early years in the United States, I would get the auspicious times for the New Year from my mother and try to make traditional *kiribath* at that time. The Sri Lankans in the United States living in major cities celebrate the New Year by getting together and observing some of the traditional customs.

There are similar festivals in India. In Banares there is the "Holi" festival celebrated to welcome the New Year, the festivals of love and life. This is one occasion when all communities irrespective of race and caste distinctions celebrate in harmony. The festival is meant to purify, regenerate, and unify the community. It is an occasion in the year, which brings about communal harmony in Banares. In Sri Lanka however, the Sinhalese celebrate separately. New Year is basically a nonreligious festival. The monks and the temple are associated only in an indirect way.

April is the month of reveling and merrymaking, the most vibrant of the twelve months. New Year is a national festival officially recognized and observed throughout the island and lasts seven days. Most activities come to a halt during this time. Town dwellers who have their roots in villages take time off to visit their parents and relatives, to celebrate together. It is a family-based ceremony with numerous observances and traditional customs: visiting parents, making peace, and beginning things anew. The customs observed at Avurudu (New Year) symbolizes unity and harmony within families, among relatives and neighbors.

ALL AT THE AUSPICIOUS TIME

Sri Lankans attach great importance to New Year customs and follow the directions in the *Panchanga Litha* (Almanac) for auspicious times. The astrologers determine the auspicious times for festivities, the end of the old year and the beginning of the new. The Sinhala Avurudu does not begin at midnight but at the time determined by astrologers. There is an interesting period of a few hours between the beginning of the New Year and the conclusion of the old year that is called "*nonagathe*" (neutral period), meaning the absence of *nakatha* (auspicious time), the period of doing nothing until the sun moves to its new astrological position. It is considered an inauspicious period. One is expected to abstain from any type of work during this time other than religious activity.

Before the *nonagathe*, fireplaces are cleaned, and the ashes are removed. Everything is made ready for a new beginning. Houses are cleaned and often color washed. There is neither cooking, eating, nor work done during this period. Any activity during this period is believed to be fruitless. The last meal has to be finished and all activity ceased before the transition time.

Alice Nona, my aunt's housekeeper, more like an extended family member, gave us a ritual bath to symbolize the end of the old year. She rubbed our bodies with a paste of magosa leaves and turmeric and poured buckets of cold water on us. According to her the herbal paste made us pretty. She applied sesame oil on our bodies and let us play in the morning sun, scantily clad. The sun before 10:00 A.M. is good for the skin. Our heads were massaged with a concoction of limes boiled with fennel seeds to promote the growth of healthy hair and clean hair roots.

Most Buddhists engage in religious activities during this time, visiting the temple dressed in white, carrying flowers, joss sticks, coconut oil, and wicks for the lamps. Because of the mystic nature of this transition period, villagers feel a need to fortify themselves spiritually and to make a success of their activities in the coming year.

One year we spent the New Year with a relative near Kelaniya, a place about ten kilometers from Colombo. The Kelaniya temple is of great significance to the Buddhists because of the belief of Buddha's visit. During the *nonagathe* period, also known as the *punyakalaya* (the time to do good deeds), we went in an open raft across the Kelani River to the temple. It was after sunset, and elders took torches to light the way. With the prospect of the coming year, all were happy and carefree. We carried white jasmine flowers and coconut oil to light the lamps. Even those who did not go to the temple regularly made it a point to go on this day. It was a way of spending this time of inactivity, which seemed sometimes lengthy. The moonlit night on the raft moving through the clear flowing waters of the Kelani River made it all romantic. At the temple we offered flowers to the Buddha, lit lamps around the Bo tree, and passed the time leisurely talking about the advent of the good time to come. We all had a common purpose, the wish for a good year.

COMING OF THE NEW YEAR

When the *nonagathe* was over, the coming of the New Year was announced with the ringing of the temple bells, the noise of fire crackers, and the sound of women playing the traditional *rabana* (drum). At the auspicious time the hearth was lit facing the right direction. Thereafter the traditional *kiribath*, Sri Lanka's quintessential festival food, was cooked for the New Year meal. It was made from the first batch of the year's harvest of rice and cooked in coconut milk. Women dressed in new outfits sat on the floor of the kitchen scraping the coconut to squeeze the milk for the *kiribath*. Mother usually lit the hearth to welcome the New Year, an important task not delegated to the kitchen staff. A pot of milk was boiled in a new clay pot. The boiling milk was allowed to pour over on all sides, signifying prosperity and plenty in the coming year. The villagers forecast the prospects of the New Year by watching the direction of the overflowing boiling milk. The predictions they made were never pessimistic. Everybody made a wish at the same time, on this same day, that their prosperity would overflow the way the boiling milk overflows.

I have vivid memories of Aluth Avurudu festivities celebrated in my aunt's house in Ratnapura, a town about fifty kilometers from Colombo. We all went to her house for the Aluth Avurudu, as it was done in traditional style observing customs and traditions. Growing up in the city, this was a fun time. The village was a fascinating place, and Avurudu customs were even more fascinating.

SWINGS, DRUMS, AND FIRE CRACKERS

The whole village took on the atmosphere of a carnival. My aunt would get *onchillas* (traditional swings) made with strong ropes tied to a sturdy branch of a rather large tree in the garden. We spent many happy hours on the swing, the older brothers pushing it from behind to reach far into the sky. It was a common site in the houses around, a typical Avurudu pastime. We sang "swing songs," which we learned from our village friends, while swinging to great heights.

> *Sura lova wimane suran paddine,*
> *Nara lova guvane naran paddine*
>
> In the heavens above the fairies swing,
> in the human world humans swing.
>
> *Onchili chili chillamale, Wella digata nellikale.*

These lines go beautifully with swinging up and far on the *onchilla* but have no real meaning.

We looked forward to going to Ratnapura, as it was the school holidays. We did not have TVs, computers, or extra classes to attend to supplement school work. We did have a lot of time to play. We were free to roam the village and watch the numerous activities. We liked visiting the humble dwellings of the villagers freshly color washed and cleaned to suit the occasion.

Then there was the potter from the adjoining village going from house to house carrying his wares for the festive season. He carried clay pots of various sizes and forms in a traditional *kada*, a long pole balanced on his shoulder with two baskets hanging on either side. The two baskets tied with strings to the ends of the pole swayed from side to side as he went along. He carefully balanced the two sides with his new pots. It was the custom to buy new clay pots for cooking in the New Year. He went from house to house. At each house he laid the *kada* carefully on the ground. In his *kada* he carried miniature pots, toys for the children to cook *sellambath*. Delighted at his arrival, villagers often treated the *kada* man with hot tea and a chew of betel.

Magginona was a woman who lived on my aunt's property and on special occasions dropped in to help with the domestic work. One day we saw her clad in a skimpy jacket, which barely covered her upper body, and a little piece of old cloth tied round her waist, which came up to her knee. It was a practical working outfit, common attire of the village women. Poor women in the village wore a minimum of clothing as though to say that they owned little. When Magginona went out of the house she wore a longer cloth on top of her short one. By her side was a clay pot of liquid cow dung, which she applied in a systematic pattern on the floor of her mud hut to give it a new covering for the New Year. She explained to us that the paste was clean and also a disinfectant.

In front of her one-room house she had a little verandah which had a piece of furniture that resembled a bed covered with a newly woven mat. This was where her husband slept. On the bed was a brass tray of betel leaves arranged in a circle, with some condiments, which she offered to her humble visitors as a mark of hospitality. Magginona was poor but was happy, kind, and content. There was a chair and a bed inside her hut. She took the ashes from her fireplace and cleaned around it. She too had bought a new pot to cook *kiribath* for the New Year. Outside the house were two large pots filled with water, their mouths covered with coconut shells. It looked as though everything and everybody were being dressed up for the New Year festival.

Avurudu festivities celebrated in villages and urban areas alike had about them a certain indefinable charm. People were extra hospitable and visited each other during this period. We had freedom to visit village houses to observe the various customs and the activities of the villagers. In one house there was a woman seated on a low stool, in front of a large frying pan of hot oil, frying the traditional sweet made with rice flour and honey, called "*konda kavum.*" She too was wearing a scanty blouse with a deep-cut neckline, which exposed her oversized breasts, I wondered if they would pop out if she bent too far forward. The colorful cloth worn tightly around her waist emphasized her thin waist and the curves of her body. Her scanty attire was not considered immodest. In the village culture things were looked at from a different perspective. She poured the dough using a coconut shell with a small hole for pouring the dough in the oil. As the dough fell into the hot oil she used a thin stick to make a shape on top, which she proudly called the *konde*. She explained how important it was to learn how to make the *konde* (knot), which comes with years of experience. As she kept frying, her *kavuns* filled the woven basket hot, fresh and sweet. Freshly cooked *kavun* is a delicacy for special occasions. We were not allowed to eat them as it was the tradition to send the first lot to the temple, and the rest would be served only at the auspicious time.

It was a custom to wear new clothes specially made for the festival according to the colors prescribed as lucky by the astrologers. Since there were no shopping malls, we bought material for dresses and shirts from door-to-door vendors, and our unmarried aunt would make clothes for us. She was called "*kalu* aunty" because her skin color was slightly darker than the rest of us. Everyone rich and poor looked forward to getting new clothes to wear at the same time. For the many poor villagers, this was the only occasion when they got new clothes.

MILK RICE FOR NEW YEAR

The first meal in the New Year was eaten at the auspicious time. It was a tradition for the family to get together for the first meal of the New Year. The tour de force was *kiribath* and other traditional curries. In some homes a *hathmalu* of seven vegetables cooked together as a single curry was made for this occasion. The table was laid with a variety of traditional Sri Lankan sweets and several types of bananas. Many of these sweets were made only during this time, and we looked forward to tasting them. At the auspicious time food was served by our uncle, the head of the household. Before we began to eat, each of us had to pick out some of every item on our plate and put it on a banana leaf. This was taken outside and placed at a higher elevation for the spirits of the dead and the birds. My uncle, who sat at the head of the table, served *kiribath* to all of us, feeding each of us with his own hand, as an affectionate gesture. This was done to emphasize family unity and a wish for good health and prosperity.

We all ate facing the auspicious direction specified for that particular year. This positioning of the family dining table at different angles to suit the auspicious direction of the particular New Year always intrigued me as child, but I did not think it was my place to ask about it. Custom did not call for blind obedience or conformity. Indeed the traditional culture made ample provision for different ideas. Moreover, families generally worked for harmony and moderation.

Offering betel leaves to elders as a mark of respect was another Avurudu custom. Betel was given first to the parents, then to the elders, and last to sisters and brothers. It was the custom for the wife to offer betel to the husband. This symbolized the asking of pardon for any misunderstandings or wrong-doings during the past year and made peace at the dawn of the New Year.

EXCHANGE OF GIFTS AND MONEY

Exchange of gifts and money was an important aspect of the New Year tradi-tion. It was traditionally referred to as "*ganudenu,*" the act of receiving and giv-ing. This custom of *ganudenu* took different forms. It was a rite of exchange. Elders gave money to the young ones, masters to the workers, rich to the poor. Members of the family too exchanged gifts and money among themselves. Along with gifts of clothes and material, coins take a prominent part in the exchange process. Coins received during this exchange were preserved till the dawn of the next year.

The dawn of the New Year was the most auspicious time. Whatever was initiated during this time would yield the highest results. A farmer may plant a tree or work in the field briefly at this time. We were made to study for a short period of time. Our aunt got new fruit trees planted around her house—usually a king coconut tree and a pomegranate plant—and would point out the trees that she had planted in previous years. She believed that trees planted at the auspicious time would bear well.

We watched with curiosity the ritual that Alice Nona performed at the auspicious time. It was her special *ganudenu* with the well. Normally a house-wife performs this task in the village, but in our aunt's household it was always done by Alice Nona. In silent reverence she dropped various types of medici-nal herbs, copper coils, charcoal, and white flowers into the well from which drinking water was drawn. Water is vital for living and hence of great signif-icance. It was of prime concern to maintain the water source in the well and keep it pure. Alice Nona then drew a bucket of water, drank a little of it, and filled a bottle with some to preserve, like the coins she received, till the dawn of the next New Year.

My uncle had his own tradition of *ganudenu* with the people who worked for him and other villagers. A man of standing and influence, he had many visitors at the Avurudu. He kept a pile of paper money of various denomina-tions and coins to give all those who visited him as a gesture of goodwill. In exchange for the betel given by the villagers, he gave a note and a coin on a betel leaf. Not to be outdone, my aunt gave colorful fabric two and a half yards long and a matching yard for the blouse to each of her female servants and the village women who worked for her, including Magginona. She gave a sarong and a banyan to each of the men. My aunt, who days ahead of the festivities had made large amounts of traditional sweets, distributed them in trays to the neighbors. In turn she received trays of sweets from them. We children were all excited and waited impatiently to taste a wide variety of delicacies. The customs are called Avurudu charitra and were observed with care. Indeed it seemed that the very air was filled with tremendous goodwill and warmth.

As I mentioned earlier, the New Year was the time to heal, time to make amends, time to appease a relative alienated by some misunderstanding. Above all it was the time for the family to reaffirm faith in one another. The children regardless of their age would go down on their knees and touch the feet of their mother and father in reverence and then offer betel leaves to each parent as a gesture of deference and respect.

After the essential rituals of the New Year had taken place, a slow-moving afternoon began. It was at this time that the women of the household sat around and played the *rabana*—beat a large round drum, a big tambourine on a wooden frame with supporting legs about a foot high. It was a custom to heat the drum from beneath in order to get better resonance.

As many as six persons could sit around the *rabana,* and the entire house reverberated with the rising crescendo of the rhythmic beat that was familiar to all. Sometimes two or three groups of players would improvise doggerel verses in rhythmic competition arousing the animated interest of an ever-increasing circle of bystanders.

> *Punchi batala getatumba kola*
> *Lida watakara bahina bathala*

This has no significant meaning but the rhythm was repeated on the *rabana.*

FEAST FOR CROWS

A New Year tradition not as universally followed as those I have described was that of feeding crows. It was believed that the crow was in a condition of perpetual hunger and that it was a meritorious act to feed it. My father-in-law, who was not particularly enthused by all the Avurudu celebrations, attached great importance to feeding crows with ghee and rice, a combination that was thought to satiate the hunger of the crows. This was organized with the help of servants. In Sri Lanka the black crow (the color black had negative associations in traditional culture) was a universal presence. The crow had the distinction of making endless cacophonous cries, hence its Sinhala onomatopoeic name *kakka.* Traditional theory did not know what to make of the crow. In a folklore derived from Buddhism, which made much of elephants, monkeys, hares, tortoises, lions, and snakes, the crow was clearly marginalized. Its unseemly scavenging habits were accounted for by a condition of perpetual hunger, which was never appeased. As a child I heard it said by sagacious elders that the benighted crow was born as such because it had in previous lives denied food to those who were hungry and had asked piteously for even a morsel.

I was told too to consider the case of the *piyakussa*, a strange bird that absolutely fascinated me as a child. It flew way up in the sky, a speck in the blue vault, and remained motionless in flight. It emitted a plaintive cry, which was barely heard. I was told that as a consequence of karmic demerits, it was in a perpetual state of thirst, constantly looking for water and strangely finding none.

As the day dragged, spurts of activity alternated with moods of quietness and repose and remembrance of things past. It was not unusual for me to see two of my aunts in a corner comfortably extending themselves on rattan armchairs reliving the yesterdays of their lives. My brothers would be playing with intense concentration a game of *pancha*, using colorful seashells as pieces, on a wonderfully crafted antique wooden game board. My sisters went through their New Year clothes and other finery. Outside the house and at a distance it was possible to hear the young men of the village playing typical New Year games. Tug-of-war, in which large numbers of them took part, always aroused frenzied shouting and excitement. At the other end of the playing field typically another group of young men would be playing *gudu*, which was in all respects remarkably like baseball but without the rich paraphernalia of the latter. Playing cards was a pastime exclusively for men. They chose to play either in the open air seated on mats or inside the house. Playing cards was an important event during the New Year celebrations.

OIL ANOINTING ALL AT THE GOOD TIME

A few days later, New Year celebrations culminated with the ritual of everyone in the household bathing at an auspicious time. They were first anointed with coconut oil mixed with extracts from medicinal herbs, specially prepared in the temple and distributed. This was the thelgana Avuruda. The anointing was done under a canopy from which branches of leaves were suspended, prescribed by the astrologer. The head of the household daubed a little of the oil on each person's forehead, facing the auspicious direction, dressed in the colors for that New Year. The person anointing oil stood on certain leaves also prescribed for the occasion as auspicious. A brass lamp was lit throughout the process. Villagers went to the temple for the oil anointing ceremony. While performing the ceremony, the monks recited the following *gatha* (stanza of benediction).

> May all blessings be upon you
> May all the gods protect you
> By the power of the Buddhas
> May you always be well.

TIME TO LOOK AT THE NEW MOON

The whole season came to a conclusion with many setting off to work and the resumption of normal life at an auspicious time. It was also a time for starting new ventures and setting off for new jobs, although in the urban areas this practice was not universally followed on account of practical considerations.

Looking at the new moon on the New Year was considered important, and a time was prescribed for this too. However, regardless of the New Year, care was taken not to look at the new moon on a Wednesday or a Friday.

Dukaduru badada, sada nobalan senasurada.
Dutuwot sada saduda, madak sapadei eta pasuda

Look ye not on the moon on a Wednesday nor on a Saturday,
should you do so suffering rewards your rashness.
If you see the moon on a Monday,
little joy will come the following day.

In the folklore tradition the wish for long life is expressed in the following poem:

Till the black crow turns white,
Till the *mongaha* [rice pounder] gives tender shoots,
Till the *hunu-sal assa* [piece of the paddy seed] grows into plant.
May you live one hundred and twenty years plus another hundred?

(De Silva 1980: 233)

FOUR

Loving Worship and Loving Kindness

LITTLE ONES

You could hardly hear them lisping the syllables, stumbling over the unfamiliar words. In age, they ranged from five to about eight. Their voices rallied only to fade away. As the lights of flickering coconut lamps fell on their beautiful faces near the *stupa* in Bellanwila, I felt a trifle sad as I saw my own childhood on their faces. Then it was the best point of life—the age of innocence. I watched the little ones taking *pansil* (Five Precepts) urged on by the stentorian voice of the old *upasaka mahattaya* (lay Buddhist) in command of the party of little devotees who were all dressed in spotless white on this beautiful Sri Lankan night.

The children were taking *pansil* in a devotion of love directed first toward the Buddha, who led mankind to freedom from suffering, second they reverenced the dharma (Buddhist religious doctrine), and third the Sangha (order of monks). At about the same time someone else was leading a party of devotees, intoning *gathas* as they circumabulated the great *stupa*, a bubble of whiteness in the surrounding ambience of darkness. Little ones could hardly understand that taking *pansil* was a devotional practice done primarily for the purification of the mind. There was also merit accruing to oneself in reciting *pansil*.

Devotional practices of Buddhists play a crucial role in their spiritual lives. They are part of the living tradition of Buddhism in Sri Lanka and take the form of worship, making offerings, and chanting the *Suttas*. Buddhists kneel before an image of the Buddha, a Bodhi tree, or some object that represents the Buddha, and reflect on the virtues of the Buddha. Offerings are made to the Buddha, the dharma, and the Sangha, for the purpose of ending suffering and gathering merit, for rewards in this life and in the next.

41

The most common ritual of the Buddhists is that of personal worship, which many devout Buddhists perform daily in their homes. On the communal level ritual worship is performed in the temple on *poya* days.

MOTHER'S SHRINE ROOM

Ours was a typical Buddhist home, made so by my Buddhist mother. We had a shrine room for worship, like a private chapel. This house of the Buddha we referred to as the "*buduge*," an alcove, which had a small platform with statues of the Buddha and other objects of veneration. There were also portraits of the Hindu gods and goddesses. In our home we took part in daily worship of the Buddha, Buddha *vandana* (Buddha worship). My mother lit lamps and gave flowers, water, and sometimes *kiribath* (milk rice) as offerings. We were told that the blessings of the Triple Gem would help us to overcome the difficulties and problems that we might encounter in our daily lives.

Some of our friends had elaborate shrine rooms. In villages there were small outhouses rather like the spirit houses in Thailand, built on the side of the main house for worshipping the Buddha, and provision was made to light lamps and make offerings. To the Buddhists this simple daily ritual is important, at the beginning of the day to receive blessings, and at the end of the day to give thanks for the blessings received. A short *metta* meditation session followed. My mother insisted that we all come together for this ritual. The eleven of us often sat in our *buduge*, in the limited space on the floor on a mat, barefooted with our mother reciting the Pali stanzas. We repeated her words like parrots. It was orderly and soothing. The meaning and relevance of the words we came to know over time, by reciting them with mother regularly, as well as in Sunday school.

Our daily *vandana* had other effects. The collective worship brought our family together, helped to resolve minor conflicts among us brothers and sisters. Worship always had an element of meditation on spreading kindness and compassion. We were reminded daily of the importance of tolerance and kindness toward each other and extending kindness to all the members of the family, and in turn to friends and to enemies. Sometimes we went into the *buduge* angry after petty squabbles but came out with good feelings for each other. My mother insisted on kindness and compassion toward the members of our family and urged us to be kind to all, including animals.

Among the many things that we offered in worshipping the Buddha, flowers were the most common. The color, smell, and quality of the flowers were important. Flowers were washed in pure water and arranged in trays for offering. Lotuses took a prime place among the flowers offered to the Buddha. Apart from the fact that lotuses are easily available—usually sold outside temples—they are thought to beautifully exemplify the Buddhist idea of transcendence. The lotus grows not in midstream but in those parts of a stream that are stagnant, muddy, and dirty. It rises above all that. Its long, slender stalk symbolizes the capacity of the human person with the proper perspective to rise above the negativities of birth and environment. It is the flower of flowers offered to the Buddha.

Flowering plants were specially planted for this purpose in the garden. It was the duty of a young maid in the household to gather a tray of several types of sweet smelling fresh flowers for this offering. As part of the offering of flowers, the following *gatha* was recited:

> With these flowers I worship the Buddha,
> by this merit may I gain liberation
> Just as these flowers fade and wither,
> so will my body undergo decay.

These words embody the Buddhist idea of impermanence. We recited stanzas in offering lamps, incense, and food to the Buddha, and in worshipping the Bo tree. When the *vandana* was over, we recited the "aspiration" stanza:

> By means of this meritorious deed
> May I never follow the foolish.
> May I join always with the wise
> until the time I attain nirvana.

Finally merit was transferred to the gods and deities and asked for their blessings and protection.

THE BUDDHIST WORSHIP

The Buddhists, to pay homage to the Buddha, take refuge in the Buddhist trinity—the Buddha, the dharma, and the Sangha—and take *pansil*. This is done daily in private by individuals or as a family collectively. A person who takes the Three Refuges and the Five Precepts is thereby a Buddhist. In Buddhist practice there is no ceremony for conversion to Buddhism, beyond the recitation of these *gathas*. One who recites these *gathas* can rightly call himself or herself a Buddhist. Observance of these precepts is considered important for religious progress.

First homage is made to Buddha by reciting the following:

Namo tassa bhagavato arahato samma sambuddhassa

Homage to Him, the Blessed One, the worthy one, the perfectly enlightened one.

Buddhists declare their reliance on the Three Gems for salvation, and they are as follows: the Buddha is the founder of the religion, the dharma is truth he discovered, and the sangha is the vehicle for preserving and spreading that truth.

> To the Buddha for refuge I go
> To the dharma for refuge I go
> To the sangha for refuge I go
> (these are repeated twice more)

There are Five Precepts that regulate lay life and are observed by the Buddhists:

> I undertake to abstain from destroying life.
> I undertake to abstain from taking what does not belong to me
> I undertake to abstain from sexual misconduct
> I undertake to abstain from false speech
> I undertake to abstain from taking intoxicants.

The first precept is about not destroying life, however miniscule it might be. The mind of a person who is regularly involved in killing animals is polluted with hatred. We are told that suffering inflicted on others will come back as karma as surely as night follows day. War, abortion, euthanasia, capital punishment, and hunting are all considered violent acts, ethically wrong, and bringing with them karmic retribution. One distinguished Sri Lankan professor was visiting us in Chicago. He was a vegetarian. We were driving along the shores of Lake Michigan and came across some people fishing for recreation. He told us that his mother had instructed him not only to abstain from such acts but also from witnessing them. In the world of Buddhism, whatever the gap between theory and practice might be, there is a universal repugnance to killing animals, however miniscule and inconsequential they might be.

The second precept is to refrain from taking what is not given and legitimately belongs to another. A theft committed by force or fraud is an act of greed, resulting in harmful consequence. Honesty in all dealings with all, be they workers, employers, consumers, or citizens, is a basis for true happiness.

The third precept is to refrain from sexual misconduct. Adultery causes pain and distress, breaks up marriages, and disrupts families. Buddhist culture frowns upon promiscuity and overindulgence in sex, which is believed to result in moral degeneration, with evil consequences.

The fourth precept is to abstain from falsehoods. Buddhists are taught to value the truth as precious. Besides lying, the Buddha condemns hurtful speech and senseless babbling as causing deep pain and social mischief.

The fifth precept is to abstain from taking intoxicants. The Buddhist teaching is that intoxicants and drugs dull and distort the mind and vitiate the intellect. This may lead to helplessness and forms of wrong behavior causing personal and social misery.

MEANING OF *PANSIL*

Being born within a tradition has its drawbacks. Due to overfamiliarity one may fail to see nuances that an onlooker may see in encountering an alien tradition for the first time. Taking *pansil* is a case in point. Many Sri Lankans I know rush through the Five Precepts at some speed as if they are taking the last train out of town. Since *pansil* is in the language of Pali, those who recite the *gathas* may not understand their meaning. Taking the Five Precepts is a moral commitment to refrain from doing acts that could harm others and contaminate one in the process. Venerable Thanissaro, who was in Chicago recently, is an American who was ordained as a monk in Thailand. He told us that the resolve to become a monk came to him when he saw on the very first morning looking down from his hotel window monks going on *pindapata* with their begging bowls. Although he found the sight distasteful and what he termed "subversive," it was the critical catalyst that changed his entire life. He lived for years in northern Thailand as a member of the legendary forest monks and told us a few fascinating stories about those rare beings. Among his many writings I came across a short piece on taking the Five Precepts: "Only if the mind is free of wounds and scars can it . . . give rise to undistorted discernment. This is where the Five Precepts come in . . . clear cut, humane, and worthy of respect . . . other people may not respect you for living by the Five Precepts but noble ones do, and their respect is worth more than that of anyone else in the world."

In the Buddhist act of *vandana*, after taking *pansil*, the virtues of the Buddha, the dharma, and the sangha (the Triple Gem) are then recited in that order beginning with Ithipiso gatha where the multiple excellence of the Buddha is recalled. In a veritable plethora of accolades, he is recognized as the Gracious One, the Worthy One, Perfect One, Buddha of Buddhas, the driver of mankind along the Righteous Path taming their negative ways. The pious devotee intoning the soft cadences of the Pali prayer also pays homage to the Buddhas of the past in incalculable dimensions of time and affirms that he has no refuge other than that of the Buddha. This segment is concluded by asking forgiveness for wrongs and transgressions.

Second, in reverence to the dharma (the second of the Three Gems), a Buddhist recites the ancient lines concerning the nature of the dharma, its characteristics, and her personal faith in the work of the Buddha. She tells herself, as her forefathers did ages ago, that the dharma is plain for all to see, that it is neither occult nor esoteric. In the recitation we are told that the dharma is timeless, that it is open to examination and empirical realization, that the knowing of the dharma begins the process of self-transformation and ultimately to achieving the nirvana of self-transcendence. The dharma is the best refuge, the best of all paths.

The Sangha is worshipped by a recitation of the virtues of the Sangha. "The disciple of the blessed one who have practiced well, who have practiced straightly, who have practiced rightly, who have practiced properly is worthy of gifts, worthy of hospitality, worthy of offerings, who should be respected, the incomparable field of Punna (merit) for the world."

For the Buddhists, the ritual of worship is the expression of respect for the greatness of the spiritual leader and gratitude for showing the way to salvation. To enjoy a happy life in this round of existence and beyond, the Five Precepts serve as a guide. In our *vandana* sessions, time was set apart to meditate as a means of mental development. The belief was that a concentrated and purified mind was a true source of happiness. The practice of sitting in a quiet place, in a comfortable posture, being relaxed was something my mother engaged in, as her daily meditation.

YASOMA'S HOUSE

Yasoma performed Buddhist observances that exemplified Buddhist ideals daily. Yasoma was a beautiful person, well matched by her inner composure and beauty. She practiced a Buddhist *dina cariyava* (daily practice) in keeping with Buddhist tradition and Buddhist teachings. She began the day by listening to *pirit* on the radio. Before leaving for work she gathered her whole family in the shrine room to take *pansil* together in a brief worship. Magilin, a servant, brought a tray of fresh smelling white jasmine flowers gathered that day, to offer to the Buddha. The flowers were grown in the garden for the purpose. The family would light a small coconut oil lamp and some incense sticks. Before they left the house, her three children worshipped Yasoma and her husband. The ritual was repeated in the evening. It kept the family together united and happy. It was beautiful.

The verse to worship the mother is as follows:

> *Dine patan ma uppanna—Mov vidi duk bahe kiyanna*
> *Dohot mudun taba menna—vadimi mavni pau arinna*

> From the time of my first breath,
> Mother went through suffering, I cannot fathom,
> I put my hands above my head,
> to worship you in gratitude, my mother.

In an identical verse, gratitude is shown to the father.

Yasoma and I taught in the same school in Peradeniya near the university. Our husbands were teachers at the university. When her husband was leaving for Australia on a year's sabbatical leave, Yasoma gave us her house. Ananda and I, newly returned from Oxford, did not have university quarters, so we were happy to accept the offer. Along with other items with which she entrusted me was her sacred worship place. She had in the shrine room a casket, which contained sacred relics, and its presence brought great blessings to the family. Yasoma explained to me the importance of continuing the religious practices as a mark of respect to the relics. She believed that the presence of the sacred relics would bring me blessings. She added that if I did not make offerings with devotion, on a regular basis, the relics would disappear. However, I was not a particularly religious person, and I failed to perform the rituals regularly. Yasoma returned from her vacation and found that the relics had disappeared. She did not blame me but understood that I was young and my personality was different. She assured me that when she resumed her normal practices, the relics would return to the casket. It is a general belief among devout Buddhists that if the Buddhist rituals are performed on a regular basis in the home, sacred relics reappear in some mystical way. As Yasoma said, it was a very lucky house. My daughter was born there, and we were happy.

MY OTHER MOTHER

Each Buddhist has his or her way of observing the ritual of prayer or *vandana*. My mother-in-law in her middle years in the 1970s showed an interest in the study of Buddhist philosophy. She was an avid reader. She read books on English and European literature, history, and less intellectual reading materials such as Barbara Cartland novels, for entertainment, which she shared with us. My father-in-law shared her enthusiasm in studying the dharma, and they organized an *Abhidharma* class in the house, the purpose of which was to focus on a deeper understanding of Buddhism. Other professionals and friends from the community were invited. It was held on Tuesday afternoons. A monk from the Asgiriya temple Dhammakanda hamuduruwo renowned for his knowledge of *Abidharma* was invited to teach. The collection of professionals, lawyers, doctors, university professors, and others interested in learning the dharma in a serious way, making an effort to study the teachings of the Buddha was an impressive sight. The living area of the house was converted into a classroom. The monk sat on a chair covered with a white sheet. (It was a gesture of lay reverence signifying the exalted purity of the dharma, and its messenger the visiting monk.) The students sat on the floor on little cushions, a tacit recognition that as you got older it was difficult to sit on the floor, in itself a theme for meditation. This practice continued for many years with the same enthusiasm.

My mother-in-law became increasingly familiar with the dharma and the practice of worship, chanting, and meditation. She became a devoted Buddhist. On my subsequent visits to Kandy she explained to me her *dina cariyava* (her daily routine), observed without a break for many years until she passed away. The session lasted three hours. After Ananda's father's death she took *atasil*, wore white saris, and gave up wearing jewelry, as a sign of renouncing. After taking *sil* she worshipped the Buddha, the dharma, and the Sangha, and she meditated for an hour. Then she chanted *pirit* and finally blessed all her children, each individually and the families collectively. She believed that her immense faith in the Triple Gem and her blessings would bring good health and other blessings to her family and protect them from any misfortune. Whenever I had any problems or concerns I would call her or write to her to remember me especially in her prayers.

MAGICAL EFFECTS OF RECITING BUDDHA VIRTUES

The Buddhists have faith in the healing, protective, and meditative powers of the *ithipiso gatha*, a recitation of the nine great virtues of the Buddha. By continuous recitation of the virtues of the Buddha, the devotee consciously aspires to cultivate in time the same virtues. There is also the belief that constant recitations of the *gathas* have talismanic effects, that they bring security and wellbeing. We were made to memorize it to recite in times of distress and despair. As children we believed most things that our mother told us. I found all this firsthand in a rather unexpected manner when we were taken on an excursion to see the botanical gardens, the zoo, and the harbor in Colombo. At the harbor, we saw the large P&O luxury liners, which carried passengers to the west via the Suez Canal. We were all excited at the chance to go around a large ship in a small boat, which carried about fifteen of us girls. When it was time to get off the little boat, we were told to get up in small numbers so that we would not topple the boat, which was heaving up and down in the choppy waters. That was exactly what happened. A few of us fell into the water, and I remember thinking vaguely in the deep water that I was drowning. I remembered my mother's instructions, to recite the *ithipiso gatha* when in distress. A diver rescued me, and it all worked out well. I believed then, as my mother had told me, that the *ithipiso gatha* worked its magic in rescuing us along with the help of the diver.

I heard many stories from victims of the 2004 tsunami that hit Sri Lanka. Some were amazing stories of survival. There were stories of women whose little children were snatched away from their hands who also remembered the *ithipiso gatha* in time of despair. I heard the same story from many women who had been saved from the waters of an angry sea. There was a story of a woman who escaped from the train on which many hundreds were washed away into the sea. (Among the dead was my dear friend Tamara from Chicago who was vacationing in Sri Lanka.) The woman who got saved from the same train was a Buddhist. She was hanging on to a luggage rack on the train carriage, which swayed from side to side by the force of the waves. She went underwater intermittently. Each time she came up she took a deep breath and continued to recite the *ithipiso gatha*. She believed she was miraculously saved by the power of the *gatha*, which stated the virtues of the Buddha. She was pushed out of the carriage and swept away by the waves flowing over the land where she managed to cling onto a tree. Her firm belief was that the power of the Buddha helped her to be swept out. Helped by others she walked over dead bodies and rubble to safety—an amazing story, and even more amazing was her faith in the virtues of the Buddha.

In Sri Lanka, there are simple and beautiful ceremonies performed in temples on religious occasions. A typical Buddhist temple consists of several significant structures. In almost every temple there is the *buduge* (house of the Buddha) with statues of the Buddha seated, reclining, or sometimes both. In front of the statute is an elevated pedestal to offer flowers, incense, and other things to the Buddha. There is always a cylindrical structure, the *stupa* (relic chamber). The *stupa* has many names: *dagaba*, *chetiya*, and *vehera*, and in the compound a Bo tree for Buddhists to worship. A building with an open hall called the "*dharmasala*," also referred to as "*bana maduwa*," for preaching the dharma, meditation, and other religious activities. Living quarters for the monks are also in the premises. We offer flowers, light lamps, and burn incense to the Buddha in the *buduge*, around the Bo tree, and around the *stupa*. These rituals help the less advanced both intellectually and spiritually to satisfy their religious aspirations.

Buddhists worship relics of the Buddha or of any *araht* (advanced being) who, in the manner of the Buddha, has attained transcendence. The relics of the Buddha are of three categories. The first consists of the parts of the body of the Buddha, second, the items the Buddha used, and third, the reminders or things that represent the Buddha.

BUDDHIST FESTIVAL OF LIGHTS

The offering of oil lamps to the Buddha is known as the *pahan puja*. It is performed in the vicinity of the Bo tree, a reminder of the power of the original tree under which the Buddha attained Enlightenment. *Pahan puja* is also done around the *stupa* in a temple. My mother believed that a *pahan puja* brought in good health, wisdom, and knowledge. As the light of the lamp dispels the darkness, so may the merits of the offering to dispel all ignorance and ill will bring blessings. A *pahan puja* is held often to avert evil influences, which may be caused by inauspicious planetary conjunctions. On the temple grounds there are special railings made for the purpose of holding hundreds of coconut oil lamps. My mother believed that lighting lamps around the Bo tree to honor the Buddha would please the gods, who in turn blessed her and her children and kept them healthy.

Sometimes elaborate *pahan pujas* are performed with the assistance of Buddhist monks to ward off disease and overcome bad times. Special offerings of a specific number of lamps with different kinds of oil, such as ghee, mustard, and sesame are made to fulfill a *baraya* (vow) or to counter evil planetary influences. Sometimes entire villages cooperate in holding a large-scale *pahan puja* to bring blessings to the village. My mother once participated in a temple *pahan puja* offering eighty-four thousand lamps to commemorate the eighty-four thousand elements of the Buddha dharma, an ancient Buddhist tradition. This is believed by many to bring great blessings to the country, especially in times of drought, distress, and famine. Special light offerings are also made on *poya* days. When I visited the holy city of Anuradhapura to worship Ruvanveliseya (the great *stupa*), and Siri Mahabodhi (the sacred Bo tree) our party made monetary contributions to light the places and were told that it was an act of great merit.

As children we have participated in the Buddha *pujas* held in temples, as a form of collective worship. The most common Buddha *pujas* is the one performed in the evening known as the *gilanpasa puja*. If the Buddha *puja* is held in the morning, items offered would include *kiribath* (milk rice) and other breakfast items. The Buddha *pujas* are held either in a shrine room or near a *stupa*, either on a *poya* day or on a special occasion. Participants contribute various items as offerings. They stand in line in front of the shrine room and pass the items from hand to hand toward the altar. The mere act of touching the items to be offered becomes meritorious. The items consist of flower trays, flower vases, incense sticks, beverages, and medicinal herbs. Usually a monk who conducts the *puja* recites the *gathas* aloud, and we all repeat them in chorus. On such occasions the monk delivers a short sermon explaining the merits of such a *puja*, and at the conclusion of the ceremony, merit is transferred to dead relatives and to the *devas*, soliciting their blessings.

THOSE FULL MOON DAYS

A full moon day, or as the Buddhists call it, the "*poya*" day is an important religious day. Some *poya* days associated with important events in the history of Sri Lankan Buddhists are more significant than others. In Sri Lanka *poya* is a religious holiday. Offices and shops are closed to encourage people to engage in religious activities, and Buddhists observe the day by visiting a temple to engage in religious activities.

We too went to the temple, wearing white for purity and simplicity, to make offerings to the Buddha. In Sri Lanka, religion is practiced more conspicuously by women and in general by middle-aged women. When young, women are engaged in studying, raising children, and making a home, and when these are accomplished a typical Buddhist woman reverts to a life of doing good deeds to take to the next world. This is the *yanathane* (place to go), and they actively prepare for it by taking *atasil* (meditation), listening to *bana* (preachings), and making offerings to the Buddha and in recalling the dharma.

My mother, like many other Buddhists, often observed *atasil* (Eight Precepts) on *poya* days. The Eight Precepts include three additional precepts to the Five Precepts: (1) to abstain from solid food after midday, (2) to abstain from dancing, singing, music, and improper shows, and from wearing garlands, scents, and so on, and (3) to abstain from the use of high and luxurious beds and seats. In this manner, at least for the duration of a single day, a layman lives the life of a monk, relating more emphatically to the monks and the spartan quality of their lives.

It was my mother's routine on *poya* days to wake up early, bathe in cold water, and wear clean white clothes to go to the temple. In addition she wore a white piece of cloth like a shawl over her right shoulder. This is the traditional *sil* dress. She took off all her gold ornaments on that day, to appear simple. At the temple, a monk administered the Eight Precepts to groups of people, in *sil* dresses, assembled to observe *atasil*. They spent the day at the temple according to a timetable of ritualistic activities, which included sermons, *pujas*, periods of meditation, and dharma discussions. It was considered good karma to feed those who took *sil*, and devotees would distribute rice parcels for their midday meal.

We went to the temple on *poya* days with flowers and coconut oil. Large numbers of women dressed in white saris walked to the temple with lotus and jasmine flowers. As a mark of respect it was the custom to remove one's shoes before entering the temple premises. To the young at heart, apart from the religious aspect, the visit to the temple on *poya* days was a social occasion.

MEMORIES OF VESAK

The most important *poya* day for the Buddhists is the full-moon day of Vesak (in the month of May). Vesak commemorates the birth, enlightenment, and passing away of the Buddha. There is the popular belief that the Buddha paid a visit to the Kelaniya on a Vesak day. Consequently, Buddhists visit the Kelaniya temple in large numbers on this day to hold special *pujas* and to witness the colorful annual procession held there. There is a saying that if you worship the Kelaniya temple once in your life, the sins of a lifetime will be forgiven. A villager would say: "*Upanda sita karapu pau nata, varak vandot kelaniye.*"

Vesak was a religious as well as a fun festival in our household. My mother insisted that we all take *atasil* on this day. The servants were given leave to take *atasil*. We pottered around the kitchen and its unfamiliar topography in their absence. Vesak was celebrated in Buddhist homes, as the grandest religious festival in Sri Lanka. We decorated our homes and lit elaborate and fancy lanterns that were made for this occasion. Having lit our lanterns, we went around on foot with friends and family to see other people's celebrations. This was the fun part of the Vesak festival. Wealthy Buddhists and commercial businesses erected large *pandals* depicting various scenes and stories from Buddhist literature. The *pandals* were illuminated with multicolored electric bulbs. Sometimes a monk with a microphone related the stories shown in the pictures on the *pandal* to the public, and there was a competition to put up the best pandal in town. Cities were transformed into a fairyland of glittering light.

It was a practice in our household to make an elaborate Vesak lantern. It consisted of a single large mother lantern surrounded by a cluster of small satellite lanterns arranged in a geometrical pattern. All my sisters and brothers sat down each evening for many weeks and worked on the lantern, each one contributing his or her part in making and assembling an intricate, elaborate lantern. My youngest brother with his tiny fingers would with great effort do his bit to paste two corners of a tissue square to form a pattern to go on the lantern. All participated eagerly and uncomplainingly to make the lantern beautiful. Male servants in the house did the heavy work of assembling the lantern and carefully hoisting it. When we lit it, which we did every year for many years, it was a magnificent spectacle, and many of our neighbors commented on its beauty and uniqueness.

A particularly enjoyable aspect of Vesak was going around the city to see the decorations. There were many lanterns of different sizes, colors, and shapes. Apart from large pandals, there were also theatrical performances with themes chosen from the Buddhist stories acted out on elevated stages. They were immensely popular. The effort involved (to entertain many in the name of Vesak) was considered meritorious. There were also humorous stage dances performed purely for entertainment.

Another charming facet of Vesak involved food. There are food distribution centers throughout the country on Vesak. They are the *dansela* or places where food is given away to all and sundry for merit. Communities form organizations and with voluntary contributions provide warm cooked meals to everyone who visits the *dansela*. Tents are erected near temples and other popular places with tables and chairs and banners indicating the presence of the *dansela*. Rich and poor, people of all castes sit together for a free meal. Buddhists give lavishly in the name of the Buddha for two days. Many pilgrims, visiting the cities to view Vesak decorations, especially poor, find the free warm meal a great boon. The idea is that no one should go hungry on Vesak.

There were devoted laymen specially assigned to solicit passersby to go to the *dansela* to acquire merit. A young boy I knew from our neighborhood from a fairly affluent family once sneaked into a *dansela* and ate rice and potato curry, his favorite food. In affluent homes this type of simple food is not cooked often. He kept eating the potato curry until he got sick and had to go to a doctor. For a time being he acquired dubious fame and a nickname.

The *dansala* for Buddhists is rather like the *langar* of the Sikhs. A Sikh temple has a special area, the *langar*, set aside where food is prepared and served to anyone who comes, whether Sikh or not, rich or poor. We went to one in Boston and ate warm, delicious *roti*, an Indian bread, with some kind of curry, sitting on the floor with all the others on plates. This is the Sikh belief of sharing and displays the equality of all human beings. Unlike the *dansala*, which is seasonal, it is a daily routine in the Sikh temples.

There is also the practice of singing *bakti gee* (devotional songs) at Vesak times, rather like Christmas carols. I remember boats made in the shape of swans decorated with Vesak themes floating in Kandy Lake carrying young girls and boys singing *bakti gee* on Vesak days.

A KING, A DEER, AND THE MONK

The full moon day of Poson in the month of June is of special significance too to Buddhists in Sri Lanka. On Poson *poya* many thousands of pilgrims flock to Anuradhapura the ancient capital city of Sri Lanka and to nearby Mihintale. This celebration was to mark the introduction of Buddhism by the great missionary monk from India, Thera Mahinda, the son of emperor Asoka, whose meeting with the then-king of Sri Lanka on this full moon day twenty three centuries ago, was the turning point in the history of the island.

The legend is fascinating. During this time King Devanampiyatissa (loved by gods), was the ruler of Sri Lanka. King Asoka, who had embraced Buddhism, was bent on sending missionaries of goodwill abroad. He knew king Devanampiyatissa. King Asoka asked his son Mahinda, who had attained arahathood, to go to Sri Lanka to preach the dharma to king Devanampiyatissa. In India when Mahinda was wondering whether it was the appropriate time to go to Sri Lanka with this mission, the Sakka, the god of gods, who plays a prominent role in Buddhist legends, approached him and informed him that the time was right. Mahinda then used his psychic powers to go to Mihintale, near Anuradhapura.

At the time, King Devanampiyatissa was in the forest hunting. He was chasing a deer on Mihintale mountain when he passed Mahinda and his other missionaries. Seeing the king, Mahinda addressed him, "Tissa come here." The king, who could not imagine anyone calling him by his personal name, was surprised. When he looked around he saw the yellow-robed monks. The king inquired who they were. Mahinda gauged the intellectual level of the king, preached the dharma, and thereby the king and his followers became Buddhists.

I may add that it took me years to understand the simple entrancing magic of Buddhist forms of worship, pilgrimages, and uniquely colorful celebrations such as Vesak and Poson. Worship over the years slowly but surely creates two elements in the mind—faith and morality. Morality ensures the purity of the mind, the ridding of the mind of defilements of gross sensual indulgence, hatred, envy, jealousy, and so on, enabling the mind to have a cleared field as it were to understand the deeper issues of insight and transcendence.

FIVE

Givers

Many Motives, Many Fruits

THE GODS SHOULD NEVER be taken for granted. As always, swift was the wrath of Minerva. Every now and then when our family made preparations to go to Kataragama, one sensed a certain tension. One never spoke aloud about how the trip was planned prior to reaching Kataragama. To go there without mishap and to return home safely was entirely in the hands of a god whose continuing goodwill and blessings were constantly and silently sought on the journey, especially by the leader of the group. We children, whose monumental ignorance and lack of tact were taken for granted, were warned about what we said once we were in the Ruhuna the *adaviya* or demesne of the god Kataragama where he reigned supreme. Using a Sinhalese phrase that is difficult to translate, we were told not to let our wagging tongues "get ahead" of ourselves.

I was reminded of those childhood trips recently when we left Kandy early on a Saturday morning in August—our destination Kataragama. My brother-in-law Harilal, and his wife, Visaka, who were taking Ananda and me to Kataragama, had planned the trip ahead, in detail. We would return to Kandy late on Sunday evening because on the following day Ananda and I were hosting a *dana* for the Malwatte monks. During the last several years this had become a routine item on our Sri Lanka summer itinerary. There was legendary lore associated with Kataragama: a saga of mysterious incidents such as flat tires; the capricious malfunctioning of brand new cars; or someone in the party suddenly falling ill, without any apparent reason, were embedded in my mind. But our trip that day, as Harilal had planned, was without event.

Was it that modern technology, expeditious modes and facilities of traveling, and the ubiquitous cell phone had somehow changed everything? The old magic of the trip and its allure (not to mention wild elephants literally standing in the center of the road) were all gone. They were the remembered vignettes of old Ceylon, the Ceylon of my childhood.

In a rather large van driven by an obviously competent driver, who hardly spoke, I could not commune silently with my thoughts. Instead of forebodings about the road ahead of us, a certain raucous atmosphere and bonhomie (ill suited for a pilgrimage) prevailed. Harilal burst into Sinhala songs and insisted on stopping the van to give rides to sundry strangers waiting patiently at bus stands along the way for buses that came late or not at all. There was a certain old world Sinhala charm to these circumstances marked by extraordinary civility on both sides. Indeed when it came time to drop off our guests, we were sorry to see them go. I loudly proclaimed that no one in his right mind would give rides to perfect strangers. My remark was met with stony silence. On this occasion at least my Sri Lankan kinsmen refrained from asking me why I continued to live in America. *Time* and *Newsweek* (commonplace in many Sri Lankan middle-class homes) provided fodder to a pervasive Third World thesis that America and Chicago in particular were terrifying places to live and morally decadent at that. Grudgingly (silent and unwilling to admit defeat in the cultural battle), I felt that my kinsmen had a point.

My fitful reveries, interrupted by the chatter in the van, ended when the van drove up to the Buttala rest house. Rest houses, relics of colonialism in old "Ceylon," scattered throughout the country, were initially meant to be resting places for weary British civil servants on "circuit." The British civil servants, away from their work in *kachcheris* (offices) and often separated from their wives and families left behind in England, relaxed in the rest house, where they were served with servility, and every need was met in a manner typical of local hospitality. Buttala had the ambience and old world colonial charm of the typical rest house far away from Colombo, which I loved in my childhood. The rest house keeper at Buttala had a flexible menu for us, a great lunch— rice and curry sans meat and a spicy *pol sambol*, a mixture of freshly ground coconut mixed with red onions and ground chilies with lime juice and salt added to taste.

The old Buttala road would take us to Kataragama. We had done well on time. It was early afternoon, and the heat was near stifling. We were in the dry zone. Stretches of rice fields, not altogether lush, were broken by gobbet-like mountains. Ananda had persuaded his brother to break the journey here because he wanted to see an *aranya* (Buddhist monastery) that he had stumbled upon the previous year. This place had affected Ananda immensely. Back in Chicago he often spoke of it. But we were not sure of its precise location. Finally, a dirt track took us to the Buddhugal Forest Hermitage. It was here in a seemingly inconsequential setting that afternoon that I stumbled on what I thought had long disappeared in Sri Lanka—an entire region held together by a monastery practicing Buddhism—especially the sterling virtue of *dana*.

A GLIMPSE OF FOREST MONKS

The grounds of the monastery were spacious, but in the opposite direction they seemed to end rather abruptly at the mountain, which we had seen for miles earlier on. Narrow pathways led to the mountain, every now and then marked by steps, that had been hewn out of the rock over the centuries. Laymen and casual visitors were not encouraged to go farther when the path became a steep ascent leading to the *kutis* in which the individual meditating monks resided. No one would be inclined to do so anyway because of the great respect Sri Lankans have for meditating monks. Here as elsewhere in Sri Lanka, unnoticed by foreign and local tourists who pretty much kept to the beaten track, was a community of forest monks. Ananda told me on the visit he made to the same place the previous year with his brother that providentially they happened to go to the place at about the time the monks were coming down the mountain for the midday *dana*. The monks walked in single file keeping their eyes on the ground. They walked at an almost brisk pace while preserving the unhurried dignity for which they are known. Ananda, who all his life had associated with the Malvatte monks, told me that he was struck by the simplicity of the saffron robes these monks wore. Ananda counted as many as forty faded robes. It was possible that the community was too poor to buy new robes for the monks. My impression of the Buddhugal Forest Hermitage was that neither the monks nor the laymen thought that the faded robes were an issue, mindful as they were of the "real thing." Those from the community knew what the "real thing" was. In successive visits to Sri Lanka I had begun to observe a greater and involved focus on the transformative aspects of Buddhism and less on popular ceremonies and rituals. At the end of the *dana*, after blessing all who had partaken of it and helped, the monks, led by the elderly senior monk made their journey back and would not be seen until the following day.

However, on this day nothing much seemed to be happening. Ananda and his brother decided to go to the office to make a donation. Visaka and I, to escape the oppressive heat of the sun, remained in the van half listening to the driver, who was trying to explain why in this particular model of van, the air conditioner was only effective in the front portion of the van.

Meanwhile, in the modest office of the monastery where visitors sat on benches, the man in charge using the only technology he had—a telephone— had just finished an arrangement and was free to talk to his two visitors. A *dayakaya* had been discharged from the district hospital but had no way of getting home. Another *dayakaya*, who was also a member of the Buddhugal monastery and had a small pickup truck, was persuaded to give the man a ride. Harilal and Ananda each made donations that were gratefully received. A genial man sporting a walrus mustache and like the rest of the lay community wearing the national dress (a white sarong and white shirt extending well below the waist) was optimistic about the financial solvency of the institution. "We somehow manage. There is a lot of goodwill around here. All the time unexpectedly out of the blue we get things." Our visit illustrated his point. Ananda received a receipt for his donation. It had about it a quaint old world charm, the format reminding me of the way printing was done in Sri Lanka in the 1950s. What interested me most about it was the benediction to the donor, which promised in return for his modest donation multiple benefits, including perfect health, long life, comforts of lay life, fame, wealth, power, and so on. The benediction concluded with the wish that Ananda in the fullness of time would understand the path (Noble Eightfold Path) leading to nirvana.

CHEERFUL LOT OF PILGRIMS

There was a bus full of pilgrims parked parallel to our van. Their leader came to us to make conversation in the Sri Lankan way. We were interested in why they were here. He in turn was curious about our presence and told us that the purpose of their pilgrimage was the day's *dana* for the meditating monks who lived in the little *kutis* (huts) in the forest far away from the village. Buddhist devotees support and admire meditating monks. These were regular visitors offering *dana* to the monks. Monks need the lay people to keep them alive. It is a continuing reciprocal process. The leader of the pilgrims made us aware that it was not easy to get a date for the *dana*, and one had to book well in advance. The pilgrims were farmers from a village several miles away. Great faith and devotion went into what they offered. Their joy at performing the *dana* and their excitement at completion of the meritorious deed was an eye-opener for us. They were people of meager means but their devotion was abundant.

The villagers had arrived the day before to prepare breakfast and a midday meal for the monks. The monks in the *pindapata* style came with begging bowls from the forest to receive the *dana*. Afterward the monks silently walked away, one monk remaining behind to bless the devotees and give the *pinanumodana* (transferring merit). He answered questions from the pilgrims if they had any, a short discourse was given, and that was all they saw of the monks.

The leader of the pilgrims spoke with enthusiasm of their next visit which would be to the Kelani Vihara for a *dana* to the *atasil* observants on the *poya* day. Their ambition was simply to rejoice in the act of *dana*. I was tempted to give a contribution to their *dana*. I felt they were poor and would make good use of the money, but I did not want to offend them. I looked around for our traveling companion and adviser, Mr. Munasinghe, the wise man. He was not in the van. Had I changed with long years of living abroad and tuned to the Western way of thinking? It was a dilemma I battled with. Later I regretted not having given some money, which I could have easily afforded. Besides this was the Buddhist way of contributing to the *dana*. Why did I not think easily and freely like the villagers? I had lost my spontaneity, god knows in the name of what. The thought haunted me for a long time.

We watched the pilgrims, both men and women, get into the bus to leave for home, happy in the knowledge that they had gained merit. The leader had told us that the pilgrims had taken the time to boil a pot of water for the next group of pilgrims, whoever they might be, so that they could have tea on their arrival after a long journey. Their concern for and thought of the comfort of others was the village way. This is real Buddhism, without middle-class sophistication, that keeps Buddhism alive and vibrant.

THE RATIONALE OF GIVING

Generosity is encouraged as an essential attribute in Buddhist teachings, a way of getting rid of craving and the desire to acquire. The Buddha taught that there are three types of meritorious deeds essential to the achievement of nirvana, the ultimate goal of the Buddhist path. The first major way of gaining merit in Buddhism is *dana*, which means literally giving. The other two are *sila* (observance of moral precepts) and *bhavana* (meditation). In Buddhist ethics, *dana* is a necessary act in one's ethical development. The basic nature of humans is to grasp. Buddhism encourages people to be generous as a way of liberation from grasping. The wholesome act of giving releases the tyranny of craving and grasping.

The tradition of giving is deeply rooted in Sri Lanka and is associated with the Buddhist doctrines of karma and rebirth. The monks in Sunday school taught us that the karmic rewards of generous acts are far greater in value than the original value of what is given. The act of giving helps in gaining wealth, beauty, and pleasure in this lifetime and better births in the future. Sri Lankan Buddhists often quote the popular sayings from the Pali texts, the Jataka stories, and Sinhalese literature, to give legitimacy to the act of giving. The rich and generous are much talked of and admired and command respect in the community.

Giving, done with understanding and consciousness, increases the benefits to the giver. This was one thing I remember understanding about Buddhism in my childhood when other things seemed difficult to grasp. The magnitude of the merit gained was supported by three factors: the motive of the giver, the spiritual state of mind of the recipient, and the quality of the gift. Therefore, we were encouraged to keep the mind pure when giving, choose the most appropriate recipient, and be aware of the quality of what was given.

At *dana* ceremonies in our home, the monks took care to emphasize that the practice of giving helped to purify the mind. When we decide to give something of ours to someone, the act logically weakens the desire or the craving for the object in general. The giving accompanied by wholesome thoughts generates good karma, which, in turn leads to happy future births. With the act of giving, the mind becomes pure and enables the giver to develop virtue, concentration, and wisdom.

GIVING IN MANY WAYS

There are many forms of giving in Buddhist culture. The concept of *Dana paramita* (a gift of generosity), a vibrant form of giving, involving the donation of blood or organs, is a common Buddhist practice. Buddhists have been at the forefront in the movement of organ donation, and it is deeply entrenched in the religious cultural thinking. Sri Lankan Buddhist lore is full of such acts of giving. Indeed, the Sri Lanka Eye Bank, first set up in a small way in Colombo, is the biggest in the world and has helped millions of people in nearly two hundred countries regain sight. My aunt organized an educational campaign in the temple to encourage and educate the villagers about the importance of donating organs, blood, and eyes.

In this context, the story of Podiappu, the gardener in Ananda's father's house, comes to my mind. He had no family we knew of. For many years their beautiful garden with exotic flowers was tended by the careful hands of Podiappu. Seasonally he would in addition to working in the garden arrange many vases with fresh-cut flowers and polish the brass. There was great activity one day concerning the gardener, as he had to go for surgery, and the hospital requested a donation of blood. Ananda believed in the merit of blood donation and also, with affection for Podiappu, was the first to volunteer. Ananda's blood donation caused concern in the household, especially by his mother. Many of us were made to accompany him to the hospital, and Ananda's older sister was asked to see that all went well and that Ananda did not face danger. I was rather amused because Ananda was a strong, healthy man, and I did not think a pint of blood less in his system would kill him. With some amount of preparation, he was made to lie back on a bed, and his blood was drawn. Ananda was embarrassed at the great attention given to him. This was demeaning, and to show his masculine prowess he got up quickly. I had left the room to go outside for a breath of fresh air, but when I looked back I saw Ananda flat on the floor and his sister in great panic. The doctor told us that nothing was the matter; Ananda had got up too quickly. I was amused at the whole episode, and it was hard to keep a serious face. Ananda continued this practice many times over and gave blood to other members of the household when requested, more or less becoming the official blood donor. Podiappu was proud that the young master of the house gave him blood.

Growing up in Sri Lanka we learned many Jataka stories that emphasized the importance of giving in Buddhist doctrine. These stories, like Aesop's fables, were often our bedtime stories. My mother delighted in narrating Jataka stories, many times over. Buddha, in his previous incarnations as bodhisattvas, had donated his life, eyes, head, flesh, and blood to others. A bodhisattva is simply one who has taken a vow to become a Buddha and fulfills ten sterling qualities of excellence over many births in attaining Buddhahood. The Jataka stories are a genre of literature that is widely known to all Buddhists. In the stories the Buddha as a bodhisattva was born in a variety of manifestations as a god, a man, or one of the higher animals. The virtuous are not born to lower forms.

HOW A HARE GOT INTO THE MOON

The Sasa Jataka story was one of the first stories we learned in Sunday school. It is also a favorite of the monks, to illustrate the virtue of giving. In the time when King Brahmadatta was ruling in Banares, the bodhisattva was born as a hare and lived in the woods. A great famine was raging. A Brahmin came to the hare and asked for food. The bodhisattva was delighted and said "Brahamin you have done well in coming to me for food. This day I will grant you a boon, which I have never granted before." The perplexed Brahamin was asked to pile up logs and kindle a fire. When this was done the hare sacrificed himself by jumping into the midst of the flames. The hare addressed the Brahamin with the following stanza:

> Nor sesame, nor beans, nor rice have I as food to give,
> But roast with fire my flesh, which I yield, if thou with us wouldst
> live.

The magnanimous hare jumped with joy in the burning fire and seemingly perished. Sakka, the god of gods, who had come to test the hare in the form of the Brahamin, used his miraculous powers to douse the flame. Sakka then said to the bodhisattva, "Wise hare, may your virtue be known throughout the whole world for many years to come." He then drew the sign of the hare on the orb of the moon so that the selfless act will be forever remembered. Buddhist villagers believe to this day that the form you see on the moon is that of the hare. In 1969 when the Americans sent an astronaut to the moon, many villagers were skeptical, as they believed in the traditional story of the hare. They would look up at the moon and try to figure out the picture of the hare Sakka drew, or at times refer to it as the *handahami* (the moon rabbit). In Buddhist teaching the highest form of giving is when one sacrifices one's life for the sake of others. The Bible says much the same thing; that there is no greater love a man may have than to lay down his life for another.

In the Sivi Jataka, the bodhisattva was born as the king of the Sivi country. He delighted in sharing his wealth with the poor. He set up free food distributing centers throughout his kingdom. He was happy with his generous deed, but he felt the need to give more. The desire to give part of his body to anyone who might ask for it came over him. Sakka read his thoughts, and appearing before him as a blind Brahmin, asked for his eyes. The king agreed to give them and sent for his surgeon, Jivaka. Amid the protests and lamentations of his family and his subjects, Sivi had his eyes removed and given to the Brahmin. When the sockets had healed, Sivi wished to become an ascetic and went to the park with an attendant. Sakka appeared before Sivi and offered him a boon. The king wished to die, but Sakka insisted on his choosing something else as his wish. Sivi then asked for the return of his sight. The eyes reappeared, but they were neither natural eyes nor divine eyes. They were eyes called "truth absolute and perfect." Sivi assembled all his subjects, and, resting on the throne in a pavilion, taught the value of generosity.

Another form of Buddhist giving is the *abhaya dana* (gift of life), or freedom from the fear of death. In the Jataka that illustrates this, Prince Siddhartha was playing with his cousin Devadatta. Siddartha was the most compassionate person, whereas Devadatta is depicted in Buddhist literature as a jealous and violent person. Devadatta shot a swan with his arrow, and Siddartha took out the arrow and saved the swan. Devadatta got angry and claimed the swan, saying, "I shot the swan, and it belongs to me." Siddhartha believed that because he saved the swan it belonged to him. Finally both had to go before a judge to settle the dispute. The judge declared that the lifesaver must be the owner of the swan. This story is popular among the villagers. Buddhists often free animals from slaughterhouses to celebrate special events in their lives: birthdays, weddings, anniversaries, and sometimes recovery from sickness. In Thailand Buddhists buy cages of birds and release them as a way of performing *abhaya dana*.

DIFFERENT QUALITIES OF GIVING

Aside from the different types of giving, monks also talk about the different qualities of giving. Irrespective of the size and quantity of the gift given, goodwill between the donor and the recipient is considered important. The recipient must not feel humiliated or hurt, and what is given must be done with sensitivity and consideration. Personal involvement in the act of giving is considered meritorious. One should give only what is appropriate and useful while making the one who receives feel welcome. When offering alms to monks, deference and respect, along with delight in the act of giving, are emphasized. What is given should be timely and useful, and it should not hurt the donor or the recipient. It should be for the well-being of the recipient. Things that result in affliction for others such as weapons, poisons, and intoxicants are not considered good things to give. Giving unsuitable foods and drinks to the sick, even though they may ask for them, is discouraged. More than what is given, the manner of giving is considered important.

MY MOTHER, A BEGGAR'S DREAM

In our household giving, even in a small way, was practiced daily. I remember—and it fascinated me as a child—in a room next to the kitchen, there was a fairly large rectangular box made of solid wood that was an heirloom of sorts passed from mother to daughter when the latter set up house. This was the *halpettiya* (rice box). As you opened it there was a detachable wooden tray with separate compartments for a variety of condiments. Below the tray, and occupying the bulk of the space, was a large quantity of rice. There were also cylindrical metal containers (one bigger than the other) for measuring the rice. These were used daily both for domestic cooking and for giving away quantities of rice to itinerant beggars or to poor people who lacked the means to buy rice. The box was opened several times a day to dole out rice for beggars. On any given day three to four beggars would turn up. The distribution of rice either for cooking for the household or for the beggars was always done by my mother, an important task never delegated to servants. I recollect that my mother in giving out the rice for cooking always gave extra handfuls for cooking, anticipating someone dropping in on that day for a meal or to be given to a beggar.

Sri Lankans also give to the needy on a regular basis. To our house the poor came for food, money, and clothes. Something was always given. The poor in need of a meal at midday would come to our house and sit outside waiting to be served. We would see the same faces on a regular basis. There were no soup kitchens in Sri Lanka or organized charity. No one was turned away begging for food. We also had a coin box kept handy, and as children we loved to run to the gate to give money to beggars.

THE MASTER SPEAKS

Buddha's teaching emphasizes the need to give to get rid of craving and attachment. But in popular Buddhist practice the act of giving often has more

than one motive behind it. Many generally give with the idea of getting
something better in the future, better births and wealth. "A noble giver is
one who is happy before, during and after giving. Before giving he is happy
anticipating the opportunity to exercise his generosity. While giving he is
happy that he is making another happy by fulfilling a need. After giving he
is satisfied that he has done a good deed." The Buddha compares one who
righteously earns wealth and gives much of it to the needy to one who has
both eyes; the one who only earns wealth but does no merit is like "a one-
eyed man."

   In the Sri Lankan society, given the pervasive influence of Buddhism,
theoretically everyone should be giving. Why one person gives and another
walks away may be attributed to what the Sinhalese call "*sasara purudda*," or
the cumulative habit of *samsaric* inclinations. In other words (though not an
inflexible rule or axiom), someone generously gives because he or she has
given in previous lives and will continue to do so by sheer force of inclination
in the *samsaric* journey until transcendence is achieved. The cynical reflection
that those who give do so only because they can afford to give is therefore
untenable. If that were so, given the immense affluence in American society,
we should have not one but a thousand Bill Gates.

THE BILL GATES OF THE GANGES VALLEY

In Sri Lankan culture a generous giver is compared to the fabled
Anathapindika, a Buddhist Croesus. Anathapindika was born as Sadaria. As
a result of his great generosity, he was given the name Anathapindika, which
means "the feeder of the helpless." He was a great follower of the Buddha
known for his generosity and lavish giving. After establishing the monastery
for the Sangha in Jetavana, he invited the Buddha to receive the donations.
When Buddha was entering Jetavana, Anathapindika scattered flowers and
burned incense, and as a symbol of the gift he poured water from a golden
decanter saying, "This Jetavana vihara I give for the use of the brotherhood
throughout the world." The Buddha received the gift and replied, "May all evil
influences be overcome; may the offering promote the kingdom of righteousness and be a permanent blessing to mankind in general to the land of Kosala, and especially also to the giver." He was assiduous in his support for the
resident Sangha. He supplied the monks dwelling there with necessities,
including meals and other requirements of clothing, alms bowls, and medicines. It is said that every day at mealtime his home was filled with saffron-
robed monks and that there was an ambience of saintliness. Anathapindika
welcomed the monks and regarded them as spiritual friends who lived for the
welfare and benefit of all beings.

GIVING IS HARD—IT WAS ANCIENTLY SO

Let me get back to my narrative of ancient times. King Kosala once asked the Buddha, to whom alms should be given to obtain the best results. The Buddha replied that alms given to the virtuous would bear the greatest fruit. Buddha specified that giving alms to the Sangha, the community of people, the noble individuals who have entered the path of saintship who are endowed with morality and wisdom, would lead to good results. Just as seeds sown on fertile, well-prepared, well-watered fields produce abundant crops, the alms given to the virtuous without expectations result in good births.

To illustrate the fact that one must not have second thoughts about giving, my mother read the story of King Kosala to us. King Kosala asked the Buddha about a rich man in Savatti who passed away without leaving any heir, and consequently all his property went to the royal treasury. Though rich, he was tightfisted and did not practice *dana*. He was unwilling to spend any money on himself, and he ate very sparingly and wore cheap clothes. The Buddha told King Kosala that in past existences too the man had been rich. One day when a monk came to his house on *pindapata* he instructed his wife to offer the monk alms. The wife was surprised because he did not give anything to anyone. With permission from her husband the wife filled the monk's alms bowl with food. When the rich man saw the substantial amount of food his wife offered to the monks, he thought that it would have been better if his servants were given this food instead so they would give him better service. He regretted his act of generosity. Because the man had offered alms to the monk he became rich in the present life, but because he regretted the giving he was not able to enjoy his wealth.

Although giving is considered a great virtue in Buddhism, some Buddhists have their own notions of *dana*. As a young adolescent, I remember our neighbor, Mrs. Perera, who believed that she was a good Buddhist and lived strictly according to Buddhists teachings. She took *pansil* every day and was a regular visitor to the temple on *poya* days to take *atasil*, but generosity was not her great virtue. She preserved and guarded with care all her material possessions, which would go to her daughter after her own death. She was known among her neighbors for her miserliness and inability to give anything to anyone outside her immediate family. It is a habit among some Sri Lankans to rinse one's mouth with water after a meal and throw it out on the grass outside the house. She too practiced rinsing her mouth after meals. She told our neighbor, Mervin, that this was an act of generosity. She contemplated that "with this mouth wash water there could be tiny particles of food, and may the *pretas* [spirit beings hungry and wanting food] use these as food and satisfy their hunger." Mervin, amused at her story, told her, "Mrs. Perera, you cannot go to nirvana on the foot board in a bus. To go to nirvana you must pay the full fare. One has to perform wholesome good deeds." Mrs. Perera was annoyed at the comment but did not see the sense of it. People in crowded buses get rides on the footboards for free. The driver tries to put them off as it is an illegal practice, but they insist on traveling, and since they are not in the bus proper, they do not feel the need to pay. There are often arguments about this, but the person on the footboard eventually wins.

THE A TO Z OF GIVING A *DANA*

A significant ceremony performed ritually in Buddhist homes is the giving of the *sanghika dana*, when alms are given to the Sangha (the order of monks). This is generally given on special occasions such as when one occupies a new house, a marriage, death anniversary, or following a *pirit* ceremony. Some Buddhists give *sanghika dana* on a regular basis, and this was so in Ananda's home. Custom generally requires the presence of at least four monks who have received higher ordination for a *sanghika dana*. But theoretically even one monk is considered sufficient to represent the Sangha. The donor goes to the monastery and informs the chief incumbent monk of the intention to give a *dana* to the Sangha. Theoretically the *dana* is for the entire order of the monks, present, past, and future; therefore it is not proper to mention any preferences of monks by name. It is the chief monk's task to decide which monks should represent the Sangha at the *dana*.

On the day of the *dana*, the monks are conducted from the temple in a procession. A layman leads the procession carrying a casket of relics on his head. The casket is taken under a canopy. Sometimes drummers participate. The head of the household receives the monks. It is the custom to wash the feet of each monk as they enter the house in reverence to the Sangha. The monks are then led to *asanas*, specially arranged cushioned seats on the floor.

The ceremony begins with the *puja* to the Buddha. A special tray of food items is arranged for the Buddha *puja*, along with an offering of flowers. The ceremony begins with the taking of *pansil*. *Gathas* are recited to offer the food and flowers to the Buddha. The senior monk gives a short discourse on the significance of the occasion and the good merit that would result in giving food to the monks. Food offered to the monks is laid on a clean mat in dishes and covered with a white cloth along with the *pirikara* (gifts) for the monks. The food offered to the monks is referred to as *sangika* food, dedicated to the use of the monks. Before serving the food to the Sangha, the monks recite the following *gatha*:

Imam bhikkham saparikkharam bhikkhusanghassa dema,

These alms along with other requisites we offer to the community of monks.

The ceremony being the midday meal for monks is offered before noon. It is considered a meritorious deed to serve the monks, so all participate. After the meal, it is the tradition to offer an *atapirikara*. This consists of the eight monastic requisites of a monk: an alms bowl, three robes, belt, razor, sewing needle, and water-strainer. All are offered to the chief monk and the other gifts are offered to the rest.

Once the *dana* ritual is over, the monks conduct the *pinanumodana* (giving merit), an important aspect of the ceremony. The monk who gives the discourse talks of the merits of giving and reminds those present of the great Buddhist devotees of the past and their generosity to the Buddha, the dharma, and the Sangha. They explain the need to have good thoughts throughout the process of *dana*, in its preparation, during the *dana*, and after the *dana*. Everyone present takes part in the merit receiving ceremony by sitting on the floor, with folded palms. The merit thus gathered is transferred to the dead relatives, friends, and deities who are waiting to receive merit, and finally the blessings of the deities are evoked.

Pinanumodana is a significant concept in Buddhist thought: the sharing of one's wholesome deeds with others so that they too can receive the benefits of our generous deeds. Buddha taught that we are not the sole heirs to our deeds. Sharing our good karma with others, friends, and relatives raises wholesome consciousness of others in our good deeds, and thereby they too rejoice in good deeds. We can also share the merits of good karma with dead relatives whereby they can receive good benefits.

THE LEARNED MONK EXPLAINS IT ALL

Once, after a *sanghika dana* in our house, Venerable Pahamune Gunananda of the Malwatta monastery who was teaching with me at Dharmaraja College, gave the *pinanumodana*, in traditional style. He related the advice given to the layman Tundila by the Buddha at Kapilavastu. The householder Tundila, and his wife, Irandati, offered alms to the order of monks led by the Buddha. The Buddha said that while it was important to give to all and sundry, it was better to give to those who lead spiritual lives. Giving to monks is considered the best kind of giving because monks lead spiritual lives and are the repository of wisdom they share with laymen. They also do not earn wages. They give spiritual guidance to the laity, and the laity has an obligation to support them. Whether born in heaven or as human beings, those who give enjoy the greatest happiness.

Venerable Gunananda said that the generosity of the giver results in the giver getting what he or she wants, akin to the wish-giving tree, *kapruka* (a mythical tree that grants everything that one wishes) or a treasure pot, which never dries up. Be generous to the poor, provide shelter to them, and give alms, and you will be rewarded. The poor need the help of the rich to survive, and the rich become spiritually richer by helping the poor. He said that the rewards of generosity come to you wherever you are, on a treetop, on a mountain, in the sky or earth, or in between, with the assurance that you will receive food, drink, and material goods.

It was a custom to invite the monks from the two main monasteries of Malwatte and Asgiriya in Kandy to my father-in-law's house periodically for *sanghika dana*. Close friends and relatives were invited to participate in the merit-making ceremony, and a feast was prepared for the occasion. The priests who knew my father-in-law were elaborate and lavish in their praise of him. Monks prayed that he would be born well in his next incarnation with wealth, fame, and glory and lack nothing. An elaborate *pinanumodana* was given, focusing on his goodness, which made the household happy and brought immense joy to all.

Servants of the household took great pains to prepare the *dana* and perform all the work of setting it up, thereby becoming an integral part of the collected merit produced by the household on the occasion, but they were hardly mentioned in the ritual of *pindima*. One might argue that the merit acquired by the servants was the greater. Although the affluent householder provided the wherewithal of the *dana*, it was the efforts of the servants that transmuted the raw material as it were into an impeccably beautiful offering. The servants showed no bitterness because our social structure accepts that due to the lack of good karma, they are born poor and as such have no claims to recognition. It bothered me, but I was never comfortable expressing my view. However, if the karma theory holds true, these servants may well be born in future births to fame and fortune.

Buddhist households in our community customarily take *dana* to the temple on an assigned day every month, the *salaka dana*, which ensures that the monks in the temple get meals on a regular basis. Although Ananda and I have lived in America for many years, we continue the practice of giving our *salaka dana* to the two neighboring temples in Kandy, on two separate days of the month. The community around a temple has an organizing committee called the "*dayaka sabava*," who attend to the matters relating to the temple.

THE MORAL OF A CHANCE DISCOVERY

My mother-in-law's story of her *salaka dana* was different from the normal practice of it, continued for over forty years. She belonged to a women's organization in the area, which visited the nearby temple. On their visit much to their dismay they saw the servant of the temple seated on a small bench cutting a Jack fruit. This fruit is hard to describe to a person who is not familiar with tropical vegetation. It is a fruit that is available in abundance and is used often as a substitute for rice or eaten with rice by the less affluent. Robert Knox (1958) in his descriptions of local fruits gives the following graphic account of the Jack fruit:

> There is another fruit, which we call Jacks; the inhabitants when they are young call them *polos*, before they be full ripe *cose*. . . . These are a great help to the people, and a great part of their food. They grow upon a large tree, the fruit is as a good peck loaf, the outside prickly like a Hedge-hog, and of a greenish colour; there are in them seeds and kernels or eggs as the Chinggulayes call them, which lie dispersed in the fruit like seeds in a cucumber. Then being cut in pieces they boil them and eat to save rice and fill their bellies; they eat them as we do turnips or cabbage, and taste and smell much like the latter. (Knox 1958:22)

The ladies were surprised to learn that since there was no *dana*, the servants were cooking humble fare for the monks' midday meal. The women were deeply moved, and they decided in the future to send the midday meal on a daily basis from their homes to the temple. There were three monks residing in this temple.

My mother-in-law continued to send *dana* to the temple for over forty years, until she passed away. I lived most of my married life in this household before coming to America. A man named Banda was appointed the task of taking the food to the temple. He would like a prayer get ready at 10:00 A.M., and he reminded everybody that the *dana* must be taken on time. My mother-in-law went to the kitchen, which was her only visit to the kitchen quarters of the house, where the *dana* was carefully prepared under her instructions. She put the food into containers for Banda to take to the temple. Whenever some special food was prepared in the house or fresh fruits brought from the estate, the best portions were set aside to be sent to the temple. This ritual of sending *dana* was broken only during the rainy reason (*vas*) when the monks had different arrangements.

There is the tradition of *sramadana* in our society: *srama* (one's own labor), and *sramadana*, labor as a form of *dana*. Sri Lankans perform *sramadana* in the temple. When there is a need for some work to be done in the temple premises, people in the community organize themselves to give their labor. The work is voluntary, and it is for merit making.

INSURANCE POLICY FOR THE FUTURE

Buddhists believe that the hardships they encounter in the present life are due to lack of *pubbetha katha punjatha* (good karma in their past births). Naturally, they are anxious this time around to remedy their situation and assure themselves more favorable circumstances in the next life. Giving to monks is encouraged, and nothing is expected in return except merit. As with my mother-in-law, the best of the garden produce such as vegetables and fruits are taken to the temple. If one gets a good gift of food, part is first set aside for the temple. Most joyful or sad occasions are followed by *dana*. *Dana* is given in memory of the dead, as gratitude and merit from the giving is always transferred to the dead relatives.

The actual task of preparing a *dana* is performed with reverence. The very best is cooked, and a lot of thought and effort are put into the preparation. The traditional food items prepared for a *dana* often include overly rich foods, but monks have to eat what is given to them. These foods are not necessarily what the monks like or nutritionally good for them, which may account to the fact that many monks suffer from diseases such as diabetes. The most common items prepared for a *dana* are a savory pickle made with shallots and vegetables and fried eggplant curry, which takes a lot of effort in cooking. The idea is that the greater the effort expended, the greater the amount of good karma to be reaped. More than once different monks indicated to me that they were not particularly fond of these overly fried and currified items, but there is no way of communicating with their devotees on matters of this nature.

WHO GIVES MORE?

I often wondered at the disparity between the rich and the poor. In the matter of giving, the poor tend to give more in proportion to what they have. I have known well to do Sri Lankans living in America who give large sums of money as donations as a means of avoiding paying taxes to "Uncle Sam." Due to good karma in the past the rich are able and blessed to give more. Does this mean that the poor never can catch up with the giving of the rich? In Christianity there is the concept of giving in proportion to one's wealth. Sister Rita explained this to me. "A poor widow came and put in two small copper coins, which are worth a penny. Then Jesus called his disciples and said to them, 'truly I tell you, this poor widow had put in more than all those who are contributing to the treasury. For all of them have contributed out of their abundance; but she out of her poverty has put in all she had to live on" (Mark 12:42–44). In Buddhism the same philosophy prevails. It is the *cetana*, or the motive, that brings the merit in giving, not the quantities.

MY FATHER-IN-LAW MADE SPACE FOR THE DEAD

There is a *dana* of a different sort. My father-in-law had many people come to consult him or seek his help on numerous matters, not always confined to legal issues. He treated all and sundry with uniform kindness and care. He had the servants give them tea, and if they came at lunchtime they were given lunch. He reminded me that this was the Buddhist way. One evening a middle-aged lady was among those waiting to see him. It was my habit to hang around and listen to people who visited my father-in-law on school holidays, as I had nothing very much else to do.

When it came to her turn, the woman introduced herself. Her mission was to represent a problem her villagers had in getting access to a cemetery to bury their dead. She listed the inconveniences and problems the villagers had to undergo when it came to a burial. People with property buried their dead on their own land, but poor villagers had to keep the body in a house for several days looking for a place to bury. There was no public cemetery nearby, and all around this area were foreign-owned tea estates. The villagers had no means to take a body many miles for burial, and cremations were costly.

My father-in-law had a small tea estate in the area, in Hanguranketha. The lady was asking for a piece of land from this estate on behalf of the villagers to be set aside for a cemetery. She reminded him that this was great *kusala karma* and that only he was in a position to give a piece of land. My father-in-law, who always thought of the poor and the less fortunate, did not take much time to come to a decision. He agreed, and after a brief discussion the details were agreed upon. When I met the woman a few weeks later, she was keen to express the gratitude of the villagers by having a ceremony of donation. My father-in-law said that he did not need publicity or ceremony, and he was glad to help. This was a great *dana*.

HARVARD DIVINITY STUDENT MISSED THE BUS?

There are also simpler forms of giving. It was in Harvard that I met Steven Jenkins, a graduate student at the divinity school working for his PhD. We became good friends. Once we were walking to the Widener Library and on the way there saw a homeless man begging. I dipped into my pocket and gave him a coin, which was all I had. Steven was intrigued at my spontaneity and asked me why I encouraged begging. To Steven this was an ethical question. He began a discussion on giving and giving to beggars without hesitation. I explained that it was my upbringing, to give to whoever asked without resorting to questions of philosophy. I also told him that if the beggars had a lot, they would not ask us. The rich never ask; it is the poor that have the need to beg. I quoted the Bible, the language that made sense to Steve: "Give to all who beg from you" (Sermon on the Mount). Steven was impressed; he in turn told me his story.

Steven was a deeply spiritual person. He was in the Notre Dame Cathedral in Paris deep in prayer. The cathedral was not crowded and was peaceful.

Suddenly he felt the strong presence of someone next to him. He had not noticed him before. A man seated next to him begged him for some money, and Steven was debating whether he should give or not. On the one hand, he thought it was shameful to beg in church. On the other hand, his inner thoughts were urging him to give something. He finally decided not to give. But in a moment Steven was smitten by remorse and looked for the beggar, who had disappeared. The church was not crowded and Steven would have seen him leave if the man had left. This was a strange experience. Steven believed that God was testing him. He observed that I did not have that problem in giving. I told him that in Buddhism we are told to give to the poor as a means of liberation from greed. Steven told me many of his spiritual experiences, which I remember well. We parted when I moved to Chicago. We believed that we were drawn to each other by some strange affinity and that we were bound to meet again someday somewhere.

VESANTARA STORY

The quintessential example of giving goes back to ancient India and is told in the Vesantara Jataka so dear to Sri Lankan Buddhists. In colloquial language if someone is overly generous they compare him or her to Vesantara. Vesantara is the Buddhist legendary giver. There are plays staged on this theme in villages and urban areas, songs are composed based on the story, and at Vesak times the story is depicted on the heavily lit pandols. Many ancient paintings are found in monasteries depicting the story as an example of perfect giving. This story speaks of the virtue of giving in its ultimate form.

In the kingdom of Savi, there was a king called "Sanjaya." He had a son named Vesantara who was known for his generosity from his birth. When Vesantara was born it was believed that a divine elephant was left in the royal stable, and that it was to bring the kingdom immense blessings, which it did. As Vesantara grew, his fame and generosity spread all over the country. Whatever was asked of him, he gave willingly. He married Mantridevi, had two children, a son, Jaliya, and a daughter, Krisnajina. In the neighboring kingdom of Kalinga there was a severe drought, which caused famine and immense hardship to the people. The king of Kalinga sent Brahmins to fetch the auspicious elephant of Vesantara. Vesantara gave the elephant. This made the people angry, and the king Sanjaya sent his son away from the palace for fear that people would harm him.

The next morning Vesantara left the city with his wife and his two children. On the way some Brahmins asked for his horses and chariot, and he gave those away along with other possessions. He proceeded on foot, and another Brahmin came to take his children to serve his wife as servants. Though he loved his children dearly, he gave them away. Then god Sakka came in disguise as a Brahmin and asked for his wife. Hesitatingly he gave his wife too. Sakka, very pleased with the genuineness of Vesantara, revealed himself and gave Vesantara's wife and children back to him. The Vesantara story is the most popular tale depicting discreet acts of excessive charity.

Thereby hangs a dolorous tale as one might say, a fitting finale to our reflections on giving. Yet the story of Vesantara has remained problematic. To Western audiences the drama runs flat. It exemplifies not virtue but extravagant behavior running counter to notions of commonsense and the Buddhist ideal of the sensible middle way of moderation. Here is a king who gives away his wife and two children (all of whom protested their love for him) as if they were chattel. In Sri Lanka, it is a heroic story exemplifying the *paramita* of *dana*, which is therapeutic and contributes to self-transcendence. Besides, the intervention of Sakka restores a state of normalcy. Everyone can breathe a sigh of relief because if it did happen no one was hurt and the moral triumphed.

SIX

Sri Lankan Buddhists and Their Rituals

BUDDHISTS IN SRI LANKA perform many rituals. Rituals are performed as a rite of passage connected with an event that denotes a change of social or religious status in the passage of life. They take many forms: a new birth, introduction to solid foods to an infant, the first reading of letters, attaining puberty, two people getting together, a loved one passing away, and so on. As rites of passage they hold together the fabric of life to make it healthy and socially acceptable. The ritual practices have made the Sri Lankan Buddhist culture rich and vibrant, giving it depth and color. They are not an integral part of the Buddhist religion. In the following section I describe two major rituals concerning Buddhist monks.

BEING BORN AND WHAT FOLLOWS

A temple and its monks are a focal point in the Buddhist way of life. There is constant interaction between the temple and Buddhists. At birth, death, happiness, unhappiness, sickness, and joy we go to the temple and seek the aid of the monks.

When my mother gave birth, the monks were brought to the house to bless her. There is a practice among the Buddhists to get the Angulimala Sutta chanted to pregnant women by a monk. Pregnant women often memorize the *sutta* to recite at the time of childbirth to ease labor pains.

The story of the *arahat* Angulimala is fascinating. On his way begging for food in Savatti, he saw a pregnant woman in difficult and dangerous labor. Returning home from the alms gathering after the meal he reported her condition to the Buddha. The Buddha advised him to recite an oath of truth by declaring that he had not intentionally taken any life from the time he became a monk. The affirmation of truth with the purest of motives was in itself an act of power.

"Sister, since I was born in the Noble Birth, I intuitively know I have not intentionally deprived any living being of life. By this truth may there be well-being for you, well-being for the child to be born."

The chanting of the sutta saved the lives of the mother and the child. Sometimes relatives chant the Angulimala Sutta to give blessing to ease the pains of labor and to distract the woman in labor. In villages where women have no access to prenatal breathing classes and training for labor, the recitation of the suttra becomes a psychological supporting device.

When a child is born in a Buddhist home certain practices are observed to ensure his or her ritual admission to Buddhism. The baby's first outing is to the temple on an auspicious day or a full moon day. In the temple the parents place the child on the floor of the shrine room or in front of a statue of the Buddha. A monk often blesses the child with *pirit*. It is a common scene in Sri Maha Bodhi in Anuradhapura and at the Dalada Maligawa in Kandy. This is done to obtain the blessings of the Triple Gem. At the daily religious ceremony in the Temple of the Tooth Relic in Kandy, I have seen mothers handing over their babies to the officiating monk inside the shrine room, who in turn holds the child for a few seconds, blesses the child, and returns it to the mother. This is the first initiation, or one may call it the Buddhist version of baptism.

When a child is born the parents consult the monks to cast the child's horoscope. A monk who knows astrology will cast the horoscope. The belief in horoscopes is endemic in the Sri Lankan culture. If a child is born at an inauspicious time, monks may suggest a *pahan puja*, a Bodhi *puja*, or a *pirit* chanting to mitigate the impact of malefic influences.

MY DAUGHTER BECAME A GOLDEN GEM

My daughter was born in Sri Lanka, and as it was the custom, we consulted an astrologer. Synchronizing with the time of birth, auspicious letters and sounds favorable to her were determined, and she was named accordingly. Some sounds are believed to be favorable and when combined with other sounds may bring good luck. The constant use of favorable sounds in a name confers good luck and helps to mitigate malefic influences during times of adversity. My friend Yasoma's husband was then the professor of Sanskrit at Peradeniya University, and she undertook to find a suitable name in harmony with the letters. We chose to call her Ranmini. Ananda's father gave her the second name Tamara. Some years previously Tamara Deutscher, the widow of Issac Deutscher who wrote many books on Marxism and a trilogy on Leon Trotsky, had visited Ananda's household. She translated from Russian the biography of Lenin, *On Lenin*. Ananda's father liked Tamara Deutscher, who was a guest in his house. Impressed with her, my father-in-law decided to name my daughter Tamara, after her.

The name *Ranmini*, Yasoma explained, meant the "golden hued gem," and she thought it was appropriate for my daughter. *Tamara* in our culture means "lotus," which is characteristically offered to the Buddha as it symbolizes transcendence.

RITUAL INTRODUCTION TO RICE

When my younger sister was six months old, the time came for her to be introduced to solid food. This is considered an important rite of passage. Rice, the staple diet of our country, was ritually fed to her for the first time. This ceremony is known among Sri Lankans as the *idul katagema*. My mother had made a visit to the temple, and the Buddhist monk well versed in astrology determined her auspicious date and time, according to my sister's horoscope. On the auspicious day monks were invited to the house. Special seats were prepared for them, covered with white cloth as a mark of respect.

Our household was busy for a number of days preparing for this event. Many kinds of traditional sweets were made. Food was given to the poor because of the belief that if the poor are fed at this time, my sister will not be in want in life. Furniture was rearranged to suit the occasion, giving prominence to the presence of the monks. The monks chanted *pirit*, a blessing for all, and especially for my sister. Since the monks are virtuous and compassionate, when they perform important rituals, good results follow. In front of the monks was laid a freshly woven mat, and on it was a large spread of food items and fruits. The most important item of special food prepared on this occasion was *kiribath*. This is a preparation of new rice cooked with milk and sugar, prepared to bring good luck and prosperity.

After chanting blessings, the monks made my sister sit on the floor. A monk took the first morsel of milk rice and put it in my sister's mouth. My sister, not used to solid food, spat it out. There were also bowls of jewels and coins on the mat along with other items. My sister, more interested in the glittering objects, soon crawled toward them and grabbed some coins. My mother predicted that she would have plenty in life, that she would be rich. The concept of prosperity is important in Sri Lankan society, for there is much want and suffering.

THE SMALL BUSINESS OF THE ABCs

The ceremony of the first reading of the letters to a young child is the *akuru kiyavima*. It is performed at the age of three or four. When my little brother

Bernard was almost three, my father, who was devotedly fond of him, thought it was the time to formally introduce him to letters. My brother was a beautiful baby with light skin and a head of curly hair. There was an inherent charm in him that attracted attention and induced even strangers to show kindness to him. He was very special, like a little Buddha. It was obvious to all of us that our father had a special place in his heart for Bernard. Even in the most difficult times my father took care to provide him with the best. Father chose an educated and saintly monk to read Bernard his first letters. We older siblings were anxious to teach him the letters, but this was not satisfactory, because the first reading of the letters should be done at the auspicious time by an auspicious person.

An auspicious day and time was set for the ceremony. There was once again much preparation. The special brass lamp was polished, and seven lights were lit. Milk rice was prepared along with the other items of food. My father made sure there was plenty for everyone. New reading books were bought in English and Sinhala. The ceremony began with the taking of *pansil* and chanting of a *pirit* blessing for my brother. At the auspicious time, the monk seated in the chair put my brother on his lap, blessed him, and made him comfortable. My brother knew something very special was happening and acted like a movie star. He loved the attention and affection showered on him. The monk made my brother repeat the letters and numbers, both in Sinhala and English. Later he was put on the mat to go around and take what he wanted as it was a day of freedom for him. He ran to the pile of books and started to turn the pages in a great hurry. My relatives predicted that he would be a learned person, and this pleased my father immensely. He rated education as his first priority for all of us. My brother is today a psychiatrist and a good Buddhist. Most of all he is a kind and compassionate person. To this day I cannot fathom why these predictions are made, but infinite and unquestionable is the faith and trust lay people have in the system of which they are a part.

As a grown woman on my visits to Sri Lanka, I have seen these ceremonies and customs performed in much the same way. In the city they often substitute an educated relative, but in villages it is always the Buddhist monk who performs this function.

PUBERTY BEYOND THE CLINICAL

Attaining puberty, or the coming of age, for a young girl is traditionally associated with the *kotahalu magula* ceremony. When I attained puberty, as is the custom in our society, there was an elaborate ritual to teach me to accept the new status of womanhood. My first menstruation was a frightening experience as I was ignorant of what was happening to me. My older sister in her mischievous way whispered in my ear that it was a terrible thing and that I would bleed to death. In the society in which I grew up, it was not the custom to warn a young person of the biological changes that were taking place in the human body. Sex was a mystery; to talk about it was taboo until puberty. My good mother kept all this secret from me. I was kept indoors for several days until an auspicious time for my coming out was determined. I was given only vegetarian food, which was rather insipid, and the whole thing seemed unreal. My horoscope was read, and my future was spelled out. Until the auspicious day I was not allowed to see any male persons. They believed that if these rituals were broken, I would have an unhappy life. My father, who did not have much belief in these customs, came to see me every now and then. During this period of enforced seclusion, I was always with a female companion, to avoid *thanikama*, being alone. It was believed by some that I was attractive to the spirits in my delicate state, so I should not be left alone. If my female companion were to leave for a moment, she left an iron axe by me to keep the spirits away. I was not sure whether in her absence I was expected to kill the spirit, if it appeared in some form. Indeed every now and then I looked at the axe. My confined stay was a vigil of sorts, and I missed the life outside and wondered what everybody was up to.

On the day of my coming out, the *dhoby* woman took the center stage in the ceremonies. It looked as though the *redinanda* "the clothes aunt," owned me. Covered from head to toe with a white sheet at the auspicious time she took me to the bathroom, where there was a large barrel of water with jasmine flowers floating on it. With a clay pot she poured the icy cold water on me. She walked around me seven times with the final pot of water, poured the water on me, and smashed the empty pot on the ground for good luck. A big branch from a Jack tree was brought to the bathroom. I was given a *manne* (a little axe) to make a cut on the branch until milk oozed out. This too was for good luck. (Milk in any form is considered good luck in our culture.)

Then a coconut was placed on a mat, and I was made to hit it hard with the *manne* to break it into pieces. The way the coconut was split would determine how many children I would have and their sex. One side of the coconut shell denoted male, and the other, female. I was then dressed in new clothes with new gold jewelry, but everything I had worn before, my clothes and my old jewelry, was taken away by the *redinanda*. I asked to keep my little earrings, which I was fond of, but was told that everything I owned prior to puberty belonged to the *redinanda*.

She then took me over to the ceremonial place where a large traditional brass coconut oil lamp was waiting to be lit. She made me walk around it three times, with my face covered. As I lit the lamp, the sheet was removed. There was an impressive display of food. I was the center of attention. I got many presents, new dresses, and jewelry. I was given *kiribath* at the auspicious time. I was made to feel special, and my aunt gave a lecture on sex and how I should conduct myself from now on as an adult woman. Among other things, I was to sit properly with my legs together, talk softly, and act like a lady. When I went to school, my female friends, who had already attained puberty, joyfully accepted me as one of them, since I now had the special status of womanhood. The *redinanda* left happily with a lot of groceries. There is a customary list of items given to her for performing this function. *Redinanda* gave me her advice that I should not eat any fried food or any nonvegetarian food for three months and not go alone anywhere for that period of time to avoid the influence of spirits. When all was over, our temple monk came to the house to chant *pirit*, bless me, and give me a sermon on good conduct for a young woman, which I remember to this day. It was a soft and gentle version of sex education. I thought this was an interesting custom, especially the fact that a celibate monk was preaching to a young woman.

In the student lounge at Simmons College, Boston, I narrated the story of how I became a woman to my Jewish friend Lyn. Lyn remarked that among Jewish women too there is a similar tradition. She showed me a clip from a book, "When a woman has a flow of blood, where blood flows from her body, she shall be in *niddah* for seven days. This is what the law says about a woman during her menstrual period." Lyn added that *niddah* meant separated, and once a woman is separated she remains so until she is "clean." Before she can emerge from *niddah*, she must be put into a *mikvah*, a ritual bath.

My brother-in-law's housekeeper, Leela, described to me the festival involving the first menstruation of her daughter, the *kotahalumagula*. This is the most important event in the village involving a daughter before marriage. It is also the announcement of the girl attaining womanhood to the village. The whole village gets involved in celebrating the event. She performed the formal rituals of separating her daughter and keeping her segregated with no male access, until a good time the *nakathas* were determined by the astrologer. Her female relatives took turns staying with her all the days she was in seclusion. Special vegetarian meals were prepared for her during this period. It is believed that eating fish or meat attracts bad spirits. There are many myths and legends associated with the ritual, which are carefully observed to keep the spirits happy and at bay. Her time of entering womanhood and the responsibilities were emphasized. From then until she is married, it is not proper for her to go out alone or associate with young men freely.

Leela performed the ritual bathing, of her daughter with a new clay pot from a barrel of fresh water scented with jasmine flowers. She was adorned in new clothes, including a traditional sari with gold ornaments. Leela invited the whole village, her friends, and relatives to a meal, which she called the "at home party." Music with loud speakers was heard throughout the village announcing the event, the coming of age of her young daughter. We all contributed to the party to help Leela to make it a success, since giving the best party was a status symbol in the village. It involves considerable expense to the villagers, and often they get into debt trying to outdo another's party. Leela reminded me that although they spend money in entertaining they also get substantial gifts of money, so it all balances out. Sometimes this ritual is more elaborate than a wedding in villages. This was in a way an announcement to the village that one's daughter is now a full-fledged woman, available for marriage. It is a common practice in villages for couples in love to "*panala yanawa*," jump the gun, literally running away (eloping), so a family may not get the opportunity to celebrate a wedding.

INFECTIONS? LOOK FOR THE SEVEN MOTHERS

There is a great deal of myth and legend surrounding infectious diseases in our culture. One time most of my brothers and sisters contacted chicken pox. We were isolated and kept away from school for fear of spreading the sickness. Neighbors were alerted. Most important, my mother made a vow to goddess Pathini, the goddess to whom one prays in matters of infectious diseases. The vow was that when we got all well, she would give a Pathini *puja* and a *dana* for seven mothers in the name of Pathini. This is known as the *ammavarungedana* (*dana* for the mothers), a traditional ritual among Sri Lankan Buddhists. With the *dana* for the seven mothers merit is transferred to the goddess Pathini. The *dana* is given at dawn, and special food items are prepared for it. Seven is considered an important number in the ritual, seven mothers, served seven rounds, with seven servings of each, seven portions set aside, and so on. This is performed to show gratitude for recovery and a thanksgiving to the goddess. The place was cleaned with saffron water, and the traditional brass lamp was lit with seven wicks. Large quantities of traditional sweets were made for the occasion. Bags of food, fruits, and sweets were given away. A special kind of sweet with milk and jaggery, called "*kiri*," was prepared for the occasion. Everything had to be in abundance to please the goddess. At *dana*'s conclusion the mothers pleased with the offerings blessed the family and prayed to Pattini and other deities to protect all from illness and bring good health and prosperity. Great attention was paid to detail to please the mothers in the name of Pattini. This was followed by an elaborate *puja* for the goddess as a thanksgiving.

When Ananda got the scholarship to go to Merton College, Oxford, a special *pirit* and a *dana* were held in his house to thank the gods for blessings and to ask for protection and further blessing for his success and good health and finally for a safe return. Ananda's spiritual mentor, Venerable Ampitiye Rahula, also gave us a special blessing for success in educational undertakings and for good health. In many ways our behavior was typical of the culture of which we were a part. While one is aware that the receiving of scholarships, awards, and even honors are all attributed to merit, there is a parallel belief that in the long run the bounties of life are really due to one's innate *punya* karma—the cumulative positive karma that one brings along in successive *samsaric* births. But the very resource has to be replenished consciously, by good acts, *punya* karma, and evoking blessings and showing gratitude.

PIN SHOTS FROM OTHERS

Pindima and *pinanumodana* are common in Buddhist practice. It is a difficult concept to translate. They literally mean "rejoicing with others" and asking all and sundry to rejoice sincerely in the good karma, and so benefit themselves. Persons doing good *kusala* karma invite others to rejoice and share the merits. *Pin or punya* are good deeds, all kinds of actions that cleanse and purify the mind of the doer and can be shared with others. *Pin* is quite unlike a pie, which disappears as it is cut up and shared. With *pin*, as you give with a good and clean heart, the *pin* increases and so do the blessings. *Pin* can be given to dead relatives or the suffering and sick to better their conditions. By taking joy in the good karma of others, the receivers too benefit. After a good deed this recitation is chanted: "May the good *punna* karma made by me be shared among all other beings. Rejoicing in this cause this gift of *punna* given by me, may all beings live a happy life free from suffering, and may all be happy."

In the summer of 2005 a dear friend lost his seventeen year old daughter under tragic circumstances. During the first critical days many religious rituals were performed to transfer merit to her. Despair like brooding clouds hung over the home once enlivened by her cheer and laughter. The Buddhist ritual of the three months commemoration bana and *dana* ceremony was held primarily to transfer merit to the dead. The occasion was made memorable by the charismatic presence of a Sinhala Buddhist monk (teacher at GTU Berkeley) invited to lead the ceremony. The monk explained lucidly the meaning and relevance of the ritual *pinkama*. He said that *pinkama* literally means an action that generates positive energy in the participants' minds. Positive energy makes one happy, joyful, and lighthearted. This energy can be transmitted from one mind to another, consciously or unconsciously, regardless of distance. During the *pinkama* by good thoughts of generosity, compassion in feeding the monks, giving gifts to them, listening to the dharma, positive energy was generated. This energy could be transferred to the young person whose life ended suddenly. Thoughts laced with boundless compassion create powerful vibrations. This energy when transferred would be felt by the living as well as the recently departed, still in the range of access and receptivity.

The mind is a powerful transmitter as well as a receiver the monk explained. Depending on the nature of the individual's cumulative karma the person may be born instantly to conditions of bliss, or states of woe, or linger in a state of limbo. Transferring merit to a person whose positive karmic gains were marginal would tilt the balance in his or her favor. In such situations transferring merit is critical. He gave an apt example of a person who may need karmic relief and another to whom transferring of merit would be of not much relevance. A parent sending a substantial sum of money to a daughter who lives in a poor and unsafe neighborhood with bleak prospects may enable the daughter to move to a better place and live comfortably, and even buy a good car. On the other hand if the daughter was living in a luxury house in a good neighborhood, the generous gift was of little avail. Still the kind gesture would be appreciated. The monk said by the same token, the Buddhist ritual of *pinanumodana* to the dear and departed has a certain relavancy built into it. He gave an analogy to show the process of transmitting good thoughts. Radio waves of media stations such as NBC and CNN transmit instant messages and pictures across space to far away places, as graphic visual images. In a similar way good thoughts could be transmitted, received, and benefit the living as well as the dead if they are in a receptive situation.

Giving normally means that the giver parts with the thing given, but in *pindima* one actually earns more merit in sharing it with others. The receiver of the merit rejoices in the good deed and earns merit. If one performs a good deed, one may earn as much merit as the giver does or even more by being sincerely pleased about the good deed. My monk friend explained this with a Buddhist story. When a famous Buddhist devotee in the time of the Buddha was donating the Jetavana Grove monastery to the Sangha a poor man watching the great deed with pure thoughts of joy earned even more merit than the great giver.

In a lighter vein, when we were working in the Public Record Office in London, and at noon we would have sandwiches made with fish paste (humble fare indeed), I would often tell Ananda that if his mother sent us good "pin shots" or made instant transfers of merit more often, we would surely get better food. Ananda's mother in her daily routine of taking *pansil*, which lasted over two hours, would routinely bless each member of our vast joint family and the numerous siblings (over fifty in all) on an individual basis. We were told about the benign blessings, journeying through seas and oceans and the boundless ether to us on a black London afternoon. Ananda was always amused at the concept of "pin shots," which was my invention.

RITUALS IN THE WORLD OF MONKS

There are also genres of rituals of a more structured sort to do with the lay relations to the culture of the Sangha, or the traditional monastic order.

At the beginning of the establishment of the institution of monks, there were no hard and fast rules to regulate the conduct of monks as I have described elsewhere. As time passed the Buddha was made aware of the difficulties the monks faced when traveling during the rainy season, which lasted three months. The Buddha stipulated the tradition of *vas* or a retreat period to keep the monks from having to travel during the rainy reason. Consequently monks observe a three-month period of retreat during the rainy season. *Vas* begins after the full moon day of July and ends in October, also on the day of the full moon. During this period monks are expected to dwell in their monasteries and suspend travel except in very special circumstances. Commonly the years a monk has spent in monastic life are reckoned by counting up the number of *vasas* he has observed. In a sense the *vas* and the ceremony held at its conclusion, the *katina pinkamas*, are the most important ceremonies in the nexus joining the laity to monks.

VAS INVITATION

It is said that in the time of the Buddha, Visaka (the chief female lay disciple) expressed a desire to offer a special piece of cloth to each monk for *vas* observation. Buddha accepted her offer. Since then the custom of inviting the monks to go into retreat, *vas aradana*, is done by offering a special piece of cloth at the beginning of the rainy period. During this period monks are provided with food, domestic facilities, medicine, and so on. These *vas* months are important for both the monks and the lay people because monks can engage in meritorious activities of dharma sessions, dharma discussions, meditation programs, and *pirit* chantings. During the period of *vas* the religious activities in the monasteries are at their peak. Offerings made to the monks during this point of time are presumed to acquire more merit and bring about happiness and a long healthy life. It is also a custom to invite prominent monks to a monastery for the *vas* period to accrue merit.

Buddhist lore has many stories relating to the *katina*. During the time of the Buddha a group of monks went to the forest for retreat. At the conclusion of the retreat they returned to visit the Buddha. On the way they were caught in heavy rain, and one monk in the group got more drenched than the others. The Buddha, seeing the monk whose robes were wet, advised the monk to accept an extra robe as a *katina*. The extra robe was always given to the one who needed it the most. There are many traditions and rituals involved in offering a piece of cloth to be stitched into a robe called the "*katina* robe" at the conclusion of the *vas* ceremony.

I remember one such occasion involving our family. Ananda was anxious to get to the temple in time and hurried us all. Aunt Lillie was his father's older sister. She was a traditional Buddhist and was a great believer in the merit of the *katina pinkama*. Traditional Buddhists believe that one has to perform a *katina* at least once in a lifetime to get the best birth the next time around. Aunt Lillie decided to build a special dwelling place for a monk and perform her own *katina*. It is the Buddhist belief that if you build a dwelling place for a monk, in future births in *samsara* you will never be in want of shelter or that if you offer a *katina* robe to the monk after the *vassa* season, you will never be in want of clothes in your future births.

When the construction was completed, she did her *vas aradana*, inviting a monk of her choice to the retreat. She undertook the responsibility of providing all the needs of the monk during this *vas* period. At the end of the *vas* retreat, a *katina puja* was held in the temple involving the offering of the *katina* robe to a monk. The *katina* robe was taken around the village in a ceremony with drumming and the playing of flutes. Aunt Lillie placed the robe on her head and went in the procession. The *katina* robe was offered to the monk, and a *dana* followed.

Another fascinating ritual is the presence of the "wishing tree," traditionally known as the *kapruka* (legendary tree of bounties, which grants one's wishes) in the temple premises. Various items for the use of the monks, including money, are hung on the tree. Whatever is offered on *katina* day is considered meritorious. Indeed it is said that one who offers a *katina* robe, even on a single occasion, will never be in want or destitution or reduced to wearing rags for want of clothes.

One of the *gathas* recited during the *katina* ceremony glorifies the greatness of the merit. It says even the solid earth or a solid rock or a piece of diamond could tremble, shake, and break at times. However, the merit obtained by offering the *katina* robe to the Sangha cannot be nullified by anything until one achieves the ultimate goal of nirvana. It is also believed that the merit, the positive karma gained by making offerings at *katina*, could reduce the negative effects of other minor bad karma one may have committed. One would be blessed with long life, happiness, good health, good complexion, physical strength, and wisdom in this life and in many more lives until nirvana is achieved.

HOW ONE BECOMES A SON OF THE BUDDHA

The ritual of *upasampada* is the higher ordination ceremony in monkhood. Initially a young boy is admitted to the order as a novice, and he takes vows to observe *atasil* (the Eight Precepts of morality). There is no set age for admission to monkhood. It is not the custom for a chief monk to refuse admission provided certain conditions are satisfied. Usually the time and the date of the ordination are determined by consulting the novice's astrological charts. The ordination ceremony is performed according to the *vinaya* rules, in default of which ordination is considered invalid, and the candidate does not become a monk. The requirements are strict, and the ceremony has remained unchanged since the time of the Buddha. It is conducted in Pali to give it a solemn formality. The ceremony is open to the public, relatives, friends, and well wishers.

A novice or *samanera* monk, after intensive training and learning, gets the opportunity to receive higher ordination. The candidate for higher ordination must posses the necessary educational qualifications and be twenty years of age or more to be ordained. The counting begins when the infant is conceived in the mother's womb. If by error a monk is ordained before age twenty, the candidate remains a novice until he comes to the proper time.

There are several reasons for withholding ordination. The list is comprehensive. If one has an infectious disease, is a slave, has escaped from jail, is wanted by the law, has not paid his debts, is in the service of the king, or is maimed, disabled, or very old to the extent that he is not capable of performing monastic duties, he is not considered a suitable candidate. The stipulation that physically handicapped people are not generally admitted to the *sangha* may be due to the difficult living conditions in a monastery.

Sirima Kiribamune, professor of history in the Peradeniya University, had many visiting colleagues from abroad. One such visitor was the distinguished Indian historian Romilla Thapar, who expressed an interest in seeing a higher ordination ceremony in a temple. I knew many monks in the Malvatte temple and agreed to take her to an *upasampada* ritual. We all enjoyed the fascinating religious ceremony.

We were given special seats from which to watch the proceedings. Before admission the candidate was made to put away the yellow robes of a novice monk and wear the clothes of a layman. He was then by question and answer examined as to his fitness for admission to the higher order. When it was determined that he satisfied requirements, he was led away to an inner sanctum and dressed this time in the robes of a monk.

The ritual began with the candidate's parents or sponsor presenting him with a robe and the mendicant's begging bowl, for one is not ordained without a set of robes and a bowl of his own. He formally asks permission from the parents, expresses gratitude, and asks for forgiveness for any wrong done over the years, intentional or unknowing. This was done by worshipping the parents. The parents give their blessing to the candidate who then approaches the Sangha, who are waiting to perform the ordination. The presence of at least five monks is required, one of whom must be a senior, knowledgeable monk, who would be the candidate's preceptor or *upajjhaya*. A senior monk on this occasion would come forward and be the monk's spiritual guide and mentor who would be responsible for the candidate's wellbeing throughout his entire life as a monk and would take care of him as a father would his son.

The next step in the ritual was a brief session of instruction about the ceremony, followed by giving the monk a new name, which was not the name his parents gave him at birth, but one that reminds him constantly of his new role and purpose in life. Two senior monks had been appointed to investigate and question the candidate's suitability to become a monk. Among the questions asked were his age, if he was suffering from an infectious disease, if he was a human being, if he was in debt, or if he was a free man, and finally if he had a robe and a bowl. If the responses were satisfactory, the general body of the monks was told that all was well. The same questions were asked in front of the gathering in an act of further affirmation.

Although similarities are often emphasized between Sri Lanka and Thailand, both Theravada Buddhist countries, cultural differences related to religion are often strikingly different. This is particularly true of ordination—in both varieties, the *samanera* and the *upasampada* ordination. In Thailand becoming a monk (taking the *samanera* vows) does not involve a lifetime commitment.

There is a legend concerning why in both traditions, the question of whether the aspirant is human is asked. A certain *naga* (a member of the serpent race) took human form and entered a monastery in the hope of being ordained as a monk. The reasoning was that if he became a monk and lived the life of a monk, the merit he acquired would enable him to realize his hopes for transformation to the human condition. It is in the human condition and in the realization of the vast potential in the human condition that one can achieve transcendence. Sadly for the *naga*, he was denied.

The two senior monks then returned to the assembly. They bowed and reported that the candidate had been examined. If the Sangha consented, the candidate was allowed to come forward. At this stage the preceptor said, "Now is the time for you to request the *Sangha* to ordain you a bhikkhu." At this command, the candidate approached and bowed three times, knelt with his hands together. He respectfully requested the Sangha to ordain him as a *bhikkhu*. He begged the *Sangha* out of compassion to elevate him up from the status of a novice. He did so three times.

The most important question asked was whether the young man of his own free will and volition was becoming a monk. The idea was that no one was forced to become a monk. The candidate then made the final request from the monks to be ordained. At this stage all the Sangha in the conclave agreed to accept him to the fraternity of monks. Within the *sima* or the delimitation of space, which belonged to the particular temple, the ordination hall in the Malvatte monastery is especially reserved for such monastic functions. This special building is set apart, and lay people and animals are not permitted to enter during the time of the monastic rites and ceremonies.

The two senior monks formally announced to the gathering that the candidate was found suitable to become a monk. This announcement was repeated three times. Should any monk in the gathering at this point object to the candidature, the ordination could be stopped. The senior monks carefully noted the time of ordination, like recording the time of birth of an infant, the new beginning for a new life. The monk's seniority would be counted from this time. In all ceremonies monks ordained even a few hours before would precede him, in the ritual order of precedence. The preceptor then advised the monk of his responsibilities. An *upasampada* ordination gives special religious powers to the monk, enlists him as a full-fledged member of the community of monks, the Sangha. Wherever he may go in Sri Lanka and beyond, and indeed in the benign *sakwalas* of boundless space, he is a monk, raised from the inferior state of a layman to that of a *bhikkhu*, a superior state of virtue and perfection. With this the ceremony came to an end. Parents and well-wishers offered gifts to the new monk.

Having witnessed a few *upasampada* ceremonies I was touched by the human dimension, while its ritualistic aspects fascinated me. When the ceremony was over I could feel the relief in the air—the joy of all involved. A son of the Buddha was born. A particularly moving scene was when the parents greeted their son, now that the rite of passage to monkhood was finally complete, reversing normal hierarchical notions, the parents worshipped their son. Many monks told me that this was a difficult moment. All through life a monk worships his parents as a mark of respect, gratitude, and affection. Now by becoming a monk, their son, in a sense ceases to be their own son and is in the exalted position of a monk—well above a layman, a *Buddhaputra*, a son of the Buddha.

SEVEN

Reminiscences of *Bana* Preaching

THE BUDDHA, HAVING ATTAINED ENLIGHTENMENT, looked for an audience to share the fruits of his wisdom and found none. He hailed five mendicants who had at first enthusiastically been part of his search for wisdom but scornfully left him when they realized that he had abandoned extreme forms of asceticism to which they attached great importance in the Brahamanical tradition. With ill-concealed reluctance, they formed a circle to listen to the Buddha preaching his first sermon, the Dhammachakka Sutta. They now became his first disciples, in a sense beginning the long history of Buddhism and the tradition of *bana* preaching.

WHAT THE BUDDHA TOLD HIS SONS

The Buddha story says the Buddha sent his first disciples in various directions as messengers of truth to teach what he had discovered for the welfare and happiness of all beings:

> Go forth, O monks, for the benefit and happiness of the many, for the good of the world, for the welfare and happiness of gods and men! Let not two of you go the same way. Preach the doctrine that is beautiful in its beginning, beautiful in its middle, beautiful in its ending. Declare the holy life in its purity, completely both in the spirit and the letter. Those beings with dust in their eyes will decline for not having heard the dharma. There will be those who will understand the dharma.

Shortly before Parinibbana (passing away) the Buddha, told his disciple Ananda, who was in a state of grief, that none should grieve over his passing away because the dharma he preached should be taken as the teacher. Since then teaching and preaching of the dharma has taken a significant role in Theravada Buddhist countries.

My mind shifts to another scene far away from the valley of Ganges, to my Sunday school days as a young adult. We learned that the Buddha asked the monks to preach with compassion, to remove suffering of humanity. Monks told us that the Buddha was a great teacher; he possessed unique qualities of preaching, charisma, and an uncanny feel for his audience. They gave us examples from the Buddha stories to illustrate these qualities. The Buddha was able to tailor make the content of his dharma teaching to suit a given situation. He had superior intellectual faculties and miraculous powers of thought reading, which enabled him to see the needs of a particular listener and the intellectual level of the audience and adjust his teaching accordingly. He had the ability to select a sermon appropriate to a person. His methods of teaching provided the Buddhist monks with examples of skillful ways to impart religious instruction.

WHAT IS *BANA* PREACHING?

Bana preaching, also called "*dharmadesana,*" is an ancient Buddhist tradition of teaching dharma to the laity, by monks to reinforce the teachings of the Buddha. In Sri Lanka, *bana* preaching is an important religious phenomenon in the practice of Buddhism. *Bana* is public religious instruction and is used as an educational instrument, a tool in traditional communities to divert human minds to religious and moral avenues. Listening to the Buddha's teachings, meditative reflection is considered an act of merit. These sessions are constant reminders to the laity to lead moral and ethical lives. *Bana* preachings help to preserve the ties between the monks and the laity and the social bonds within the community. They are seen by the laity as rituals directed to the attainment of present and future rewards both material and spiritual, worldly and otherworldly, human and divine.

Dharma preaching is the main instrument used by monks to educate lay people. Buddhist concepts such as 'karma,' 'rebirth,' '*dana*,' 'mediation,' 'compassion' are used as topics in the preaching of *bana*. The importance of observing the Five Precepts and living a spiritual life is taught by means of this media. *Bana* helps Buddhists to be virtuous, inspiring them in ways to avoid negative actions in life and engage in positive deeds with the aspirations of making life better in the future.

A monk once explained to me with clarity the point of it all. *Dana* (giving) is a cardinal virtue extolled in Buddhism. It is usually associated with giving money, food, items of clothes, or gifts in kind to the poor, the needy, and would occur spontaneously in one's mind. Such forms of giving are meritorious acts in Buddhism bringing immediate states of joy to the person giving away this or that altruistically. The monk reminded me that the Buddha said that nonetheless the most meritorious form of giving was the giving of the dharma or what the Buddha taught. The gift of dharma excels all other gifts because knowledge is transformative and has the potential to change the attitudes and mind of the receiver.

The purpose of any form of *bana* preaching is twofold: first to reinforce what is already known in the mind of the listener, and second to clarify and implant a new thought or perspective. Both objectives lead to reinforcing and expanding the mind, which is the key to living a virtuous life, and to achieving peace and happiness in this life, ultimately leading to transcendence. The monks further explained that it was the unbroken tradition of *bana* preaching—for over two thousand years—that made the population at large knowledgeable about Buddhism and its core concepts of ethics, morality, and social values. But for the monasteries and the monks who live in them, the agrarian communities in Sri Lanka, who live simple lives with a functional literacy, could not on their own have had access to the dharma. The knowledge was always confined to a minority of the laity.

Bana has multiple purposes. Politicians in Sri Lanka use this medium as a means of attracting large Buddhist audiences for important events. It is used as an instrument in appeasing the Buddhists prior to commencing a public venture. Politically minded monks are used by politicians for the purpose of putting forward their individual agendas. Often the opening of the new parliament sessions inaugurating new government ventures are begun with a *bana* session followed by *dana* and blessings. *Bana* sessions, like other Buddhist rituals, were held to give blessings to soldiers engaged in the ethnic war in the last two decades. *Bana* is preached to celebrate happy occasions as well to grieve for losses.

My mother regularly invited monks for *bana* preaching ceremonies. Friends, relatives, and neighbors were invited to share the benefits of listening to the dharma and making merit. Birthdays and anniversaries were celebrated with *bana* followed by *dana*. These sessions usually took the traditional format. Monks when choosing a topic for the sermon used a Pali *gatha* from the Buddha teachings. Its meaning was translated and explained with illustrations. This session lasted one hour, and at the end there was an expression of aspiration that the good merits acquired helped all to gain good health, prosperity, and joy in this life. Merit was transferred to the dead relatives who might be anticipating merit and unable in their condition to create merit by good acts, and finally all could attain nirvana in the time of the next Buddha named Maitriya.

TALES MY MOTHER TOLD ME

My mother had interesting stories. The story of Mattakundali was an unforgettable popular story, and often quoted. According to this tale, each morning the Buddha entered into a trance of *mahakaruna* (great compassion) to survey the world to see beings who suffered most intensely and those that needed guidance as well as those ready to benefit from his teachings immediately.

Mother related many other stories to illustrate Buddha's *mahakaruna*, which was one of her pet topics. In the city of Savasti, during the time of Buddha, there was a rich Brahmin (person of high caste). His name was Adinnapubbaka (nongiver). One is reminded to be aware of the virtues of giving and conversely the bad effects of miserliness. (When one is overly miserly, one is referred to as an "Adinnapubbaka.") He had a lot, but he was not willing to part with anything. He had a son whom he loved dearly. As the son became older, it was the custom for the father to give his son a gold ornament. To have an ornament made, he had to get a craftsman. He was not willing to do this, since he would have to give the man a place to stay, feed him, and pay him. Since all this would cost too much money, Adinnapubbaka decided to make the ornament himself. He got gold and beat it up to look like an ornament and made his son wear it as earrings. So the son acquired the name Mattakundali (one who wore the flat earrings).

When Mattakundali was about ten years old, he was anemic and ill. His mother wanted to consult a physician, but the Brahmin would not hear of it, as it cost money to provide food and pay him for the service. Instead Adinnapubbaka went to a physician, described the son's sickness, and asked for a remedy. The physician, who understood the problem only too well, was annoyed at the father's selfishness. Since he did not get proper medicine, Mattakundali lay dying. Now the Brahmin thought that when his son died, those coming to the funeral would see his wealth all stored in the inner rooms and think that he was tightfisted. So he moved his dying son outside to the porch. The Buddha in a state of *mahakaruna* (special individually focused great compassion) saw Mattakundali on his deathbed. The Buddha asked of himself, "What benefit will come from my going to the boy when I appear before him? His mind will be made tranquil by my presence, and even if he had not done any other meritorious deeds, this tranquility will help him to be born in a better realm." As the story continues, Mattakundali, having seen the radiance of the Buddha was pleased, died peacefully and was born in a happier situation.

HOW THE WORD OF THE BUDDHA IS UNFOLDED

Bana preaching was the height of activity of the temple on *poya* days. As in all temples in Sri Lanka, our temple too had a *dharmasala*, a special hall dedicated to *bana* preaching. A *dharmasala* had four entrances, for devotes who would come form all four directions, giving the deeper meaning that it was open to all, and all were welcome. It was a simple bare hall. Devotees sat on the floor on mats irrespective of caste or social status. In the *dharmasala* all devotes had equal status and wore white to further eliminate distinction (white in Sri Lankan culture denotes purity, it is auspicious and sacred). There was a prominently displayed seat, architectured with elaborate design on a raised platform, the *dharmasana*. It was distinctive in appearance and specially constructed for the preaching monk. Although distinctions of class and caste are integral elements of Sinhala culture, in the *bana maduwa*, when everyone wears white and sits on the floor without footwear, an egalitarianism of sorts is achieved, at least for the time being. This was a sharp contrast to high-caste converts to Christianity in Bengal and elsewhere in India, insisting that the pews in churches be arranged to accommodate caste distinctions.

In the Sinhala village sitting together on level implies social equality. For only people of the same caste can sit together. People of the so-called "low castes" do not sit on a level with those of the so-called "high castes."

In the temple, however, everyone, irrespective of his or her caste distinctions is made to sit together. This is achieved by making everyone sit on the floor on mats. Sitting on the floor is also a mark of respect for the monk. Thus, when people assembled in the sermon hall to listen to a monk's sermon, they all sat, almost touching each other, on mats spread on the floor. It is said that even members of the royal family had to sit on the floor, along with others, when they visited the temple" (Disanayake, 1993:104).

Devotees gathered in large numbers at the temple for the *dharmadesana*. Usually an educated, well-known Buddhist monk was invited for the occasion, and the event was announced by means of a printed advertisement. We sat in the *dharmasala* to listen to *bana*, on mats laid on the floor. We girls wore appropriate clothes suggested by my mother, long skirts that enabled us to sit modestly. Any type of clothing that would distract the opposite sex was considered inappropriate. Simplicity was emphasized. Men and women sat separately on either side of the hall. Between the *dharmasana* and the audience was an empty space, and it was the custom to select a knowledgeable man to perform the function of being respondent to the monk exclaiming every now and then the Sinhala equivalent of "Yeah" to the preacher. His role was more like a spokesman representing the laity.

The monk was brought to the *dharmasala* in ceremony. With the beating of the drums the devotees cried out loud "*Sadhu! sadhu! sadhu!*" Three times they would intone the words as an expression of joy. This also expressed the idea that the time has come to listen to the *bana* and pay attention. The monks often held fans in front of their faces, which served to depersonalize the sermon. The idea was that one focused on what was said, rather than on the speaker. Buddhist lore is full of charismatic and attractive monks who were an attraction to the women; monks took great pains to "play down their attraction." I recall how girls were attracted to one particular charismatic young monk who came for *bana* preaching to our temple. His mother was friends with our mother. They both took *atasil* on *poya* days together. Girls came up with the story that he became a monk because he was rejected by a woman he loved. Later we were disappointed to hear that the monk had taken to robes at the age of nine.

To get back to my narrative, the preaching began with the administration of the Five Precepts, which symbolized the ethical and moral discipline as the foundation of Buddhist spiritual life. The monk recited the invitational *gatha* to begin the sermon. "*Dharmassavana kalo ayam padanta*" (the time is appropriate to listen to the dharma), a solemn opening refrain.

The actual *bana* preaching took a well-structured predictable format. First the monk recited a Pali *gatha* rhythmically from a Buddhist text and established the theme of the discourse. He then proceeded to explain the meaning of the *gatha* in Sinhala and illustrated it beautifully with a masterfully appropriate Jataka story and anecdotes and finally gave a moral and ethical basis for the contents. Some monks were great instructors. At the conclusion he elucidated the merits of attending to *bana* preaching and conducted the *pinanumodana*. The monks transferred the merit of this act to the dead relatives and friends. Finally he blessed the audience so that they would have good health, happiness, peace, and joy. Appeal was made to the gods to share the merits, shower their blessings, and give protection to all.

The practice of listening to *bana* preaching was first introduced to us in the Buddhist Sunday school, as first lessons in Buddhism. As part of the dharma instruction program, the *dharmadesana* was well crafted, relative to the age and maturity of the students. Relevant stories were included with moral lessons attached. The stories given as illustrations touched the emotional and spiritual chords of young adults. The Sunday school always began with the Buddha *vandana* and a sermon by a monk. We did not have the intellectual maturity to understand the value of what we were then learning. Looking back I now realize that *bana* preachings were an educational experience, the way we learned Buddhism, and its core concepts.

Before television came into vogue, a popular form of listening to *banas* by Buddhists was the weekly *dharmadesanas* on the radio. There were also reminders of the Buddha word at the beginning of radio programming every morning, called the "dharmachintha" (dharma thoughts for the day). There were two *dharmadesanas* for the week, one in midweek, and one on Sunday mornings. Monks well known for their oratorical skills were chosen for the task. As a family we listened to the regular *bana* preachings on the radio, which lasted about an hour. My Buddhist mother encouraged us to listen, and later the salient points were discussed at the dinner table. I remember how my younger brother Bernard, who had Buddha-like kindness, was greatly influenced and attracted to *bana* preaching. He would cover himself with a white cloth and sit under a tall table, which we called the "teapoy," a typical colonial item of furniture in the house, pretending to be a monk. He insisted we all sit to listen to his *bana* preaching. He was serious about what he was doing, although he was only seven years old. It was amusing, but we were not allowed to make fun of him for fear he would be hurt. My mother wanted to make him a Buddhist monk, but my father decided that he should become a doctor and serve the people.

THE ART OF IT ALL

I particularly remember the sermons of Venerable Pitakotte Somanada. Devotees looked forward to his *desanas*. He preached the most complicated concepts of Buddhist philosophy with simplicity and clarity. His preachings took a set format. He would define his objectives, recite a Pali *gatha*, and explain the meaning in context. He then elaborated the philosophy in the *gatha*, interweaving his theme with relevant Jataka stories and memorable anecdotes. Finally he would cleverly summarize the entire sermon and deftly connect it all to the central theme. The whole hour would pass, and we would be glued to our chairs with interest and often discussed the contents later at a family meal. He was a prominent and popular preacher for many decades.

Among the literary treasures of Buddhism, the Jataka stories hold pride of place. The Jatakas consist of five hundred and fifty stories (*pansiya panas*) about the previous incarnations of the Buddha in both human and animal form. The Buddha himself related the Jataka stories, of his previous lives as a bodhisattva. At the end of each story, he identifies the role that he himself played to his disciples. These were transmitted orally for centuries, and when they were written down, they took the form of story and moral commentary. The stories are used widely in Buddhist instruction, to explain difficult concepts in Buddhist philosophy.

A significant feature of *bana* was that at the end of the preaching, the monks transferred merit to the gods, devas, spirits, and dead relatives by reciting the *gathas*. Finally the monk would bless the audience by chanting the following Pali verse:

> *Icchitam pattitam tuyham sabbameva samijjihatu*
> *Purentu cittasankappa cando pannarasi yatha.*

May all your hopes and wishes quickly succeed!
May your aspirations be completely fulfilled!
Just as the moon on the full-moon day.

MATAKABANA

A significant Buddhist ritual in *bana* preaching is the *matakabana* (homily of remembrance), associated with funerals. Monks are invited to homes to give a

sermon on the seventh day after the death of a person to console the mourning relatives and friends and show how the living can help the dead spiritually.
Monks explain the Buddhist concept of 'death' and how human life can be
explained only by reflecting on death. Often on such occasions they explained
the Buddhist teachings of impermanence:

Anicca Vata Sankkhara, Uppadavaya Dhammino, transient are all compo-
nent things; subject are they to birth and then decay.

This is always followed by the transference of merit to the dead to help
them get a better birth and to the gods asking for protection and blessings. The
closest relatives huddle together in the presence of the monks pouring water
from a large receptacle to a smaller bowl until it overflows.

At the end of *bana* preaching the listeners recite the *pratana* (aspiration).
Mundane aspirations and deeply felt wishes take many forms: to attain nirvana
some day in the future, to be reborn in the time of the next Buddha, designated
as Maitriya in the tradition. Buddhists believe that while erudite monks could
explain the dharma in all its deep dimensions, only a Buddha had the total
capacity to explain it best, leading to instant illumination leading to transcendence. Listening to a Buddha in the far future, one could attain transcendence
never to be reborn in a world of woe, enjoy happiness in the six heavens, enjoy
the happiness in the divine world of *devas*, and while in this life and in lives to
come enjoy happiness, health, and wealth and lead a religious life free from suffering in *samsara*. Benefits of listening to *bana* are either future centered or for
proximate worldly gain. The ceremonies serve even today as a rich social, cultural, educational, and religious means of guidance and inspiration.

Matakabana is a continued practice. Sri Lankan Buddhists repeat this ritual three months after the death of a person and on the one-year anniversary
of the dead and annually thereafter. In our homes annual *matakabana* and a
dana on the following day was prepared in the memory of parents to show
gratitude, and merit is transferred by the pouring of water.

Once I had a long discussion with Venerable Labuduwe Siridamma of
the Getambe Vihara in Peradeniya, on the subject of the popular Bodhi *puja*
ceremony. It was an intellectual discourse, which helped me to clear a number
of myths and legends involved in this popular Buddhist ritual. After the discourse I asked him a question that had bothered me for some time, about nirvana. He skillfully explained that we need not go very far. We had been talking about an hour on topics of dharma. During this time we did not have bad
thoughts. We were compassionate and indulged in intellectual and meaningful conversation. We practiced mindfulness. He described this as a temporary
state of nirvana. He said we should try to practice this over a longer period of
time and that it was the right path in understanding nirvana. The monk had
made the point so beautifully, I still remember the evening clearly—a soft
breeze stirring the leaves of the splendid Bo tree through whose leaves I saw
a beautiful star-studded tropical night.

SRI LANKAN VIRTUOSOS OF THE ART

The Buddha instructed the monks to engage in the mission of preaching the dharma for the good and happiness of the many. Buddhist monks are trained over many years in the skills of preaching to spread the word of the Buddha. Most monks possess a deep knowledge of the Pali Canon, and the Tripitaka (three baskets) which enables them to enrich their *dharmadesana* with interesting and apt quotations in Pali. It is often a treat to see how various teachings are skillfully meshed into an hour of nonstop preaching with an eloquent flow of thoughts and words.

Monks of the Vajirarama temple in Colombo were an example of popularizing the practice of *bana* preaching and bringing Buddhism to the day-to-day lives of the Westernized middle class in Sri Lanka. Venerable Narada and Venerable Piyadassi stand out prominently among the monks who carried out this mission within the country and later to the outside world. Apart from conducting *dharmadesana* on public and religious occasions, the monks regularly visited schools and universities to educate and inspire young minds. These discourses taught us moral and ethical lessons. Interest in Buddhism among the college and university students was a new phenomenon in the 60s. The lucid *dharmadesana* with their clear, simple, and analytical expositions of the Buddha's teachings were directed to captivate and educate the young minds. Well versed in Pali texts, the monks translated the ideas of philosophy into simple formulae. Remarkable communication skills, pleasing personalities, and fluent knowledge of English helped the monks.

Peradeniya University campus was a beautiful spectacle on *poya* days. Students in large numbers wearing white, especially the young women in white saris, went in procession carrying white temple flowers, which were available in abundance in the campus. The *bana* preaching drew large crowds, and the largest lecture hall was commissioned for the event. On one occasion, Venerable Narada was invited by the University Buddhist Brotherhood for *bana* preaching. Targeting his sermon to an audience of young, rather sophisticated, self-absorbed women of the Peradeniya campus, he focused on the impermanence of the physical form of youth. In illustrating the Buddhist doctrine of impermanence, he related to us a colorful story of Rupananda, a beautiful woman who lived in the time of the Buddha. Rupananda, a great beauty with a charming personality, was obsessed with her physical form. She never visited the Buddha for fear that the Buddha might criticize her beauty and comment on her obsession. Rupananda entered the order of *bhikkhuni* not out of conviction but because her relatives had done so. She went to see the Buddha believing that she would be able to avoid the Buddha's eye by hiding behind her relatives in the crowd. The Buddha with his divine eye saw Rupananda, and reading her thoughts, he decided to focus his sermon to benefit her.

Using his super powers, innate in a Buddha, he created a young woman to stand before him with a fan in her hand, swinging the fan back and forth. Only Rupananda was able to see the beautiful woman fanning the Buddha. Rupananda had the desire to be as beautiful as the woman holding the fan. The Buddha gradually transformed this woman to a middle-aged woman and subsequently to an old woman. Feeble and old she fell to the ground and died. Rupananda was disillusioned and became disenchanted. The sermon of the Buddha and the illustration brought enlightenment to Rupananda. She came to think of her own physical form: "In this very place this woman has come to old age, has come to disease, has come to death. Even so, to this body of mine will come old age, disease, and death."

Venerable Narada used the story to show the young undergraduates that youth was not a permanent state and that beauty was transient. It made much sense to the audience, and we talked about this sermon long afterward, until once again earth-shaking undergraduate concerns and grand visions of reforming the world took over our minds elsewhere.

Recently, on my visits to Sri Lanka, I observed the use of television media extensively by popular, learned monks with exceptional communication and oratory skills like Venerable Maduluwawe Sobitha and the late Venerable Soma. People flocked in thousands to listen to Venerable Sobitha, who was widely known for his preaching skills. The monks used the media to inculcate Buddhist values and sometimes share their political agendas with the Buddhist public. These programs were watched by many young audiences. Their charismatic personalities and excellent oratory skills were mesmerizing.

Venerable Soma with his two television programs, *Aduren Eliyata* (From darkness to light) and *Nana Pahana* (Wisdom), which were discussions and discourses based on current problems of the country in daily life, became popular among millions of Sri Lankan television viewers. Venerable Soma preached the fundamental Buddhist values with emphasis on simple ethical living associated with the orthodox forms of religious beliefs. His presentations were clear and audiences looked forward to his preachings and programs glued to the television. Although the technique of spreading the Buddha's word through preaching was not new, he had the magical power of voice and oratory skill to entice the audience, especially the young, in an innovative way.

BUDDHA IN CYBERSPACE

Bana preaching is popularized in modern Sri Lanka with television and other media. Popular dharma teachings are available widely on audiocassettes, video cassettes, CDs, and DVDs. Less popularly known media are the Internet sources, which disseminate special *dharmadesanas* from many parts of the world, especially from the monastery in western Australia, on a variety of topics, and has become a way of listening to *banas* in audio MP3 format. A sophisticated Buddhist living in the West could purchase a year's worth of dharma talks from the Buddhist monastery in western Australia on MP3 format or CD for a few dollars. They are available by downloading to CDs, free of charge, a technique familiar to computer-savvy Buddhists living abroad. The new inventions help to quench the thirst for a dose of *bana*, for Sri Lankan Buddhists living outside, especially in America.

On a recent visit to Sri Lanka in the summer, I stayed in a rural area in the house of a family who are clearly the elite of the village. On a three-day weekend, they took me to listen to more than one *bana* preaching at two beautiful *vihares*, where as of old, the charm of ancient traditions still remained seemingly very much in tact. Dressed in white, with my new hosts, I sat in a *banamaduwa* (preaching hall) listening to a village monk. It was a copybook performance with the stage props of a beautiful moonlit night and the muted chorus of a thousand *rahaiyas* (cicadas). I felt good, a trifle humbled to realize that after all, stripped of my illusory pretensions, I was like the rest—all wayfarers seeking the solace of the dharma.

And yet in a disquieting way I became aware that maybe at some not too distant time in the future, the fine old monk and the unpretentious *banamaduwa* would be rendered obsolete. There are the new vistas of cyberspace. These days the dharma unimpeded criss-crossed the ether, the common property of all humanity. Without the intermediary of the traditional monk and the *banamaduwa* and splendid nights of a thousand cicadas, one could, seated at my desk (alas, the banality of it all) as the phrase goes, download digitally the dharma via audio MP3 format be it from Perth in western Australia, Washington DC, or Los Angeles. The old distinction between the *magul sakwalas* (worlds in which one was within earshot of the dharma, the road to redemption) and the *pitasakwalas* (where the benighted dwelt beyond the call of the dharma) is visibly melting. Everything is in a state of flux.

EIGHT

Buddhist Pilgrims' Progress

BUDDHISTS MAKE PILGRIMAGES to worship the sacred *dagabas* (relic chambers) in Sri Lanka on a regular basis, inspired by instructions given by the Buddha in the Mahaparinibbana Sutta (his last discourse) to his trusted disciple Ananda, before he passed away, on how his relics should be treated after his cremation. The pronouncement gave sanction to the erection of *dagabas*, which enshrine relics of the Buddha and have become special objects of veneration.

LISTEN UP ANANDA

"This Ananda is the way they should treat the remains of the Tathagata (the Buddha). A *dagaba* should be erected over the remains of the Tathagata. And whosoever shall there place garlands or perfume, or light or make salutations there, or become in its presence calm in heart, that shall long be to them, a profit and a joy."

After the death of the Buddha, the relics of his body were collected from the funeral pyre and divided into eight parts, distributed to the rulers of eight territories in northern India, where the Buddha had traveled and preached. Legend states that ten *stupas* (bell-shaped symmetrical structures) were erected to house them. The practice of pilgrimage in Buddhism probably started with visits to these places. The Emperor Asoka, three centuries after the physical demise of the Buddha, divided the Buddha relics into eighty-four thousand portions and vowed to erect a *stupa* for each portion in his great empire. Asoka, a convert to Buddhism, indeed established a number of temples and monasteries that became important sites for Buddhist pilgrimage. For two millennia Buddhist devotees have aspired to visit these places of worship during their lifetime, to acquire good karma, to be reborn in a better place.

According to the Mahavamsa (chronicle of the history of the island), the Buddha paid three visits to Sri Lanka. At Mahiyangana, he left a few strands of his hair, and after his demise, his collar bone also miraculously found its way to Mahiyangana. Both items are enshrined in the *stupa*. Nagadipa, according to the beliefs of Buddhists, has the seat from which the Buddha preached. There are altogether sixteen places the Buddha visited, and all are popular places of worship in Sri Lanka.

A VILLAGE ON THE MOVE

On *poya* days Buddhists visit the village temple. On special days they make pilgrimages to significant places of worship. These are social and religious events. I remember with nostalgia villagers making preparations during the season of *na mal* to make the pilgrimage to a well-known *stupa* a few miles away. *Na* is a beautiful tropical tree with glowing red young leaves, which bear fragrant white flowers in season. The fragrance is distinctive and is considered sacred. Villagers offer the fresh *na* flowers to the Buddha. A pilgrimage to offer *na* flowers to the Buddha is a romantic day trip. The pilgrimage centers round the decorated bullock cart, which traditionally is the affordable means of transport available to villagers. Flowers and other offerings are carefully packed along with a lunch for all. Women sit in the cart, and the men walk behind it. Young men and women get acquainted with each other on the pilgrimage, and often relationships get cemented, with parental approval. Pilgrims wear clean white clothes. Preparations for the trip are made in advance, with enthusiasm, as it is a rare occasion when villagers get together for an outing away from routine life.

Buddhists in urban areas also make regular pilgrimages, in groups. Sometimes a well-organized pilgrimage includes a monk from the temple who serves as a knowledgeable guide. Some pilgrimages last a week, with visits to many places of worship. An appointed leader takes charge of the pilgrimage, and a bus or a lorry is used. Simplicity in attire and meals is emphasized. The group collects items for the *pujas* for different places they are going to visit. Sharing and kindness are emphasized through the journey.

Customarily the group leader makes a vow before setting off for a safe journey in ritualistic style. He leads the group in reciting devotional stanzas throughout the journey. They take precooked food items, generally vegetarian, and spend the night at places of rest for pilgrims. In major places of worship these days facilities for preparing meals are available and often are provided for a nominal sum.

Buses are decorated to resemble pilgrim vehicles. Arecanut flowers, which are considered auspicious, are stuck in front of the bus along with the Buddhist flag made up of stripes of blue, yellow, red, white, and orange. In addition, pilgrims take white and colored flags made out of materials stitched into a long string and paper flowers to offer at the various places of worship. Villagers believe that the flags make merit as they sway in the wind. The pilgrimages of large groups traveling for a common purpose in some ways help to promote community harmony and good will. Personal relationships improve, and friendships become more binding.

The idea of going on holiday once a year is a Western concept. Most Buddhists go on pilgrimages at regular intervals. These are joyous occasions. We had eleven children in our family, enough to make a crowd for a pilgrimage.

The Buddha during his third visit to Sri Lanka rested in eight places, *atamsthana*, in deep meditation in Anuradhapura. Later shrines and *dagabas* were built at these sites. Pilgrimages are made to these places, especially so during the month of Poson. At the various shrines, pilgrims worship with the following stanza:

> *Vandami cetiyam sabbam sabbatthanesu patitthitam,*
> *Saririka dhatu maha bodin Buddharupam sakalan sada*

> Standing in every place,
> I worship every shrine,
> the bodily relics, the great Bodhi tree,
> and every image of the Buddha.

A MOUND OF GOLDEN SAND

To the Sri Lankan Buddhists the most sacred of the *dagabas* is the Ruvanvaliseya *dagaba* (the *stupa* of gold), built by King Dutugamunu in the holy city of Anuradhapura. The Mahavamsa describes the process of construction in detail, in the form of miraculous stories, which are familiar to villagers. The king decided to construct the *dagaba* soon after his victory over the Tamil king Elara. Due to the ravages of war the country was impoverished, and the king could not begin the work. Legend has it that the gods provided the king with the necessary materials and that gems appeared miraculously in various places. Relics were enshrined in the *stupa* along with many treasures. Before its completion the king fell ill. His brother Saddhatissa ingeniously covered the *stupa* with an immense white cloth and made it look complete to rally the spirits of the dying king.

PILGRIMAGES TO SRI PADA

Sri Pada (Sacred Foot), the footprint of the Buddha, is on a holy peak, the second highest mountain in Sri Lanka, and is one of the sixteen sacred sites for

Buddhist pilgrimages. Buddhists believe that the Buddha visited this mountain and left his footprint, which is preserved to this day. The pilgrimage to Sri Pada is a combination of worship of Buddha and devotion to the god Saman, the guardian deity of the mountain.

My father, who did not neglect our education in culture, which was so much a part of Sri Lanka, took us all to climb Sri Pada. Also called "Adam's Peak," it is situated 7,360 feet above sea level in the central hills of Sri Lanka. It offers an unobstructed view over land and sea, overlooking the south-central mountain ridges. Legend and folklore are a great part of Sri Pada. It is the only mountain in the world that has followers of three great faiths—Buddhists, Muslims, and Hindus—and it is universally known.

To the Buddhists, Sri Pada is the footprint of the Buddha on the summit of the peak. Muslims refer to it as Adam's Peak because they believe that when Adam was driven out of paradise, he alighted on this peak. The Hindus claim it as the footprint of Shiva. Emerson Tennent, who as a result of his long sojourn in Ceylon (as the island was known in British times) had a great feel for the place and the nuances of the indigenous cultures, makes the interesting reflection that in early Muslim literature, Sri Pada was not identified with Adam's place of exile. Probably during the first centuries following the ascendancy of Islam, Ceylon was unknown. Later, with developments of trade across the Indian Ocean, Arab traders and sailors became increasingly aware of Ceylon and its topographical features and in time staked a claim of their own.

Buddhists have immense faith in the miracles and blessings of Sri Pada, a place of great devotion and faith. Sri Pada is also known as Samanala kanda (the mountain of butterflies) due to the clusters of butterflies which abound on the mountain with the start of the season. The pilgrim season commences in December and runs until the start of the southwest monsoon in April. During this season a steady stream of pilgrims and tourists makes the weary climb up the countless steps. There are three traditional routes to reach the peak. I remember we took the *punchi kochiya* (the little train) that ran on narrow gauge tracks to Ratnapura from Colombo.

Young and old women carrying children and men and women who appear physically disabled all climb to the top strengthened in the belief that they are doing an extraordinarily meritorious deed, with the god Saman's blessings. We climbed in the night as most people did. Our climb was not a pilgrimage but an adventure. Lamps lit the trail. Pilgrims' rests and refreshment stalls made the climb easier. There were willing helpers and first-aid stalls on the way to the top. My family, with many good-looking girls, had unsolicited help from young pilgrims throughout the climb and on our way down, much to the annoyance of my father. This made the climb all the more joyful and effortless.

There are many resting places, *ambalamas*, along the way at various points on the path where pilgrims could rest or cook a meal. Pilgrims follow a number of traditions and customs on the journey. It is customary for pilgrims to wear white clothes and take the ceremonial purificatory bath in the *seetha gangula* (torrent of icy water), an important landmark on the route to the summit. We washed our faces and hands and felt refreshed to start the climb. Here the pilgrims observe *pansil* and make obeisance to the god Saman, the guardian deity of the area. Tying *panduru* (a coin washed in clean water wrapped in clean white cloth as a talisman for protection and safe journey), they begin to ascend the mountain to reach the summit.

The next point of respite is Idikatupana (place of the needles). The devotees stop to hang threaded needles on shrubs by the path's side. The practice originated from the time when the trail was obstructed with thorny bushes, and the caring pilgrims would leave needle and thread for those who followed to mend their clothes. In time it has become an established ritual. From this point, a long line of concrete steps leads to the summit.

Before modern safety improvements were put in place, we heard stories of disasters that happened every now and then, on the climb up. The final ascent to the summit was made by clinging onto iron chains and virtually scaling the cone. In bad weather when there were strong gusts of wind, the chains swayed perilously. I have read an account of a tragedy. A party of pilgrims from a village decided to visit the peak at the beginning of the off season when the fury of the monsoon unfolds. As they were scaling the summit, gusts of wind made the chains sway perilously like ropes of hemp. Unable to hold on, one by one the children went hurtling down the mountainside, followed by the old and infirm. The women were swept away. The men grimly hung on only to be swept away in turn. When the last cries of agony were heard no more, a chilling silence prevailed.

It was believed bad form to ask how far it was to the top. Instead pilgrims just exchanged the greeting *karunavai* (peace). Sri Pada and the surrounding ambience is part of the *adawiya* (territory) of the great god Saman, the presiding deity. Those who visit this place of worship do so with reverence and devotion constantly mindful of Saman. The belief is that the kindness and compassion of Saman would get them to the top safely. Devotees have tremendous faith that if a vow is made here, it will be granted provided it is made with devotion. Even the most impossible wish is granted, according to tradition.

To make the journey less tedious some enlivened us with stories. I remember one story vaguely. According to the Mahavamsa, the first person to climb the sacred mountain was King Vijayabahu (1058–1114) who having climbed to the summit saw the footprint of the Buddha. The king had seen in the early hours of the morning angels gathering flowers in his royal garden. When questioned, one had replied, "We are gathering flowers to worship the footprint of the Buddha in Samanalakanda."

The pilgrimage is done with extreme *sarda* (devotion). Pilgrims abstain from eating meat or fish for at least a week prior to the journey, in order to purify themselves by way of preparation. We felt guilty as we had not observed any of these rituals with my father, not having much faith in them. I am sure Saman with his *karunava* (compassion) had mercy on us. We had fun singing the devotional songs, which we learned on the way in making friends with other young people.

GUARD YOUR TONGUE OR ELSE

All the way to the top pilgrims recited devotional rhythmic songs aloud. Others joined in. It was also done to make the tedious journey less of an ordeal; it was a distraction. Usually the *nadegura* (leader of a group of pilgrims), well versed in reciting the verses and *gathas*, led the crowd. The pilgrims followed, reciting the verses in chorus, and complied with his instructions. The climbers were advised to guard their tongues. "*Kata varaddaganna epa*," was the advice given to all by the *nadegura*, especially to the novices. Some words were taboo, especially those voicing complaints or expressions of doubt or fear. The leader would lead the way. One had to have faith. Saman would take care of them all. The main theme all the way up was kindness and compassion in the name of Saman. Pilgrims chanted all the way up and down:

> *Ape Budun api vadinna; Saman deviyo pihita venna*

> To worship our Buddha may god Saman help us.
> They sang "*karunavai*" (kindness) all the way, repeatedly.

> *Karunavai, karunavai, saman devindu karunavai*
> *Vandinta yana me nadeta Saman devidu karunavai.*

> God Saman, Lord of this demise
> As upwards we trek to worship our Buddha
> Grant us the grace of your compassion
> Show our group of pilgrims your protective kindness.

The young eagerly helped the elderly. If one had difficulty in walking or climbing, others came to their aid. Drinking water and food were shared without thought of one's own needs.

Pilgrims and tourists attempted to reach the summit before dawn to view the effulgence of the rising sun, the grand phenomenon known as the *irasevaya*. The sun like a ball of fire came out of the eastern horizon causing a shadow of the mountain to fall on to the valley in the opposite direction, like a cone. It was a breathless sight. There is a large brass lamp at the top of the mountain, kept burning day and night during the season. This is the *dolosmahapana*. Pilgrims put oil in the lamp and also take oil from it for medicinal purposes. In villages where medicine is hard to come by, the oil from the lamp serves as a healing medicine. Religious rituals of prayer and meditation are performed in the summit, near the footprint of the Buddha. At the summit is an enormous brass bell. Pilgrims ring the bell with pride to claim the number of visits they make to the holy place. It was our first time, so we rang it once.

BUDDHA'S INDIA

And yet, it is not Sri Lanka but India—the beloved Jumbudvipa—that boasts the most sacred places of worship. Buddhists are fond of quoting certain passages from the Mahaparinibbana Sutta, in which the Buddha tells his chief disciple Ananda there are special places

> that a devout person should visit and look upon with reverence, Here the Tathagata was born. This Ananda is a place that a pious person should visit and look upon with feelings of reverence. Here the Tathagata became fully enlightened in unsurpassed, supreme Enlightenment, this Ananda is a place that a pious person should visit and look upon with feeling and reverence. Then the place where Tathagata set rolling the unexcelled wheel of the dharma and finally the place where Tathagata passed away. These Ananda are the four places that a pious person should visit and look upon with feelings of reverence.

The words of the Buddha have inspired millions of Buddhists to make the pilgrimage to the remote part of the Buddhist world. Braving all hardships they venture to the sacred places where the feet of the Buddha once trod. The four holy places of pilgrimage are specially cherished. First there is Lumbini, where the Buddha was born; second is Buddha Gaya, where Buddha defeated Mara and attained Enlightenment seated under the Bo tree. This is by far the most sacred place of all to Buddhists. The third, *locus sacralis*, Saranath is the deer park where the Buddha preached his first sermon known as the *Dhammachakkasutta* "setting-in-motion the wheel of the good law." The wheel is a fundamental symbol to Buddhists, standing for the dharma, the eight spokes in it signifying the Noble eight-fold path. Finally there is Kusinara, where Buddha passed away in his eightieth year among *sal* trees.

It is considered an unrivaled meritorious deed to have made this pilgrimage in one's lifetime. My aunt, who was fortunate enough to do so, was sad that she could not take all eleven of us with her. She decided to share her merit with all of us by her continuous *pindimas*, or conscious merit bearing blessings. We were rewarded for listening to her *pindimas*, which were repeated many times over.

A LITTLE KINGDOM WITH A GREAT TOOTH

The Temple of the Tooth Relic in Kandy in Sri Lanka is a great place of reverence to Buddhists. This temple was built to house the Tooth Relic of the Buddha. Monks of the two great monasteries of Kandy, namely Asgiriya and Malwatta, alternately perform the *puja* ceremonies, which are held daily in elaborate fashion, to honor the relic. The morning *puja* commences at 5:30 A.M. and is announced by the beating of drums. It is the time of the *thevava*, when first the *wattorurala*, the leader of the ceremony, carrying the keys to the shrine, proceeds to the shrine room. When the doors are opened, the *puja* begins by handing milkrice to the officiating monk to be offered to the Sacred Tooth Relic. Until the rituals are over, the drumming continues. Thereafter the devotees are allowed to go in and make offerings until 7:00 A.M. when the doors close. The doors next open at 9:00 A.M. for the *dana*. A *dana* of thirty-two curries is offered daily to the Buddha as *puja* in this shrine. Then there is the evening *gilanpasapuja*.

August is the month for the Esala *perahera*. The word *perahera* simply means "festival" or "procession," both of which are commonplace throughout Sri Lanka. They are usually organized by a specific temple and are participated in by the members of the particular temple community. They center around the ceremonial exposition of a specific holy relic kept by the organizing temple and are accompanied by a sumptuous display of finery and color.

The Esala *perahera* in Kandy, held in honor of the Sacred Tooth Relic of the Buddha, is the most colorful and magnificent procession in the country. According to the legend, one of the Buddha's teeth was taken from the smoldering funeral pyre by a devotee and then smuggled into Sri Lanka in the hair of a Brahmin princess around 300 A.D. King Meghawana received the tooth with great honor and laid it in a gold urn. Since then the Relic of the Tooth has been moved around temples of the island. Rulers of Sri Lanka laid emphasis on the possession of the Tooth Relic in order to legitimize their rights to the throne. It has great religious and political connotations. It is used to prevent famine and make rain. The *perahera* to celebrate the Sacred Tooth Relic, conducted annually in July (Asala), constitutes the grandest festive ritual of the Dalada Maligava, the Temple of the Sacred Tooth.

The program of the Esala *perahera* is drawn up by the *diyawadana nilame*, the lay custodian of the Tooth Relic, in consultation with the *basnayaka nilames* of the four devales. After consulting with the astrologers, auspicious times are worked out to perform the rituals. The first ceremony is the planting of the *kap*. This is done in the premises of the *dalada maligawa* and the four *devales*. *Kap* is a stump of a Jack, *Rukattana*, or *Esala* tree, which is planted within the premises as a pledge to the deities that the *perahera* will be conducted in accordance with the relevant rituals. After this, the *perahera* is conducted on five consecutive days within the respective premises in which the *devale* kapurala officiates. On the sixth night the *per-ahera* is taken to the streets.

The initial *peraheras* are the Kumbal *peraheras*, conducted for five days. These go around the temple premises only. Little children are taken to see the first Kumbal, in the belief that witnessing it will help in getting rid of all diseases. People from all walks of life line the street and wait patiently to witness the spectacle. After five days of Kumbal, the most spectacular *perahera*, the Randoli takes to the streets, for five more days. It all ends in the day *perahera* and the water-cutting ceremony of the temple.

On our visit to Kandy I persuaded Ananda, who was born in Kandy but did not have much enthusiasm to see the *perahera*, to accompany me. Many tried to persuade us not to go. Some said you could see it better on TV. Others said it was not safe; a bomb might go off. Some others said that we could see it from our house across the lake. I was fortunate in that my brother-in-law got an invitation to see the *perahera* from the Bank of Ceylon building. This clinched the issue, and Ananda could no longer refuse to go and see the *perahera* after twenty-five years. While waiting for the procession to begin, which was a few hours away, we were treated to a large assortment of delicious Sri Lankan pastries, sandwiches, and cakes, along with tea and coffee. We had a window to ourselves on the second floor of the building, and it gave us a spectacular view. I noticed men quietly sneaking to another floor to have a drink. Drinking is done discreetly, and only by men. From time to time men in the crowd disappeared and reappeared.

I watched from the window and saw below us enormous crowds, five deep, seated patiently for many hours waiting for the *perahera* to pass. I felt guilty enjoying my vantage point and seeing the inconvenience millions go through to get a glimpse of this magnificent spectacle. There was a fear in me that a suicide bomber might be lurking around some corner. I spotted a dark-skinned woman standing in the crowd, and I imagined that she was wearing a cyanide capsule round her neck, which could blow up at any time. I worried about the crowds below. I wondered if anyone in the five-deep crowd would have the need to use a toilet and where they might find it. There are no portable toilets in Sri Lanka for such occasions. I worried too that if it rained, all these thousands of people would have no shelter. I prayed that it should not rain till the procession was over, although there were threatening clouds. It was the full moon day, and the bright, round moon was peeping through clouds as if to get a glimpse of the spectacle.

Young boys in different colored tee shirts denoting the particular organizations they belonged to, distributed water, making sure that those who wanted would have a drink of water. I was proud to see some of them were from the school where I had taught, which took pride in social work. There were also groups of young people carrying stretchers providing first aid services.

Despite my worries, I had a good time waiting for the *perahera* to pass. The people around me obviously belonged to the privileged class in society. I recognized that the bank manager was a staff member of the school I had taught at many years ago. People around me talked about politics and cricket, as it was the test match season.

With the sound of the drums, the procession began at the auspicious time. The ancient protocol was strictly adhered to, and the Tooth Relic was taken along a long prescribed route with customary fanfare. Whip crackers led the Maligawa *perahera*. These were muscular, barefooted, and bare-chested men in white sarongs. Their bodies swirled to the whirling of the whip, which met the ground in a loud crack. They led the way and announced the approach of the *perahera* by the cracking of their whips. I remembered that many years ago there had been a little man, a midget, who led them. I was told that he was no more. Then came the flag bearers representing the regional flags, about thirty of them in rows of five followed by the *peramunerala*, the official who kept records of the tenants, with the temple's tenant and property records, riding the first elephant, huge and regal in a heavy elaborate gown moving gracefully forward. Drummers playing festive music *magulbera* followed him. Gaily decorated dancers with necklets, bracelets, and anklets moved in rhythm to the beating of the drums. They were of several traditional schools of dancers, *ves* dancers, wearing elaborate headdresses. *Uddekki* dancers, *pantheru* dancers, and *naiyadi* dancers who perform in the Vishnu and Kataragama *devales*, flanked the procession. The few instances in which women took part in the *perahara* was when it came for the *pattini devale* section, where beautifully dressed young women danced to drums.

The most spectacular among the 150 elephants that went in the *perahera* was the Maligawa tusker carrying the golden casket containing the sacred relics. The temple tusker, a majestic elephant richly dressed and carrying lighted electric bulbs, moved to the rhythm of the music proud that he was the one chosen to do the privileged task. On his side were two other elephants dressed the same way walking rhythmically at the same pace. A canopy was held over the tusker and *pavada* (white cloth) was spread in its path for it to walk on as a mark of respect.

Elaborately adorned elephants cloaked in sequined velvet of rich blues, vibrant reds, and exotic ambers moved gracefully along in threes. At times their trunks were tucked away, folded in their mouths, and others swayed to and fro giving the appearance of dancing to the drums. Baby elephants, dressed for the occasion, went in the procession, dancing to the tune of the drumming along with the young dancers. They swayed their long trunks with seeming merriment and joy.

The men lighted the entire procession with torches. They were carrying huge wooden poles with iron baskets attached to the ends filled with lit copra (dried coconut). They remained upright as the flames from their iron containers soared many feet into the air. At regular intervals they would lower their poles to refuel them with fresh copra shells. The heat and light generated was intense. It kept the coolness of the air away and dispelled the darkness of the night.

The procession continued with elephants, dancers, and drummers. Sometimes it would stop for a while and the drummers and dancers would do wonderful kinetic swirls for the crowd. When the performance was over, the procession went on, and the elephants adjusted to the speed and the rhythm. The *basnayaka nilames* (custodians) from the Kandy *devales* followed in turn. The first was the procession of the god Natha, the benevolent god believed to be the next Buddha. This was followed by the Vishnu *devale*, the protector of Buddhism in Sri Lanka, followed by the Kataragama *perahara*, and finally the procession of Pattini, who is a deeply cherished goddess of purity, chastity, and health. It took two and a half hours for the *perahera* to pass from our spot. Afterward, we had to walk home, which was not far, but we had to wait almost an hour for the sea of people below us to move on.

NINE

Karma in Popular Buddhist Culture

IN SRI LANKA, IN A SENSE, I grew up with karma. The culture was permeated with karma. Every action and its reaction was connected to karma. Fortunes, misfortunes, accidents, sickness, bad luck and good luck were related to karma. It was an axiom. Villagers would complacently refer to an unfortunate state of things they face in daily lives as *labaupanhati* (born to the state of things), and it was all due to karma and could not be helped. It is a common term among Sri Lankans. Believing in karma is a way of accepting that things happen because of previous karma, and prospects of making thing better are unrealistic. However, the interpretation of karma bordering on fatality is not quite the Buddhist explanation.

Karma has spread beyond its traditional cultural boundaries and has become a core concept in Western New Age thinking. It is in common usage, among broadcast journalists, often in mainstream television programs, and in the movies. It is in a way associated with the idea of "What goes around comes around." People throw it around: "Oh, it is bad karma," or one might hear someone say, "I guess it's just our bad karma," or "I landed a good job; it is my good karma." To these sorts of sundry situations karma is applicable more as a figure of speech.

My eye fell on a large colorful advertisement in a city bus in Chicago, which read "Specialty Karma." I was puzzled by the use of the word *karma* and looked around trying to decipher the context in which it was used. It was to solicit contributions for the Chicago Food Depository to feed the hungry. If you made some sort of a donation, the reward was good karma.

Having lived many years in the United States, I realized that the perception of karma was entirely of a different order from that of the Buddhist world. Like the term *nirvana* (loosely used to describe a situation that had brought the user, or in anticipation is likely to bring the user, ecstatic joy),

113

"karma" is used in a tongue-in-cheek manner to explain flat tires, unforeseen contingencies, or running into traffic jams and similar mundane afflictions.

In the seventies the newspapers in London, detailing an accident captioned, the article "So Is This Karma?" It was an accident of extraordinary coincidences. A young wife accompanied by her little son and a friend went to Heathrow airport to drop off her husband who was a pilot scheduled to fly a plane the next morning. On her way back to London, having got more than a few minutes delayed by traffic, she died in an unusual accident caused ironically by her husband. His plane, having difficulties and loosing total control, crashes onto the highway many miles away from the airport, precisely in the area where his wife's car was traveling. The wife died, as did her little son, but the companion miraculously escaped death. The husband, of course, died in the fiery inferno.

The Taliban authorities destroyed ancient Buddha statues in Afghanistan because idols were anathema to Muslims. The destruction of the two Buddha statues caused international outrage. The larger of the two statues, which stood 175 feet, was believed to have been the world's tallest standing Buddha. The other statue measured 120 feet. Both were among Asia's great archaeological treasures. Many Buddhists in America saw the allied invasion of Afghanistan and the elimination of Taliban rule as some sort of karmic retribution.

GOOD AND BAD KARMA

'Karma' is a Sanskrit word that basically translates into "action." According to Buddhists, karma is an outcome of a person's good or bad actions. *Kusala* karma (good action) involves positive acts, such as generosity, righteousness, and meditation, which bring about good results and happiness in this life and in future lives. *Akusala* karma (bad actions) such as stealing, killing, or sexual misconduct conversely engender mental torment, stress, remorse, and the probability of being born in states of woe. Karma links one's actions with one's fortunes, either in this life or another. This is the basic meaning of karma.

The Buddha said to the monks, "*Cetanaham bhikhave kamman vadami.*" "O monks it is the thought that directs karma." All actions are not karma related. Involuntary, unintentional, or unconscious actions do not constitute karma because of the absence of volition. The weight of karma is determined by variables such as frequency, repetitive action, intentional action, and action performed without regret.

In a recent Buddhist sermon I attended, a monk from Malaysia was invited for the New Year celebrations in Chicago. He explained the concept of 'karma' by referring to a Pali *gatha* from the Buddhist scriptures, which he translated as: "Owners of their deeds (*kamma*) are the beings, heirs of their deeds, their deeds are the womb from which they sprang, with their deeds they are bound up, their deeds are their refuge. Whatever deeds they do— good or evil—of such they will be the heirs." He went on: "There is one who destroys living beings, takes what belongs to others, has unlawful intercourse with the other sex, speaks the untruth, is a tale-beater, uses harsh language, an empty prattler; is covetous, cruel-minded, follows evil views. . . . Thus it is with the rebirth of beings, according to their actions (karma) they will be reborn. Reborn, they will experience the results of their actions."

KARMA: A SELF-GOVERNING SYSTEM

The monks in Sunday school explained to me that the law of karma is a self-governing system of justice that automatically generates the appropriate future effects in response to the present actions. It is different from the laws and legal system of a country, where misdeeds are found, tried in courts of law, and punished accordingly. Karmic law is subtle. It punishes misdeeds and rewards good deeds whether they are known or are not. Monks gave examples. A man commits a murder or robs a bank and is never caught in the eyes of man's law, but he will not be able to escape karmic law. Inevitably he will face the consequences of his deeds through the law of karma. Anonymous givers will be rewarded, although we may not know the giver's names. Those who drop gold coins in the Salvation Army till will be justly rewarded. Some winning lottery tickets are popularly attributed to good karma.

As children we were told constantly that it was bad karma to harm others. We were reminded that bad actions come back to hurt us and good karma bring us good. Karma is action, and its result is *vipaka*. Karma is the cause, and *vipaka* is the effect. I could however, never comprehend how I should be punished for something I did in a past life that I do not even remember.

Because good deeds lead to good fortunes, Buddhists perform good deeds with the attainment of good fortunes in mind. As discussed earlier, this is making merit. Merit can be made by something as small as helping someone to cross the road or by visiting the Buddha's place of birth. Accumulation of merit to the soul is like taking regular exercise to the body. Buddhists have a spiritual bank account. Making merit, or *kusala* karma is like a deposit, and doing *akusala* karma is like making withdrawals. In Sunday school the monks explained karma to us this way: "According to the seed that's sown, so is the fruit you reap there; doer of good will gather good; doer of evil, evil reaps; sown is the seed, and thou shalt taste the fruit thereof."

Buddhism teaches that birth and death are the essence of the *samsaric* cycle. Every person must go through a process of birth and rebirth until he reaches the state of nirvana whereby he breaks this cycle. What one will be in the next life depends on actions in this present life. A virtuous woman may be born a man in a next life or acquire wealth in this life or in a subsequent life. The inequalities in the world, such as some being born to a condition of affluence, endowed with fine mental, moral, and physical qualities, while others are born to poverty and wretchedness, are all due to karma. This explains why virtuous people are often faced with ill luck and misfortune, and the less virtuous and foolish are rewarded with all forms of good fortune.

LEGEND OF LOVE AND BORN LOW

As children we enjoyed the story of Prince Saliya, a popular love story in Sri Lanka. Prince Saliya, who was the son of the great and heroic king Dutugamunu, married a *chandala* (outcast) woman, Asokamala, described in the *Mahavamsa* (the country's primary historical epic), as a woman of peerless beauty. The prince fell in love with her, rejected royal life, and with his gypsy bride is said to have escaped the royal city of Anuradhapura through a secret tunnel in a local cave. King Dutugamunu was angry about the marriage and had nothing to do with his son Saliya for a period of time. When the king eventually visited the son, his wife, Asokamala, came forward with a bowl of water to wash his feet. The king, astonished at her beauty, thought she was more a goddess than a human being. He forgave the son, saying men in love know no caste barriers. This story is often used to show how by bad karma even though born low good karma made her beautiful. The negative and the positive effects of karma in this instance played their parts, the power of good karma elevating Asokamala to regal eminence. This is a popular story in Sri Lankan lore, many songs are made and sung based on this romantic story.

Then my mother's perennial favorite, the tale of Prince Kusa, who was subject to much humiliation owing to his ugly appearance. Prince Kusa was extremely talented but had an ugly face. He married a beautiful princess, Pabhavati, on the condition that she should not see his face for some time after the marriage, until a child was born to them. But Pabhavati was determined to see the face of Prince Kusa. Discovering that Kusa had an ugly face, she ran away. Prince Kusa tried his best to get her back, but Pabhavati would have nothing to do with him. Kusa followed her and finally won her back by his wisdom and prowess. This is a well-known story often quoted in popular Buddhist literature, as an example to show how negative and positive karma could interact in a person's life. Kusa, as a result of his good karma, was born to princely life. He gets a beautiful princess. But he cannot, however, escape the negative karma, and so he was born with an ugly face.

The Theravada Buddhist perspective is that we, and we alone, are responsible for our actions, (volitionally conceived and deliberately acted on) and that no one can contaminate us but ourselves.

MONK NAGASENA'S ANSWERS TO KING MILINDA

The Pali literary text *Milindapanha* records a dialogue between a Buddhist monk, Nagasena, and the Greek king, Menander or Milinda. Milinda asks a series of questions highlighting what seems to be anomalies and contradictions in Buddhist doctrine. To each question Nagasena gives a clear, ingenious answer. The effectiveness is enhanced by similies included in the answer.

> The king said: "Why is it Nagasena, that all men are not alike, but some are short-lived and some long-lived, some sickly and some healthy, some ugly and some beautiful, some without influence and some of great power, some poor and some wealthy, some low born and some high born, some stupid and some wise?"
>
> Nagasena replied: "Why is it that all vegetables are not alike, but some sour, and some salty, and some pungent, and some acid, and some astringent, and some sweet? I fancy, Sir, it is because they come from different kinds of seeds. And just so, Great King, are the differences you have mentioned among men to be explained. For it has been said by the Blessed One: Beings O brahmin, have each their own karma, are inheritors of karma, belong to the tribe of their karma, are relatives of karma, have each their karma as their protecting overlord. It is karma that divides them up into low and high and the like divisions."
>
> "Very good Nagasena!" (Rhys Davis, 1969:1:100)

Buddhists attribute all the variations that occur in life to karma. However, they do not believe that everything is due to karma. Buddhism teaches that individuals have within themselves the potential to change their own karma. The question sometimes asked is, Where is karma? In a lifetime a person performs a magnitude of actions, either moral or immoral, and in this way accumulates a lot of karma. Where is all this karma? Where is this stored? In answer to the question of Milinda, Nagasena replied: "Karma is not stored somewhere in this fleeting consciousness or in any part of the body. But dependent on mind and body, it rests, manifesting itself at an opportune moment, just as mangoes are not said to be stored somewhere in the mango tree, but dependent on the mango tree they lie, springing up in due season" (ICIB 1998:26).

Karma in this way is a potential, is transmitted from one life to another. Buddhists believe that the sorrow and happiness one experiences are the natural outcome of one's own good or bad actions or self-inflicted wounds.

DIFFERENT TYPES OF KARMA

In Sunday school in a dreary cheerless way we first learned about the five varieties of karma. The *pancanantari* karma, involve five grave offences. They are killing one's father, mother, or an *arahant*; injuring the person of the Buddha; and causing schisms and dissension in the Buddha *sasana*. These will cause miserable karmic consequences. There is *ditthadhamma vedaniya* karma, the type where the good or bad results are experienced in this life, in contrast to the karma where the results will be experienced in the next life, the *upa-padya vedaniya*, or subsequently. The karma that will result in the lives following the next life is the *aparapariya vedaniya*, indefinitely effective karma. The final form is *ahosi* karma, ineffective karma where the results will be shown in an undetermined life. However, a person's karma may be altered by making amends for previous misdeeds and by leading a good life. There is an idea that with good deeds one can mitigate the bad effects or neutralize bad karma. The *ditthadhamma vedaniya* karma is this kind. The idea is the basis of certain types of Buddhists devotion, rituals, and good actions. Leading a virtuous life, giving *dana*, feeding the poor, kindness, and compassion to all are good karma that may mitigate bad karma. Sinhala legendary king Dutugamunu was supposed to have committed bad karma of an enourmous magnitude in his war with Elara to free the country, which is *pau*, but in the process saved Buddhism, which is *pin*. In repentance he built monasteries in Anuradhapura and an immence amount of good deeds that far outweighed his bad karma. He was born in heaven, to remain there until the time of the next Buddha Maitri. In this way his bad karma was never effective.

Sri Lankan Buddhists believe that things go wrong because of bad karma. They seek worldly remedies to mitigate its bad effects. In a culture where the belief in astrology and horoscopes is pervasive, bad times predicted in the horoscopes are attributed to negative karma brought from previous births. Leading a good life, helping others, going on pilgrimages to sacred places, giving *dana*, and observing *sil* are done in order to change the karma by the virtues of spirituality. In such situations Buddhists also seek divine help to manage karma. Special *pujas* are made to the gods and to the Bo tree, or a *pirit* chanting is done. They pray for the removal of obstacles in life's path. Gods are believed to be capable of giving blessings in times of difficulties by divine guidance.

BANDA'S KARMA

In spite of the stratified society in Sri Lanka, there is no great resentment toward the rich and wealthy by the poor and unfortunate. To some extent this may be attributed to the belief in karma. I have often heard people say they were blessed with all the good things because they have done good karma in the past. The poor work in rich households as servants. They are loyal and grateful to their masters, take care of property, perform numerous tasks, and look after the sick with affection. We have Banda in our household. He has been in our house since Ananda was born. Banda had a clear notion of who did what in the division of domestic chores. An otherwise rather mild man, he would not tolerate departure from the system and would become angry.

Banda believed that he belonged to the household, and it was his assigned duty to keep the place running smoothly, doing whatever he did and had been doing for over sixty years. Banda was paid a very small wage for all the work he did, but as compensation he was looked after as a member of the household. I often wondered if we were committing collective bad karma by getting Banda to work for us. Are we to pay a debt to Banda in our future births?

When we returned from Oxford, Banda was anxious to update us about his life events. The very next day he made us sit and listen to his saga. In the years we were away he had married a Kandyan woman according to Kandyan laws, which were commonsensically simple. The Roman Dutch law governs the rest of the country. His new wife had a difficult time adjusting to Banda's ways, which were set and rigid. He refused to share his towel with her, and a host of other things. A few months later she suggested a separation. Banda went in front of the government agent and declared three times he did not want the woman as his wife. The marriage was dissolved. All this was under the prevailing Kandyan marriage law. His argument that he did not want a woman who did not want him sounded logical. Banda subsequently married again but never left our house for more than two days. He felt it was his house, and he had a commitment to perform his duties, including taking *dana* to the temple daily. In my more thoughtful moments I wondered if this was Banda's karma. He had little and asked for little. Banda was a good simple Buddhist and was free of resentment and anger. He lived an ethical and moral life, content with the little that life had given to him.

There is an old Bo tree in our garden. It is said that this particular Bo tree, together with a few others in the vicinity, was planted in the days of the Kandyan Kingdom, in the sixteenth century. Its ancientness is matched by a certain calming ambience surrounding the tree. As the wind rustled it always seemed to me that it whispered the secrets of an age long gone. Banda had the unfailing habit of lighting a lamp under the tree. On Vesak days Banda made decorations round the tree, and we were all called to share his simple joy. Some days he would tell me in great earnest, "He was there today." When I asked him, "Who was there?" he looked surprised at my ignorance and may have felt sorry that I was not on his wave length. He believed he saw the deities in the tree. Some of the other servants also said that deep in the heart of the night they would see moving flashes of light clustering around the Bo tree. Like Banda they all accepted these phenomena as a matter of course. It was Banda's simple belief that the offerings he made to the deities would result in good blessings to all. His simple message to me was that he was happy, and I was being looked after.

MONK EXPLAINS KARMA CAN BE CHANGED

Ajan Brahmavamso, an English monk who is currently the head of the Buddhist Society of Western Australia, explains how karma can be changed. Our happiness is completely in our hands. It is indeed in our power to overcome some effects of karma. Like baking a cake, karma defined what ingredients you have and what you have got to work with. A person with unfortunate karma may, as a result of past actions, not have many ingredients, maybe some old stale flour, a few raisins, and some rancid butter. Another person might have good karma, all the best ingredients that you could wish for, whole-wheat flour, butter, brown sugar, and many kinds of dried fruits and nuts. But even with the meager ingredients one can bake a beautiful cake by mixing them all up well. The other, with all good ingredients, might bake a cake that tastes awful. Ajan explained that karma defines the ingredients that we have got to work with but does not define what we make of them.

ACCEPTING ONE'S LOT AS KARMA

When we were in Sri Lanka we often went to Kurunegala on Sundays with Ananda's parents. We walked around the coconut estate in the morning hours, and at noontime and enjoyed the sumptuous village-style meals prepared by the man who oversees the land. The traditional meal consisted of new rice from the fields, with a *dhal* curry, dried fish preparation, and freshly ground coconut sambol. We were sitting in the verandah of this modest house one day, its roof thatched in traditional style with sheaths of dry coconut palm woven into a pattern, which maintained the coolness of the interior. It was too hot to do anything but sit. I have a vivid memory of a young, attractive woman rather well made walking toward us with a heavy basket on her head. She wore the traditional village dress: a short cloth tightly wrapped around her waist (she had large hips to hold it up) and a skimpy jacket to cover her abundantly blessed breasts. According to urban middle-class thinking, it is not modest to show one's midriff and hips, but this is not so in the villages. She looked feminine and attractive.

She walked toward my father-in-law, laid the large basket in front of him, and started to measure the grain in it. It was the produce from the land she had been given to cultivate. According to the *ande* system of cultivation the people who cultivated gave half of the produce to the landowner. This was her honest way of sharing the produce of the land with my father-in-law, the owner of the land. She was grateful to him for letting her use the land, and she said that it was her good karma. She was not resentful that she had to share the produce. In another context I heard her mention that they were poor because of her past bad karma, and they had to work hard for little. My father-in-law was not in the least bit interested in the grain or the quantity; his thoughts were far away. He walked away. I felt sad for the woman. She was attractive, yet born poor, so she had little in life. Seated on a stool she sipped tea in the village style, with a little sugar on the palm of her hand, occasionally licking it with the tea to get the sweet taste. This was the way to make sugar go a long way. I was amazed at her attitude. She was not resentful of us for having more than she had.

I read an interesting petition, which was sent to Queen Victoria when Sri Lanka (then Ceylon) was under British rule, in the London Public Records Office, while doing research for my husband. The petitions the natives (to use the nomenclature of the colonial period) sent to Queen Victoria drew attention to injustices done in the name of the queen. They were fascinating and threw light on the social history of the island. The colonial secretary would conscientiously answer each.

A certain native functionary in the district of Dumbara had whipped a group of women while he was riding on horse back for wearing cloths to cover the upper part of their bodies. These women belonged to the lowest caste in society, the *rodyias*. They were rather like gypsies. They lived in the remotest parts of the country and were not allowed to be seen or mingle with the rest of the population. They had no education or opportunities to get jobs, therefore, the majority lived by begging. One of the grossly unjust rules of this incredible system was that women were prohibited from wearing anything to cover their breasts. *Rodiya* women were generally known to be very beautiful, and the officer must have resented the fact that he was deprived of the pleasure he might have received by seeing their bodies during his rural rides. The secretary of state was not pleased and ordered the governor to chastise the officer concerned.

Rodiya women were generally treated unkindly and were deprived of their basic rights. I met a *rodiya* woman in Kandy who came begging to our house. She was outside the gate, as *rodiyas* are not allowed to enter the compound. The servants hurriedly gave her some money and sent her away, recognizing her caste from her dress and the dialect she spoke. They are not allowed to roam freely even to beg. There are legends of *rodiya* women carrying charms to attract the men folk of a house. For this reason they were feared. When I heard the commotion I went to the gate and called the woman in to give her money and clothes. She was charming and quite different from anyone I had seen. She did not resent the fact that she was chased away and instead accepted it all as her karma. She insisted on telling my fortune, for they are known for their ability to forecast the future. She gave me a little talisman, which she said was for my protection. I kept this secretly hidden for a long time. I was young and could not fathom Buddhists who while believing in the effect of karma could treat their own people this way, adding to their baskets of bad karma.

The fear of karma induces people to engage in good deeds. Karma can be a teacher. Killing animals would result in shorter life spans, and that the children of butchers may suffer from accidents and short life spans was a common belief in our society. Karma consciously deters one from doing negative acts and is an incentive to do good. Its utilitarian orientation is plain. Ananda told me the story of a rich Muslim butcher in Kandy, my father-in-law's client. He was butchered and killed by robbers in an inhuman way. He added that he cried in pain in a way similar to the cries of the animals he butcherd daily.

BEING BORN A WOMAN IS BAD KARMA

Past actions determine one's wealth, power, beauty, talent, and even sex in future births. In popular belief, one is born a woman because of bad karma in the past. The notion deeply ingrained gives religious sanction to the inferior status of women. It is not unusual for a woman to aspire to be born a man in the next birth after meritorious deeds are performed. In my marriage I accepted the superiority of my husband. My husband and I often had disagreements on certain matters when we were young. Once when I told my mother about this, she listened to me very intently and said I should treat my husband well and take care of him and then I will get a better partner in my next birth or that I would be born a man. I used to repeat what my mother said to my husband who on such occasions tried his best to conceal his amusement. He would tease me by saying that he kept a secret score card of my performance and that someday I would know the final tally.

ANGULIMALA'S KARMA, GOOD AND BAD

The story of Angulimala is the story of how karma may be changed in one's own lifetime. When Angulimala was born, his father, in casting his horoscope, discovered that he was born under the "robber constellation." This indicated that the boy would have a tendency to commit robbery. He was named Ahimsaka, which meant "harmless" and was given a good education. His parents gave him lots of love and encouragement. Ahimsaka was well behaved and intelligent. He eventually went to Taxila Univesity, a famous university in ancient India. He served his teacher with respect and humility. His fellow students were, however, envious of him and told the teacher many stories to poison his mind. These attempts failed, but as a last resort they made up a story that Ahimsaka was plotting to get the teacher's job as professor. The teacher believed the story and began to think that maybe the only way to retain his position as a renowned guru was get rid of Ahimsaka. There was a tradition in those days that upon graduation the *sisya* or pupil would give the guru a very special gift—possibly something in which the guru had expressed an interest. The guru summoned Ahimsaka and asked him to bring him a hundred little fingers excised from the right hands of his victims. The teacher, aware of the horrific nature of his unreasonable request, nonetheless said that this would be a token of gratitude for all that he had taught him.

Ahimsaka, in a dilemma pondering how he could please his teacher, was disinclined to cause hurt to innocent people. However, the teacher quite cynically and coldly insisted that if the stipulated reward was not forthcoming, Ahimsakas's education would be incomplete. Reluctantly, Ahimsaka decided to do what he was bidden, but his idealistic heart broke, and he became disillusioned and cynical. He could have gone to the cemetery and collected fingers from the dead bodies, but he did not think of this. Instead he collected swords and knives and went into the Jalini forest to wait for victims. He waited on top of the mountain for people to pass by, and he killed them and cut off their fingers. He threaded the fingers into a necklace and wore it around his neck. He was given the name *Angulimala*, in reference to the necklace of fingers. He went to village houses by night to kill or maim people in order to get their fingers. People left their homes for fear. They complained to the king, who sent the army to capture him.

Nobody realized that the robber was Ahimsaka. His mother, however, had a suspicion and urged his father to go in search of Ahimsaka and advise him to change his ways. Ahimsaka's father, angry with his son said, "I have no use for such a son. Let the king kill him." His mother's heart was soft, and she set out to the forest to warn her son of the impending danger. Angulimala, having collected nine hundred ninety-nine fingers, was waiting for the last one to complete his teacher's request. He would not have hesitated to kill his mother to get the last finger, which would have been the most heinous karma that one could commit and would have taken him to hell.

The Buddha with his psychic powers was able to see the plight of Angulimala and with great compassion resolved to help him. The Buddha was warned when he was approaching the forest that Angulimala would not spare even monks. The Buddha went on the desolate mountain path in silence. Angulimala saw a woman approaching. He approached his mother. The Buddha appeared between them as a monk. Angulimala decided to kill the monk instead. He began to go behind the Buddha to get his finger. The Buddha with his magical powers created the visual illusion wherein however fast Angulimala walked he could not catch the Buddha. The Buddha walked at his normal pace, and Angulimala, walking as fast as he could, was unable to catch up with the Buddha. Exasperated, Angulimala shouted, "Stop monk, stop." The Buddha replied, "I have stopped; Angulimala, you should stop too." Angulimala was perplexed. Then the Buddha said, "Angulimala, I have stopped forever. I gave up violence. I showed compassion to every living being, but you have not. That is why I have stopped, and you have not." When Angulimala heard the words of the Buddha, he was deeply moved and listened to the dharma. He said, "I will renounce all evil." He threw his sword and asked the Buddha if he could become his disciple. The Buddha replied, "Come Bhikkhu," so he became a monk.

As they were leaving the forest they saw the king and his army intent on capturing Angulimala. The Buddha asked the king if he was going to capture another kingdom. The king replied that he was going to capture Angulimala. The Buddha then asked the king, "If you were to see Angulimala with a shaven head, wearing the saffron robes of a monk, having vowed to abstain from killing living beings, from stealing, from lying and deceiving, and living the holy and blameless life, how would you treat him?" The king then replied, "I would pay homage to him and offer my protection, but how could such an unvirtuous person of evil character have such virtue and restraint?" The Buddha pointed to Angulimala and said, "Great king, this is Angulimala. Do not be afraid; there is nothing to fear." The king said to the Buddha, "It is wonderful, sir; it is marvelous how the Blessed One subdues the unsubdued, pacifies the unpeaceful, and calms the uncalm. He who we could not subdue with punishments and weapons, the Blessed One subdued without punishment or weapon."

Who are we then? All the talk of karma should not free us from taking the responsibility for our actions and their mathematically calculable consequences. Karma can easily be confused with fatalism and negative social attitudes. Buddhism seems to be saying that mindfully living our lives conscious of our every act takes care of "the things that happen to us." The linkages of our thoughts and where they might end is well expressed in the following well known stanza attributed to the Buddha:

> Watch your thoughts; they become words
> Watch your words; they become actions
> Watch your actions; they become habits
> Watch your habits; they become character
> Watch your character; it becomes your destiny.

TEN

To Die Only to Be Reborn

THE FOLLOWING ARE THE haunting lines of a song that was popular when I was growing up: "*Epida mare yali epide; nothira sasara sagare.*"

In a vibrant voice, the popular singer W. D. Amaradeva is telling us that one is born only to die and be reborn again and again in the boundless ocean of samsara, an ocean devoid of a shore. Buddhists regard rebirth as a fact. They believe that each person has lived many lives and will continue to do so.

I recall also the popular song of Victor Ratnayake sung at his spectacular music event popularly termed "SA." The opening of the song translates as "We never really die, as long as there is sun, moon and stars, we too will be here. If by some chance we die we go to a divine world and come back after a time, with a new name, a new family, new place and a new lineage. It is just a change of scene. We just go round and round in deaths and births in a never-ending cycle appearing and disappearing, but we never really die."

Trixie, my cousin, was intensely in love with her boyfriend. She was unable to conceive of a time when she would have to part with him in this life. She was thinking ahead. She prayed to be born again to love him and crave him in the next four births (I wondered about the number) to come. She sought refuge in the Buddha for help in her prayers. A few years later she had to seek the assistance of the law to separate from him. Recently in conversation I reminded her of her *prattana* (wishful prayer) and asked her if the wish had changed. She laughed in embarrassment. Sri Lankan Buddhists pray for association with people they love and cherish in future births, thus establishing their belief in rebirth as a given fact.

In a recent discourse, an ordained female Buddhist nun, Bhikkuni Kusuma, explained to a gathering that such a wishful prayer is really unrealistic. We meet in this world and have good relationships; we crave the same in future births. The chances of meeting the same person are rare. She explained by a metaphor: You dip your finger in the cool waters of a flowing river and feel the fine sensation. The river waters flow to join a bigger river and then the great ocean, and that water is lost in the mass of immensity. To expect to get the same partner in the next birth is like expecting to dip the same finger in the same water. What you get is new water as the old water has flowed away, and new water has taken its place.

WESTERN SKEPTICISM

Westerners in general are clearly skeptical about rebirth. This concept, so much an integral part of the Asian religious tradition, does not fit into Western ways of thinking. However, at a popular level, the notion of rebirth is romanticized, especially among the young who tell each other (indeed as we did too, long years ago) that the current passion is but a phase in an ongoing tryst in ageless cosmic time. It is, when all is said and done, a beautiful idea. However, rebirth is not taken seriously in a culture powerfully influenced by the weight of centuries-old Judeo Christian traditions.

A FISH TALKS ABOUT REBIRTH!

The prevailing ambivalence was nicely illustrated in a remarkable story that appeared in the *New York Times* recently. The venue was the New Square Fish Market in New York, serving a predominantly Jewish community belonging to a Hasidic sect. One of two fishmongers was about to kill a twenty-pound carp, which would be used to make gefilte fish for the Jewish Sabbath dinner. Unaccountably however, the fish, which was surprisingly still alive, put up a terrific struggle and successfully got away from the slaughter bloc. It thrashed around and finally got back into the very box from which it had been taken. To the amazement of the two fishmongers, the carp began to speak in Hebrew, cautioning in apocalyptic vein that the end was near and that everyone would have to account for themselves. The carp urged the fishmongers to pray and revealed that in the previous year he had been a member of the Hasidic community and had died childless. Investigations revealed that there had been such a man who was himself a regular customer frequenting this particular shop. Nonetheless, the carp was caught and slaughtered.

In numerous radio talk shows in the days following the incident—which alternated between belief and downright disbelief—great consternation was universally expressed that the fish had after all been killed and not kept alive somehow. As the dust settled, and the incident was quickly forgotten, some wondered whether the whole thing was not a prank to coincide with the Jewish festival of Purim, which was a time for pranks anyway. The more thoughtful, however, were struck by the fact that a humble fisherman was chosen (if that is the correct word) to hear a message of such profundity. One might wonder whether the predisposition to believe or to disbelieve is simply a matter of conditioning of the mind brought about by a conniving culture.

LOSING A CAMPUS FRIEND

As I put my own thoughts together, my mind goes back to the month of May in Peradeniya. We were young undergraduates living in residence halls. It was after the harvest season, a beautiful time in Sri Lanka, when everything looked serene and fresh and there was an appearance of abundance. The mango trees of many varieties on the university campus were drooping heavy with luscious fruits. It was also the avocado season. We had returned to the campus after the Sri Lankan New Year vacation. There was an air of enthusiasm and hope and the promise of new things.

It was more by habit that every Sunday we went to the Buddhist Brotherhood meetings with our friends. Indrani, my good friend, my soul mate really, was prim and proper and always did the right thing. In everything she was ethical and never crossed the line, even in lighthearted moments. She gathered us that day to go for the special *bana* by the eminent Venerable Narada who had been invited from Colombo to address the students on the topic of rebirth. Venerable Narada, was well known for his eloquent style of preaching and his saintliness. The day turned out to be special in many ways.

As young adults, we seldom talked about death. We were aware in an abstract cognitive way that we needed to think philosophically of death, but it had not hit our doorstep yet. Besides, life in Peradeniya was too much fun to think of dying, or for that matter, to think of what happened after death.

However, the concept of "rebirth" was fascinating to our young minds. Some had firm belief in a life after death, and there was no need to question it. If you were born a Buddhist you believed in rebirth as an axiom. My upbringing however, was mixed, with a variety of beliefs and confusing ideas. I had always had doubts about rebirth as a young adult. I wondered often what would happen to us when we die. The English nun, Mother Calumba, who taught religion to us in the Catholic high school I attended, gave us comforting answers to these difficult questions. She told us that God had a plan for us. He sent us here for a purpose, and when it was time, he recalled us to join him. We had a place to go, especially prepared for each one of us, with him. God determined the time of our parting. We needed to trust God, and to doubt was a sin. When we died angels would come to escort us to our loved ones, and all would be united. To our growing minds, these were comforting thoughts.

The death of Hemalatha, who had committed suicide in the residence hall the previous semester, shocked us. We knew that she was in love, that her boyfriend had found another girl. I recollect as a freshman, in the evenings, a handsome young man would come to fetch her, the fabled prince charming, her boyfriend. The romantic affair continued for a while, until suddenly he stopped visiting her, which made her unhappy. The trauma of rejection was unbearable to her, loosing her lover and having to face the gossip and questions that went with it.

Our young minds were fascinated with love and wanted stories to end "happily ever after." Romantic stories were a popular topic of conversation. We wondered whether the loss of a lover was a reason to commit suicide. Hemalatha was a pretty woman and was much liked by her friends. She wore pretty saris to lectures, tightly wrapped around her beautiful body, emphasizing her thin waist and broad hips, signs of oriental beauty. Her hips swayed rhythmically from side to side as she walked in her high-heeled sandals. I thought that if she wore the sari a little lower, like a hipster, it would make her even more attractive. Hemalatha was conservative and had an air of freshness about her. In the evenings she came to the student study room to listen to Sinhala songs from the old movies, to break the monotony of studying, a rather romantic person. Indrani reminded us that we needed to be especially attentive to the *bana* to transfer merit to Hemalatha's soul, in the ritual of *pinanumodana*, which would follow the *bana*, which was our obligation to transfer merit to her.

TO MEET A MONK WHO KNEW IT ALL

The explanations and stories I had heard in Sunday school and from my mother did not quite satisfy my thirst for information about life after death. We were taught in the Buddhist Sunday school that when we die we are reborn elsewhere according to the good and bad deeds we committed in this life. We needed a better answer as to what would happen after death. We wondered why Hemalatha could not come back to tell us what she was doing or where she was. Some students made up convincing stories of a pretty young woman in white appearing in the night, then disappearing into darkness, vaguely resembling Hemalatha. Others reported seeing this figure standing on the balcony in the night on their way to the bathroom. As the stories spread details were added.

We came to breakfast, dressed in white saris, to leave for the *bana* immediately after. It was a beautiful morning with the sun mildly spreading its gentle rays to take away the coolness of the air. We young women would always walk in groups in an atmosphere of sisterliness. We showed affection and concern for each other, holding hands and touching each other. We exchanged the most intimate emotional stories and feelings with each other. Lesbian life styles and such views were not known at this time or may not have come out of the closet. In matters of dressing, those who were not comfortable with wearing the sari got help from others. We all had to look nice and proper. If you did not have a white sari, others were forthcoming in lending one. We gathered at the front hall to walk together. As we walked down the steps of the Peiris Hall hill, beautiful pink flowers in bloom on the cherry blossom trees seemed as though they too were blessing us. The fallen pink blossoms provided a pink carpet to walk on, like the traditional *pavada*.

Pink-clad cherry blossom trees were not native to Sri Lanka. They were planted for the beautification of the campus, along with other exotic flowering trees. We went down the hill one following the other. The Obeysekara Hall girls soon joined us on the way, in a white clad procession. Here and there we saw male students wearing white joining us. All were going to listen to the *bana*. We talked a lot in groups, the topic, rebirth. Some, as good Buddhists, had no problem believing in rebirth. Those who had doubts expressed them.

Venerable Narada was seated on the stage dressed in saffron robes, calm, serene, and composed. He had the appearance of a little Buddha, above all human problems and sorrows. The sermon began with the administering of the Five Precepts and a few minutes of *metta* meditation. The *bana* preaching followed, a lucid explanation of the difficult concept of rebirth in Buddhist teaching. He began the sermon by saying that rebirth was a part of the Buddhist teaching that many found difficult to accept. Rebirth was central to Buddhist teaching and it was useful for each person to grasp its meaning.

The monk said that Buddhism generally teaches the way, and it is open for anyone to empirically test out what it says. As Buddhists, we are not required to believe in rebirth; we had to discover it for ourselves. In the bigger scheme of things, it is important to know what happens to us when we die and more so to find out where we came from. All this is possible in this life with the right effort. He said those who have followed the path of the Buddha teachings have found out for themselves.

The monk reminded us that the Buddha, when he sat at the Bo tree, by training his mind through meditation, and empowering his mind, was able to see his previous lives. He saw the reality of life and then finally attained Enlightenment. The Buddha, with the newly acquired wisdom, could see that all beings are subject to certain natural laws and are trapped in an endless round of existences. Death is just one phase of this cycle and is invariably followed by rebirth, which is yet another phase or moment of an endless *samsaric* cyclical round.

He gave interesting examples on how to train the mind. He urged us to be aware of the mind, which travels all over, and to practice bringing the mind back to the proper place, each time it runs away. He said we too, like the Buddha, can train the mind by practicing mindfulness, to find the basic truths, even see our previous births. But he said it involves a lot of discipline and hard work. We are involved in daily activities, problems of studying for exams, going to lectures, reading, and we do not have the time to develop the mind or pay attention long enough to what we are doing. The mind travels faster than the speed of light. In Buddhism this untrained mind is compared to the "monkey mind." Generally our attention span is short, and the depth of concentration is weak. He explained that a trained mind could be put to efficient use.

He went on at length to explain the benefits of the trained mind, such as the ability to sustain it on one thing, for a long period of time. It could be tested, by trying to call up the earliest memories. The monk shared with us some of his earliest memories, and in the process of mindfulness, meditation how he had a glimpse of his previous lives and where he came from, his past lives. The truth of this, he added, puts everything into proper perspective. As a monk, he said, rules prohibit him from sharing these with us, but we can all try it for ourselves. "Once you see this, you will see for yourself that rebirth is true, and you will no longer have doubts." We may not be able to convince anyone else, but we will know that rebirth is true. We will know that we have lived before and that we are going to come back. This is how one discovers the truth of rebirth, he added.

He connected rebirth to karma. It is like coming back to the house to pick up the mess. He said it was important to live a good life, practice generosity, kindness, and compassion. What is important is not how long you live but how well you live. He also said that we are together here, because we had been together before. If you did good deeds together you will meet again to reap the benefits.

There was a young, attractive lecturer in the university who was the first to receive a first class in his department, and therefore it was sensational. He was much sought after by the female undergraduate community. Young, attractive, accomplished; pretty women sought his company. This was not unusual. To everybody's amazement he liked a rather simple, composed, small-made girl from his class. There was nothing distinctive about her but her simplicity and goodness. The more glamorous, wealthy women felt angry and slighted. The young man paid no attention to them. He pursued his love. This type of attraction the monks would explain as a phenomenon of rebirth. They had been together before, and here they were again.

It was an illuminating *bana*. We were convinced that rebirth had validity, but we had to put off practicing the meditation that was a prerequisite for its discovery to a later day. Now we had other things to do: write tutorials, read the required texts, and study for the exams and the trillion issues of immediate survival. We had to find careers and get married to our boyfriends. To the young undergraduates, this was not possible then and there. The *bana* taught us valuable lessons, especially the practical usefulness to train the mind to remember what we read better. The lesson was memorable and rewarding.

A CULTURE PRONE TO REBIRTH

Belief in rebirth is almost a birth inheritance of a Buddhist. People often say in conversation, "I must have been so and so in my previous birth," or, "I must have been someone related to you in one of my previous births." Often in the most casual of conversations someone will say, "It is my good karma or bad karma arising from previous birth karmas that such is such." Buddhists believe that rebirth takes place continually until all craving is overcome and one attains *nirvana*. The ultimate goal of Buddhists therefore is to get off *samsara* (the wheel of rebirth). By good karma this process is gradually eliminated by being born in better and more favorable situations. The aim in the process is to reduce greed, hate, and delusion.

Buddhists give legitimacy to their belief in rebirth in indirect and coincidental ways and scenarios. One such is the concept of "*sasara purudda*" or *samsaric* inclination or connection; a term popularly used among Buddhists in relation to the idea of karma and rebirth. The concept is thrown around to explain many phenomena. Monks would explain it through examples. It is not a dictionary term with a specific explanation or a concept that can be proved in a laboratory by clinical tests. It is belief, largely faith based, with rather vague connotations. If we meet someone under extraordinary or coincidental circumstances and form bonds and meaningful relationships, the assumption is that we may have previously met and had associated with them in previous births. As a karmic connection we meet them again and maintain connections. The idea of continuity of birth experiences due to karmic results is an accepted theory. Buddhists do not demand explanations or proof but assume them as unexplained phenomenon. These can be favorable or unfavorable, pleasant or unpleasant, good or otherwise.

It is said that the Buddha acquired two sorts of insight, the ability to recall with visual clarity his previous existences and the ability to do so in the case of anyone else. He remarked that the continuum of births was so lengthy that it did not make sense to fathom where the process all began. Following his instructions his disciples also developed this knowledge through meditation. In the Jataka stories, which are familiar to Buddhists, the Buddha's previous life stories exemplify the theory (fact) of rebirth.

However, questions about the beginning of birth were a problem, which for example my son, Channa, as a child could not quite comprehend. He studied at Trinity College, Kandy. Ananda's father insisted that he attend the scripture classes and know the Bible well before he studied Buddhism. Being in a Buddhist household, Channa often heard rebirth mentioned. When he had troubling questions, Channa often went to his *seeya* (grandfather). He had faith in his grandfather and his ability to find answers to all his questions.

Before going to school one day, Channa went to see his grandfather in some haste and found him shaving, getting ready to go to work. Channa asked his *seeya*, "If you say there is a thing called rebirth, when did this all begin? There must be a beginning to everything." He talked of the creation, the story of Adam and Eve, and said that he could not comprehend the theory of rebirth. Seeya invited Channa to have breakfast with him. Banda had laid the table with plates for everyone, and Channa too had his plate. Seeya asked Channa to examine the plate carefully and find the beginning of it. The plate was round, and Channa carefully and seriously examined the plate to find a beginning. Then he said, "Seeya, there is no beginning to this plate. I cannot see it." Seeya then told Channa, "Do you remember the question you asked me? The answer is similar. Channa, there is no end or beginning to birth and rebirth. The plate is like *samsara*. The process goes on and on." Channa was satisfied for the moment, worshipped his grandfather, as was the custom, and went on his way to school.

MY ENGLISH FRIEND

Venerable Sobhita once explained that there are millions of people of different races and religions in this world. We meet and become intimate only with a few. Did we really choose our parents, our children, our friends, or was this a pure accident? He said that we met here in this birth because we have met before somewhere, maybe in a previous birth. He explained all this as karma. Our forming strong bonds with people we have not met before is often rationalized on this basis. He said that we meet under strange circumstances because of our previous associations. He asked, "How else would you explain this?" Rhetorical questions are notoriously difficult to answer, and one feels quite helpless.

My friendship with Anna Hood in my student days at Oxford was enigmatic in its own way. I was young, married, with family obligations, while most of my colleagues were unmarried. I accepted the obligations without question. The idea of sharing domestic tasks was a foreign concept to Sri Lankan husbands. Being a full-time student I had little time for socializing outside my family. However, Anna insisted on cultivating a friendship with me. She made time to go with me to the park or accompany me to the bookstore. She had an old Morris Minor car, and she took me around to show me places in and around Oxford. Sometimes she persuaded me to join her and her other friends to go to an English pub, which I liked very much, to have a beer and discuss schoolwork. I felt comfortable with her, although we were culturally far apart. It seemed as if I had known her for a long time.

She invited us many times to visit her family in Salwarpe, Worcestershire. It was our custom always to go with our husbands. When I told all this to Ananda, he did not show much enthusiasm and dismissed the idea, saying he did not like going to English homes because the women in the house have more dishes to wash with us there. I innocently repeated this to Anna. She said that her mother did not wash dishes since they had a staff of servants. Anyway, I managed to convince Ananda to join us. Anna came to meet us. She had already bought the train tickets for all of us. We took British Rail to the city, and her father picked us up at the station in a fancy Rolls Royce. They were the most hospitable people I had met in England.

The Rolls Royce rolled through winding country roads to a beautiful mansion, the like of which I had seen only in pictures. Anna made us comfortable and put us at ease. They did have staff to do the chores, and the entire setup was all very lavish. I had no idea that Anna was so wealthy because she had never talked about wealth or showed any signs of it. My husband, a historian by training, knew British history well. Looking at the enormous portrait hung on one side of the wall in the dinning room, he told me with surprise that it was a picture of Lord Hood, who was associated with Admiral Nelson. So it turned out that Anna's father was a descendant of Lord Hood. They were aristocratic by birth and behavior, but never was there any mention of their lineage. We stayed the weekend with them, and they became our good friends. They took care of us as an extended family, and we made many visits to them over the next four years. It was a one-way hospitality since as students we had no way of reciprocating.

There was a marriage arranged for Anna with an equally distinguished family. She met Peter at a foxhunting ball. Peter was also with us in school, and he showed great affection to Anna. Peter, I might add, was the son of the governor of the Bank of England. In contrast to Anna's ebullient spontaneity, Peter was staid and somewhat settled in his ways. When they were together the contrast was striking. Anna had one ambition at this time, which was to go to India for voluntary service. Politically, Peter was conservative, and Anna was strongly liberal. She once told me that unearned wealth was unethical. It took me some time to clearly understand her thinking. She was born to wealth, but her heart was for the less fortunate. Anna's mother complained to me that Anna hardly ever used money, which was deposited in the bank for her expenses. Anna's life style was simple. I did not think going to India to do voluntary work was a good idea, and I did my part to dissuade her.

The same year that we returned to Sri Lanka, Anna arrived in Bangalore on her mission. On her frequent visits to me from Bangalore, she had no complaints except that Bangalore was too industrialized, and she wanted to spend another year in a small rural village, more typical of India. She found an ideal place in Kerala in Mitranikethan, a self-sufficient rural community. She told me that there they had tapioca for breakfast, lunch, and dinner, and she too got used to tapioca. While in India she got accustomed to wearing the sari woven by the community in which she lived. She fitted in with the community, and her face glowed whenever she told me stories of her experiences living there. My friendship with Anna was beautiful. I believe it was something made in heaven and often wondered if I had had close associations with her in a previous life. I lost touch with Anna, but I strongly believe that I will meet her again someday, somewhere, an example of a *samsaric* connection, brought about by some shared karma.

A SON AND A FATHER

Ananda's family was associated with Richard Gombrich. We met many years ago in Oxford when Richard met Ananda at a graduate seminar. He was interested in studying Sinhala, and his research was to be based on Buddhism in Sri Lanka. Ananda introduced him to his father. Ananda's family took a liking to Richard, and his father felt he was the long-lost son come to visit him. Ananda's father was interested in helping Richard in any way he could with his research, which was centered in Wewegama, a village in the outskirts of Kandy. Richard soon became part of the household. Having done his investigative research, Richard went back to Oxford. During the time we spent with them, we formed close relations with Richard and his wife Dhosha. They were the most wonderful and generous friends one could hope to have. Was this *sasara purudda*? With Richard and Dhosha as friends, we really did not need any other friends at Oxford.

When we went back to Sri Lanka in the late sixties, Richard made his second visit with his family and lived in Wewegama. Whenever Richard needed a break from village life, he came to Ananda's house, and the household accepted him as one of them. People called him *sudu nilame* (white nobleman) or *sudu mahattaya* (white master).

Richard and his family returned to England, having completed his research, but continued to visit Kandy. Richard made trips to the village laden with food stuffs. He would take a veritable cornucopia of food items and get one family to cook and feed all his friends. On these occasions my mother-in-law would ask me to accompany Richard to the Kandy market when he went shopping. I spoke the colloquial Sinhalese better (Richard and Dhosha both spoke Sinhala), and she believed Richard got better deal on prices and good quality fish when he was with me. Normally it is not the custom for a young married woman to go alone with a young man in Sri Lanka. It could become a topic of conversation. I was not allowed to go with anyone. My mother-in-law, although conservative, did not think of Richard as an outsider. People looked at us because we looked so different. Richard was a handsome young man in native attire, tall and white, impressive, and I was a small Sri Lankan woman in a sari. The casual observer might have thought that Richard was a reincarnation of Robert Knox: gone seemingly native but appraising the local culture with perceptive eyes.

Ananda's father believed in the strong karmic connection with Richard. When he was saying farewell to him on his last visit in the early seventies in the traditional way by bowing down to greet him with folded palms, I remember Ananda's father with great emotion and sadness said, "Richard, we met because of the *sasara purudda*, and we will meet again some day in *samsara*."

Connected to this is the idea that if we owe a debt to someone it must be paid, or else it will have to be paid in a future life. Servants in households who have strong bonds to a master work for a small wage with loyalty, with no complaints, presumably paying off a *samsaric* debt. This may not make much sense in a modern society with its emphasis on scientific analysis and proof. Within the milieu of popular Buddhist belief, however, making the connection itself would serve as proof. Rebirth in Sri Lanka was an axiom. Proof was superfluous. It was clearly reductionist, but all the same a charming idiom of social interaction—a cosmic visiting card.

There are also some people who spontaneously develop the memory of their past births and remember fragments of their previous lives. In hypnotic states some relate experiences of their past lives. Sometimes people have strange experiences, which cannot be explained other than by rebirth. We often meet persons whom we have never met before and yet instinctively feel that they are familiar to us. Sometimes we feel we know places even if we are visiting the place for the first time. Attachments are explained as previous connections. The overall rationale is complex.

REBIRTH AND BUDDHIST STORIES

At the time of death, according to the karma one has done, the place of rebirth is determined. There are six realms in which one may be born after death. They are the realms of gods, demigods, human beings, animals, hungry ghosts or *pretas*, and hells. These realms include the three happy or fortunate states and three less fortunate or woeful states. The realms of the gods, demigods, and humans are considered the fortunate or happy states. In general it is believed that good actions such as good moral conduct, generosity, and mental development result in the rebirth in happy realms such as gods, demigods, and human condition that has the potential for spiritual growth. Unwholesome actions such as immoral conduct, miserliness, and cruelty cause rebirth in unfortunate realms as animals, ghosts and *pretas*, and in hells untold.

Of all these realms, to be born a human being is considered the most fortunate. It is the only birth form where one can do good karma and make one's way to attain nirvana. According to Buddhist teaching, people are born and reborn endlessly in *samsara* in one realm or the other. There is no permanent rest in this cycle of rebirth and death. One is advised to follow the Noble Eight-fold Path taught by the Buddha and put an end to craving and attain *nirvana*, the only way to end the cycle and attain permanent happiness and peace. But most Buddhists do not think of attaining nirvana in this birth. It is a difficult goal sensibly put off for a future occasion to be tried later, giving Sri Lankans Buddhists a curiously laid back attitude.

The Buddha spoke of the rarity and the precious nature of opportune birth amongst human beings. I remember a story where the Buddha had used the simile to illustrate the difficulty of being born a human being. The story is of a blind tortoise seeing the full moon. The ocean is vast and on the surface is a yoke floating about, blown about by the wind. At the bottom of the ocean is a partially blind tortoise, which comes to the surface of the ocean once every hundred years. The tortoise has to come to the surface on a full moon day and place its neck through the opening of the floating yoke to see the full moon. The yoke too has to be in the correct place. Just so rare is the opportunity and the combination of circumstances for someone to be born a human being. A verse from *Loveda Sagarava* is very much on the lips of the Buddhists:

Kalakini Budukenekun upadinne; Dukakini minisath bava labaganne

Rare indeed it is for a Buddha to born.
To be born to human condition needs great striving.

REBIRTH AS A STORY IN SCIENCE

Yet another way of providing proof for rebirth in the Buddhist world is the belief in past life stories. In Sri Lanka one hears reported incidents of children talking about their previous births. These are highlighted in newspapers and attract attention.

The stories of rebirth always interested me. In Sri Lanka in the seventies I had the good fortune to attend a lecture given by Dr. Ian Stevenson on rebirth stories, an altogether intriguing experience. His presentations were illustrated with slides. He discussed his research, especially the methodologies and assumptions, and shared several cases as examples of reincarnation that he had investigated in Asia and Europe. He categorized them into three major groups. In many case studies there were presumptive evidences of rebirth in another place. He had done extensive investigations involving children who claimed to remember their previous homes and families. He would verify the claims and often send research assistants to look up birth and death registration to establish the basic facts.

He talked of a case in India of Gopal Gupta born in Delhi India, in 1956. His parents were members of the lower middle class with little education. Soon after Gopal began to speak, his father asked him to remove a glass that a guest had used. Gopal startled everyone by saying, "I won't pick it up. I am a Sharma." (Sharmas are members of the highest caste in India, the Brahmins.) He then went into a temper tantrum in which he broke some glasses.

When Gopal was asked to explain his rude behavior, he related many details about a previous life that he claimed to remember having lived in Madura, a city about 150 kilometers from Delhi. Gopal said that he had owned a company concerned with medicine and gave its name. He said he had owned a large house and had many servants. He had had a wife and two brothers, and he had quarreled with one of them, and the latter had shot him.

Gopal's family had no connections with Madura, and all this made little sense. His father felt indifferent to Gopal's assertions but spoke about it to his friends. Eventually Gopal's father went to Madura in 1964 for a religious festival. While there he inquired about the company and the family to which Gopal had referred. What Gopal's father said impressed the manager of the company because one of the owners of the company had shot and killed his brother some years before. Subsequently Gopal visited Matura, and during these visits, Gopal recognized various persons and places known to the family. The Sharma family in Madura was particularly impressed when Gopal mentioned an attempt of Shaktipal Sharma (Gopal) to borrow money from his wife to give his brother, who was a partner in the company. He wanted to give money, but his wife objected. The brother became angry and shot Shaktipal. The details of the family quarrel were never publicized and probably never known outside the family. These stories and other statements and his recognition of persons convinced the family that Gopal was Shaktipal Sharma reborn. Dr. Stevenson presented this as an example of a proven case.

I remember another story told by Dr. Stevenson. This was of a little girl who had drowned and in later lives had a remarkable fear of bathing or any activity concerning water. Her name was Shamlini and she was born in Colombo. Her parents lived in a village about sixty kilometers from Colombo. Shamlini was also afraid of buses and cried when she saw one even at a distance. The parents were concerned about these phobias but explained them as traumatic events from her previous life.

When Shamlini began to speak she told her parents and others about her previous life. She had lived in a village about two kilometers from where she currently lived. She gave the names of her parents and her sisters and of two companions from school. She described the house in which she had lived and how she had died. She described how she had gone to buy bread and the road was flooded. A bus splashed water on her, and she fell into the paddy field and was drowned. After investigation they verified that a girl named Hemaseeli had drowned in the village in circumstances similar to those Shamlini described. About a year later she recognized Hemaseeli's sister and her school companions. As the years went by her memories faded, and she stopped talking about her previous birth memories. Dr. Stevenson presented this as a case that plausibly supported rebirth.

He mentioned that birthmarks and birth defects related to the previous personality provided the strongest evidence in some cases he investigated. He

talked about the age and manner of speaking about the previous lives in children he investigated. The children who talked about their previous lives
always did so between the ages of two and five. It is a commonplace that as
we age, newer experiences and the sheer cumulative weight of such experiences tend to phase out of the mind earlier experiences, especially when our
minds in our younger phase could not quite make sense of these experiences
and if the latter were "felt" rather than in strict actuality experienced. Put in
another way, the newborn child is no more than the old man who died yesterday. Significantly subjects mispronounced the words and compensated for
the lack of vocabulary with gestures. Subjects usually remembered the names
of the previous personalities and names of places.

Godwin Samararatne, Dr. Stevenson's research assistant, was known to
me, and this whole episode kindled an interest in me to be more receptive to
reincarnation stories. I brought to Godwin's attention for investigations several cases that I had heard of and knew about personally. Dr. Stevenson men-
tions that persons who claim that they remember a previous life were found
in India, Sri Lanka, Burma, Thailand, and Middle Eastern countries. It was
not as if stories of rebirth were confined to either India or to Buddhist countries, where there is a certain cultural predisposition to believe in rebirth.

When children began talking about a previous life, the initial reaction of
the parents depended on their convictions concerning reincarnation. The
Christian parents did not believe in rebirth, and often such incidents were
attributed to psychological problems or childhood fantasies. Ananda had
friends who were tea planters in the hill county of Ceylon. On one of our visits, I met a little two year old, he had a tremendous fear of guns. There were
no guns around, but he had fear of them. At certain times of the day, usually
in the evening, he would go into a trance-like state and hide behind the heavy
curtains in the living room, pretend to shoot through the window, and at the
same time dodge bullets. This went on for some time with great intensity and
concentration. He talked of war and the other mother he had had in his previous life. This did not please his parents, who were embarrassed and tried to
stop the child from talking nonsense. All this was quite contrary to the belief
system of our friends. They mentioned that this boy often got into an agitated
state. When the child insisted on talking about his previous life, a servant was
called in to remove him from our company.

Another incident I brought to the attention of Godwin was of a child
from an upper-class, affluent home claiming to have been born previously in
a poor village near his house. This posed difficulty. The family lived in Peradeniya, and the father was the curator of the botanical gardens. Ananda knew
this family, and we visited them frequently. Their three-year-old daughter,
Shanti, went into a trance-like state and talked about her previous life. They
were Buddhists of the bona fide traditional variety. She talked about her
mother, who wore a cloth and a jacket (the traditional village attire of poor

people), and spoke of her kindness. She said her house was a hut and did not have all the luxuries that were there in the house she lived. She referred to the previous life house as "my house" and mother as "my mother." She mentioned the village, which was not too far from Peradeniya. In fact I knew exactly where the village was situated. She pointed out the direction and talked about her father, who cultivated land, and their cow Tikiri. Our friends had difficulty in accepting that their beautiful daughter could have been born to a very poor family in her previous life.

I have lived many years in America, but have not come across similar rebirth stories. In his writings, Ian Stevenson has pointed out that children in the United States begin to relate similar stories but are strongly discouraged by their parents because of the embarrassment such stories may cause within the milieu of the Judeo-Christian tradition, which of course does not countenance the idea of rebirth. Consequently, as it happens in traditional countries, recollection of previous births tends to fade from memory as the child grows older. It is also possible that in the West in general persistant talk on rebirth may be taken as a symptom of a disturbed child. Fascinatingly in the culture of rebirth it is an old man who speaks in the mind of the child.

ELEVEN

Death

Buddhist Ways and Other Ways

A BEAUTIFUL PARTING

THE DRAMATIS PERSONAE numbered many: a bitter cold Chicago winter morning; the sun deceptively filling the world with light but yielding little in warmth; the sidewalk taken over by mounds of overnight snow, already turning a dull, ugly gray; an endless procession of vehicles, the crunching wheels scattering the ice in cascades of crystals; an old man threading his way along the sidewalk, every step a perilous voyage, fear writ large on his ancient furrowed face; the parking lot opposite the Greek Orthodox Church—our destination—with just one parking space as if by providence left for us. A hundred steps led to the portals of the great church, the stairway of marble gracefully winding upward to the main church, the great altar at the far end, the somber groups of men and women huddled together in subdued conversations, and finally my friend Penny, the now widowed wife of George, her two handsome sons, Plato and Steve, their sorrowing eyes red with endless weeping.

I lit a candle in keeping with tradition and waited for Ananda. Someone appeared from nowhere to invite us all to go in and sit. There was plenty of space. The endless rows of pews on either side of the aisle seemed like battle lines awaiting the signal to march forward. We did not have to wait long. Everyone rose to their feet as the pall bearers carried the casket toward the altar, walking it seemed to me, at a brisk stride. Once the casket was positioned, its lid was opened to reveal the figure of George lying within serene and composed.

Two priests on the left hand side of the altar in firm vibrant voices intoned in Greek. Immediately two others standing to the right translated the words into English for the benefit of those who, like ourselves, did not belong to the Greek Orthodox tradition. They asked God in his infinite mercy to forgive George and receive him, a truly worthy man. Then George spoke for himself in the same suppliant terms to declare that he had led a good life harming none and never looking away when asked for help. I was moved because that was truly the George I had known for years, an open, goodhearted, genial person always anxious to help.

After the dialoging was over, one of the priests, older than the others, stepped forward, and, standing next to the open casket where George lay, began a memorable homily, his gentle, coaxing voice becoming increasingly assuring, as he continued.

> Brothers and sisters, I can sense your sorrow. Our beloved brother George is gone. In mortal form and flesh we can only understand life and the sorrow of death when it comes to those that we love, and finally to our own selves. Yet, we must have faith in God, our savior, and the promise he gave us that death is only the gateway to heaven. A dying man often dies in pain, and in sorrow, gasping for breath and may too easily forget that God awaits him with open arms even as our spirit soars, leaving our bruised bodies grown old with time. There is another world awaiting us.

A FROG AND A WORM

Let me tell you a story. Once upon a time, a frog and a worm lived in a pool of water and were the best of friends. Every now and then, the frog would leave the pool and go about the land. One day the worm said, "I don't know how you get about on the land, because you once told me the land is not full of water. I cannot imagine anything living, other than in water." The patient frog replied, "Well, everybody up there lives on air. They breathe air." The poor worm asked, "What is air? Is it like water?" The frog said it was not and added reflectively "It is hard to describe. You cannot touch it. You cannot see it. But it is there all over the place." The worm, taking courage, replied, "If all that is true, it does not exist, and much as I like to believe you, I don't understand how you can believe something exists, which cannot be touched or seen and which is not an object. You must be pulling my leg, and that's funny because I have no legs. Ha! Ha!" There the matter ended. At least for the time being.

Next day the frog announced that he would be gone for a long time because he had many things to attend to on land. The little worm said nothing but smiled to himself thinking, My friend the frog is growing old and is now beginning to imagine things. The frog left, and the pool was quiet. All of a sudden a bold idea came to the worm's mind. Why don't I go up to the land and see for myself? At first he dismissed the idea as a wild plan. But strangely it increasingly gripped his mind. So the worm resolved to make the journey upward to the land. He had never swum so much, and as he painfully got closer to the rim of the pool, he felt exhausted. Somehow he carried on and finally crawled up to the surface and lay dying. A small pool of water spread around where he lay and soon dried up because of the rays of the sun. Too late he regretted his folly. Life was ebbing away, and he was in intense pain. He felt sad. When he thought it was all over, miraculously, his little body shuddered, and out of it emerged a beautiful little butterfly. He was so happy he cried for joy and with his beautiful wings began to fly. There was no pain, no sadness but absolute joy, and the little worm (now a butterfly) knew a happiness he had never known before.

Such, my brothers and sisters, is heaven, which follows death, a place that as we in our faith say surpasseth all understanding. Look beyond death to a heaven that one day we all will know in the sturdiness of our faith and in the grace of God. It is there that our dear brother now stays and will see us all who loved him in the fullness of time. Go your ways in peace.

ALL IS BURNING: THE FIRE WITHOUT AND WITHIN

The Buddhists have their own stories, the stories I have heard many times over from monks trying to explain death. The stories of Patacara and Kisagotami are the ageless ones about mothers overpowered with grief. Patacara was going to visit her parents with her two infant children. Her husband was bitten by a snake and died on the way. Patacara had to go with the two children, one newly born and the other a year old. She was weak, having recently given birth to her second child. She had to cross a river, and she could not carry them together, so she left the elder child on the bank and waded through the water with her newborn with difficulty. Having reached the other side she left the newborn there and returned to get the older one. She had hardly reached midstream when a hawk swooped down on the newborn baby and carried it away. When Patacara saw this she cried out in grief, raising both her hands. The elder child on the other bank, thinking that his mother was calling him, ran into the water and was drowned. Patacara, now alone, weeping and lamenting, decided to proceed to the house of her parents.

On her way she met a man returning from her hometown. She questioned him about her parents. He gave her the sad news that due to the heavy rain storm the previous day her parents' house had come down, killing all her family. As he spoke he pointed to the smoke coming from the funeral pyre in which her mother, father, and brother were burning. Patacara, in deep grief, ran about like a mad woman with no regard to the clothes she was wearing. She finally reached the Buddha and explained her plight. The Buddha told Patacara that this was not the first time that she had wept over the loss of her husband, wept over the loss of her parents and brother, just as today, so also through this round of existence she has wept over the loss of so many countless husbands, sons, parents, and brothers that the tears she has shed were more abundant than the waters of the four oceans. As the Buddha spoke these words of wisdom Patacara's grief grew less intense, and finally she overcame her grief. Patacara realized the universality of death.

FOR WANT OF A MUSTARD SEED

Kisagotami was born poor but married into a wealthy family. She did not bear children and was scorned by her in-laws. It made her very sad. But after some time she conceived and gave birth to a son, who became for her a source of boundless joy. Everyone in her husband's family accepted her now that she had brought forth an heir to their wealth. But after a few months the child died, and Kisagotami became distraught. She refused to believe that her son was dead. Convinced that he was gravely ill, she went around everywhere asking people to give her some medicine that would bring back life to her child. The villagers ridiculed her as one deranged. Finally she came to the presence of the Buddha with the dead body of her child in her arms. She pleaded with the Buddha for advice on bringing life back to her baby. He told her he could make some medicine for her son, but she had to bring one ingredient, mustard seeds from a house where no one had ever died. In her grief she thought this was the medicine that could cure her child, that it would be easy to get. At every house she went they gave her mustard seeds very willingly, but when she asked if any death had taken place under that roof, they had many relatives who had died. She went to many houses. In each she was told of a mother who had died or a son or some relative. By sunset she was tired, and she began to realize the hopelessness of her task. She came to see that death was the universal fate of all living beings, not a unique calamity that had befallen her. She went back to the Buddha with no mustard seeds. He cured her grief, and she became calm and was ordained as a nun. In time she was known as one of the best nuns in the Buddha's circle of disciples.

I have attended many funerals and seen many faces of death. I was told as an adult that it was part of our culture to pay last respects to a person by attending a funeral, sharing the grief with the party. In America I have heard my friends say, "I don't do funerals," but in my culture one has to "do funerals." It is an obligation.

FAREWELL TO ARCHIE

There was a funeral service in America for Archie, the husband of my friend Valerie. It was different from the funerals I had attended in Sri Lanka or those of my Sri Lankan friends. It was a memorial service, a celebration of his life. There was no casket, no body to weep over. He had been a good person, a simple human being who had helped many and touched the lives of many. It was attended by people from different walks of life. There were stories about his goodness, his contributions, both humorous and affectionate. Hymns were sung, especially those he had liked, and finally all gathered in the basement of the church to share a meal in his honor. I learned many things about him and how people loved and respected him in death as much as in life.

CHILDHOOD MEMORIES: TEARS OF DEATH

My earliest memory of death was that of an unknown woman crying following the death of her mother, indelibly etched in my memory. I was too little to attend the funeral—I may have been six or seven years old—but I remember the enormity of sorrow at her loss, expressed by plaintive weeping and wailing. It was more an amazement to me, and the novelty of the situation stuck in my memory as deeply marked as charcoal on white paper. Although I had not seen a dead person then, I reckoned that death was a sad thing, a sad parting.

The woman had lived with her mother in a small house at the edge of our garden. For many days she appeared near the door of her house with one hand holding to the side for support. Leaning on the door, she wept for her mother's loss. She cried aloud as if to get it out of her chest and to tell the rest of the world of her loss. She wept that she was alone and that life was unbearable now. She said beautiful things about her mother. The lamentation continued for several days. My sister and I would go near her house from the opposite side of the fence to watch her and try to say something. She did not hear us, nor did she see us, engrossed in her own world of grief. After a while my sister nudged me to say it was time to move on. I was sad for the woman. I watched her for a long time intently in silence. I went into our house and looked for my mother. She had my little brother on her lap. I looked at her and wondered if she would die too. Would I feel as sad? The thought disappeared, and I went on to play.

At the end of the large garden was a cemetery. Our house was in the middle of the garden, and on either side were two gravel roads that led to the cemetery. We had seen people carrying coffins and villagers following in a procession, beating drums in plaintive somber tones. In the night too there was activity in the cemetery of a different sort. I heard from Edwin, a servant who was a permanent adjunct in our lives, that some people do black magic in

graveyards. I remember seeing men in this cemetery in the night with homemade torches, chanting aloud, swaying rhythmically. Edwin told us that these
were bad people, and we should not go near the cemetery. He had horror stories to frighten us from going there, but my brothers were curious. They made
clandestine visits during the day to see what had been going on at night. I too
followed. As children we were fascinated with the cemetery and its goings on.
The fact that the cemetery was forbidden territory made it all the more attractive. We went to see the dead buried with flowers on top of their graves. The
rich had nice gravestones, flowers, and slabs of marble, the poor only a mound
of elevated earth with a forlorn flower or two, a mound that would soon
become indistinguishable from the rest of the ground.

We were not taken to funerals as children. We persuaded our grandmother,
always inclined diligently to have fun with us, to take us to a village funeral
house when we were holidaying in Anuradhapura. Grandmother took us to
many such places when my mother was resting in the afternoon. The funeral
was a sad occasion, and there was much weeping and crying. Villagers express
their emotions aloud. We looked like a bunch of strange inquisitive characters
from the city who had no business being there, but the villagers were tolerant
and ignored us. We thought the loud rhythmic weeping and wailing was "cool."
In the early afternoon six strong men carried the corpse out of the house, and
drummers preceded them announcing its arrival. Villagers solemnly walked
behind in procession. On the way to the burial place, when they approached a
junction, they turned the corpse several times. This was to confuse the dead
man's spirit so that it would not be able to find its way back. They also cut large
branches and left them at different places in the junctions to confuse the spirit.
They loved their relative when alive but did not want his spirit to return home.
Finally they reached the place of burial. They carried the corpse round the grave
seven times before easing it down. The Buddhist monks began the funeral ritual, typically a sermon—a mix of a eulogy and a homily focusing on Buddhist
themes—followed. But on such occasions our escapades were short lived since
we had to get back before my mother got up from her afternoon siesta.

When we were children holidaying in the Catholic village of Tharala,
death was talked about in a different way. Our cousin Theresa told us beautiful and consoling stories of what would happen to us when we die. Being a
devout Catholic she explained that God loves us all. We are his children, and
he has prepared for each a special place in heaven with him when we die. We
did not have to fear death. We had to do good, kind deeds, and he would take
us to him where there is no want, sorrow, or sickness, but eternal life. This was
consoling. It gave us a fixed place to go to, a beautiful story.

In Sunday school, back in Colombo, we had the Buddhist version, which
was one of responsibility and accountability, along with the concepts of karma
and rebirth. We had to be accountable for our present acts, and after death, we
will be reborn elsewhere, determined by our actions. One gave us the respon-

sibility, and the other relied on divine authority. Metaphorically speaking, tired of all this shopping in the market of religious beliefs, I did not know which to believe. Theresa's interpretation seemed easy to live with.

The Tharala cemetery was at the edge of the village. It was the most well kept place in the village, organized by families, beautifully and lovingly tendered. However poor, the families bought plots of land to bury their dead. Families were buried together in clusters as it were. They all had headstones with the family name etched in, the grandmothers, grandfathers, aunts, uncles, and the rest. When you die, although you leave home, your family, in the cemetery you are forever with relatives. Tharala Catholics were pre-Vatican in their beliefs. They firmly condemned the practice of cremation, as they believed that one day far into the future God would come and resurrect them and the families would be together. It was a beautiful, consoling thought. Tarala folk were simple people. I jokingly asked my friend Bridget why we should be resurrected in our old and sick bodies. Would it not be nice to have a pretty body like Jennifer Lopez or Cindy Crawford, sexy and pretty? She thought I was being blasphemous. She privately no doubt reflected on the ignorance of her Buddhist friends, all of whom she warmly loved.

HOW BUDDHISTS COPE WITH DEATH

We learned in Sunday school to meditate. One form of meditation was to contemplate on the impermanence of things and on death. However, it did not make much sense to us, and we often questioned the relevance of what seemed to be an unproductive exercise. On *poya* days older women dressed in white sat by the Bo tree counting on a beaded chain, rather like a rosary, and meditated on death and impermanence. *Nawagunawela* was a beaded chain used in meditating on the nine great qualities of the Buddha. We thought that these women had a lot time at their disposal, and this was a way of keeping themselves occupied—devotion to religion.

Buddhists regard death as an occasion of major religious significance. For the dead it is the moment of transition from one birth to another. When death occurs, all the good and not-so-good karma a person has committed comes into force to determine the next birth. To the living it is a reminder of the Buddha's teaching of moral and ethical responsibility.

Preparing for death is an important concept in Buddhist thought. Ceremonies are conducted as a means of assisting the dead person to get a better place of birth. There is a belief that the last thoughts of a dying person are important in determining his or her next birth. Monks are invited to chant *pirit* and give short discourses to the dying at the time of death as a means of inducing the right state of mind for the dying. It is considered a gift to give the dying positive and wholesome thoughts. My aunt was a religious woman who led a spiritual life. When she was terminally ill, she requested that at her time of death she should be left alone, in peace, to focus on the Buddha's teachings and to be mindful of her good karmic deeds, to leave this life with positive energy and lightness of heart. She kept journals of her good deeds, like a dairy of events and activities. Buddhists call this the "*pinpota*" (book of meritorious deeds). It recorded in detail the pilgrimages she had undertaken, the *danas* she had performed, the rituals in which she had participated, and the merit gathered. This is a common practice among Buddhists. These are to be read at the time of death, as recollections, in purifying the mind. King Dutugammunu, we read in local history books, kept a *pinpota*, which was read and reread at his deathbed so that the great monarch would be mindful of the good he had done, especially since in battle many had met their death at his hands.

Buddhist monks over the centuries have continued to effectively console the bereaved. My mother-in-law associated with many educated monks during her lifetime. These included Venerable Piyadassi Thero, Venerable Nannaponika Thero, and Venerable Balangoda Ananda Maitriya, who in spite of his advanced years visited her when she was sick. They recited special teachings from the Buddhist scriptures and meditated with her. The teachings and words of wisdom brought her peace and comfort. Venerable Dhamapala, who was the chief incumbent of the nearby *vihare*, chanted *pirit* for three sessions, and few hours after the final *pirit* session, she passed away.

When my mother-in-law, a deeply spiritual person, was facing the end of her long life, Ananda and I visited her to spend time with her. She reflected on death, meditated on the impermanence of things, and was not afraid to die. In the absence of a *pinpota*, I took the opportunity to remind her of her good deeds throughout her life, which was an exemplary spiritual one. I reminded her of what a good mother she had been to all of us and her kindness and compassion to everybody who came into contact with her. This made her happy. I sat by her bedside, held her hand, and chanted the Karaniya Metta Sutta. She was happy, smiled with me many times, and held my hand tight. Monks I knew well told me that chanting creates an atmosphere of peace, and it was important to appease the mind. She was beautiful when alive, and she looked peaceful and calm in her dying moments.

One morning when Ananda was alone with his mother in the hospital a conversation took place. "Now mother take comfort. Be at ease. We are taking you home today away from this place, this uncomfortable bed, to be in your own bed, your own home," Ananda said. Mother, who off and on groaned in pain, stopped and with great force, calmness, and clarity said, "What home Ananda? There is no going, no home. Don't you see it is all so clear there is only now." Ananda said he was startled by his mother's clarity and vehemence and sudden change of manner. We, with his brother Harilal and our friend Godwin Sammararatne, long pondered what these words meant. Was this the final moment of lucid illumination?

After a pause the sad caravan moves on. My mother one evening after dinner related a story. A man was so overwhelmed with grief after losing his son that he went every day to the cemetery and wept near the charnel ground where his son was cremated. The Buddha surveyed the world every morning with the Buddha eye, with extreme compassion. That day he saw this man. After the alms round he came to the doorstep of the layman with one other monk. When he saw the Buddha the man invited the monks to the house and prepared a seat for them. The Buddha asked the layman why he was so sad. The Buddha urged him not grieve. That which is called death was not confined to one place or to one person but was common to all born into this world. No one or nothing was permanent; therefore, one should not give oneself up to sorrow, but recollect. "That which is subject to death has died; that which is subject to destruction is destroyed." He advised the layman to meditate on this concept. He said, "As children cry in vain to grasp the moon above, so mortals idly mourn the loss of those they love. While he burns he does not know the lamentation of his kin or their woe. Because of that do not mourn; destined to birth he's gone to be reborn. A broken pot of earth ah! Who can piece it together again?" He pointed out that lamenting about the dead, depriving oneself of food, and abandoning occupations was not wise. Instead diligently meditate upon death. "Grieve not at the thought that your son is dead, for where there is attachment there is sorrow." On that occasion the Buddha recited the following stanza.

> From endearment springs grief, from endearment springs fear;
> For one quite free of endearment, there is no grief or fear.

FUNERAL TRADITIONS

A traditional Buddhist funeral I remember was that of my aunt. She lived in Ratnapura in a rural setting, some fifty kilometers from Colombo. She had lived there most of her life and owned land. Everyone knew her, as a part of the landscape. She had no children and considered the eleven of us her own. Although her death was anticipated, as she had been ill for some time, it was to us a sad occasion. Our family—all my sisters and brother with their families—came to Ratnapura to grieve together the death of our aunt. In addition, our relatives, friends, neighbors, and almost the entire village took part in the rituals. Villagers were eager to help in whatever way they could, and such was the tradition. We were all there as a family to perform the traditional rituals and customs related to paying her last respects.

The body was laid in an open coffin in the main living room, which was made bare of all furniture. The family photographs were turned over to avoid distraction, and the mirrors were covered. The focus was my dead aunt. The brass lamp filled with coconut oil was lit and placed near her head. The lamp had to keep burning the whole time my aunt's body was in the house. The body was dressed in a white lace sari with a long-sleeved white blouse. She had white gloves on her hands and white socks on her feet. Only her peaceful face was exposed. The coffin was to face the west. In normal times it is auspicious to sleep with the head of the bed pointed to the east, and never to the west. The rising sun as elsewhere is a positive force in our culture. She had given specific instruction emphasizing simplicity in all matters relating to her death.

Buddhists observe many dos and don'ts when it comes to funerals. They do not bury or cremate the dead on Fridays. My relatives discussed how important it was to make sure that the coffin fitted the body in the belief that if there was any extra space it was ill luck, or maybe another would fill the space. Outside, adjoining the verandah, was a temporary tent constructed to accommodate visitors, and many chairs were set in rows to seat them. There was a steady stream of villagers dressed in traditional white, lining up to visit. Some wore white saris, and the village women wore cloth and a jacket, the traditional Sri Lankan dress for women. Men wore white trousers and shirts or a white sarong. All went past my aunt's coffin with palms folded together bending and inclining their head to pay respect.

We wore white saris, and with our husbands stood in front to greet the visitors, a sign of appreciation for sharing our grief. Customarily the hearth is not lit or food cooked when the body is in the house. The villagers brought us cooked vegetarian food at meal times. It is considered improper to bring meat, fish, or eggs to a funeral house. Some others brought rice, coconut, tea, and sugar, as contributions to the *malabatha* (collective feast of remembrance).

The visitors were offered soft drinks, cigarettes, and the traditional tray of betel, for chewing. Some accepted drinks, and others chose to chew betel. In the evening hot tea and coffee were served to all. This went on all through the day and night; we took turns to keep up. On the day of the funeral there was much activity. We gathered to say our formal farewell to our aunt by going down on our knees to worship her. When this was over, the coffin was closed and carried to the place of cremation by six male relatives. We walked behind the coffin in silence. It was a long procession. Ahead were drummers and a man playing the flute in a plaintive tune heard only at funerals.

The cremation site was at the end of the property about half a mile walk near a lake, a lonely, bare place. Some distance away were the coconut trees, and in the far corner stood the structures built to commemorate our grandfather and grandmother. My aunt was to join them. We saw at a distance the funeral pyre, constructed in a traditional design. It was a platform made of wood, in this case sandalwood. The whole pyre was draped with white cloth in a special traditional design and looked like a little house. All the way to this site were lines of young coconut palm leaves strung on ropes on either side of the road.

When we reached the cremation grounds, monks who were brought from the temple performed the Buddhist rituals. The family offered the traditional *matakavastra* (a white cloth) to the monks, as part of the funeral rituals. The senior monk gave a sermon, a rather long eulogy focusing on the good and generous deeds and the spiritual life of our aunt. We all sat on the floor and held a jug of water that we poured into a smaller vessel until it overflowed as the monks recited the *gathas* to transfer merit. This ended the religious ceremony, and the monks were taken back to the temple. Our uncle had had eulogical verses with Buddhist sayings printed, which were distributed to all.

THE SUNDERING RITUALS OF DEATH

The *matakavastra puja*, a traditional Buddhist ritual, is performed at the time of burial or cremation, for which a Buddhist monk's presence is required. This is the offering of the white cloth, twenty yards in length, to the monks on behalf of the dead person. This is performed in the home of the dead or in the cemetery. The ceremony begins with the administration of the Five Precepts followed by a short sermon on the significance of death in Buddhism and urging all present to reflect on the impermanent nature of all things. Throughout the sermon, participants remain silent reflecting meditatively, while the monks intone in unison:

Iman matakavattam bhikkhusanghassa demi

I give this corpse-clothing to the Sangha of monks.
At this the monks spread the cloth out across the coffin and chant
   the Pali *gatha*:

Annicca vata sankara uppadavayadhammino
Uppajjitva nirujjhanti tesam vupasamo sukho

Impermanent are formations, subject to rise and fall.
Having risen, they cease; their subsiding is bliss.

This *gatha* is supposed to have been recited by Sarka at the death of the Buddha. The verse is recited by all present in a chorus. After this the immediate relatives of the dead sit on a mat and perform the ritual of *pinanumodana* (transmission of merit) to the deceased by pouring water. Water is poured slowly from a small jug into a vessel until the vessel overflows. While the water is being poured everyone recites these *gathas* along with the monks.

Yatha varivaha pura, paripurenti sagaram
Evam eva ito dinnam, petanam upakappati

As the full water-bearing [rivers] make the ocean full,
so may that which is given here go for the benefit of the dead (*preta*).

Idam me natinam hotu. Sukhita hontu natayo

Let this merit go to our relatives; May our relatives be happy.

When the water has overflowed the monks stops chanting and everyone says "*sadhu*." The ritual is meant to transfer merit to the dead so that they may find relief if born in an unhappy realm. In the ceremonies and rituals of death, rites of chanting, reflection, and kind words have meaning for the people involved. These rituals help them to come to accept with grace the passing of a loved one. They help to acknowledge the truth of what has happened, that a final separation from that person has occurred. In that acceptance they come to peace.

It was sad to see my aunt's body taken and laid in the funeral pyre all ready to be lit. The custom is for two nephews to light the fire. My brother and my brother-in-law, dressed in white with their heads wrapped in a white cloth, were given two long torches, to perform this task. They stood at the entrance holding the lit torches. They began to walk backward in opposite directions to one another three times round the pyre. When this ritual was complete they lit the pyre and went away without looking back. All these are ancient traditional customs observed with great attention to detail. We watched sadly as the flames caught and the coffin that held our aunt began to burn. The roaring fire spread quickly all around, making it all one red blaze inside the white-covered structure. When all was over we greeted the visitors and invited everyone to our aunt's home for the *malabatha*. It was important to join in the partaking of this meal to confer merit to the dead.

When the body was removed, those who remained in the house hurriedly cleaned up the place using saffron water as a disinfectant. The space was prepared to light a fire to cook the traditional *hathmalu* (seven-vegetable curry). In addition a complete meal was cooked to feed those who would return from the funeral. The traditional items used for this meal are dry fish, pumpkin, dhall (lentils), and curries served with rice. There were a large number of people. They all sat on the floor on mats, and food was served on banana leaves. Before consuming the food they set aside a portion of food, which was left outside for the spirits or *pretas*. This is also a mode of conferring merit to the dead. With the partaking of the meal, the ceremony was over.

Commercial funeral homes are new to Sri Lanka. Keeping the dead in a funeral home is considered abandoning the person at death. Ideally, the dead body is kept in the house. Coconut oil lamps are kept burning near the corpse, which is never left alone. In the night friends and neighbors gather to share the vigil. Often villagers read Jataka stories, throughout the night, to keep up their spirits and relieve the tedium. Nandasena, who had a good voice sat all night, reading the *yasodarawata* (the story of Yasodara queen of Siddhartha,

in poetry form) aloud to pay respect to the dead, and drive the lingering spirits away, for three days after the funeral. This is a village custom. Finally the
spirit of the dead is let go.

The Buddha taught that the greatest gift one can confer on one's dead
ancestors is to perform acts of merit and to transfer these merits to the
departed. Every now and then Buddhists remember departed friends and relatives by performing meritorious deeds in their memory. They invite monks
and give *dana*, gifts of basic necessities. Buddhists share merit when they perform meritorious deeds.

TRUTH STRANGER THAN FICTION

The idea that we who are living should do something to alleviate the distress
of those who have died and are in some manner suffering, is in a sense not
unique to Buddhism. In the Catholic tradition there is for example, praying
for the souls of the dead to reduce their stay in purgatory. But a story I read
some time ago in the *Times Literary Supplement* surpasses belief. It happened
in France in the eleventh century in a community of Jews. One day a rabbi,
walking through a cemetery, saw a curious sight: a naked man who was black,
carrying a pile of wood on his head. When questioned, the man said that he
was already dead but that every day he was sent out to chop wood. He knew
the reason why. When he had been alive, he was a tax collector by profession
and had been hard on the poor, and indeed was partial to the rich. He could
end his damned condition if he had a son who would say prayers before the
congregation intoning the Lord's praise and asking for blessings. He told the
rabbi, however, that he left his wife who was pregnant and was unable to say
whether she gave birth to a son. He could not be sure that the boy had been
taught the Torah, a task that in ideal circumstances would have been undertaken by a close friend on his behalf. The rabbi, who was greatly moved, privately resolved to somehow find the child, which he was able to do because he
knew all his parishioners. Although the child, who was indeed a boy, had not
been brought up as a Jew, the resourceful rabbi was able to bring him back to
the fold, instruct him in the Torah, and persuade him to make the necessary
recitations before the congregation. The story ends on a happy note. Sometime later the dead man appeared in a dream to the rabbi to say that he had
been saved from hell.

DEATH RARELY PRIVATE, THE CONCERN OF ALL

There are the social customs relating to funerals and death. Paramount is paying the last respects to the dead, which is done by attending funerals. As a

young adult, I attended many funerals with my father-in-law, involving his clients in villages in and around Kandy. Some of them I did not know. Whenever my mother-in-law was unable to attend, I represented her. Often when attending funerals in the villages there were many problems of access to the houses. Sometimes we had to walk long distances across paddy fields, but my father-in-law always made it a point to attend them, and I followed him. It was considered an obligation, to share grief. I recollect once balancing on a coconut trunk, laid across as a bridge to cross a stream (*edanda*). It was no easy task for city dwellers especially in the attire of a traditional sari. I had to hold the sari up with one hand and carry my sandals with the other to walk on the *edanda*. It needed concentration, to avoid falling into the stream, a balancing act on the coconut trunk. The villagers were good at this. Many men tried to lend me a helping hand, but it was unbecoming for a young woman to hold the hand of a strange man. My father-in-law was concerned, but it was not appropriate to hold his hand either. I managed with difficulty without falling into the water. Villagers were honored by my father-in-law's presence. When we returned home from the funeral there was a cleansing ritual. A basin of water and fresh limes cut in halves was left at the entrance to the house to wash our hands to ritually clean ourselves before entering the house.

Large-scale participation is considered a good thing at funerals. Funerals of the famous and rich have many mourners. Friends and foes all go to a funeral. Even if you do not attend a wedding, a funeral is a must. The rich advertise funerals by means of printed notices. Friends and relatives often travel many distances to attend funerals. I have heard the questions being asked of people returning from a funeral, "Were there a lot of people? Was there a lot of crying?" and so on. There is a period of mourning following the funeral and close relatives refrain from wearing ornaments, attending social functions during the mourning period. Close relatives mourn for three months or even a year.

THE MANNER OF THEIR MOURNING

Great emotion is openly expressed at funerals. It is a custom to weep as an expression of grief. My school friend Manel's father died in a car accident. Her mother had strained relations with him, and indeed not many people there were inclined to cry. This was considered a sign of disrespect or lack of caring, so they had to hire women to weep. Primarily Catholic areas near Colombo have a tradition of professional mourners, who could be hired by affluent families in Colombo to weep at funerals. They come in groups to service funerals for payment. They were easily recognizable as they wore black and were mostly middle-aged. Manel's father's coffin was kept in the house in the main living room. As the guests arrived, the mourners in a group came to the front of the coffin, wept, and wailed aloud for short periods of time. This act was repeated and looked absurdly artificial. Nevertheless it served the purpose. There is a popular saying that if you are unkind and selfish no one will weep at your funeral. A well-attended well-wept funeral is considered a successful funeral, in Sri Lanka. Robert Knox (1958) describes the weeping he observed in the Kandyan villages:

> Their manner of mourning for the dead is, that all the women that are present do loose their hair, and let it hang down, and with their two hands together behind their heads do make an hideous noise, crying and roaring as loud as they can, much praising and extolling the virtues of the deceased, there were none in him: and lamenting their own woeful condition to live without him. Thus for three or four mornings thy do rise early, and lament in this manner, also on evenings. Mean while the men stand still and sigh. These women are of a very strong courageous spirit, taking nothing very much to heart, mourning more for fashion than affection, never overwhelmed neither with grief or love. And when their husbands are dead, all their care is where to get others, which they cannot long be without. (Knox 1958:185)

Funeral houses are decorated with white flags and sometimes banners with pictures of the dead person hung with information about him especially the services he had rendered to the community. Sometimes a banner may have the picture with the *prattana*, the wish that he may attain nirvana. The villagers or the community do this as a mark of respect. It is also a custom to decorate the road leading to the house with white flags and with young palm leaves. It is not uncommon to see leaflets describing the religious activities or the spiritual life of the dead person, distributed with some Buddhist sayings at funerals, often as a eulogy with the statement at the end "May you attain nirvana." To confer merit to the dead, leaflets or booklets with religious instructions are distributed. The elaborateness depends on the monetary capacity of the dead person.

In Kandyan villages it is a custom of those visiting the funeral house to take items of food, such as tea, sugar, and powered milk. For poor families these items help provide refreshments for the visitors. A funeral is a burdensome expense to villagers and often money is collected on their behalf.

THE HOMILY OF REMEMBRANCE

Important customs are the *bana* given and *dana* performed by the relatives on the seventh day after the death of the deceased. *Dana* is taken to the temple on the third day after the death. The seventh day *bana* preaching is called the *matakabana* (remembrance sermon). Apart from the act of commemoration, the sermons deal with the concept of death according to Buddha's teachings and are intended to console the mourning relatives and show ways that the living can help the dead. The focus of *matakabana* normally is to explain that human life cannot be fully understood without reflecting on death and the Buddhist doctrine of impermanence. The sermon usually lasts an hour, and relatives and neighbors participate. After the sermon the monk is offered a gift and gathas are recited to transfer merit to the dead person. This is normally followed by the *matakadane*.

Normally, three months after the death, monks are invited to the house for a *bana* sermon and a *sanghika dana* in memory of the dead to transfer merit. This is repeated annually.

TWELVE

Bodhi *Puja*

All for the Sake of a Tree

THE PIPAL TREE (*ficus religiosa*), a native tree of India, is popularly known to Sri Lankans as the Bo tree or Bodhi tree. It got these names when Siddartha Gautama (2,550 years ago) sat under this tree for many weeks in meditation resolving not to arise until he reached his goal of attainting Enlightenment. He defeated the evil forces of *mara* (death) and their attempt to break his resolve and achieved victory. This state of awakening, realization of the truth or Enlightenment, is Bodhi. Siddartha became a Buddha, after his Enlightenment, the Awakened One. The Bo tree thereafter became a sacred object of worship to Buddhists, symbolizing wisdom and Enlightenment.

BO TREE BECOMES A VERY SPECIAL TREE

The Bo tree, belonging to the Banyan family, is a large tropical tree spreading branches to represent an umbrella providing shade to animals and humans. It attains great size and age and has leaves that hang from long, flexible petioles which rustle in the slightest breeze. Having attained Enlightenment under this tree, it is said in Buddhist literature that the Buddha, as a show of gratitude, spent many days mediating and looking at the tree. Paying homage to the Bo tree has now become a popular ritual in Sri Lanka. *Pujas* performed to a Bo tree are called Bodhi *pujas*. The ceremony is meaningful to Buddhists and fulfils the devotional needs of the pious devotees.

Tradition records that Theri Sangamitta brought a sapling of the original Bodhi tree from India to Sri Lanka during the reign of King Devanampiyatissa in the third century B.C. when Buddhism was first introduced to Sri Lanka. It was planted in Anuradhapura, and since then the Bo tree has become an object of great worship and is a feature in every Buddhist temple. According to the *Mahavamsa* the first Buddhist king of Sri Lanka, Devanampiyatissa, held magnificent ceremonies after planting the Bo tree in Anuradhapura symbolically offering the entire island to the sacred tree, a practice followed by some of his successors.

Sri Lankan Buddhists believe that powerful deities of the Buddhist pantheon inhabit these trees, and by making offerings and prayers to them they will be blessed and their wishes fulfilled. Over time, the tree has become a symbol representing Buddhism itself. Every Buddhist temple and monastery in Sri Lanka has its Bo tree. There is usually a flower altar nearby and facilities to light lamps around it. At many wayside shrines with Bo trees, there is provision for offering a *panduru*, and travelers in the hope of a safe and successful journey make contributions to deities of the Bo tree. My father-in-law's driver always stopped at the Gatembe Bo tree, as we left the town of Kandy, to drop a coin in the *pinpettiya* (merit box), praying for a safe journey. No one asked questions, and he did this as something that he always did.

RAGING WATERS RECEDE FROM A TREE

Sri Lankans are prone to believe in miracles. In 1947, days of pitiless incessant monsoon rains in the central highlands caused the waters of the Mahaveli River, which passes Kandy at Peradeniya, to overflow its banks and flood the surrounding areas running at a level of twelve feet above the roads. Everything in sight was under water. Miraculously the famous Gatembe temple right at the edge of the river was spared, the ravenous waters somehow swirling around it. It was considered a great miracle. From this time great veneration has been shown to the tree and the temple. Most vehicles passing to and from Kandy drop coins in the donation box for a safe and trouble-free journey. *Pujas* are held every day at the Bo tree. The widespread belief is that the tree has miraculous powers. With the income from the coin boxes, *pujas*, and patronage, the temple stands out with an air of affluence and modernity. There is a great demand to have a *puja* for this Bo tree, and it is not easy to have a date set apart for a Bodhi *puja*.

When one is subjected to astrologically bad periods (*asuba* times), the commonly recommended remedy is to perform a *puja* for the Bodhi to get blessings. In terms of efficacy, the Bo tree in Anuradhapura, popularly known as the Sri Maha Bhodiya, surpasses all others because of its association with the Bo tree in India. A Bodhi *puja* performed in the vicinity of the Sri Maha Bodhiya is considered especially sacred and as an agent of great merit. The Bo tree, here the oldest historical tree in the world, has survived over two thousand years. It is also the most sacred place of pilgrimage in the island. Buddhists believe in the miraculous powers of this Bo tree. My friends, married for many years without a child, made a special pilgrimage here to make a *puja* to be blessed with child.

HEALING AND REVERENCE TO A TREE

Bodhi *pujas* are done at a personal level to get relief from sickness, injury, and reversals of fortune or from situations of suffering in general. Sri Lankans visit astrologers in times of sickness or misfortune or in situations of expecting something good to happen. Astrologers detect bad times and recommend performing a Bodhi *puja* or several of them on consecutive days and seek blessings. It is believed that in reciting the virtues of the Buddha and invoking thoughts of goodwill and compassion in the ritual of the Bodhi *puja*, merit is generated. The merit is inexplicably transferred to the deities who are thought to reside in the Bo trees. In reciprocation, the deities grant to worshippers the relief for which they ask.

The traditional Bodhi *puja* involves the participation of one person or a family, sometimes with the help of a monk. The *puja* to the Bo tree takes the form of offering flowers, incense, and lighting lamps around the tree. Devotees would worship the Buddha in the traditional way reciting the *gathas*. Pouring water for the tree, referred to as "bathing the tree," is also a part of the *puja*. The ceremony often gets elaborate depending on the enthusiasm, knowledge, and popularity of the monk conducting and the affluence of the party involved.

When I was living in Sri Lanka in the early 1970s, my aunt in consulting the horoscope of one of my children found that the child was under a negative planetary configuration, which required mitigation by means of a Bodhi *puja*, which venerable Unduwavela Chandananda Thero of the Asgiriya temple in Kandy undertook to perform. It was an involved Bodhi *puja* focused on the nine astrological planets commonly called the "*navagraha* Bodhi *puja*." Here nine separate ceremonies are performed, simultaneously to the nine planets.

Since it was evening, drinks and beverages were offered as *puja* items. This was in keeping with the meal habits of the monks. Incense by means of joss sticks and pungent *sambrani* powder sprinkled over live coals were offered. The sacred smoke drove away bad spirits to usher in influences of the benign spirits. In a metal receptacle the aromatic incense was taken around the tree in repeated acts of circumabulation. As mentioned earlier, betel was another offering made in *pujas*, with arecanut, and items such as cloves, nutmeg, and cardamoms.

Yassamule nisinno va, Sabbari vijayam aka
Patto sabbannutam satta, Vande tam bodipadapam.
Ime ete mahabodhi Lokanatena pujita
Ahampi te namassami bodhi raja mamattu te.

I worship this Bo tree seated under which the Lord Buddha attained
    Enlightenment by overcoming all inimical forces.
I too worship this great Bodhi tree, which was honored by the
    Buddha the Leader of the world.
My homage to thee, O King Bodhi.

The ceremony was concluded with the chanting of *pirit*, to evoke blessings. The monk acted as the mediator between the deities and us. Offerings
were made to please the nine deities of the nine astrological placings. The
merit gathered from this *puja* was transferred to all beings, especially to the
deities in charge of overseeing the nine planetary positions. Another popular
aspiration or benediction with a wider societal reach was chanted to conclude
the ceremony.

BOY FRIENDS, GIRL FRIENDS, AND THE TREE

Bodhi *pujas* are also performed on happy occasions to get blessings. One
would go to the temple for a Bodhi *puja* before sitting for an examination,
going to a new job, or birthdays and anniversaries. Vows or promises are made
to be fulfilled in the future, when favors requested from the gods, such as a
good husband for a daughter, or a birth of the child for a couple wanting one,
are seemingly fulfilled. Young girls offer *pujas* to get the boyfriend they desire
or overcome parental objections. Once a girl I knew went to Gatembe temple
for a Bodhi *puja* with her boyfriend to overcome parental objections to their
love affair. Meanwhile the parents, unknown to the girl, were making another
elaborate Bodhi *puja* to the gods to break the affair. If the wish was granted,
they promised to make more *pujas*. The two subsequently eloped, confusing
the parents and the gods.

BILL AS MASTER OF CEREMONIES

In my world of Bodhi *pujas*, Bill was the monarch of all he surveyed. He and
his wife knew the art of conducting a Bodhi *puja* in a style of their own. On
our visits to Colombo this was a source of socioreligious entertainment to me.
To Bill it was a serious ritual, and absolute devotion was a must. Bill and his
wife, Anula, got the necessary flowers, garlands, and essential ingredients for

an evening *puja* to the Bellanvilla temple. The Bo tree in the premises at Bellanvilla was massive and over the years had received numerous *pujas* from devotees. Bill invited his friends to participate, in the belief that the greater the number of participants, the greater the merit and the potency of the *puja*. Anula had an entourage of helpers. The servants were busy folding and preparing the *panthira* (pieces of cloth folded in a pattern like a thick thread) used to light the oil lamps. These were made of clean white cloth folded thin to absorb the oil in the clay lamp.

Bill began the *puja* by offering the elaborately arranged trays of flowers and lighting many lamps around the tree with different kinds of oil. Mustard oil, sesame oil, and ghee are of special value. Seven clay lamps with each kind of oil were lit, as well as many more with coconut oil. He took *pansil* and worshiped the Buddha with many *gathas*. He recited the *gathas* to worship the Bo tree aloud, and we followed him in sonorous chorus. He was the undisputed leader, and all present followed him—such was the protocol. The whole process took a long time. He prepared the *kiri kalahatha* (seven pots of water) mixed with milk and scented with special ingredients. He held his pot over his head and went around the Bo tree seven times (seven being a significant number in rituals). We followed him one behind the other carrying our pots of water. He chanted *pirit* and recited the blessings all the way. Finally we poured the water for the bathing of the tree. We all gathered around Bill. The merit acquired by this great *kusala* karma (good deed) was transferred first to our dead relatives, who might be anticipating merit, and then to the deities and other beings from whom we asked for blessings and protection.

A CHARISMATIC SUPER STAR MONK

My father-in-law's house was on one side of Kandy Lake. Across the waters, one could see the Vishnu *devale* at a distance. Sarath, knowledgeable about Buddhist rituals, a great devotee, and altogether a kind and gentle person, volunteered to accompany me to the *devale*. We bought jasmine and lotus flowers from a vendor near the Dalada Maligawa and joined the flowing crowd of white-clad devotees. In a matter of minutes the grounds were full, with people of all ages and classes. Some had evidently come from distant places in buses. The place was beautifully lit, and decorated with festive flags. There was to be a Bodhi *puja* in the *devale* premises, a ritual that always fascinated me.

It was to begin at sundown, officiated by none other than the well-known monk Venerable Ariyadhamma. He was a young, attractive, charismatic person, kindness and compassion radiated from him. The special purpose of the Buddha *puja* in the vicinity of the Vishnu *devale* Bo tree was to bless the country in general. Sri Lanka was going through economic hardships, political turmoil, and a sense of malaise in the seventies and the decades that followed.

People from all walks of life attended in large numbers to Bodhi *pujas* for relief from stress.

When the monk took the microphone, a magical silence prevailed. His voice was calm, unperturbed, clear, and had a hypnotic effect on the crowd. He urged those assembled to concentrate on the virtues of the Buddha and to have kind thoughts throughout the ceremony. The ceremony began by taking refuge in the Triple Gem and administering the Five Precepts. His voice and intonation were deliberate and clear. He repeated the verse:

> *Datha nalale bada, vadum labanne,*
> *Sama denahata pinketa vane*
> *Neka maha gunayen babalanne,*
> *Sadhu sadhu budu himi namadinne*

> For all beings, a field of blessings,
> shinning with manifold goodness,
> my hands folded on my forehead,
> I worship the Buddha, The Dharma and The Sangha.

The crowd cried out "Sadhu! sadhu! sadhu!" which echoed and vibrated. The monk sang several stanzas describing the virtues of the Buddha from the popular poem *Loveda sagarava*. The crowd repeated them. The sayings were well orchestrated and deliberate. He went on to describe the great virtues of the Buddha and the birth of the Buddha in verse form. After every interlude he blessed the crowd with tangible compassion, with the words: "May by the virtues of the Buddha, the dharma and the Sangha, you overcome all obstacles, may all your wishes come true. May all your good and spiritual expectations come true; may all your problems be resolved, all your obstacles to happiness and success go away, and may you be content and happy. May all of you be blessed with good health, and may the county prosper, and may there be peace." Its simple language invoked devotion of the crowd.

There were many aspects to the *puja*, offering of flowers, lamps, and incense to the Buddha, but its centerpiece was the worship of the Bo tree. Each segment was followed by an elaborate blessing session. It lasted over an hour, and the crowd dispersed peacefully and looked happy. This was my first encounter with the famous Ariyadhamma Bodhi *puja*, which the charismatic monk had perfected, almost as an art form.

BODHI *PUJA* FOR THE STRESSED

In the seventies there was a dramatic rise in the popularity of these *pujas*. With the depressed economic and political climate of the country, unemployment had risen rapidly. Large numbers of university-qualified youth remained unemployed, causing a great deal of stress among them. In these uncertain and unsatisfactory times, people in large numbers were drawn into the Bodhi *puja* movement led by the charming Buddhist monk Venerable Ariyadhamma, who hailed from the coastal town of Panadura. Bodhi *puja* which was hitherto an individual *puja* took a strikingly collective form under his direction. It took the pattern of a public performance with hundreds of people participating for a common purpose and common blessings. The success of these was measured by large attendances and enthusiasm of the devotees. Disgruntled youth participating in such religious ceremonies in large numbers was a new phenomenon that added to the popularity of the *pujas*. Encouraged by large crowds, the monk regularly performed in major cities.

The monk's pleasing appearance, his dynamic personality, his melodious voice, and his organizational skills drew the dissatisfied urban youth in droves to his *pujas*. Being a young person himself, he had a good understanding of contemporary society and the problems of disgruntled youth. He had the compassion and kindness of a Buddhist monk and the desire to end the suffering of the society by creating the Bodhi *puja* cult, which had extraordinary appeal. He provided a collective means of expression and thereby laid solid foundations for the popularity and appeal of this type *puja* in the future.

Young men and women attending these popular *pujas* found it an occasion for romance and socializing. It was an opportunity to get dressed up and meet others of similar background, problems, and understanding and to share a commonness of feeling and empathy. It was a place to make acquaintances. The television was yet to appear on the scene. Other than movie theaters or musical concerts, such as Victor Ratnayake's "SA" there were few avenues of entertainment. In this setting the Bodhi *pujas* became a great attraction to the youth of Sri Lanka.

Venerable Ariyadamma conducted the *puja* sitting with the congregation in lotus position, in front of the Buddha's statue to show humility and a sense of community. Venerable Ariyadamma used the commonly understood language Sinhala for his repetitive verses, inviting crowd participation. He led the singing, and the devotees followed. It reminded me of a Harry Belafonte concert I attended in Chicago, where he got the audience to sing with him in chorus popular songs. The verses were repetitive and had an easy-flowing, smooth construction, enabling memorization.

Buddhist *gathas* are generally in Pali, the language not meaningful to the devotees who repeated them without understanding their meaning. Venerable Ariyadhamma's Sinhala verses were in simple language, chanted melodically, and in form and content had immense appeal to the young. His voice was carefully crafted to rise, drop, rise again, and fade away. All this added to the mystic appeal of the *puja*. The congregation repeated verses in chorus form. Phrases such as "May all beings be happy," and, "May all beings be well," "May all your aspirations come true" were first sung softly by the monk and then by the congregation. The thoughts and words of kindness, compassion, and comfort were prominent in his verses. He was soft and gentle and generated mass appeal, in a culture that made a virtue of gentleness.

Devotees came to the Bodhi *pujas* in busloads, traveling many miles. There was much publicity in the newspapers. The *puja* took place under a Bo tree in the evening. When the charismatic monk took the microphone, devotees were ecstatic, his rhythmic voice echoed and reechoed aloud, spreading over the entire village. Young and old flocked by hundreds following him from one Bodhi *puja* site to another. The ceremony included decorating the Bodhi with flags and other ornaments, lighting a large number of coconut lamps around and in the vicinity of the Bo tree, and offering flowers. Water and milk often mixed with fragrant ingredients in special pots were used to bathe the tree. By the offerings and the chanting with devotion, participants believed that their wishes would be granted and that they would receive blessings. Blessings apart, it was a great distraction. The *puja* had multiple benefits, merit, good blessings in this birth, good rebirths in future, and finally *nibbanic* bliss.

The movement was popular among the young middle class. There were tape recordings of the Venerable Ariyadhamma Bodhi *puja* for sale, and Buddhists, especially women, listened to them in their homes and traveling in cars. Leaflets were published for sale. There was popular demand to learn the new form of worship, which was soothing and comforting and spread compassion—all the more necessary since the country was experiencing economic hardships, such as a shortage of essential food items, milk products for infants, sugar, salt, and flour. Due to restrictions of imports, there were long lines for the essential items of food such as bread, milk products, and sugar. Bread lines were legendary during this period. When society and politics were unkind, the compassion and kindness of the monks made an oasis in the harsh desert. This was the time when people took part in protest marches:

> *Mokada pute adanne, lunu natuwai adanne.*
>
> Why do you cry my son? I cry for the want of salt.

There is a tradition of *kavikola* in Sri Lanka, a popular form of vernacular literature. These are verse publications of current, historical, social events and scandalous gossip of popular interest written in lucid verse form. These were sold particularly at bus stands. In Sri Lanka waiting for a bus is a story in itself, and people spend a lot of time in long-suffering patience. The *kavikola* man was the popular entertainment at the bus stand. A man with a good voice did well and earned a living selling the doggerel verses to the passengers. To this genre was added the Bodhi *puja* literature, and it was a good sell.

THE TREE, THIS TIME IN LONDON

After the untimely passing away of Venerable Ariyadhamma the new style Bodhi *puja* took root in the Buddhist community. It has spread to other countries where Buddhists reside and become a popular form of collective worship. In the absence of a Bo tree, sometimes miniature trees are used on stages, but the concept no longer needs the presence of a tree.

I was delighted when my friend Jayanthi decided to take me to the new style Bodhi *puja* ceremony in London. She knew my interest in Bodhi *pujas*. This one was officiated by Venerable Dhammaloka, a follower of Venerable Ariyadamma, in 1998. Starved for a Bodhi *puja*, London Buddhists flocked to the place, and devotees lined up to get a date to have their own *puja*. The monk was specially invited to perform the ceremony. Venerable Dhammaloka's melodious and easily understandable, meaningful verses and the blessings, followed by an eloquent and soothing *bana* preaching touched the hearts of the devotees. The hall was decorated with Buddhist flags and banners displaying Buddhist messages. I have not seen anything so spectacular outside Sri Lanka. There were no chairs, and all the devotees sat on the floor. There was even a Bo tree on the stage and several Buddhists monks. Venerable Dhammaloka performed the *puja*, amidst a large crowd, to invoke blessings upon themselves and on Sri Lanka and to pray for peace and harmony in the mother country. The *puja* was a great success, and some devotees were already beginning to feel the good effects from the evening. I thought it must be stressful to live in London, and they must yearn for their familiar rituals for relief.

THE WAR GODS SEEK THE TREE

In recent times, during the periods of communal unrest, many resorted to large-scale Bodhi *pujas* to invoke blessings on the armed forces and to bring about peace and unity to Sri Lanka. Prominent monks from temples of the country lead such activities to bring peace and unity among all ethnic groups. These ceremonies bring large numbers of Buddhists together. Usually it begins with the Buddha *vandana* (worship) taking refuge in the Triple Gem and observing the Five Precepts. This is followed by the Buddha *puja* and sermons remembering the devastation caused by war, the tragedies and untimely deaths of thousands of soldiers, physical and emotional devastations experienced by many Sri Lankans. Monks lead the *metta* meditation and *metta pirit* chanting with the blessing for the army personnel and extending it to all Sri Lankans irrespective of race and religious affiliations. *Suttas* are chanted for peace and tranquility and for blessings to all. Large-scale Bodhi *pujas* were held in well-known temples such as Bellanvila and Kelaniya to bless the country, to bring about peace and finally transfer merit to the gods and other beings and appeal to them for the protection of mortals.

Ariyadhamma passed away as a young person, but his Bodhi puja lives on as a vibrant tradition. Like John Brown of old, he lives on in Sri Lanka (where his memory is cherished and his prescriptions are acted on), and in different avataric manifestations in the lives of the burgeoning Sri Lankans expatriate communities, here in the United States, and elsewhere. So long as angst is the unwelcome visitor dropping in to torment our lives and minds, there will be Ariyadhammas, his successors, and heirs ready to perform the necessary ritual Bodhi *Puja* to relieve human stress, by praying and blessing for relief of the mind and body.

The new Ariyadhamma of our times might be a young monk, Venerable Thalangama Devananda, of the Buddhist Institute in Forte Wayne, Indiana. Both in his charismatic person and in his unique orchestration of rituals, recitations, his eagerness, and most of all his compassion and concern for all those who come his way, he is a worthy successor to Ariyadhamma. He is personable, tall, and fair skinned, more so than the typical Sri Lankan Buddhist monk. His voice, and the rise and fall of the cadences as he relates Buddhist homilies, blessings, and great *suttas* gathers up his hearers, weaving them together as common humanity with the gossamer threads of loving compassion. The altar he presides over, sitting for an hour and more in the enviable asana (lotus) posture, is a simple affair. There is a rather small Bodhi tree made of silver beside a towering beautiful terra cotta statue of the Buddha. Oil lamps flicker to and fro, and swirls of incense rising upwards and sideways fill the room. He focuses on the words of the Buddha, and has great personal faith in both their talismanic and transformative powers. Not surprising, his CDs are high in demand and increasingly difficult to obtain. So what matters more, the words of the Buddha or the art and skill of the presenter, the person? I have never been able to answer this question. It baffles me as I suppose it did 2,550 years ago when ordinary folk were listening to the Buddha somewhere in the beautiful valley of the Ganges.

THIRTEEN

Pirit Chanting and the Holy Thread

PARITTA IN PALI OR *PIRIT* in Sinhala means "protection." *Pirit suttas* are canonical scriptures that are regarded as records of discourses delivered by the Buddha, and are chanted for protection, security, prosperity, and well-being. The Buddha taught the monks to use the spiritual energy generated by chanting the Buddhist scriptures and reflecting on the virtues of the Buddha, to relieve suffering both physical and mental. To Buddhists in Sri Lanka, or living elsewhere in the world, chanting of *pirit* is a ritual, believed to have the power of healing and warding off evil influences, relieving stress, and bringing peace of mind. It is one of the most popular Buddhist rituals.

Buddhists have faith in the power of the Buddha's word. The Buddha was totally free from the defilements of desire, anger, and ignorance. Listening to the word of the Buddha is a path to *nirvana* (deliverance). It has dual purpose: to obtain happiness in this life and in the next. The essence of the *pirit* ceremony is the ritualistic chanting of Pali *suttas*. The *suttas* are collected and arranged in a particular order in the Book of *Parittas* or *Piritpota*, which contains twenty-four *suttas* such as Ratana, Maha Mangala, Karaniya Metta (three together chanted as the *Maha pirit*) Dammachakka, and Atanatiya.

At the time of the momentous millennium celebrations, I was in London. After the thirty-first night parties and fireworks over the river Thames, my brother, who lives in London, and his English wife, Muriel, decided to take me to the Buddhist *vihara* (temple) in London on the first of the year. It is a Buddhist practice to go to the temple as the first act in the New Year. There was a sense of muted excitement in the air. The Buddhist community in London is large, and the *vihara* is well patronized. A traditional octagonal structure, which in the Buddhist world is called the "*pirit mandapa*," was constructed conforming to traditional and ritualistic rites. There was a seven-day continuous *pirit* chanting, and Buddhists from many areas came to the *maha pirit* (main chanting session) involving the chanting of the three major protective *suttas*. Over five hundred devotes sat on the floor in two rooms in composed silence, eager to absorb the spirit of *pirit* and get their share of blessings for the New Year. We were in time to catch the main *pirit* chanted before the midday *dana*.

The devotees formed a line to get a piece of the sacred thread. There were two monks, one distributing the *piritpan* (holy water), and the other tying the thread on the devotees' right wrists. It reminded me of the Holy Communion in the church waiting for bread and wine. I often wondered how any blessing would be statically stuck in a thread and kept for many days. Listening to *pirit* was soothing, healing, and a meditation. Buddhists attach much importance to the power of the *piritnula* (sanctified thread). The monk tying the holy thread on the wrists was catering to human anxieties and fears. The chief monk, who knew Ananda and his family sent a piece of the thread for him.

A REMEDIAL DEVICE FOR ALL SEASONS

In Sri Lanka and wherever Buddhists live, social functions, religious festivals, and ceremonies are considered incomplete without the recital of *pirit*. *Pirit* ceremonies are also held on many other occasions, such as prior to building a house, a house warming, starting a new job or project, illness, misfortune, drought, flood, marriage, and birth. Predictably it is also popular among politicians and is used sometimes to establish legitimacy and attract popular support. *Pirit* is a classic example of religious legitimization in politics. After an election victory, opening of a new parliament session, or starting a new government venture, politicians often resort to a *pirit* ceremony to get blessings. During the war with the Tamil Tigers, *pirit* ceremonies were held to give blessings to the soldiers and to the country in general for peace. Sometimes these ceremonies are large and attract much publicity and crowd participation. Before leaving the shores of Sri Lanka, Buddhists get monks to chant them *pirit* for protection and a safe journey. They can be recognized in airports anywhere in the world as they wear the *pirit* thread around their right wrists.

It is a common belief among Sri Lankans that misfortunes are sometimes due to malignant beings or malefic astrological formations, and the chanting *pirit* would ward off these forces and promote good health and prosperity. Chanting *pirit* invokes protection by stating the spiritual qualities of the Buddha, his miraculous deeds, and above all his compassion. The *pirit suttas* state the truth and power of the teachings of the Buddha. Finally *pirit* focuses on the spiritual goodness of the Buddha's followers, the Sangha. The goodness and power of the Buddhist Triple Gem is evoked to get blessings and protection. All three generate power and spread loving kindness, which in a sense is the core essence of all *pirit*: selfless loving kindness is one's protection.

In chanting *pirit*, the chanters must have love and kindness toward the listeners, and the listeners in turn must listen with respect and attention to get the best results. *Pirit* is also chanted for mental well-being and help those who are ill to get better. Regular *pirit* chanting and listening to *pirit* gives joy and enhances personal confidence. Devotion or *sarda* energizes life. The core force of *pirit* is loving kindness, a panacea to ward off evil influences, heal illnesses, and promote health and prosperity. Stanzas of conferring blessings include the following *gatha*: "By this *pritta*'s virtue, may no ill come to pass through cosmic forces, demons, powerful nonhumans, or opposition from planetary antagonism. May all misfortunes cease to exist."

In recent times due to the unrest and disturbing events in the country, the temples have resorted to many activities of a religious nature to bring about peace and harmony. One hears the chanting of *pirit* in temples with the use of loud speakers to spread peace and bring blessings. This starts at six in the morning and is repeated in the evening.

During the recent disaster caused by the tsunami, which affected the Sri Lankan coastal seaboard, monks traveled in vans chanting *pirit* to comfort the destitute and to prevent the spread of disease. Whenever there is a disaster of this nature monks contribute to the healing and protection process by chanting *pirit* and spraying holy water.

It is stated in the *Culavamsa* (an ancient Sri Lankan chronicle) that in the time of King Upatissa *pirit* was chanted by monks to bring about rain during a period of drought and disease. The monks walked the streets throughout the night chanting the Ratana Sutta and sprinkling holy water. At sunrise clouds gathered, and there was a downpour of rain bringing great relief to the people. There was much rejoicing at the sight of rain; the king was pleased and issued the decree: "Should there at any time be another affliction of drought and sickness in the land, do ye observe the like ceremonies."

In our homes, we woke up in the morning to *sethpirit* played over the radio. On special occasions, monks were invited home to recite the *paritta suttas* for a simple *varupirit* (sessional *pirit*) when *pirit* was recited in several consecutive sessions. *Pirit* was also chanted, for the entire night continuously, and sometimes for three or seven days. The *varupirit* sessions were generally conducted in three, five, or seven sessions, each lasting about an hour. In this ceremony maha *pirita* was chanted, which includes three suttas of the Buddha, Maha Mangala, Ratana, and Metta Suttas, and a few benedictory stanzas. There were certain requirements for chanting *pirit*. If the *pirit* is a *varupirit* the number of monks should be not less than three and, if it is the all night *pirit* there must be an even number of monks, eight, ten, or twelve, and so on. The all night *pirit* begins in the evening and ends in the morning.

MY DAUGHTER CURED BY *PIRIT*

When my daughter was little, she got sick often as she was born premature. Monks were invited to the house to chant *pirit* for her, for good health. Accepted traditions were followed in this ceremony. A pot of water was placed on the center of the table, along with white jasmine flowers and a coconut oil lamp. White, twisted strands of thread were wrapped around the pot of water, the *pirit* thread. The pot of water, the *piritpan* and the thread, the *piritnula*, were all sanctified during the chanting of *pirit suttas* and were used thereafter as a protection against evil and to bring blessings. A statue of the Buddha was placed on the table. The thread was passed through the hands of the chanting monks and was held by the persons on whose behalf the *pirit* was chanted. We all sat on a mat with my daughter holding the thread in her tiny hands.

The monks began the session by administering the Five Precepts and recited the three main *suttas*, the Maha Mangala, the Ratana, and the Karaniyametta, as well as the Jayamangala gatha. Finally they chanted the victory stanzas. This *gatha* was repeated three times for blessings:

> All ill-luck, misfortunes, ill omens, diseases
> Evil planetary influences, blame, dangers, fears
> Bad, undesirable dreams—may they all come to an end
> by the power of the noble Buddha, dharma and Sangha.

At the end of the chanting the monks blessed my daughter and transferred merit to the dead relatives and to gods and spirits. They appealed to the deities to receive the merit and give blessings to my daughter, while inviting *devas* and others to participate and share merits: "May all the beings inhabiting in space and earth, Devas and Nagas of mighty power having shared this merit, long protect the dispensation."

There was also the conferring of merit to those who had passed away, and finally there were the beautiful abstract blessings to the world at large and mankind:

> May rain fall at suitable times,
> May the world progress
> May all be happy and peaceful,
> May the king be righteous.

After each session the thread was rolled back and placed on the pot of water. At the last session benedictory refrains were recited, *piritpan* (water) was given to all, and the *pirit nul* (thread) was tied. The session was concluded by a *dana* to the monks. The monks chanted *pirit* with kindness and great compassion. My daughter got better and remained healthy for a long time.

The sounds of chanting are regarded as a penetrating and an effective force. The power of good thought and compassion, in which it is chanted, is believed to soothe the mind, to bring tranquility and peace.

NEW HOUSE AND ALL NIGHT *PIRIT*

When we completed our new house, Venerable Dharmapala, who was virtually our family priest, advised us to have an all night *pirit* chanting to bless the house and its occupants, which is a traditional custom among Buddhists. Wherever this ceremony is conducted, traditional customs are followed, and the villagers participate willingly with devotion for merit and blessings. A temporary octagonal enclosure was built in the main hall of the new house, which we call the "*pirith mandapaya*." The enclosure was decorated with paper cuttings and fresh leaves. The entrance to the enclosure faced east for good luck. The pavilion was decorated with varieties of betel and Na leaves. Its roof was covered with a white canopy from which hung cuttings of arecanut flowers, young coconut leaves, and other traditional leaves. In the *mandapa* chairs were kept for the monks. A table was placed in the center covered with white cloth. Five kinds of flowers, the *ladapasmal*, were scattered on the table, consisting of grain, broken rice, white mustard, jasmine flowers, and panic grass. A pot of water was placed on the center of the table. A post, the *indrakila*, was planted securely and fastened to the chair. Clay pots with coconut and arecanut flowers were placed outside the *mandapa* structure at each entrance, and small coconut lamps were left on top of the pots over the coconut flowers.

PIRIT FROM A TO Z

Monks from the temple came in a procession in the evening. Ananda and his friends went to the temple to escort the monks, who arrived in single file in order of seniority to the sound of drumming. At the head of this procession, a layman carried a Buddha relic in a casket over his head in veneration. An umbrella was held over the relic. When the monks entered the new house, Ananda washed their feet, and a servant kneeling next to him carefully dried them. We lit the lamps inside the *mandapa*. The casket containing the sacred relics was placed on the table, with the *piritpota* (book of protection) written on ola leaves. The relics represented the Buddha, the *piritpota* the dharma, and the reciting monks the Sangha, the disciples of the Buddha. These three entities represented the Triple Gem.

Before the commencement of *pirit*, the monks were offered a tray of betel leaves with arecanut, cardamoms, nutmeg, and other sundry items as an invitation to the ceremony. The senior monk accepted the invitation on behalf of the entire Sangha. To make the invitation formally valid he had the lay devotee repeat after him the following Pali *gatha*, requesting the monks to begin the ceremony:

> *Vipattti patibahaya sabbasampatti siddiya*
> *Sabbadukkavinasaya—parittam bruta uttamam*

> To heal all suffering
> To achieve prosperity, success
> To avoid misfortune
> *Pirit* will be chanted.

The thread was drawn around the interior of the pavilion, around the casket, around the neck of the pot of water, and finally to the *piritpota*. The purpose was to maintain unbroken communication from water to the relic, to the *piritpota* and the monks. The thread was then passed on to the listeners.

The monks sat round the table, and their hands were ritually cleaned with special liquid made out of sandalwood paste, milk, and water. The monks instructed the devotees to clean their hands with the mixture. The chanting began with the observing of the Five Precepts and the worshipping of the Buddha, dharma, and Sangha. Then in moving, sonorous refrain the gods were invited to listen to pirit.

> *Samanta cakkavalesu, attragaccantu devata,*
> *Saddamman munirajassa, samntu saggamokkadam.*

> In all the world systems, may all the *devas* come to listen,
> The good law of the king of sages gives divine and nibbanic bliss.

After the auspicious drumming, the *magul bera*, the chanting began. The monks in unison chanted the *maha pirit*. Thereafter a pair of monks commenced reciting the remaining *suttas* for two hours. They would then retire to be followed by another pair for two hours. Two monks constantly officiated so that the chanting lasted unbroken till dawn. When the time came to chant the *dammachakka sutta*, a special *sutta*, drums were beaten, and incense was burned ceremoniously. This was the very first sermon preached by the Buddha. The ceremony continued from dusk to dawn, Atavisi piritha, Jinapanjaraya, Jayamangala Gatha were also chanted. The *atanatiya sutta* was recited at the conclusion of the ceremony, which is thought to have a power to pervade a million world systems, was recited with great fervor. This sutta is considered the most powerful and there are rituals observed in reciting it. Merit was given to the gods and spirits and those present.

The ceremony came to a close with the distribution of *pirit* water and thread. The thread sanctified by the *pirit* chanting was cut into pieces and distributed among the listeners to be tied around their wrists. The sanctified water from the pot was sprinkled on all, and some drank the water and in addition sprinkled it on their heads and necks as a symbol of protective power. *Pirit* water was sprayed around our new house for additional protection. Monks were given the morning meal followed by a *sangika dana*.

THE MAGIC TOUCH OF THE MONK SIVALI

We were advised by the monks to hang a picture of the Sivali Thero in the new house in the most conspicuous place, visible as one enters the house. Sri Lankans and Thais regard Sivali Thero as the greatest fortune-bringing monk. A picture of the Sivali Thero would bring good luck and the Sivali *pirit* is chanted for good fortune. It is often engraved in bronze and kept in houses to serve as a charm for good luck.

The legend about Sivali is interesting. At the time of the Buddha, there was a righteous king, Koliya, and his queen, Suppavasa. When the queen was with child, the unborn child brought great fortune to the kingdom. The kingdom became prosperous. Crops grew in abundance, and rains came at the right time. However, when the time for birth arrived, Suppavasa failed to deliver. She grew uneasy, as there were no signs of birth. She asked the king to consult the Buddha by inviting him and his retinue of monks for a *dana*. After the *dana* the Buddha blessed the queen:

> May Suppavasa, daughter of the Koliya clan,
> Be happy and healthy and give birth to a healthy son.

The queen gave birth to a beautiful, healthy son. The prince was named Sivali. On a later date, Sivali became a monk with his mother's blessings. The monks soon noticed a strange phenomenon when they were with Sivali, Sivali always seemed to have an abundance of rich, fragrant food and the other requisites (robes, shelter, and medicine), which the other monks were able to share. Wherever Sivali went people flocked around to prepare food for him.

Once Sivali and his retinue of five hundred monks were in an uninhabited forest for seven days but were not short of food. Similarly when Sivali was traveling through the desert his needs were somehow provided. The Buddha, seeing that Sivali was reaping the benefits of a good karma from a previous birth, declared that he was foremost among monks in obtaining the requisites, food and fortune. The Buddha also instructed monks who were traveling on long, hazardous journeys through uninhabited terrain to be accompanied by Sivali, as they would have adequate provisions.

On another occasion the Buddha, accompanied by thirty thousand monks, was traveling and had to cross an uninhabited forest. Ananda Thero, fearing that they would not be able to obtain food in the jungle for such a large number of monks, questioned the Buddha about the journey. The Buddha assured Ananda that if they had Sivali with them, they had no cause to worry, as there would be no shortage of food. Buddhists venerate Sivali Thero and often keep a picture, statue, or a discourse known as the *Sivali Pirit* in their home to ensure an abundance of food and prosperity.

Buddhists believe that the sound waves of the *pirit* chanting have the power to soothe the mind and body. There is the belief that bad spirits who cast an evil eye, affected by the chanting of *pirit*, would leave the premises and treat us kindly, being grateful for receiving merit, which in their woebegone condition they are unable to acquire.

Buddhists perform all night *pirit* ceremonies on special occasions. These are festive occasions, when neighbors regardless of class and caste distinctions participate, creating harmony and cooperation, to acquire blessings and merit. There is a sense of commonness of purpose and sharing. However, to hold an all night *pirit* ceremony one must have a spacious house, the means, and the ability to get the assistance of neighbors and friends. These factors limit the ceremony to a class marked by affluence in society. The ceremony also fulfils a social function, an event for people to get together. When we were young we looked forward to *pirit* ceremonies as occasions to get together with our friends. We sat on mats around the *pirit mandapa* drinking cups of tea and enjoying the homemade sweets throughout the evening. The company of other young adults in the neighborhood made the *pirit* ceremony enjoyable.

The seven-day *pirit* is normally chanted in temples with much ceremony, with the entire community participating. In times of infectious diseases, a drought, or any other natural disasters, monks bless the community by chanting *pirit*. Once I remember in the late sixties in Kandy there was a cholera epidemic. Many lost loved ones, and the disease was spreading. Temples organized *pirit*-chanting ceremonies to bring blessings to the community. *Pirit* was broadcast over loudspeakers from temples at regular intervals. Groups of monks went around the city in buses chanting *pirit* to the community and spreading holy water as blessings. In the recent tsunami disaster, the monks in Sri Lanka traveled in vans chanting *pirit* to the victims as a means of relieving stress and protecting them from disease.

VARIETIES OF *PIRIT* AND THEIR RATIONALE

As mentioned earlier, chanting of *pirit* is done in times of sickness. According to Buddhist legend, the Buddha asked monks to chant the Bojjhanga Suttas (four in all), where the Buddha discusses the seven factors of Enlightenment as a meditative practice to heal the human mind and body. Chanting of these *suttas* is believed to provide a means of relief from physical suffering and achieve serenity of mind. The Buddha himself did the chanting of these *suttas* when his senior disciples, Maha Kassapa and Maha Mogganlla, were sick. The monks listened to the Buddha's recitation and recovered from the illness. Ttaditionally the *suttas* are recited by monks to lay devotees in the hope of protecting the listeners from sickness and in times of epidemics.

The *sutta* that is most often memorized and chanted is the Mahamangala Sutta. It is recited for protection and deals with thirty-eight auspicious signs and blessings. It is said that when the Buddha was in Savathi at Jeta Grove a certain *deva* came to Buddha in the night and in spreading his radiant light, and brightening up the entire Jeta Grove requested that the Buddha chant a *sutta* for protection and well being.

Once in the time of the Buddha there was scarcity of rain in Vesali, and many died from the effects of famine. The offensive smell from the dead bodies brought demons and ogres into town. To make matters worse a disease, like the modern plague, spread, and there were more deaths. People thought of ways and means of counteracting the disease. They decided to invite the Buddha to come to Vesali from Rajagaha. The Buddha arrived with a retinue of monks. When the Blessed One arrived at the gates, there was a huge downpour of rain, which washed away all the corpses, and the town became clean. Venerable Ananda had learned the Ratana Sutta, and, on arrival at the city gates, he recited it and walked round the city, sprinkling holy water from his bowl every now and then. All the evil spirits were driven away from the city, and it was rendered free from disease and drought. Such was the power of the Ratana Sutta. It contains *gathas* in praise of the Triple Gem. It is recited to ward off dangers and to secure prosperity.

THE POWER OF *PIRIT*: LOVING KINDNESS

On another occasion, when the Buddha was staying in Savthi, a group of monks who had been instructed to go to the forest to meditate during the *vas* season returned. The monks complained to the Buddha that evil forces in the forest were harassing them when they were meditating. The tree deities inhabiting the forest were worried by the arrival of the monks as they had to descend from the trees and dwell on the ground. They wanted the monks to leave and harassed them in many ways during the night to scare them away. The Buddha taught them the Karaniya-Metta Sutta and told them to cultivate the meditation on loving-kindness. The Buddha instructed the monks to return to the forest, assuring them that the beings would now wish them well. The monks as instructed by the Buddha spread radiant thought of *metta* (loving kindness). The deities, affected by the power of love, allowed the monks to meditate in peace.

The *sutta* spreads loving kindness to "whatever living beings there may be, feeble, strong, long, stout or of medium size, short, small, large, those seen and those unseen, those dwelling far or near, those who are born as well as those yet to be born. May all beings have happy minds. Let him not deceive another nor despise anyone anywhere. In anger or ill will let him not wish another ill. Just as a mother would protect her only child with her life, so let one cultivate a boundless love towards all beings."

This is a popular *sutta*, which is memorized by Buddhists and chanted in situations of anxiety and ill health. This is also used as a *metta* meditation at the end of meditation sessions. Buddhists chant the *sutta* in times of distress and despair as well as during normal times as a meditation in spreading compassion.

The Buddha living near Savatti at Jetavana monastery addressed the monks as follows:

> Monks eleven advantages are to be expected from the release of heart by familiarizing oneself of loving-kindness (*metta*) by the cultivation of loving kindness by constantly increasing these thoughts by regarding loving kindness as a vehicle of expression, something to be treasured and putting them into practice. The eleven advantages are, the Buddha said, "He who practice living kindness sleeps well, he wakes in comfort, he sees no evil dreams, he is dear to humans and nonhumans, *devas* protect him, fire, poison, and sword cannot touch him, his countenance is serene, he dies without being confused in mind, he will be born in a good realm.

It is the practice in Sri Lanka to have *pirit* chanted by monks to evoke blessings and ward off evil influences. Buddhist ceremonies begin or conclude with the chanting of *pirit*. This is the most important single blessing-evoking ceremony in the Buddhist world.

In answer to king Milinda's questions on the effectiveness and benefits of pirit the monk Nagasena replies:

> Oh King, "And when Pirit has been said over a man, a snake, ready to bite, will not bite him, but close his jaws. The club which robbers hold aloft to strike him with will never strike; they will let it drop, and treat him kindly. The enraged elephant rushing at him will suddenly stop. The burning fiery conflagration surging towards him will die out. The malignant poison he has eaten will become harmless, and turn to food. Assassins who have come to slay him will become as the slaves who wait upon him. And the trap into which he has trodden will hold him not." (Rhys Davis, 1969:1:216)

JUST A PIECE OF THREAD, OR WHAT?

There could be nothing simpler than a piece of thread. Yet it becomes something else when wound round a human wrist. A spectacle I recently witnessed in the Thai temple in Kingery Road, which Sinhalese Buddhists patronize because in Chicago there is no Sri Lankan *vihare*, set me thinking. The evening was rendered memorable because a Sri Lankan monk made a fine presentation on karma, pointing out that the great drama of karma was played out in the theater of the mind: the genesis of karma, the initial thought so pregnant with karmic potential; its execution as a deed; the aftermath, when in guilt long after the deed, the troubled mind is incessantly plagued with both unease and remorse. The monk constantly emphasized the importance of keeping one's mind (thoughts) pure without the defilement of harmful, negating thoughts. The monk concluded his sermon by inviting all of us to walk over to an adjacent hall, where after refreshments he would tie the sacred *piritnul*.

Sitting as a bystander and enjoying *kiribath* (milk rice) and *lunumiris* (hot sambal) served in generous proportions because it was the first day of the New Year, I counted as many as two hundred Sri Lankans patiently waiting their turn for the *piritnul*. Many of them—friends and associates of many years—had often told me that because they did not know Pali (the language in which the *suttas* were recited), they could not understand the monk's recitations that preceded the tying of the sacred *pirit* thread. Ironically, the words did not matter, but the belief that a piece of thread was somehow endowed with magical properties did matter. Indeed in crowded concourses in airports and in mixed gatherings, one could always make out a Sri Lankan bearing the talismanic thread as if it were an insurance policy with copper bottom guarantees.

I did not join the line that evening; my mind in the days that followed returned to the words of the good monk that the best protection was the purity of one's mind. But then the quick fix will always beguile the mind. I lingered on in the barn-like hall. The chairs were all put away, the monk had retired for the night, and silence reigned. I walked to the parking lot, haunted by the words of the monk. My eye fell on a piece of the *piritnula*, which had fallen from someone's wrist. It lay forlorn on the damp grass.

FOURTEEN

Sons of the Buddha

DESIGNATING ONESELF AS A BUDDHIST, or being a Buddhist, leads a person to focus on the Buddha, the dharma, and the Sangha—the epiphanous Triple Gem. From a philosophical and teleological point of view, since transcendence is the ultimate goal in Buddhism, its attainment is dependent on the grasp of the Buddha nature and, as important, on an understanding of the dharma. Would this leave the order of the Sangha out in the cold, as it were?

BUDDHA AND THE ORDER OF MONKS

Buddha attained Enlightenment after a long and difficult process. The purpose of his Enlightenment, the realization of truth, was not only for his benefit but was also for the broader purpose of teaching what he had learned and realized, to serve mankind with universal compassion. As part of attaining Enlightenment referred to as "Buddhahood" (supranormal state of being), the Buddha was able to see far into the deepest recesses of an unborn future (Buddhist literature refers to this as "*peradaknaganaya*"). He realized that Buddhism, or more accurately the dharma (his teachings), would only survive in the minds of men and women if someone were around to preach it in the manner he did. With foresight, he established the institution of the Sangha (order of monks). From a pragmatic point of view, the very existence and survival of his teachings depended on the Sangha, his disciples who could grasp the dharma, preserve it, and teach others, a reality that the Buddha understood with remarkable insight. The Sangha was indispensable in the preservation and spreading of the Buddha's teachings during his lifetime and long years after, to the present day.

The Sangha, who would be perpetuated by an unbroken tradition of ordination, would be the means of ensuring the survival of the dharma leading
to a benign social order encapsulated in the elusive term *Buddha-sasana*—
an order of things governed by a Buddhist consciousness of justice, equity,
harmony, and above all compassion. The monks, the guardians of the
dharma, become the world's oldest surviving monastic order.

THE SONS OF THE BUDDHA

But who is a Buddhist monk, and who are the Sangha? In the countries of
South and Southeast Asia, where Buddhism is predominant, as in Sri Lanka,
Burma, Thailand, Laos, Cambodia, and Vietnam, a Buddhist monk is easily
recognized by his tonsured head, shaved eyebrows, carefully draped saffron or
yellow robe, begging bowl carried at dawn to collect the means for his sustenance. He is a Buddhaputra (a son of the Buddha) in the grand lineage of the
archetypical figure Prince Siddartha who renounced home and hearth and
became the Buddha, and for forty years roamed the valley of the Ganges
spreading the dharma, the fruits of his hard-won Enlightenment. Generation
after generation, by means of Spartan rigors of simple living, the monks
sought to emulate the master in walking the path of transcendence, with
boundless compassion for a suffering humanity.

This chapter deals with the order of monks, the rules and regulations
governing the order, and defines who monks are. It also deals with what happens on a daily basis in their lives, interweaving both theory and practice with
a wealth of personal reflections and reminiscences.

In the second section, I deal with change, a fascinating revolt in the temple. The centuries-old, seemingly somnolent, order of Sri Lankan monks
decided to become persons in their own right, making a deliberate commitment to be politically conscious and be part of the political process, as a means
of safeguarding their interests and that of the *sasana*, which they believed the
state has failed to secure. I deal with the powerful impulses that have led to a
critical attitudinal shift of possibly a permanent nature.

YELLOW ROBE AND SHAVEN HEAD

Monks and the monasteries they live in (temples), were very much a part of
my growing up. The temples were pleasant, welcoming places. Lay people
went to monks for spiritual guidance and mundane problems. They were
always forthcoming with good advice and held rituals to soothe the aching
mind and body. The rich, the poor, and the powerful all came to the temple.
The monks were willing and patient listeners.

The life style of a monk is different from that of a layperson, designed to be conducive to spiritual development, learning, and dedication to service. It is a simple life, free from family obligations, and geared to a routine. Monks begin the day before dawn. They devote the predawn hours to meditation, chanting, and other spiritual activities. At daybreak they walk the streets to gather food offered by devotees going from house to house. According to the *vinaya* (monks' code of conduct) they eat only between daybreak and midday. They spend much time teaching and studying. Although the monk's life is simple, it is never idle. They have duties and responsibilities to perform both as individual members of the Sangha and also as spiritual leaders. Once a monk enters the order to become a *bhikkhu*, he distances himself from society, from family ties and lay life. He is a free man without bonds, a "son of the Buddha." He leads the life of a person dedicated to the study of the complex dharma. He is an Ariya, or one who is made noble by his knowledge, wisdom, and virtues.

NEW NAMES AND OLD IDENTITIES

Monks have very different names from laypeople. They do not carry a family name or have family affiliations. On becoming a monk—as part of the rite of passage—a monk assumes a new name. In the nomenclature of monks in Sri Lanka, some clue is given regarding the village in which the monk was born. One of Ananda's favorite monks was Venerable Ampitiye Rahula, who hailed from Ampitiya in Kandy where Ananda was born. We have Venerable Walpola Rahula, Venerable Welivitiye Sorata, and Venerable Olande Ananda (Ananda from Holland), not to omit mention of an expatriate poet who hailed from Tibet and wrote in Sinhalese, Tibet S. Mahinda. The emphasis on the place of origin shows how much the monk in Sri Lanka is part of a community. On becoming a monk he becomes a different person with diminishing attachments to lay life: a different and a distinguished genre of its own.

"Just as O monks, the great rivers Ganga, Yamuna, Acirvati, reaching the ocean lose their earlier name and identify and come to be reckoned as the great ocean, similarly, O monks, people of the four castes who leave the household and become homeless recluses under the doctrine and discipline declared by the Tatagata, lose their previous names and identities and are reckoned as recluses who are sons of Sakya" (Udana 55).

Buddhist monks wear saffron robes and shave their heads. In my incarnation as a teacher at Dharmaraja in Kandy, I enjoyed the friendship of monks in the faculty. I asked them about the significance of the saffron robe and the shaven head. They explained that these symbolized the abandonment of one's claims to stand out as a special individual, to be a "somebody." The aim of the *bhikkhu* is to eliminate the ego and the need for self-identification. Since monastic life is meant to be simple and burden free, shaving the head helped. Hair is an object of vanity and pride not appropriate for spiritual practice. Layman's clothes, hairstyles, and ornaments in subtle ways assert identity and self-image. The *bhikkhus* give up their personal identity to blend harmoniously into a larger anonymity, the Sangha. The saffron robe and shaven head are also themes of daily reflection, that they lead a life that is different from that of the lay people, a life of self-control and restraint.

When laypeople choose colors for clothes, saffron is not considered appropriate as it is sacred and virtually the privilege of the *bhikkhus* to wear. When the ancient Indians looked into the jungle they could always tell which leaves were about to drop from the trees, because they were yellow, orange, or brown. Consequently, in India, yellow became the color of renunciation. The robes of monks and nuns are yellow so they can act as a constant reminder of the importance of not clinging, of letting go, of giving up. Robes are sacred items of clothing only worn by monks. Originally monks used the discarded clothes left in the charnel grounds before a body was cremated to stitch a robe together.

The long career of a Buddhist monk begins when he becomes a *samanera* (novice monk). There is no hard and fast rule indicating the ideal age for a male child to become a *samanera*. It varies from seven to thirteen. I heard a saying that a young boy capable of chasing a crow away is old enough to be ordained as a *samanera*. It is hard not to think that on such occasions the elders applied some sort of soft pressure to make them monks. I read about a recent campaign launched with much fanfare and official government blessings to recruit two thousand male children to boost the dwindling ranks of the monkhood.

OVER THE SHRUB AND JOURNEYING BACK

A monk is allowed to give up the robe and rejoin the lay world if he so desires, at any time. The absence of elaborate processes of divestiture would suggest a lack of compulsion. According to accepted tradition, a monk who is inclined to leave the temple permanently would simply throw his robes over a shrub and depart. His fellow monks understand what is happening. There is no follow up. However, a monk is honored for staying in the order for a long time, and the vast majority do so. The lay attitude of veneration to monks is a tacit recognition of the rigors of monkhood. Correspondingly a monk who leaves the order tends to be stigmatized. A few years ago a graduate student known to us who gave up his robes on obtaining a higher degree was proposed as a suitable marriage partner to a relative of mine. But discovering that he had given up robes was a factor in his disfavor. It is interesting that in both Burma and Thailand relinquishing the robes does not carry the same sense of muted censure, because of the widespread tradition of temporary ordination in those countries.

CODE OF CONDUCT: THE *VINAYA*

In its early years the Sangha did not have elaborate disciplinary rules because it was not a large organization. With the growth of the community, some monks did not know what they should and should not do. There was a need therefore to implement rules to correct monks and to show them the right way for their own welfare and that of those who would enter the order after them. Being pragmatic, the Buddha gave monks rules to govern their individual and collective conduct, known as the *vinaya*, rules, which have survived to our day and time. The Buddha wisely did not make them a rigid, draconian code but left their interpretation in the hands of the monks themselves in each generation, which may account for their survival.

The Buddha did not set out a code of rules all at once. Instead he formulated rules one by one, on an ad hoc basis, in response to particular situations. Behind the pronouncement of each rule was an interesting anecdote, which helped to explain its rationale. For instance, the rule forbidding lustful conduct between monks and women shows that the Buddha did not view women as somehow inferior or unclean. Rather the rule originated after an incident where a monk was reported to have been fondling the wife of a Brahmin who had come to visit his hut. The Buddha wanted women to feel safe in the knowledge that when visiting monasteries that they would not be in danger of being molested.

RULES AND THEIR RATIONALE

In the Buddhist order, monks were originally allowed to go on *pindapata* begging for their evening meal. In doing so, however, monks in the Buddha's time encountered all manner of difficulties and misadventures—coming to physical harm, falling into cesspits in the dark, being mistaken for robbers, and undergoing sundry harassments. Reacting to mounting empirical evidence, the Buddha put in place the rule that the monks should not partake of solid food after they had their midday meal. Abstaining from eating in the night, it was evident, was conducive to contemplation and meditation.

With time the rules governing monks grew in number, and some Buddhists, headed by Venerable Upali, gathered the major rules into the compendium *Patimokka*. There are altogether some 227 rules regulating the relationship among the brotherhood of monks, their mutual interactivity, and more significantly, the conduct of monks in interacting with laymen.

The 227 *vinaya* rules are classified into eight categories. They involve the expulsion of monks from the Sangha, meetings as a community, confession of misdemeanors, rules for training and for resolution of disputes. A good monk has to observe the rules throughout his life as a monk, and penalties are laid down for violation of the rules. Then, and possibly more so now, the rigors of monkhood were proverbial. The Buddha was very much aware of this and compared a committed monk to one who was battling the current to swim against the tide. The task seems hopeless.

THE SINS OF MONKHOOD

The most important of all the *vinaya* rules are the four *parajikas*, the violation of which results in an expulsion from the order. They are that a monk should not indulge in sexual intercourse, commit theft, deprive a human being of his or her life, or claim to have suprahuman powers. A monk who falsely claims to have attained any superior human state loses his monkhood forever and is no more in communion with fellow monks. These rules are of equal ethical weight and share the same potential for the contamination of the mind. If a monk breaks any one of the more serious classes of rules, he is put on probation for six days, during which time he is stripped of his seniority and is not trusted to go anywhere unless accompanied by four other monks of regular standing. He is required to confess his offences to the monks in the monastery. At the end of his probation period, twenty monks are convened to reinstate him to his original status.

There are also a variety of other rules, such as those concerning the robes a monk should wear, prohibitions concerning use of money, the bowl a monk carries, his use of medicine, and others of a seemingly trivial nature. The bare essentials a monk could possess are clothing (three robes), food, shelter, and medicine.

BEGGING FOR FOOD: PINDAPATA

As discussed earlier in this text, the monks do not cook for themselves but instead go out to houses of the laity begging for their food, eating whatever is given to them regardless of preferences and tastes. The practice is called *"pindapata."* The *patra* (begging bowl) used to go on *pindapata* has become the universal symbol of Buddhist monkhood. The bowl should more properly be called the "merit bowl" because a layman acquires infinite merit by giving a monk food for his sustenance, since the monk and his brethren feed mankind with the food of the dharma. In acknowledgment the monks recite a standard benediction blessing to the laypeople and wend their way back to the monasteries. Whatever is given is consumed both for breakfast and for lunch. A beautiful sight I saw in Chiang Mai in northern Thailand was a procession of monks coming down from their mountain abodes, going on *pindapata* or the ritual rounds of begging for food. I was struck by their serenity and the devo-

tion of the laypeople. What was offered was modest since in rural areas people eke out a living as vendors of simple commodities. In the Buddhist tradition it is said that once when the monk Pindola was going on *pindapata*, he
stopped at the house of layman afflicted with leprosy, a fact of which the monk
was unaware. But knowing made no difference. With perfect equanimity he
accepted what was offered. Back in the monastery, while eating the food, the
monk found a human finger but with composure finished his meal. If theory
accorded with fact, which was not always the case, a Buddhist monk, a son of
the Buddha, was an admirable human being with the capacity to rise well
above the limitations of the human person.

While in Thailand the practice of *pindapata* thrives, in Sri Lanka it has
virtually become obsolete. In the cities one hardy sees a monk begging for
food. A monk I interviewed told me of an instance when a man put cow dung
in the begging bowl, which caused the monk considerable distress. It took a
long while before he resumed the practice of going on his rounds. A reason
for reluctance to go on *pindapata* is the changed attitude of the laity, a lack of
sardava (devotion) on the part of the laity.

However, in recent times there has been an attempt to revive the practice
of *pindapata*. I witnessed a ceremony in Kandy recently, where hundreds of
alms bowls were donated to monks to encourage and revive the practice of
begging for alms, emphasizing the need to renew the old traditions. The practice of *pindapata* would enable even the poorest of the poor to offer a meal to
one or two monks and thereby gain merit without incurring the expense of a
dana, when several monks are invited to a house—a practice more typical of
affluent Buddhists.

I remember nostalgically how as a little girl I would eagerly join my
mother in offering *pindapata* to a monk whose shadow fell across our front
door, just when the house was filled with the wonderful aromas of a typical
middle-class Sri Lankan midday meal. My mother would put aside the choic-
est morsels for the monk whose visit she routinely anticipated.

Monks observe a code of discipline and form when eating, which I
observed at *dana* ceremonies in our homes. In deciding where to sit at a *dana*,
monks observe meticulously the rule of seniority. Monks arrive punctually and
with great decorum await the arrival of the others. They follow certain table
etiquette. Reasonable amounts of food are accepted, and they see to it that all
the other monks too are served. The monks eat appreciatively and methodi-
cally from one side of the plate to the other. Monks chew silently in unhurried fashion with mindfulness. The process from the beginning to conclusion
is disciplined and orderly.

Recently when a monk teaching Buddhism in a university in England
stayed with us for a period of three weeks, his manners at mealtime deeply
impressed me. During the entire period I had no way of knowing what the
monk liked and did not like. He was always appreciative of everything I gave

him and invariably said the food was good. I tried with every means I knew to find out if there was any particular type of food he may have liked as a good *dayakaya*, but he always gave me the same answer, that what I offered him was very good. There is no waste, and little or no food remained on the plates at the end of the meal.

A RHINOCEROS OR AN ELEPHANT?

There are also rules to do with their moral and ethical conduct such as lying, using abusive language, slandering, having unsuitable dealings with women, destroying any form of life, and proper observance of rules pertaining to collective life in the monastery or when a monk goes forth as a solitary wayfarer. Indeed two modes of living had to be provided for in the laying down of rules. Initially many of the monks were single wanderers. The Buddha, anxious to spread his dharma as widely as possible, urged the monks to go in separate directions with no two going the same way. He famously urged the individual monk to "fare lonely as a rhinoceros." The phrase intrigued me. In India the rhinoceros is the animal known for its solitary ways, its obvious strength, and its skill as a survivor. But of course the rhinoceros was not a friendly animal, and typically Indian peasants who went into the forests to gather firewood or honey were wary of the animal.

The Buddha's similie did not quite fit the role of the monk. In idle moments, when my mind rambled on, to dwell on all the animals who frequently recur in both Buddhist texts and in the more widely known genre of folklore, I would try to visualize an animal that could be best compared to a monk. There were lions, tigers, snakes, birds, the ubiquitous monkey, and of course the elephant. No choice would be perfect, but I feel the elephant, with its impressive demeanor, attributes of wisdom, dignified unhurried walk, sense of power, and general air of nobility, best resembles a monk.

WHEN MONKS CONFESS

Besides these rules that are designed to regulate the daily life of the individual monk, there are others concerning the organization of the order. Some are the rules of admission into the order, rules for confession, for spending the retreat during the rainy season or *vas*, rules about the use of footwear, methods of settling disputes and conducting legal proceedings, and so on. Such rules regulate the external life of the monk.

The monks are expected to be the watchdogs of their own conduct and actions. For example, provision is made for a fortnightly assembly of *bhikkhus* known as the *uposatha*. It is the ceremony of unburdening one's conscience.

The Buddha required monks to make a confession of their trespasses so as to receive the absolution of the order. A fault, if there be one, should be confessed by the monk who remembers it and desires to be cleansed. This requires the monks living in a specific locality, formally marked out by a *sima* (boundary), to meet, to recite in conclave the *vinaya* rules, and confess to any breach of rules. Since confessions have to do with minor departures from this or that *vinaya* rule, punishments are light.

The Buddha said, "The *patimokka* must be recited in this way: Let a competent monk make the following proclamation to the Sangha: 'May the Sangha hear me today is *uposatha*, the eighth or the fourteenth day of the month. If the Sangha is ready, let the Sangha hold the uposatha service and recite the *patimokka*. I will recite the *patimokka*.' And the monks reply, "We hear it, and we concentrate well our minds on it, all of us." Then the officiating monk continues, "Let him who has committed an offence confess it; if there is no offence, let all remain silent, from being silent I shall understand that the reverend brethren are free from offences." The formula is repeated three times.

Major offences however carries heavy censure, sometimes involving expulsion from the order. The confessional aspect of this is to some extent redundant. Those who confess might well be the very monks who have a high-souled and conscientious awareness of what is expected of them and are therefore not driven by a sense of guilt per se. Such persons are not likely to repeat their transgressions. When it comes to the other variety, whose infringements of the law are so outrageous, logic suggests that their actions are already public knowledge, in which case the act of confession is purely pro forma. Moreover, how the tradition of confession functions in fraternities of monks, which are typically hierarchically organized, is intriguing. It is clear that the periodical recitation of the totality of the *vinaya* rules reinforces their collective awareness, quite apart from preventing a monk from pleading ignorance of the law as a mitigating consideration.

THE ART OF DEALING WITH THE OTHER

A significant difference between a Buddhist monk and a layperson is that a monk is celibate. Sexual activity of any kind is forbidden to a monk. Women are a source of sexual attraction and temptation for monks, who are to observe strict rules regarding association with them. Women are expected to avoid all physical contact even of an indirect nature with monks. Ideally when a woman offers a book or a glass of water to a monk it is done indirectly by placing the glass on a cloth or a tray. In buses and trains special seats are reserved for monks to minimize the risk of their having physical contact with female passengers. This does not prevent women from making daily food offerings to the monks or from attending ceremonies at the temple.

In the time of the Buddha, the good devotee Visaka, once in visiting the Anathapindika grove where for long spells of time the Buddha lived with his fellow monks, saw a certain monk, Udayin, in a secret, secluded place with a young woman. When Visaka remonstrated with the monk, Udayin ignored her. The matter came to the attention of the Buddha, who banned such trysts, likely to create the impression of a sexual liaison even if the thought were absent from the mind of the monk. Outward appearance and what was perceived to be true was often in human affairs regarded as potential fact.

In general the monks enjoy a superior status over laypersons in society. There are conventional terms of address used to refer to a monk or to directly address him. In modes of direct address, without exception, the honorific terms *obavahanse* and *hamuduruvo* are used. These terms with their feudal associations are used in traditional Sri Lankan society when people of inferior rank address superiors. Similarly there is a special terminology when laypersons describe the simple acts of the monks such as eating, washing, and sleeping or resting. When a monk passes away, a special term is used to refer to the monk's death. In every way, the superior status of a Sri Lankan monk is constantly emphasized.

SERVICE TO THE COMMUNITY

Urban Buddhists perceive monks as an entity apart from them, and therefore different. Their expectations of the behavior and life styles of this other (monks) create problems and lead to hyper criticisms. However, this is not so in the villages, where people understand the value of the monks and treat them as worthy persons following the path of the Buddha. They appreciate their dependence on the monk to perform rituals connected with daily life, the services they give the community, and the void they fill. Even on occasions when a monk deviates from the *vinaya* rules, sometimes even committing a serious breach of the rules, villagers try to understand and often say that after all they too are *pratagjana* (human) and that to err is human. Villagers say the monks observe *kotiyaksanvasasila*, meaning hyperbolically a million countless positive virtues. It is the latter perspective that enables the laity to be tolerant of minor misdemeanors or even major failings retaining a balanced perspective helping the continuity of the larger tradition. Villagers are grateful for the enrichment of their lives by the presence of monks and the numerous Buddhist services they perform.

We went to Ratnapura to stay with my aunt during school holidays. She was closely connected to the temple in her village. As young adults we heard stories and observed things in the village, especially happenings in the temple. The chief monk, attractive and flirtatious, spoke freely to young village women who visited the temple. Villagers did not pay much attention. Later we heard that the monk had an intimate relationship with a village woman and even had a family. Although according to *vinaya* rules this was a grievous offence that called for expulsion from monkhood, no one really paid much attention. Villagers talked about the valuable services the monk rendered to the community and thought of him as an indispensable person. They were ready to forgive him and made the excuse that he was only human and entitled to make mistakes. In fact they blamed the woman unfairly for tempting the monk to indulge in sexual misconduct. Villagers have the notion that monks can do no wrong and are ready to make excuses for their faults and failings. It's all Eve's fault!

REFORM AND RULES OF CONDUCT

The question is often raised, particularly in the West, should the rules of *vinaya* be modified to suit modern times? Should formal dress be made optional, and could monks visit homes and behave like normal lay people, as in the Catholic clergy? Monks living outside Sri Lanka have made adjustments to the *vinaya* rules. There are monks who work during the day, one as a driving instructor, to earn money to pay the mortgage of the temple; some others wear layman's clothes and go to work during the day and wear robes for religious ceremonies, more like part-time monks. Others live in their own apartments and spend time traveling and teaching meditation to foreigners. They maintain bank accounts and drive cars. Overall these instances are exceptional.

Some liberal minded Sri Lankan Buddhists express the view that the monastic tradition and the *vinaya* rules are archaic and are based on a hodge-podge of arbitrary rules and customs that obscure the essence of true Buddhist practice. This view misses one crucial fact. It is the unbroken lineage of monastics that have upheld and protected the *vinaya* rules for over twenty-five hundred years. But for the *vinaya* rules and the monks who continue to keep them alive, it is possible that we would not have Buddhism today in its institutional form. Whenever an issue arose in a monastery the senior monks dealt with it with foresight, tact, and resilience. It has been my experience that the bonds binding monks are strong in ways our secular mind, habituated to notions of individual rights, would find hard to grasp. Until modern times, traditionally in monastic institutions, monks regardless of their rank, kept daily diaries recording their activities and interactions. These diaries reveal the nature of conversations between senior and junior monks. Sometimes contrary to what we may think, the junior monks in a reversal of roles kept errant senior monks on the paths of rectitude.

In these matters Buddhists may not be alone. In the Christian tradition, increasingly, clergymen have abandoned their distinctive religious dress or wear it for religious functions alone. They would say, "We can better approach people when we look like them; We will not offend people who are not of our faith; it is uncomfortable to wear a habit because it is cumbersome; It is unsuitable for cold weather; You should not wear the habit to certain places or the people who see you will be scandalized." I have routinely heard such comments.

In one of his homolies in 1979, Pope John Paul II stated,

> I say: rejoice to be witnesses to Christ in the modern world. Do not hesitate to be recognizable, identifiable in the streets as men and women who have consecrated their lives to God and who have given up everything worldly to follow Christ. Believe that contemporary men and women set value on visible signs of consecration of your lives. People need signs and reminders of God in the modern secular city, which has few reminders of God left. So do not help the trend towards "taking God off the streets" by adapting secular modes of dress and behavior yourselves!

The pope prudently added that this was not his view alone but was the "desire of the Church often expressed by so many of the faithful" (Pope John Paul II, 10/7/78).

The late Venerable Walpola Rahula advocated the revision of the *vinaya* rules, pointing out that many of the rules of the *vinaya* were out of date and needed to be revised. These rules, he said, were formed some twenty-five hundred years ago when the monks were wandering ascetics in India. The Sangha now live in a secularized society and interact with the community at various levels. The social, economic, and political condition of the country has undergone many changes, and attitudes too have undergone much change. The *vinaya* rules are out of date and need to be revised to suit modern society. The idea was opposed by more conservative elements of the established Sangha. The question is not one of simple options. One may be taking too narrow a judicial view of the *vinaya* rules, at the risk of ignoring its spirit, which was to ensure a sense of compassionate harmony.

CIRCUMSTANCES ALTER CASES

It may well be that as in the case of monks living abroad, monks in Sri Lanka too should be permitted (without the heavy hand of extraneously imposed legal fiat) to make sensible compromises or adjustments.

Slowly but surely the attitudes of lay Buddhists toward the monks seem to be changing. There is a general acceptance that some changes need to be made. Along with globalization, quick and easy travel to other parts of the world, communication with other Theravada Buddhist countries, the image of the Buddhist monk and the attitudes of the laity would surely change. Sri Lankan monks in urban areas have taken an increasingly important and active role in the field of social services. Monks are involved with drug rehabilitation programs and counseling, especially after the ethnic war. Monks take on the role of healers and counselors. These factors have contributed to monks having to reinvent themselves to suit social, political, and economic changes affecting their role in society.

Recently, under the patronage of Venerable Maduluwawe Sobhitha, temporary ordination of monks was introduced in Sri Lanka. As mentioned earlier, in the Thai tradition, a monk is not obliged to remain a monk for life, nor is stigma attached should he decide to return to secular life. It has long been a Thai custom for Buddhist males over twenty to be temporarily ordained as monks, generally during the annual rain retreat (*vas*). I read in the Thai papers that some government offices, the armed services, and large private companies make temporary ordination easier by granting their employees a three-month leave with full salary. The temporary ordination, ranging from five days to three months, is available to all from the Crown Prince to the farmer's son alike.

EVEN ANTS HAVE A KING

For centuries Buddhism and Buddhist monks have received great support from the state. The traditional function of a king in a Buddhist country was to foster and protect Buddhism. He was the dharmaraja (righteous ruler). It was the duty of the king to give patronage to Buddhism, and to do nothing that would be detrimental to its interests. However, after several centuries of foreign rule, Buddhist temples and monks in Sri Lanka have lost the traditional patronage they received from the rulers and the state.

In Thailand, I could not help contrasting the Thais with the Buddhists in Sri Lanka. The splendor of the wats (temples), the gentleness and grace of the Thai people, and the visible authority of the monks guiding the laity and rulers betokened a different order of things. Perhaps not so long ago, the Sinhala people, who were preponderantly Buddhists, were that. It is a lost world. In 1815 when the British conquered the Kandyan kingdom, the monarchy, which had ruled Sri Lanka for over two thousand years ended. In history one can reconstruct an event, a certain period, but never the mood and mental ambience that went along with it. An unknown Buddhist monk who lived in the Degaldoruva Vihara not far from the city of Kandy expressed a sense of shock at the loss of a king in 1815.

> O ye happy ants, a king you own;
> We humans grieve, for we have none.

> We are desolate.
> But should our fates a monarch once more grant,
> With banners, drums, and solemn chant;
> We will celebrate!

The lament to the ants may not have been altogether in vain. Independence in 1947 did not bring about a Buddhist order of things. However, there was always the simmering yearning for it: a wish thwarted; a mission unaccomplished.

Traditionally, the ruler was integrally part of the *sasana*: the three elements, the king, the state and Buddhism, were in harmony. Whenever the state (as personified in the king and his policies) was out of step, the monks asserted themselves and became politically active until the particular issue was resolved and the state reversed this or that course of action. If tradition is to be believed, in medieval Sri Lanka, a king who had committed patricide and usurped power invited the monks to the palace for the ritual offering of *dana*. The monks sat down with customary propriety and decorum but with upturned begging *patras* (bowls) and therefore could not be served their meals. The king got the point and tried his best to placate the monks, who pointedly showed their displeasure of the unrighteous lay ruler.

REVOLT IN THE TEMPLE

Monks have realized the impossibility of returning to the status quo of kings where Buddhism and the order of the monks received undisputed patronage. In order to survive according to a code of discipline with a history of twenty-five hundred years, the monks needed the patronage of the state and the traditional support from laity. It was meant to be so when the rules were established. The attitude of the laity too had changed over the years due to changes in society and economic conditions of the country. Monks in the circumstances in time had no alternative but to resort to nontraditional means to save the order of the Sangha, Buddhism, and the *Buddha-sasana*.

We may take a cue form the example of other Buddhist monks, notably in the metropolis of Colombo, who seek solutions for the condition of Buddhism in contemporary Sri Lanka by invoking the Buddhist ethic of self-reliance. An interesting genre of monks have begun organizing job training; patronizing job-generating economic ventures begun by affluent Buddhist entrepreneurs; campaigns for drug rehabilitation; organizing funds to support the indigenous segments of the Buddhist laity; schools for vocational training and social service activities. These efforts in the long run are likely to bring the laity and the monkhood in a closer relationship. In the provincial areas, monks, partly in order to be less dependant on the Buddhist laity (who are already pressed by economic hardships) have made available temple preaching halls for fee levying commercial classes to help make young Buddhist men and women more competitive in a changing job market and in the process provide an additional means of income for the temple. Some young, educated monks took to teaching jobs, and some started business ventures considered forbidden for monks according to the *vinaya* rules. In this way, there was a shift in focus.

CHRISTIAN PROSELYTIZATION: QUID PRO QUO WAY

More recently, charismatic and politically conscious monks skillfully shifting their focus from the broad abstract issue of the state of Buddhism in post independent Sri Lanka, concentrated on a single specific question of Christian fundamentalist proselytization and unethical conversion. In doing so they were able to attract greater public support from the Buddhist laity at large, especially in the urban areas where any forms of public protest had greater visibility. On another platform, a younger generation of monks, to resolve specific issues that they believed affected the survival of the *sasana*, became radically politicized, resorting to nonviolent means of protest and adopting Gandian techniques. One such issue that particularly troubled them was what they called "unethical conversions" by groups of Christian evangelical organizations, which became unusually active in Sri Lanka. I heard stories from poverty stricken villagers, providing a common thread of a clear quid pro quo understanding in semi-urban and rural areas. Generous help was offered to the poor to complete their houses, resolve land disputes, provide schooling for children, and relieve them of crushing debts to the village store, on the strict condition that they become converts to Christianity. They were also asked to bring out the statues of the Buddha that they had owned for generations and burn them in a bonfire in front of their homes. Villagers, though desperate for help, were upset by the thought of burning their treasured Buddhas.

In dignified silence, monks walked in single file, epitomizing Gandian nonviolence. Two Buddhist monks with charismatic appeal—Venerable Omalpe Sobitha and Venerable Rajawatte Wappa—launched a fast unto death occupying the premises of the Ministry of Buddhist Affairs in the heart of Colombo. An interesting feature of the fast was the continuous broadcast by means of loud speakers outside the ministry premises of the recorded speeches of the Venerable Gangodavila Soma, protesting unethical conversions. It was widely believed that the dynamic, vigorous, and youthful Venerable Soma had died the previous year under mysterious circumstances on a visit to St. Petersburg, Russia, while attending a Christian-organized interfaith conference. The two issues now dramatically coalesced. In spite of their resolve to deal with the situation, the party in power within twenty-four hours visited the monks, the prime minister, and the senior ministers. The monks were persuaded to call off the strike. The government agreed to a demand made by the fasting monks that a committee be appointed within fourteen days to draft legislation banning Christian proselytizing.

A BUDDHIST STATE IN A BUDDHIST COUNTRY

In narrating the troubled course of these events, it often seems to me that the new clearly politicized Sri Lankan monkhood, and its popular front may not really appreciate the difficulties confronting any government in Sri Lanka, which must be secular in outlook and be fair to all sides given the reality of the pluralistic society in Sri Lanka. One might also take into consideration the volatile nature of Sri Lankan politics since the beginning of the 1980s which makes decision making and policy formulations extraordinary difficult.

The elections of April 2004 surprised all. The Buddhist monks formally put together a political party of their own, the Jathika Hela Urumaya. Mindful of the elections, on March 2, 2004, in the historic city of Kandy, the collective Buddhist monks launched their manifesto for restoring Buddhism to its pristine glory, among other objectives. It was done at a special religious ceremony attended by thousands of Buddhist monks and lay people all sharing the single mission of restoring Buddha-sasana (Buddhist state) and promoting Buddhism. Monks like their counterparts in the past have come to the forefront to protect religion and society in a time of decadence and instability. Through a plethora of publications and public pronouncements, what the Jathika Hela Urumaya stood for became evident. It was explained that the monks had taken politics as a last resort and with reluctance.

The party's aim is to form a Dharmarajjaya, a society ruled according to Buddhist principles. The protection of Buddhism should be the foremost duty of the government. The party is deeply concerned about the division of the country and declared as its objective the need to safeguard the independence and sovereignty of the nation and its territorial integrity. The Buddhist state, while granting the Sinhalese their hereditary rights, also pledges to protect the rights of other communities. As its economic objective, the monks favored an economy founded upon Buddhist principles. The monks, said Lord Buddha, had upheld a good lay life: monks are attempting to remind the people and the leaders of their duties. The monks believe that the spiritual degradation in the country could be overcome only by the strong application of the Five Precepts of Buddhist practice.

In April 2004 Jathika Hela Urumaya won nine seats and an impressive percentage of the popular vote. History was made in more than one way.

Keeping to their original resolve, the monks drafted a bill prohibiting forcible conversions. It proposed stiff penalties (including seven-year prison sentences and heavy fines) for anyone convicted of forcible conversions. Meanwhile another bill was tabled on behalf of the government by the minister for Buddhist affairs, which was approved by the cabinet but was not formally presented to the parliament. The Supreme Court, which reviewed the Jathika Hela Urumaya bill, declared two of its clauses unconstitutional and called for a new draft. In the alternative the court pointed out that the petitioners could call for a national referendum. If the referendum was successful another obstacle was to be overcome, which was to get a two-thirds majority of the entire parliament before the anticonversion bill could become a law.

Clearly a stalemate of sorts is the order of the day. Are the modern monks of Sri Lanka irreversibly politicized, or are they playing the role they always did in Sri Lanka's long and chequered history, by combining monastic involvement in a secular crisis with routinely attending to the spiritual comfort to the laity? It is not difficult for monks to become actively involved in a national crisis, especially if it threatened to jeopardize the well-being of the *sasana*, and somehow bring about its successful resolution, and then go back to the simple regimen of being a monk. In the process they would do what they always did best, which was to attend to both mundane and transmundane angst of their *dayakayas*.

THE POWER OF THE ROBE

In Sri Lanka, given the chronic volatility of the political situation, the issue of the Buddhist monks becoming involved in politics continues to be a matter of public debate, significantly more in the English media, and conspicuously less in the vernacular Sinhala press. I had a fresh insight into the problem, when on my recent visit to Sri Lanka in summer 2005, I met with Venerable Aluthnuvara Anurudda, the chief incumbent of the Rajamahavihare in Kotte.

I was aware that the monk was actively involved in reconstruction work, building cottages and establishing a village for displaced tsunami victims. I expressed an interest in seeing the tsunami-ravaged areas along the southern coast. I went with the monk from Colombo to Galle, a journey of around one hundred miles. The monk was anxious to show me firsthand the catastrophic destruction wrought by the tsunami. He was familiar with the area, having frequented it many times. I saw the endless canvass of destruction and devastation, a resigned hopelessness writ upon the faces of the victims who saw us with dazed, unseeing eyes. We stopped on numerous occasions, albeit briefly, because—with the exception of the monk—I felt that our presence was an unwarranted intrusion. The victims still lived in different colored tents donated by various countries, awaiting some miracle. They were aware that there was a generous outpouring of aid and resources of one sort or another from foreign individuals and agencies, but because of bureaucratic delays or (as was widely alleged) the siphoning off of aid monies to powerful political groups, they had not received it.

Venerable Anurudha's life was devoted to serve the community. He firmly expressed the view that this was the role of a monk. He was incredibly compassionate and had an ear for everyone. He told me stories of the tsunami, the role the monks played when the tsunami ravaged the land. He said that when disaster struck the villagers in the hundreds of thousands instinctively moved by an ancient cultural reflex, made their way—with their clothes in tatters, ripped off in battling the waves—to temples and monasteries situated near the sea coast. Caught unaware the monks welcomed all. Many of them tore their robes and offered their inner garments to provide the naked victims with some semblance of dignity. The monks organized volunteer *dayakayas* to go to every conceivable store to get food items and cooking facilities to feed all.

We visited a new settlement that the Venerable Anurudda was setting up on elevated ground not too far from the sea for victims of the disaster. Twenty-four new two-bedroom cottages had been completed with electricity. The monk was fighting with the local government agencies to get water for the villagers. He was determined to continue to build more. Here and there was an air of hope and resolution. My daughter, Ranmini, had sent money to build a cottage for a family. So many needed these little houses. Our giving did not seem to make a dent in the problem, but it was a beginning.

It was on the way back that Venerable Anurudda asked me my views on whether monks should take part in politics. I said that it was not a bad idea to fight for the protection of the Sasana. He was surprised at my answer. With great forthrightness he expressed his view that monks had no place in politics. He explained to me the nature of the political process. He was concerned about how the fair reputation of the monks was likely to be tarnished in politics. He explained that politics, which meant constant manoeuring for power, had the potential to corrupt the best of men.

He championed a power of another sort for all monks, which he called "*syura balaya*" (the power of the robe). He said that the average monk was sitting on a pot of gold—the potential of the dharma and its actualization by individual example and irreproachable conduct. If all the monks oriented themselves in this way, their individual and collective power could and would make the monkhood and Buddhism immune to political and secular power. He added that the most valuable role for a monk is to serve the people.

I spent much time in the temple and with the monk. I was fascinated by his love of nature and elephants. His face gleamed when he talked of his collection of elephants, all given to the temple as gifts from Sri Lankan heads of state.

Venerable Anurudha wryly remarked, that strange though it may seem,- the elephants in their behavior reflect the temperament and idiosyncrasies of their distinguished donors. One was quiet, dignified as if above the fray. The second was extraordinarily particular about appearance and cleanliness and could never be coaxed to soil his person by going over marsh land. The *Mahout* (trainer) has to somehow go round the obstacle. He would not get into unclean water to bathe and resented harsh words and loud behavior. The third was an animal of moods and outbursts of temper, but was at other times capable of a certain charm and docility. When I identified the three donors the monk trying hard to conceal his amusement said with mock gravity "well you said it. I still say nothing."

FIFTEEN

Varieties in a Single Saffron Robe

SHORTLY AFTER THE BUDDHA attained Enlightenment, he established the order of Buddhist monks. Beginning with five of his original disciples, over the next forty years of his active ministry, the Buddha transformed an amorphous conglomeration of monks into a well-knit, self-regulating order governed by rules that later became a code of conduct and discipline (*vinaya*), handed down from generation to generation. However, we would do well to look beyond *vinaya* issues to see the richness in the lives of monks.

After the passing away of the Buddha, the monks could not easily follow his example. A study of the Buddha's daily regimen would show that while he devoted a great deal of time to laypersons, as much time was spent in personal meditation, reflections, and reclusive isolation. He shared his own transcendent contemplative experiences with the erudite disciples who lived with him, and he often encouraged them to share their experiences. In time, however, in the slow unraveling of the post-Buddha period, the monks came into greater contact with the lay community, thereby becoming more socially engaged. The demands made by laypersons left the monks little time for meditative reflection as Buddha anticipated. In effect the alluring vision of the world renouncing *Siddartha* receded to the background.

SO WHERE ARE YOU GOING MY LITTLE MONKS?

Little children as monks always intrigued me. On visits to Buddhist temples I saw little novice monks hanging around the chief monk, playing, engaged in minor chores such as sweeping the premises or acting as messengers. They seemed happy and content. They behaved, played, and shared their wishes and anxieties like all other children. In Sunday school they were our playmates. We played hop-scotch, a game that the young play. The saffron robes the monks wore were no obstacle. We all joined in playing hide and seek. Senior monks did not object to the little monks playing with girls and boys of the same age. They shared the candy from the temple, usually the *dana* leftovers, with us. When school was over they would come to the gate and watch us leave, and I often felt sad to leave them behind. They seemed sad if we talked of going to a movie or a play and often expressed a desire to join us. We refrained from making too much of our life in the outside world. On the whole they seemed content and happy. We told them our stories, and they shared their stories. Some even made us privy to the idiosyncrasies of the older monks, and we shared common laughter. As children we bonded with them and loved them as equals. I often wondered why the little boys chose to live in the monastery, whether coercion masquerading as parental authority was a possible explanation. Were there other reasons that were somehow eluding me? The monks with whom I broached the subject gave me a wide range of reasons to account for why they took to the robes.

I was with a friend attending the *vas* ceremonies in Thailand during the season when little boys were ordained for a short period of time. Pason, a Thai friend, told me the story of how he became a monk for a brief period when he was seven. Thais believe that when they die they will go to heaven by holding onto a monk's robe. Pason was made a monk to help his grandfather go to heaven. Young boys in Thailand also become monks during the school holidays. Pason said he was scared at the thought of becoming a monk. Before his ordination he had to learn new things such as the Ten Precepts, which a novice monk was required to know. On the big day of the ordination, he went to the temple with his family. They shaved his hair and his eyebrows. Everyone took turns cutting a strand or two of his hair, and a monk completed the shaving. During the ceremony Pason had to repeat some Pali verses, which he did not understand. Later he was helped by a monk to change into robes, and the ceremony was complete.

Later the monk took Pason to the place where he was to sleep, a *kuti* (room), which he shared with two other monks. There was cable TV, a Play Station, a radio, bookshelves, a refrigerator, a sink, and a clock. The bed was a thin mattress on the floor. He was surprised when he saw the monks play games on the Play Station. He too was allowed to play. When he went to bed he was hungry because he was not given food after noon. He had to get up at 5:00 A.M. to take a bath and put on robes. Then he had to meditate for thirty minutes. He had not done this before and felt uncomfortable sitting down cross-legged with eyes closed. Later on in the morning they went on *pindapata*. Pason had to stop many times to enable everybody to offer something to the monks. When people offered food, they were not allowed to say "Thank you" in the conventional manner. Lay people offered food for merit, and the monks blessed them.

On the last day his parents came to take him back. He had a special ceremony where the monk recited verses in Pali, and he took off the robes and wore his own tee shirt and shorts. Pason said that although he enjoyed his stay as a monk, he was as happy to get back home because he could eat after lunch in his own home.

SHORT CUT TO NIRVANA:
HOLDING ON TO THE ELEPHANT'S TAIL

In Sri Lanka, traditionally, the majority of the monks hail from rural areas, comparatively less influenced by Westernization and modernization. Opportunities for social mobility, which have a great deal to do with learning English, are few in rural areas. If one continued to live on in the village, it was the temple that provided an education of a more traditional sort, which turned out to be interestingly an alternative path of mobility. Many of the monks I refer to in these pages, who ultimately became famous for their learning and erudition, used the temple and the undeniable excellence of its educational facilities as a springboard for their mobility.

Apart from education and economic motives, acquiring merit was a major factor in giving a son to the temple. In rural families I have seen instances of parents making the brightest male child a monk. This was *kusala* karma (good deed) and a way to salvation. There is a traditional religious belief that if one member of a family becomes a monk, the merit acquired thereby would be sufficient to send *hataravarge* (four successive generations of that family) to nirvana, or at any rate to *divyaloka* (the happy celestial abode of the gods). The seeming loss of the child to the parents was more than compensated by the anticipation of great merit and the feeling that their child was the recipient of opportunities that the parents could not themselves provide.

Monks I knew while recapitulating their childhood experience as novices in the temple confessed that they were often overwhelmed with the multitude of tasks—studying the scriptures, daily chores such as taking care of the temple, performing rituals, and the disciplined life in the temple. Many times some of them, unable to withstand the strict discipline of the senior monks or after petty squabbles with other novice monks, ran away from the temple only to be brought back. As children they had to get used to eating two meals a day and felt hungry in the evenings. They were taught to think of food not as something craved for, or something that they did not like, but functionally as food to stop feeling hungry. They also mentioned that the pain of separation at this early age from their parents especially their mothers was unbearable at times, but they got accustomed to it and built close relationships with the spiritual masters with whom they came into contact. Many monks expressed their gratitude for the educational opportunities they were able to get.

THOU SHALL BE A MONK, THE STARS DECREE

According to an endemic belief widely prevalent in Sri Lanka, the *kendare* (horoscope) plays a critical part in one's life. Birth time is carefully recorded, and with consultation of almanacs, and astrological calculations, a *kendare* is made. According to practitioners of the profession the configuration of planets at the time of birth becomes a critical factor in casting the *kendare*. The future life of the newborn child is forecast by reading the *kendare* and is used in making decisions in a person's life. The good times and unfavorable times are predicted by the astrologer according to the planetary positions in the *kendare*.

Kendares, which are so much a part of the lives of the people of Sri Lanka, also play their part in making a son's enter the monastery. A male child might be born with a bad horoscope portending all manner of misfortunes, which would bedevil his life. Such a child would be sent to the temple where he would in time become a monk, thereby mitigating the malefic effects in his horoscope. Moreover, a unique and unusual configuration, the *hatarapalu kendara* (absence of stars in four critical position where they ought to be) could be indicated. Such a horoscope is not a good one for worldly life. In such cases, for the well-being of the person, to avoid bad things happening to the family, astrologers often advise parents to make the child a monk. This involves a virtual removal of the child from the parents by giving him over to the monastery at a young age. The life of a monk is considered hard, and therefore this step is a form of expiation, preventing calamities such as bad luck and ill health. The blessings one would get by being in contact with the Sangha and their constant evocation of good and compassionate thoughts would circumvent ill luck.

Venerable Uduwawala Chandananda, a prominent monk from the Asgiriya fraternity of monks of the Kandy temple complex while disputing the authenticity of the *hatarapalu kendare*, agreed with the general assumption that monks who enter the Sangha may have negative horoscopes, indicating subtly that the life of a monk was not easy. In a lighter frame of mind he showed us his modest quarters and posed a question: if my horoscope was good would I live like this? At the back of my mind was the bland assumption that monks occupying significant positions lived in luxurious and well-appointed quarters. This is the general belief in Sri Lanka. What I saw was a simple, stripped to bare essentials, unostentatious room. It had a simple bed, a reclining chair, a bookcase, a wooden table, and a chair. The monk observed my disappointment. I thought to myself how wrong I was in assuming that the monks in high office as a rule lived in luxury.

Venerable Chandananda proceeded to share the not-so-attractive side of the life of a Buddhist monk. Monks do not get to eat what they like or wear the attractive and bright clothes laypersons wear or go anywhere at any time.

He liked the life of a mendicant but pointed out that this was difficult as it involved many sacrifices. However, having entered the monkhood he enjoyed its peace and the opportunity to serve others. He said he would not trade his life as a monk for any other.

In answer to my question of why children are given to a temple, I was told of instances when a child was unruly, and parents had problems of disciplining him, they gave him to the monastery to be brought up in an orderly and disciplined manner. The routine of discipline demanded from a monk is a training experience in orderly life. It is rather like sending young sons to military camps. One monk said that his horoscope predicted that he would be inclined to be unusually obsessed with sex. His parents, in what is best described as a preemptive move, handed him over to the temple at an early stage. He said all this in an easy manner conveying the impression that somehow sex had never been a problem to him. I was also told of instances where the opposite was true. When a horoscope predicted person was unfit to lead a successful domestic life because he had a weak sex drive, he was given over to the temple to become a monk. All these were predicted in the horoscope reading. Advancing years, the sense of malaise that sometimes comes with it, an unhappy marriage, and the vicissitudes of life of one sort or another are among other reasons why men choose to live the life of a monk.

A candidate for ordination requires the permission of his parents if he is a minor. There are no other prerequisites. The spiritual or educational requirements for entry into a prestigious order are minimal. However, persons with physical disabilities are not known to be ordained. Since a monk is required to be completely self-reliant on day-to-day living, one could see why physical disabilities would virtually prevent someone from effectively functioning as a monk.

THE BUSINESS OF CASTING A ROBE ON A TREE

Those who become monks do not always remain in robes. Many monks in Sri Lanka who received university education cast away their robes. Some who received higher degrees and exposure to English education did not remain as monks. The majority of the monks who came to America for postgraduate education gave up robes and returned to lay life. I knew a monk in America who worked in a government office. He came from a remote village with moderate means. The parents thought that if he became a monk he would be exposed to a world of opportunities. He received his training and education as a Buddhist monk in a secular university in Sri Lanka. He came to America to serve in a temple but ended working for the local government under an influential politician. All these opportunities were available to him because he was a Buddhist monk. His American superiors took pride that a Buddhist monk, in saffron robes, a culturally authentic exotic entity, worked for them. He earned the respect and regard of the people with whom he worked. I met his American wife who told me how she fell in love with the monk while he was in robes. She knew little about Buddhism and much less of Buddhist monks. She had no idea that Buddhist monks were supposed to be celibate and as an invariable rule have little or no contact with women. He associated with her for a few years and married her. He told me how he left the robes on a high branch of a tree and walked away almost saying goodbye to a monk's way of life.

However, by giving up the robes he now became an ordinary man of minority status, and everybody noticed that he spoke English with a strong accent. Out of his robes all this mattered. As an ordinary citizen he faced discrimination of the sort a minority member in society faces in America. When he was in robes he belonged to the class of monks untouched by social distinctions, but as a layman he became an ordinary, recognizable citizen. I knew his family, and I was saddened to witness how hard he had to work to provide for a young family. On one of my visits I found him in a pair of shorts, digging the garden to plant vegetables to augment the family income. It was a beautiful family, but I wondered why he gave up the enviable, trouble-free life of a monk, to embrace all the hardships and struggles of lay life. As the Romans would say, so many men, as many opinions and ways of looking at things.

SWIMMING AGAINST THE TIDE

As mentioned earlier, some monks I interviewed spoke about the difficulties of adhering to the *vinaya* rules formulated over twenty-five hundred years ago. They wondered if these rules should be modified to suit modern times and conditions. They talked about the difficulties they encounter on a regular basis while performing their monastic duties. Routinely, monks have to attend to obligations such as rituals related to funeral houses in the villages. On the seventh day after the death of a person, a monk is invited to the house to deliver the *matakabana* (homily of remembrance). This was a widely attended ceremony done primarily to console the grieving relatives and to confer merit to the dead. Often the villagers have no means to provide private transport, and monks have to depend on public transport. Some told me of the difficulties of getting to remote villages by buses to perform religious obligations. Buses in Sri Lanka do not run frequently and do not follow a strict time schedule.

Once a monk got delayed going to a funeral house because the bus was old, and it broke down. There was no way of getting a mechanic to repair it, so the monk decided to walk a distance of several miles to the house. The offended and disappointed villagers were critical of the monk for arriving late for the function. In America some monks drive cars donated by rich devotees, but these facilities are not available to monks in Sri Lanka. Much is expected from the monks, but there is little understanding and generosity of spirit when it comes to their failings. Monks are not supposed to wear wristwatches but are required to be on time. Lay people expect punctuality from the monks regardless of the circumstances, although traditionally Sri Lanka is not a society where much is made of the virtue of punctuality, and great laxity prevails.

A monk related his experience in attending a *matakadana* seven days after the death. The food offered was spoiled as there was no refrigeration, and the sanitary conditions of the village home were unpleasant. Being a monk he had to bear it all in silence. In village homes the dead body is kept in the house for several days, giving an opportunity for the relatives to pay their last respects, and the body is not often embalmed. Funeral homes are unknown in villages. While laypeople have the choice of either going to a funeral house or refraining from doing so, as well as the option of avoiding food in such circumstances, monks have no choice.

Monks can never refuse to attend a ceremony. The ceremonies are many. During the monsoon season and the flooding that invariably follows, villages become inaccessible. Under difficult conditions monks make visits to remote villages to perform obligations. Monks related incidents to me of times they were subjected to insults without any provocation. Some people do not like Buddhist monks and with no reason insult them. Buddhist monks have to bear patiently all the slings and arrows as it were, with compassion and loving kindness. It is a superhuman task for a monk committed to a spiritual life.

CHITRA'S STORY

Buddhists in Sri Lanka and elsewhere have interesting ideas regarding the power of monkhood. Chitra's story is one such tale. We lived in London in the same house in rented flats. Her father was a Buddhist monk. One day she received a pretty tablecloth from Thailand from him. She told me how he became a monk. Her father was a heart patient and survived several heart attacks in the days before open-heart surgery and angiograms. One time he was so gravely ill, having done everything possible in the hospital, the doctors asked that he be taken home. Her family was desperate and helpless. Her father made an unusual request from Chitra's mother, which was to make a vow that if he came out of this crisis he would become a Buddhist monk for the rest of his life and lead a life of spirituality serving the community. Chitra's mother agreed.

Chitra's father recovered, but when the time came to carry out the promise, her mother protested and was angry. She did not know how to deal with her husband becoming a monk. Her father was determined to keep the vow and entered the order. Her mother refused to see him. Whenever he visited the house to see the family, her mother did not come out, showing her disappointment. Chitra's father lived on for many years and experienced no heart problems.

Such stories are not uncommon. When I was traveling to Sri Lanka via Hong Kong to see my mother, I was seated next to an Asian woman. I was for a long time engrossed in reading, but later on into the flight, my eyes fell on the book in Thai script the woman next to me was reading. She started a conversation and asked me if I was a Buddhist. She explained that the Thais pray to the Buddha and repeat the verses in Pali concerning the virtues of the Buddha. She tried to convince me of the effectiveness of praying to Buddha for blessings.

Her story was fascinating, and I wondered if it could be true. Thais have a practice of making vows during times of illnesses. Her mother was gravely ill, and the doctors had given up hopes of her recovery. In desperation her family decided to make a vow. If her mother recovered from her illness, her younger brother, who was then sixteen years old, would become a monk for six months. She said their mother was the pivotal person at that time in their family, and without her the family would fall apart. The next morning, to the amazement of the doctors, her mother recovered. She explained to me that this was a normal practice among Thais, and that later, on another occasion, she also made her seven-year-old son a monk for a similar cause.

WATCH OUT! MONKS CAN BE ATTRACTIVE

It is not uncommon for young women to be attracted to monks. As a young girl, I attended a Buddhist girls' school in Colombo in the late 1950s. The medium of instruction was English, and there was no religious education in schools. The headmistress of the school was a young, anglicized, sophisticated Sri Lankan woman. She decided to introduce Buddhist ethics and morals to her girls. We formed a Buddhist society that periodically invited well-known Buddhist monks from the temples in Colombo and its vicinity. The girls were excited because it was an opportunity to see a person from outside.

A saintly monk visited us on a regular basis, looking like a little Buddha. He often challenged us with questions. He was very popular, attractive, and compassionate. There was an aura around him, or so it seemed to me. He talked about Buddhist ethics and morals, which he illustrated with interesting Jataka stories. We were allowed to do extra homework if we so desired to extend our knowledge. Among the girls there was Jinasili, who was conservative, pretty, and ultra religious. She did all the extra work, got attention from the monk. The girls nicknamed her "Saintly Sumana." We respected the monk immensely but also kept our distance. That was what we were taught to do. The monk too took extra care to maintain a distance, but as the months went by, Jinasili, in her seductive and gentle way, got closer to him. She was attentive and would offer him a drink after the sermon and follow him sometimes to his car, carrying books, while continuing their conversation.

By the end of the semester we could not help noticing Jinasili's attraction to the monk. The monk too looked a little disturbed with the distraction. He visibly lost his aura and his composed nature in my mind at any rate, and became a normal person. The school holidays came, and we all went home. Jinasili, having done well in the exams, entered the university. We later heard that their friendship continued, and the monk did not know how to handle the temptation. He eventually gave up his robes. Once he gave up the robes Jinasili was no longer interested in him and found it was a source of embarrassment and even a nuisance when he visited her in the university as a layman. No one spoke about the monk, and he faded out of the picture. We lost a good monk.

A MONK ABROAD: THE FALLEN IDOL

Young Buddhist monks who come for higher education to universities in America are faced with many obstacles of identity in trying to fit into the American culture and the temptations of intermingling with attractive women. Western unfamiliarity with the sight of Buddhist monks, their way of life, celibacy, and yellow robes make living among them difficult and trying. I knew of a Buddhist monk student, whose chief monk in Sri Lanka was a prominent person from my hometown. He sent the young monk, his *golanama*, who was designated to be his puppilary successor, to America for higher education to study under an American professor who was a close friend of the monk. The chief monk was proud of his *golanama* and looked forward to his return hopefully with a doctoral degree to serve the community, thereby giving the chief monk great prestige. The young monk, however, had difficulties fitting into the student culture and adapting to the American life style. The professor too had doubts about the celibacy of monks and often expressed his opinion that celibacy was not a natural way of life. The monk attended church on Sundays in a well-cut Western suit to learn about other religions and their rituals. All this was encouraged as part of his education by the American professor, who was a clergyman. I met the young monk in a bookstore wearing a tee shirt and pair of jeans. He looked rather cute. He was a little startled and embarrassed, but I quickly put him at ease. He told me that the yellow robe was too conspicuous and that conventional Western dress helped him to mingle with other students and thereby make friends. He added that he did wear the robe for formal occasions. He had a bicycle to get about on the campus and was comfortable. I understood his predicament. When in Rome, one must do as the Romans do. Besides, in the larger scheme of things, making sensible adjustments to suit difficult circumstances made sense, although there was an infringement of the *vinaya* rules. All this may have been a harbinger to what followed. The monk in due course received his doctoral degree and went to England, where he disrobed and began his new life as a layman.

It is not an easy life for monks who have to go about in public places in robes in America. American society is not used to the sight of monks attired in saffron robes in spite of the repeated professions of multiculturalism and tolerance. Nor are the robes conducive for survival and comfort in colder climates, especially in winter. Often when I took Buddhist monks around, disparaging remarks would be made about their attire. In some conservative areas, where they had not seen a Buddhist monk, they made embarrassing remarks such as "Look a man in a dress," or "a man wearing a sari." They also hailed them, "Hari Krishna." One little boy, aggravated by the strange sight, remarked "Why can't you wear normal dress?" Much as the monks tried to take all this in stride, they were pained and perplexed. Despite such manifest inconveniences, by and large monks who come to America stoically endure these hardships and remain monks. Most never wear anything other than a robe and are proud of it. One must have the personality, stature, and commitment to endure this. However, the majority of the monks who come to America from Sri Lanka for higher education having received their higher degrees give up their robes. Only a handful remain monks. They would not be able to come to these prestigious universities were they not in robes.

NO COOKIE CUTTER MODEL

There are in Sri Lanka several major categories of monks serving society in different capacities. The majority of the monks remain in village temples and serve the community, by attending to spiritual needs and by performing rituals. These rituals are many and are an essential part of the practice of religion. They get involved in the life of the *dayakayas* (laymen) who patronize the temple sharing the travails and tribulations of lay life. The monks are ubiquitous, going wherever their ministrations are required, to take part in domestic ceremonies and rituals or to simply make themselves available as counselors and mentors. They in effect meet the psychotherapeutic needs of the laymen among whom they live.

Ajan Bramavamso, of the Buddhist Society of Western Australia, in the course of a public lecture at which I was present, related this story:

> Once, when he was a young monk in Thailand, a man came into the monastery and asked him, "Can I stay in the monastery for a few days?" The monk thought he wanted to meditate, so he said, "Oh you want to meditate?" "Oh no," he said, "the reason I want to come to the monastery is

because I've had an argument with my wife." So he stayed in the monastery. Three or four days later he came to the monk and said, "I feel better now, can I go home?" The monk said what a wise thing that was. Instead of going to the bar and getting drunk, instead of going to his mates and telling them all the rotten things that he thought his wife had done, thereby reinforcing his ill will and resentment, he went to stay with a group of monks who didn't say anything about his wife, who were just kind and peaceful. He thought about what he had been doing in that peaceful, supportive environment, and after a while he felt much better. This is what a monastery sometimes is. The monk added it is a counseling center, a refuge, and the place where people come to let go of their problems.

There are also monks who focus primarily on meditation. These monks generally spend most of their time in seclusion and are hardly seen in public, indeed making it a point not to participate in public ceremonies. A good example of this may be found in Udavattekele aramaya deep in the heart of a forest of that name which had somehow survived the rapacious hand of modern developers and town planners in Kandy. With the surge of interest in meditation, a hitherto reclusive retreat of monks began to be accessed by the people, to whom the meditating monk living in a forest was always an object of admiration.

Similar retreats exist elsewhere on the island. The monks would teach lay people the basics of meditation, tacitly showing that meditation is the real thing vis-à-vis rituals and ceremonies. It is also the practice of some of the monks to disappear for months in the wilderness of Laggala to live in cells or *kutis* in an elephant-infested region far away from civilization. Curiously, in the summer of 2004 I was part of a group of people who escorted a monk from Udavattekele, whose journey's end was the Laggala wilderness. At the edge of a beautiful stream, which he crossed unaided, he waved goodbye to us. We waited until the receding saffron figure was seen no more. It was early evening. The symbolism of the scene crossing the stream of transcendence was not lost on me or on anyone in our small party as we began the drive back to Kandy. For a long while nobody spoke. This too is a vignette of Buddhism in Sri Lanka.

AN ARTIST MONK

The sibilant whispers of the sum of my yesterdays leap this time to Ratmalana, a vibrant metropolis of Colombo. The charismatic Venerable Mapalagama Vipulasara was the chief incumbent of the Ratmalana *vihara* where my mother was a longtime *dayakaya* (lay patron). The *vihara* was a well-known monastic school founded in the late nineteenth century. The monks transformed the monastery to resemble a modern religious institution, but it looks more like a mansion. It is modern with all the amenities of modern living. I have beautiful memories of visiting this monastery as a child. Venerable Mapalagama Vipulasara's artistic abilities fascinated everyone. He sculptured Buddha statues of all sizes and was a well-known artist in the East. He traveled widely in Asia and the West and had many connections with foreigners. Adjoining the temple, he constructed living quarters, to provide accommodation for his foreign friends and visitors replete with all modern amenities. He had many connections with Japan and was influenced by ideas from the Japanese.

Needless to say, Vipulasara was not a traditional monk. He was often not clean-shaven. He spoke aloud and laughed a lot. He moved swiftly, and his robes flew about him. We were in the airport once in the seventies to meet my mother returning from a pilgrimage to India. Venerable Vipulasara recognized my mother and walked toward her briskly with his robes flying. My mother told him that she was waiting for custom clearance. The monk went inside and got permission on behalf of my mother in a moment. He believed that his *dayakaya*, my mother, should not be unnecessarily inconvenienced. We were able to get out quite soon with his intervention. My mother, who had nothing to declare anyway, was impressed and grateful.

WEDDING IN THE TEMPLE

A Danish artist working in the southern sea coast of Sri Lanka had fallen in love with a Sinhalese Buddhist girl in the early seventies. He was a friend of Venerable Vipulasara. He had no relatives in Sri Lanka, and his newfound girlfriend was too poor to afford a wedding ceremony. The monk took the initiative to perform a marriage ceremony in the temple. It was the first of its kind. The occasion was much publicized, and there were many journalists. Venerable Vipulasara was an influential person, granted many favors to the *dayakayas*, and helped them in many ways using his political influence. Although a wedding in the temple was novel, an untraditional event, no one questioned him.

In his charismatic way, combining an indomitable will with effusive charm, he visited my mother and informed her of the upcoming ceremony and solicited her patronage. He convinced my mother that Buddhist monks had involvements in wedding ceremonies from ancient times. This surprised my mother, who was conservative, but her respect for the monk kept her from questioning the new idea. When my mother's friends questioned the validity of having a marriage in the temple, my mother quickly came to the defense of the monk. He went to his patrons in the community and urged them to provide the necessary items such as food. A committee was organized, and the tasks pertaining to the ceremony were assigned. There was a food committee, a decoration committee, and even a person designated to dress the bride.

Venerable Vipulasara designed a beautiful *poruwa* (traditional altar of marriage), which was constructed with young palm tree leaves and lotus flowers. The monk was in his own right a talented artist, and the ceremony was lavish and beautiful. On the day of the wedding ceremony, according to auspicious times, an elaborate ritual was performed under the patronage of the Sangha in the temple premises. We all took items of traditional food and milk rice and had an enjoyable time. Immediately after the marriage ceremony was concluded the young couple worshipped the monk and the other monks present, and the couple listened to the *pirit* chanted to them as a blessing. They then worshipped the Buddha in the shrine of the temple. Venerable Vipulasara, the master of ceremonies, took center stage and delivered a sermon to the couple about marriage and Buddhist teachings from the Sigalowada Sutta, explaining the reciprocal obligations of the newlyweds, husband to the wife and wife to the husband, the Buddhist way. He affirmed that marriages too were in ancient times conducted by monks. Love may make the world go round, but marriage in our culture makes the social world possible.

POLITICAL MONK

Venerable Baddegama Sumana was in Chicago, an invited guest of the State Department. He was passionately involved in the contemporary politics of Sri Lanka. He taught in a university in Sri Lanka, was also fluent in Japanese, having lived many years teaching Buddhism in Japan. Strictly speaking, monks cannot live in the houses of laypeople. I was aware that the State Department had made a reservation in a downtown hotel for venerable Sumana. Nonetheless I had already got the spare room in our apartment ready for him. To our relief (and as it turned out joy), he consented to stay with us. He had never stayed in a lay house and found the experience unique. He was conscious of *vinaya* rules in his daily activities. When I offered to wash his robes in the washing machine, he said that it would not be in accordance with the *vinaya*. By the same token, whenever I tried to serve him an evening meal, he politely declined. In this context he remarked that laypeople always talked about food. If they were not eating, they talked about food, evaluating the quality of the food they like. To the monks, Venerable Sumana said, food was not all that important.

During his brief sojourn in Chicago, I took Venerable Sumana grocery shopping and to a variety of shops in the shopping mall. Being a monk with simple needs he was amazed at the availability of the multiplicity of goods and American consumerism. He observed the competitive display of goods to attract the customers. Living with us was an eye opener to difficulties and problems of lay life. He confided in me that in his weaker moments he had often wondered if he had made the right choice by taking to robes, as the lay way of life appeared attractive. He thought that married people lived peaceful, harmonious lives, had many material possessions, wore beautiful clothes, got about freely, and had many friends. Our way of life may have disillusioned him. He saw me juggling a full-time job and being a housewife with children. While shopping, trying to make choices to please everyone, dealing with children's problems, balancing the finances, meeting societal obligations, and trying to get along with my husband. He said that this was a great eye opener to him and remarked that the lay way of life he once thought was rosy was evidently not so.

He observed all the complications that went into the process of packing a bag for Ananda to go to California with him. I had to match the shirts to the trousers and ties and then find outfits for evening and formal wear. All this complicated business of dress and dress codes with color coordination with design was a new concept for him. He remarked how simple it was for him to travel anywhere as he had only the saffron robe and shaving items with toothbrush and paste. He traveled so light it would make anyone envious. He did not have to wait in lines for security checks and checked baggage at the airports. Here was a lesson on simple living with few wants.

Venerable Sumana was a great storyteller. Politics was in his bones. He told me many stories relating to the history of the Sangha, the part the Sangha played in the political arena to protect Buddhism. He emphasized the need of the Sangha to be conscious of the state of Buddhism in the country; therefore it was the monks' duty to be interested in the political situation. He had definite political affiliations with the conservative party in Sri Lanka, the United National Party (UNP). In the 1970s, Sri Lanka underwent a period of political upheaval, and the opposition party that came to power banned the UNP from holding meetings. Large gatherings were prohibited. Venerable Sumana ingeniously conceived a means of overcoming this obstacle.

Gradually I got used to Venerable Sumana's flair for a certain turn of phrase. He once startled me by saying that people got the best ideas, those flashes of illumination, while sitting in the bathroom or while in the shower. One such idea was to circumvent the restrictions imposed by the ruling party to prevent his own party from convening election meetings. He thought of having the eighty-four thousand *pahan puja* (oil lamp lighting ceremony) in the temple in order to get a large number people to the temple. This ceremony is a tradition in Buddhist culture, coming down from the times of the ancient kings and is considered a great meritorious deed. Resort to it was rare. Venerable Sumana spread the word around, and the supporters of his party (big business men in the city), waiting for such an opportunity, gathered together in large numbers. The supporters of the UNP brought to the temple large quantities of coconut oil and clay lamps needed for the ceremony by stealth in the night. A temple was considered sacred ground and therefore not subject to search or surveillance.

On the day of the great *pahan puja* ceremony, thousands came to the temple. Venerable Sumana, an eloquent speaker, taking advantage of the religious event, made his political pitch and gave his political leaders an opportunity to be heard. The next day the authorities questioned him, but being a popular monk in the village there was little anyone could do to hurt him. This was the beginning of a trend, which continued, and his party won the next national elections. Venerable Sumana got the opportunity to wield great political influence and was able to put much of his social reformist program into action. He needed nothing for himself, but he skillfully used this opportunity to help his people. He got new industries started in the village to provide employment to the villagers and found employment for village youth. He worked on heath care for his villagers using the backing of the party in power.

MONK TURNED THERAPIST

Venerable Sumana wore many hats. A young woman visited him with her parents one evening. Having performed the customary rituals in the temple, they were in the waiting room to meet the monk. Customarily a layperson would not sit in the presence of a monk but as a practical compromise law chairs and stools are provided for them in the temple. Venerable Sumana spent time with the family and agreed to speak to the young woman separately.

The parents had arranged a suitable marriage partner for the daughter with the assistance of a professional marriage broker, who had compared their horoscopes to ensure harmonious union focusing on the issues of caste, the social status to determine compatibility, and finally the dowry of the girl. Having decided that everything was satisfactory the marriage was contracted. The man had a good income from a professional job, and they all thought all these factors would make a good marriage and that the girl would be materially comfortable. A few months later Venerable Sumana saw that the girl had returned home. This was a puzzle to the parents, the monk, and many others. He realized the anxiety, shame, and stress that the girl's parents were suffering to have their married daughter come back home. Marriages, especially the arranged ones, are supposed to work and end happily-ever-after. Villagers were curious, it became a topic of conversation and gossip. It is not possible to keep secrets in a village. The girl would not tell her parents the reason for her return, and the new husband claimed that he was cheated into a bad marriage. Sri Lankan society topics related to sex are taboo. The possibility of a sex-related problem was the last thing that came to their minds. It was not normal for a marriage to break up in middle-class society for reasons of sex. Women hardly spoke of the sexual inadequacies of men. In the absence of a child the woman was presumed to be barren and stigmatized. Problems of sex were hidden or patched up. Public scrutiny had to be avoided at all costs.

Venerable Sumana spoke to the girl in a fatherly fashion, and in the end the girl confided in him. The girl was born with deformed sexual organs, and she was never shown to a doctor. This is not unusual in Sri Lanka. Young women do not go to the doctor for gynecological examination. The problem went undetected, and the girl did not have the courage to confide in her parents. Sex was not a topic discussed with parents. Venerable Sumana, through his influential friends, helped the parents to contact a well-known gynecologist, she got necessary treatment, and she went back to her husband. In one of my subsequent visits to Sri Lanka I was told that the marriage was satisfactory, and the couple was blessed with a son.

In conversations with venerable Sumana, I saw another side of his personality. He was rather aggressive and forceful when it came to defending the sasana. Talking about the separatist movement in Sri Lanka he was forthright and stated that it was the right and the duty of the Buddhist monks to defend the Buddha sasana. If the well-being of Buddhism was at risk the monks would not hesitate to take up arms as the last resort.

PATRIOTIC MONK: AN ANCIENT BREED

There were other Buddhist monks who had similar views on politics. Venerable Maduluvave Sobitha was one I knew fairly well. He evoked an image of a fearless monk vowing to protect the country. He often said it was the duty of the monk to come bravely forward to fight injustice. He once told me that the monks had no possessions, no families to protect, no homes, and are committed to serve the country and the sasana. Emphasizing the importance of the interdependence of the Buddhist Sangha and the Sinhala nation, he said that there would be no Buddhist Sangha without the Sinhala race and no Sinhala race without the Buddhist Sangha. Much is written of him as an extreme monk, with violent ideas during the recent ethnic crisis. When I met him in the summer of 2004, there was no violence about him; he was subdued, compassionate, and not too politically active. Had he changed and mellowed over time? Had those fleeting moments of emotion misconstrued as violence defying all logic of reason passed on too?

Venerable Sobita too was invited to the United States as a distinguished guest, and on his journey through America he stayed with us for a brief period. Venerable Sobita was not strictly a political person. Monks, like everybody else in Sri Lanka, are interested in politics. Talking to Venerable Sobitha, who traced the political developments in Sri Lanka with skill and clarity, I felt that it was unreasonable for people to think that Buddhist monks should keep clear of ethnic politics. The anxieties of both monks and laymen were augmented when it became apparent that the major political parties were not disinclined to cut deals with Tamil militants and separatists to further sectarian political interests. Given the fact that the elite elements in Sinhalese society were themselves disinclined to do anything about the acrimonious ethnic issue, the vacuum was filled by Buddhist monks who had (at least for the time being) to abandon their reclusive cloistered ways. The sheer prolongation of the ethnic conflict created in the minds of an articulate anglicized minority the misconception that monks were stepping out of the *vihares* and monasteries to be part of frenetic public protests, rallies, and calls to arms.

Venerable Sobitha in his conversations with me emphasized the difference. The sasana in Sri Lanka (as of old) was a totality. It stood or fell as one single entity. The monks could no longer be passive bystanders but had to be participants in the process. To both Venerable Baddegama Sumana and Venerable Sobitha the archetypical example was Theri Pubbatha, who joined the army of King Dutugamunu but reverted to monkhood after the wars were over and the sasana was saved. Much as I listened to Venerable Sobitha with mounting skepticism, I felt that he had a point. The truth was that postindependent Sri Lanka had failed to produce an activity-involved class of laypeople who (using the advantages of wealth and elitism) were part of the political process.

A MONK'S PRESCRIPTION FOR NATIONAL UNITY

I listened to Venerable Sobitha, fascinated by his imagery and by the force and ardor that were so much part of the man and his speech. When I spoke to him often an outpouring of eloquence was followed by silence as if he was thinking deeply about what he said. After one such spell I asked him to tell me what sort of Sri Lanka he visualized. His answer surprised me and made me also think sadly of how widely he had been misunderstood and misinterpreted. Here then was the truth: Venerable Sobitha, a man of balance and fairness. He said that both the Sinhalese and the Tamils would have to compromise. The Sinhalese should not seek to impose their will on the Tamils by force. This would do great injustice to the rights and aspirations of the Tamils. The Tamils for their part should abandon their dreams of separation, extravagant territorial claims, and their unilateralism. Neither party would be able to have its own way. He made the interesting point that the problem was not the ethnic issue but that of the need to stand up to arbitrary governments in Sri Lanka. The constitutional rights of the people were being violated. Slowly but surely these rights and their human rights were being eroded. Both the Sinhalese and the Tamils were adversely affected by these developments, and the ethnic issue seemed to be providing an excuse and cover for governments to keep on acting unconstitutionally. Venerable Sobitha thought that the enactment of the bill of rights and the creation of a truly independent judiciary that could not be touched by executive authority would bring peace to Sri Lanka. If this were done, the ethnic problem would disappear, and peace would prevail.

FENDING OFF BODILY BLOWS

Venerable Sobitha repeated to me something he had told Ananda on the very first day they met that made me very sad. The government had brutally broken up a huge protest rally in Colombo attended by prominent trade unionists, university professors, and radical monks of Venerable Sobitha's caliber. In the violence that ensued, to the dismay of the countless Sinhalese who loved him, Professor Ediriweera Sarathchandra was beaten, and heavy blows were repeatedly directed at Venerable Sobitha's head. As a result, he has since suffered headaches, dizzy spells, and the inability to sleep through the night. With almost child-like trust he turned to me and asked whether he could have some medical attention before he left the United States. I got in touch with some doctors, but the shortness of his scheduled stay in the United States was a problem. When I met him in my most recent visit to Sri Lanka, he said he was well and did not have the headaches.

The time finally came for Venerable Sobitha to leave us. The afternoon he was to fly to Los Angeles he spoke with great affection to my teenage daughter, Ranmini. I drove him to the airport, and when my daughter and I watched him leave he walked with serenity of purpose and immense dignity. My daughter, watching him disappear, remarked, "From the days of my childhood you spoke to me of the Buddha and told me stories about him. So is this man then a Buddha? If not, who is he?" Looking back I often wondered what the answer to that question might be.

Moving on to more recent events, two days after the tsunami hit Sri Lanka, monks in yellow robes, led by well-known Buddhist monks such as venerable Maduluwawe Sobhitha and others, went on the *pada gamana* (journey by foot) from house to house with their begging bowls to collect alms to the help the victims. A beggar seeing the monks begging for the tsunami victims, said, "Normally I beg, and today the monks are begging," and emptied his collection into the monk's bowl. Monks pledged to build houses for the victims throughout the country from Jaffna to the far south of the island. They declared that the angry sea had given a signal to us that we should do good deeds, avoid enmity, and walk a path of righteousness.

MONK FOR ALL SEASONS

Postcolonial trends and developments in contemporary Buddhism in Sri Lanka may be seen in the order of monks, where one would least expect to see such trends. In the storehouse of things remembered, as I write, I see the clearly defined contours of another charismatic Sri Lankan monk. I saw him in Colombo when my companion and I battled our way through a vast crowd to get as close to the open air stage as was humanly possible. Venerable Gangodavila Soma was to address thousands who had gathered there patiently awaiting him. At first it seemed that Venerable Soma did not have about him the gravitas once associated with Sri Lankan monks of an older generation. He was not diminutive in stature but was big and muscular. Later I was told that he had played rugby for his school, Isipathana Vidyalaya, the other Royal College in Colombo. He smiled genially and was relaxed. In a soft, coaxing voice rising in measured cadence, he spoke clearly and was soon the master of the situation and all that he surveyed. He was an altogether remarkable man. Unfortunately, his life was cut short prematurely under dubious circumstances, involving veiled hints at dark and demonic forces.

Soma was born in 1948 and was ordained in 1974 at the age of twenty-six and as if by *sasara purudda* (those subtle inclinations of the mind that prompt us to do in life what we really wish to) was attracted to the temple and the ambience of things associated with Buddhism. He came under the influence of two well-known Sri Lankan monks, his mentors, Venerable Madihe Pannnaseeha and Venerable Ampitiye Rahula; men of stature in an older world of Sri Lankan Buddhism. For a short time he was a lay preacher, a period of apprenticeship that gave him the initial skills and training to become an eloquent monk, but with a remarkable penchant for clarity of speech. Later listening to many of his numerous recorded sermons on CDs and audio cassettes it was clear that he was setting his sights on retraining and retooling Sinhala Buddhists to reflect on the basics of Buddhism. He often drew attention to the simple formularies of Buddhist worship, such as taking refuge in the Triple Gem and taking the Five Precepts, to see their true intrinsic depths of meaning rather than to treat them casually as a prelude to Buddhist rituals that followed. His message was that as Buddhists, one did not need to turn to any higher power, as Buddha has shown the way to peace and contentment through the dharma. After he was ordained, this was a conscious theme. His purpose was to create a new level of individual and collective Buddhist consciousness.

The conspicuous element in his formal sermons and in the vast informal network of lay connections he had built up was to gently chastise the Buddhists, especially the influential and articulate urban segments, for mixing up Buddhism with Hindu rituals and the popular cult of Sai Baba. No monk in recent times in the monasteries in Colombo and greater Colombo, who were dependent on middle-class Buddhist support, had dared to touch on this sensitive area so evident among upper middle-class Buddhists. Venerable Soma's mission was to make society a better place in which to live. He explained that by following the Five Precepts people could lead simple, ethical lives and he emphasized how easy it was to follow the Five Precepts.

The turning point in the life of this remarkable monk came when he made a casual visit to Australia in 1989 and remained there till 1996. In Australia, dealing with expatriate Sri Lankans, and increasing numbers of Australians, his work took on more enduring, instutionalized forms leading to the serious study of Buddhism and the disciplining mores of its practice. Like other erudite monks before him, especially Venerable Piyadassi and Venerable Walpola Rahula, he felt that the Western mind, uncluttered by worldly oriented rituals, would see Buddhism with greater clarity and insight.

But fate (if that is the word for it) once more took a hand in the monk's life when he returned to Sri Lanka in 1996 to be with his ailing parents, especially his father, who had been ill for a long period. He stayed on in Sri Lanka longer than expected, returned to Australia briefly, but returned to Sri Lanka where he remained until his death. While in Sri Lanka, Venerable Soma became aware that Buddhists and the dharma were under siege from various outside influences. He was deeply moved by the plight of the rural people, especially those living in areas under threat from terrorist attack. To support and sustain the villages, he organized the local Buddhist monks at the village temples to help the villagers in various ways. In Australia he launched a campaign to finance the rehabilitation of village water tanks and irrigational canals on which the village rice cultivation depended. He worked tirelessly in Sri Lanka to awaken the nation, especially the younger generation, to Buddhist teachings. He traveled widely and everywhere he went his sermons were well attended.

It was widely believed by the Buddhists that there were widespread conversions brought by Christian missionaries, easily gaining entry into the country as part of foreign-funded NGOs (non governmental organizations), and that the fundamental evangelical movements in the United States directed this newly inspired Christian missionary thrust into Sri Lanka. Their open and brash activities of conversion by offering financial aid to complete half-done houses, private education, and extensive medical aid to the poor and needy in the rural areas, caused widespread concern among other religious groups especially among the Buddhists. The new converts were locally termed "rice Christians," a term by which Christian converts had been known in South East Asia in the nineteenth century.

Aware of these widespread Buddhist concerns Venerable Soma virtually decided to abandon his activities in Australia and focus on the problem of neo-Christian proselytization. He raised the level of Buddhist consciousness. He was forthright and active in his denunciation and infused almost a sense of militancy in the ranks of Buddhists. He used his enormous charisma during the last five years to raise the level of collective consciousness about neo-evangelical influences in Sri Lanka. Departing from his somewhat idiosyncratic views and practices, which interestingly characterized his activities on this particular issue, he made common cause with active, politically-minded Buddhist monks, especially in the Colombo area, who were organized in their opposition against the thrust of evangelical conversion. In the process he created powerful enemies. He met an untimely death in St. Petersburg, Russia, where he had gone to a conference sponsored by a Christian interfaith organization. Buddhists all over the world were shocked and deeply grieved.

Venerable Ellawela Medhananda, representing the largest sect of Buddhist monks in Sri Lanka, the Siyam Nikaya, delivered the funeral oration at the cremation of Venerable Soma. He accused the Ranil Wickremesinghe government for failing to introduce legislation in Parliament to prevent what he termed "unethical and immoral" conversions by foreign-aided Christian fundamentalists, despite repeated requests made by the monks. He said that the government should take the responsibility for its inaction, which had led indirectly to the death of Venerable Soma. He reminded the audience that it was the duty of the government to protect Buddhism, monks, and the laity of the country. On behalf of the Buddhists of Sri Lanka he demanded that a committee be appointed to investigate the death of Venerable Soma. The fact that this was not done increased the angst of Sri Lankan Buddhists. The unresolved passing away of Venerable Soma was followed by skepticism, doubt, and endless speculation.

An epitaph of sorts was best expressed by a columnist writing in the popular English newspaper the *Island*, in December 2003: "Today all the streets are saffron colored. There was no street, lane or by-lane from which an orange colored flag does not flutter . . . every street, every town, every vehicle, every home, every dirt track in every village"—the sad decorations abounded. The writer added that a saffron flag fluttered in his own heart and that he was inspired to humbly study Buddhism all over again and thereby reorient himself as a worthy person.

SIXTEEN

Quid Pro Quo Worship

Kali the mother:
O terrible and tender and divine
O mystic mother of the sacrifice
We deck the somber altars of thy shrine
With sacred basil leaves and saffron rice
All gifts of life and death we bring to thee.

—Sarojini Naidu

A TRYST WITH A GODDESS AT DAWN

IT WAS MY AUNT'S HOUSE. At 5.30 A.M. on a Wednesday, a *kemmura* day, an auspicious day for the gods, there was confusion in the house. To those who worship gods in Sri Lanka, Wednesdays and Saturdays are days of special sanctity. It is widely believed that on these days, the power of the gods is most felt arising out of their personal presence. My aunt and her entourage were going to Puttalam (a place about forty miles from Colombo to the Kali temple popularly known as the Muneswaram *devale*) to make a special offering to the goddess Kali. Here more than elsewhere, the living presence of Kali is felt. As I discussed earlier, my aunt was a good Buddhist, who observed *sil* on *poya* days and had a shrine room in the house where she worshipped the Buddha. As always for religious offerings, she was preparing for this journey with devotion. Since I was to go with her, I had a cold bath and dressed appropriately, in a long skirt. I wore my sandals, as no foot coverings were allowed in places of worship, and sandals were easy to pull off. No one talked much as they were concentrating on the journey ahead. Getting there on time for the *puja* was uppermost in everyone's mind. Servants had gathered white and colored flowers, arranged in trays. There were bottles of coconut oil and trays of fruit prepared carefully for the *puja*. Later I learned that this was to make a *bharaya* (vow) to goddess Kali, invoking her blessings, to enable the family to find a suitable groom for my aunt's daughter, who was of a marriageable age. There were many suitors, but my aunt thought it best to seek the help of the goddess Kali to get the very best.

PARADOX OF GODS IN BUDDHISM

Sri Lankan Buddhists have a complicated systems of beliefs, which are confusing to even those who are bred within the tradition. In times of despair they pray for help from many gods and goddesses. Beliefs vary from village to urban areas and among different social classes.

During his lifetime, the Buddha attained extraordinary supranormal powers, through Enlightenment. Having attained Enlightenment, he preached the Four Noble Truths, focusing in particular on suffering and its cause and the way to end suffering, the middle path for righteous living. He emphasized transcendence and rigorous self-reliance as means of salvation. He showed the way to nirvana, the final redemption, by eradicating craving and attachments and thus ending suffering. However, to the vast majority of his followers, nirvana is an ultimate and not a proximate ideal to be attained in a single lifetime.

The Buddha was not a suprahuman being. Buddhists do not have a god that they can appeal to in prayer over the day-to-day difficulties in life such as when they need a good harvest, a good wife, good health, a job, a child, or economic prosperity. Ordinary people have a need to appeal to a higher power for assistance in times of despair. In the Buddhist pantheon, there are many gods with higher powers with specific agendas ready to help those who seek their help. I often wondered if at some point in Buddhist history the Buddha was exalted to the position of a god—a superhuman figure in the full sense of the term or analogous to God in the Christian sense—whether the gods of the Buddhist pantheon would be rendered redundant. In the Judeo-Christian tradition, one can appeal to a suprahuman God. In Christianity, although Jesus Christ was born, lived, and died as an ordinary person like the Buddha, Jesus emphasized the divine nature of his origin and the truth of salvation. His own resurrection and ascent to heaven were the ultimate irrefutable proof of his teachings. Christians are bonded by the seal of heaven. As a result in the ultimate analysis there is a divine God to whom one can pray. This divine God is merciful and forgiving and can be accessed for help in difficult times.

HOW BUDDHISTS RELATE TO HINDU GODS

To my Christian friends in America, the belief in God is paramount. In conversations, if you are not a believer in God, you can be regarded as an inferior being. The importance of the belief in God is even conceptually equated with law and order. Many people cannot comprehend that Buddhists though "nonbelievers" have clearly defined notions of morality.

In the practice of Buddhism in Sri Lanka, the day-to-day observances broadly fall into two major categories. There are the *laukika* (worldly) practices, the observances for survival in this world, and there are the *lokottara* practices, the acts for the next world, for ultimate salvation. I will discuss here some *laukika* practices and beliefs of the Buddhists.

Sri Lankan Buddhists, like the Hindus, have no one god; they pray to and seek comfort and refuge from various gods and deities in difficult times. Those who go to the temple on *poya* days to worship the Buddha make visits to the *devale* (house of gods) that is attached to the temple. Devotees take white, fragrant flowers such as jasmine, sepalika, and frangipani to offer to the Buddha in worship, blue flowers to the Vishnu *devale*, and red flowers to the Kataragama devale. Flowers are taken to the shrine of the Buddha, and bowls of fruit are taken to the *devale*. The Buddha *puja*, the symbolic meal offered to the Buddha, is not eaten after the ceremony. By contrast when food is offered to gods, *devapuja*, a part is returned, by the *kapurala* to the devotees (*prasad*) charged with special powers, and is considered healing to eat, blessed by the *devas* (gods). Devotees first worship the Buddha by taking *pansil*, with the offering of flowers. Having done so, they go to the *devale* to transfer merit to the *devas* and ask for their blessings. None of this is a contradiction. Two systems exist side by side, complementing each other.

GOD WORSHIP IS QUID PRO QUO

Over the years Buddhists have incorporated various gods into their belief system, which has enriched the practice of Buddhism in Sri Lanka, making it colorful and interesting. Buddhists pray to gods and deities for worldly help in times of despair, in sickness for a quick recovery, for justice when injustice is done, and many more mundane things. In the study of religion, it becomes clear crossculturally that when people ask gods for this or that they make in effect a legal contract, a quid pro quo between themselves and the gods. It is presumed as fact that the divine party to the contract consents. Robert Knox puts the point well.

> Sometimes in their sickness they go to the house of their Gods with offering, with which they present him in entreating his favor and aid to restore

them to health. Upon the recovery whereof they promise him not to fail but
to give unto His Majesty (for so they entitle him) for greater gifts or rewards,
and what they are, they do particularly mention; it may be land, a slave, cat-
tle, money cloth, etc. . . . If after this he fails on his part, and cannot restore
them to their health, then the fore-promised things are to remain there
where they were: and instead of which perhaps he gets a curse, saying, He
doth but cheat and deceive them. (Knox 1958:132)

THE INTERMEDIARY
BETWEEN GODS AND OURSELVES

Offerings to gods take the form of flowers, trays of fruit, milk rice, or monetary contributions. In worshipping the Buddha no middle man is required, but
the gods are generally contacted through an intermediary, a *kapurala* (lay
priest, always male) who is presumed to have special contact with the god and
knows the language and the ways of the gods, being in constant service to
them. The *kapurala* is mostly a hereditary position endowed with lands
belonging to the *devale*, for his upkeep. The *kapurala* has exclusive privileges
in entering the inner sanctum of the *devale*, thereby claiming special contact
with the gods. A *kapurala* is therefore respected for his unique position and
also feared for his powers. His services require an undetermined fee, and in
return he makes incantations with offerings on behalf of the devotees, in a
special language and style. Anyone who wishes to be associated with the blessings is required to give a *paduru* (offering) which entitles the worshipper to be
mentioned in the *kannalavva* (invocation) to the god for his welfare. The
invocation takes the form of eulogies addressed to the resident deity followed
by the recitation of the particular problem. Rich devotees give large amounts
of money, conspicuously displayed in the *puja* trays to the *kapurala*. The belief
is that if more is offered in the form of *pujas*, greater rewards can be expected
from the gods. The extent and value of the offerings depend on the ability of
the giver, but something must be given to get something.

Apart from promises to the gods in kind, the devotees engage in various
acts of merit they confer to the gods: lighting lamps around a Bo tree in the
premises and giving *dana* to beggars and other pilgrims. Some resort to acts of
sacrifice and penance in exchange for help. The rich and the poor, high and
low, men and women of all religions seek the assistance of the gods in Sri
Lanka. All forms of offerings are accepted, and favors are granted without discrimination, so the faithful believe. In actuality there is little egalitarianism
here. The rich and powerful enter the *devale* through the back door or get special *puja* opportunities and *darshan* of the gods. *Kapuralas* make exceptions to
accommodate them, while the poor stand in lines in the tropical sun and monsoon rains, with patience waiting their turn to get into the sanctum sanctorum.

The gods the Buddhists pray to are below the status of the Buddha. They are not immortal beings. They are mythological persons, once human, who by acquiring merit have became *devas*. While they remain *devas* they supercede humans in power and longevity but are also finally subject to birth and death. Although they possess suprahuman powers while they remain gods, ironically they do not have the advantages of human beings, either to do meritorious deeds or to reach nirvana. Although the *devas* possess power, they are themselves ultimately subject to birth and death and have to be born as human beings to attain nirvana. The rationale is interesting. In spite of the ambrosial delights the gods or *devas* enjoy, it is only in the human condition that they could understand suffering and set about achieving self-transcendence leading to salvation.

Devas help humans and in return expect merit to be given to them to maintain their superior position. The good and virtuous get the help of the gods, hence those who tread the holy path have the good will of the gods. The benevolence of the deities also takes the form of protecting those who follow the teachings of the Buddha and those who lead a spiritual life in general. This is also a subtle form of quid pro quo. Buddhists pray to the multitude of gods of Sri Lanka collectively, to evoke blessings by reciting this popular prayer.

Sidda kihirali saman boksal vibhisana siv varan rajanithi
Sidda mahababu sacra isivara kataragama devi yanuth sithaaruthi
Sidda pattini dolaha deviyo badra kali devi ganapathi
Sidda sirilaka mehama deviyo memata asiri laba den nithi

May the blessing of the gods, Vishnu, Saman, Boksal, Vibishana and
    the four gods who protect the four corners of the earth,
along with the most powerful Lord Brahma, god of gods the Sakra,
    Ishvara, and the most beloved Lord Kataragama;
Well meaning goddess Pattini along with the twelve gods, Badrakali
    and none other than the Devi Gamapathi,
May all these benevolent Gods of Sri Lanka bless me eternally and
    keep me well.

In addition to helping humans, the gods are presumed to safeguard the Buddha *sasana*, the state of Buddhism and all that it encompasses. In Sri Lanka there are four major protectors of the Buddha *sasana*: *Vishnu, Kataragama, Saman, and Vibhisana*. Sri Lanka is divided into four precincts for the four *devas*.

GODS ARE GOOD FOR BUSINESS

Sometimes the *pujas* to the deities take a simple form. The gods are where one's heart is, as it were. The owner of a small grocery store or tea shop, for example, chooses a suitable place in the premises for a statue of the Buddha or a picture of a deity, thus creating a miniature shrine, often over the cash counter. Each morning the owner offers flowers, fruit, and incense while uttering mantras or *gathas*, invoking the blessings of the gods. (Incense powder is burnt over hot coal to make smoke. This smoke is held over the shrine and at the entrance to the shop to drive away the bad spirits and bring in good fortune. This is a common sight before beginning the business of the day. It is a reminder to the gods to protect the business, and in return the *pujas* are offered.) When we were children, Edwin, our trusted servant, told us how the local undertaker made a little prayer offering to his gods, which was placed above his cash register.

My mind travels to Thailand's omnipresent spirit houses. Beautiful young Thai women and men daily offer water, food, and flowers to the spirit houses before leaving for work.

The Hindu god Vishnu is respected and venerated as the guardian deity of Sri Lanka, entrusted with the task, by Sakka, the god of gods. Many legends are associated with Vishnu, and many shrines are dedicated to him in various parts of the country. Vishnu is considered the god of home and hearth and the protector of the Buddha *sasana*, representing mercy and goodness, stability and order. He is a benign god but wields enormous power. Politicians, the rich and the famous who have much to lose, and the mobility conscious bourgeoisie are his patrons. The poor also pray to Vishnu to cure the sick or ward off the effects of malefic planets.

THE ICONOGRAPHY OF THE GODS

Vishnu is the color of the blue lotus and carries four symbols in his four hands—the discus, conch, club, and lotus. The discus and club are weapons signifying the might of Vishnu in destroying evil. The lotus represents fertility and regeneration, which occurs through devotion to the deity. The conch symbolizes purity and auspiciousness. Vishnu's wife, Lakshmi, is the goddess of abundance and prosperity. The legend has it that Lakshmi was born out of the sea of milk, the cosmic ocean, bearing a red lotus in her hand. She is depicted standing on a lotus and holding lotuses in her hands. Each member of the divine triad—Brahma, the creator, Vishnu, the preserver, and Shiva the destroyer—wanted to have Lakshmi for himself. Shiva's claim was refused as he had already claimed the moon, and Brahma had Sarasvati, so Vishnu got Lakshmi. Often she is shown residing on his chest, showing their eternal connection. She is the center of Vishnu's life, the fortune of his heart. Lakshmi's four hands represent four spiritual virtues and are always extended in blessing. Sri Lankans, like the Hindus in India, believe that Lakshmi personifies good fortune and wealth and make *pujas* for her.

THE POWERS OF KALI

Kali is encountered in many guises. Kali, also referred to as Bhadrakali is believed to end what is bad and restore justice. In Sri Lanka, Kali is seen as an entirely benign and helpful goddess, in contrast to Kali of Kerala in South India or Bengal who possesses terrifying demonic powers. The concept of 'kali maniyo' (mother) is prevalent in Sri Lanka, and devotional practice denotes a gentle disposition. Generally Kali's help is requested to punish misdeeds, as she is perceived as the destructor of evil. Buddhists do not worship Kali on a regular basis. She is normally sought after, more or less on an ad hoc basis, in times of need. Although her appearance seems frightening, Buddhists who worship Kali do not consider her fearful. She is depicted with matted hair, carrying a sacrificed animal in one hand and a sword in the other, wearing a garland of decapitated human heads. She is mother all the same because she comes to the aid of the injured, to maintain justice, and especially to women who need help.

My oldest sister is a devotee of Kali and believes that whatever she asks is granted. The main temple for Kali in Sri Lanka is in Munneswaram near Puttlam, a city about fifty miles from Colombo. Festivities for Kali are held in July. I once accompanied my sister during the festival time to the place where the American film *Indiana Jones* was made in the 1980s. One scene in the film attempted to depict extravagant Kali worship in South Asia. Devotees in large numbers from all over Sri Lanka belonging to different faiths gather here to pray to Kali during this special time, as it is believed to be the most effective time to get favors. The month-long festivities include Rambadeema, where devotees shoot at a banana tree specially erected near the temple for the festival, and they eat the pieces of banana for blessings. This act celebrates goddess Kali's victory over evil. At the end of the festivities two chariots of the gods are taken through the city streets to the Deduru River, and the statues are immersed in the waters as a ritual bathing before they are taken back to the *devale*.

Darshan also makes the images of the goddess Kali important to devotees. *Darshan* (seeing) the image of the deity in a devotional way does not merely mean using one's eyes, but it is also a dynamic act of awareness beyond the act of mere seeing. By the ritual *darshan* Kali bestows blessings upon the worshippers. By seeing Kali, the devotees have made themselves receptive to the transfer of her grace. Devotees believe that Kali blesses each person individually even in the midst a great concourse.

Devotees often appeal to Kali to punish a wrong doer, in the belief that she is a just goddess and will punish only those who deserve punishment. Her punishment is swift. My friend Sumana, an upper middle-class woman, appealed to Kali for help in breaking the association of her only son with a girl who belonged to a lower caste and was therefore socially incompatible and perceived as evil. For Sumana, her son deserved the best and a marriage contracted ideally only with her approval. Sumana did not consider the feelings of the other party. Kali simply had to do justice and save her son. In return she promised many offerings of value to Kali. Sometimes devotees consumed with anger ask Kali for punishment of others with vengeance.

AS FAR AS THE MIDDLE EAST

With the large-scale egress of young Sri Lankan women seeking employment as domestic servants in Middle Eastern countries, there has been an increase in the number of people going to Kali for help. They make vows for the success of their venture and safe return. They believe that Kali gives quick results and positive solutions to problems. Many who want to find employment abroad are cheated by organizations promising to get good employment for a fee but disappear with their money. Often they are poor people. Young women pray for a kind master and mistress, aware of the documented dangers that befall those who go to the Middle East for employment. They also visit Kali to repay her upon receiving their first salary. In their absence a close relative often fulfils the obligation.

THE GENTLE GODDESS PATTINI

Pattini, by contrast a kinder and gentler goddess, is also popular in Buddhist worship. There are many *devales* for Pattini scattered throughout the country. The best known is in Navagamuwa, about twenty-five kilometers from Colombo. Women in particular seek Pattini's *pihita* (help) as she is kind and understands their problems. Women who have difficulty conceiving look to her for help. Devotees also go to Pattini in times of infectious diseases such as chicken pox and measles.

An important ritual connected with Pattini is *gammadu*, a harvest festival. The first portion of the paddy harvest is offered to the goddess to get rid of evil influences, attain prosperity, and guarantee fair harvests in the future. The *gammadu* ritual differs from region to region. I witnessed the ceremony at my aunt's house during the Sinhala New Year. In the ritual, the farmers reward the gods for allowing a bountiful harvest. Paddy is the staple crop of the Sri Lankan villagers and is treated with great respect. Gathering paddy after the harvest is a communal effort.

Near the Buddhist temple in the village, a special place was prepared with the construction of a *thorana*, a simple pandal of sorts. It was built with banana trunks and decorated with young coconut leaves. Many types of bright-colored flowers were hung to make it festive. The traditions and forms of the ceremony familiar to the villagers were carefully adhered to. A fire was made under the *thorana* to boil milk in a new clay pot. The boiling milk was allowed to overflow in all directions throughout the night for good luck. Dancers performed in the name of Pattini, and offerings were made. With beating drums the dancing went on until dawn. The Pattini *devale kapurala* came to grace the occasion dressed in white to represent the goddess, wearing the traditional *padasalaba* (foot ornament) associated with the goddess. This foot ornament, or anklet, made a soft ringing sound as the *kapurala* moved around. Villagers sat on the ground, around the thorana to watch the performances. The traditional *kiribath* was made, using some of the milk from the boiling pot. After offering it to the gods and the monks, it was shared by everyone else.

THE STORY OF A GOLDEN ANKLET

There are several colorful legends associated with Pattini. The story about her unswerving fidelity to her fickle husband is popular. In Kerala, India, a daughter named Kannagi was born to a rich and high-caste family. When she came of age she was given in marriage to Kovalan, a wealthy man also of a high caste. Although Kannagi agreed to marry the man to conform to custom, she decided to remain pure and chaste. She would not have any sexual relations with her husband. There is also the legend that she was born out of a mango and therefore could not satisfy the desires of a man. For whatever reason Kovalan turned to a mistress called Madavi. After wasting all his wealth indulging in an extravagant lifestyle, he decided to return to his wife. Kannagi received him with love and affection in spite of his adulterous behavior. They were now poor, and as a last resort she gave Kovalan a gold anklet to sell.

Kovalan took the gold anklet and promised to return in a few days. Strangely, at this time, the queen of the country had lost her gold anklet and was offering a handsome reward for its recovery. Kovalan, unaware of this, took the anklet to the goldsmith. The goldsmith thought that it was the queen's missing gold anklet and took it to the queen to get the reward. The king inquired about the incident and decided to put Kovalan to death, believing he was the thief. Kovalan was to be hanged under the *kohomba* (margosa) tree, which is associated with sanctity.

Kannagi, having waited in vain for her husband's return, ventured out in search of him. On her way she came to a river that she had to cross. But the king, having heard of her search for Kovalan, had instructed the boatman not to take her across. Thereupon she prayed to the gods and the deities in heaven and dropped her ring into the water. The water miraculously parted, making a path so she could cross to the other side. Later the boatman, who was stricken with smallpox, appealed to Kannagi for help, who with great compassion cured him.

Finally Kannagi arrived at the scene where her husband was put to death. She found the dead body and wept bitterly, appealing to the gods. Due to the

power of her chastity and her faithfulness to her husband, Kovalan was miraculously brought back to life. (Chastity and purity are associated with the goddess Pattini. When a woman is chaste, she is compared to Pattini in local
usage. When a woman is unfaithful to her husband, it is said that she is no
Pattini.) When Kovalan came to life he asked for his mistress, Madavi, which
angered the everpatient, loving Kannagi. She denounced him with passion. It
is said that the *kohomba* tree made an opening and swallowed up Kovalan.
Since Kannagi failed to get the blessings of her husband and was disrespectful to him she did not become a god, in the preferred male form, instead she
went to heaven to be born as a goddess.

People pray to Pattini for help when an infectious disease breaks out. I
have described elsewhere the *dana* traditionally given to seven mothers in her
name after such illnesses. Leaves of the *kohomba* tree are used in connection
with infectious diseases. A paste is made of kohoba leaves and turmeric. This
mixture is supposed to heal sores and make scars disappear.

HOW GOD GANESH GOT AN ELEPHANT'S HEAD

Then there is the legend of the elephant god Ganesh, brother of Kataragama
and son of Shiva. My daughter, Ranmini, who was taken to Kataragama, as a
three year old, was unusually curious and spouted a fountain of questions on
everything on which she laid her eyes. Nothing escaped her observation. Having attended the *puja* in the Kataragama *devale*, she was tired from the noise
of the brass bells, the heat from the lamps, and the crowds. I carried her on
my hip, the way Sri Lankan villagers carried their children. (The Sinhalese
culture says that Brahma, the creator, endowed women with broad hips, to
carry children.)

The Ganesh *devale* is connected to the *devale* of God Kataragama.
Ganesh is the remover of obstacles. Ranmini, fascinated by the appearance
of Ganesh, loudly asked me, "How can the god have an elephant's head and
so many heads and multiple hands?" She believed that I had answers to all
her questions. I promised to tell her about this later, which made her silent
for a while.

I had heard many fascinating stories, each differing from the other, about
how Ganesh got an elephant's head. I took her out of the *devale* and sat under
the shade of the Bo tree with her on my lap to tell her the story. The great god
Shiva, father of Ganesh, one day left the house on an errand. His consort, Parvati, was instructed not to leave the house or let anyone come during his
absence. However, he was late returning. Parvati could wait no longer and
went to the nearby pond to have a bath. She created a handsome young man
to look after the house in her absence. She gave him a rod for protection and
instructed him not to let anyone enter the house.

In the meantime Shiva returned, and he could not find his wife. Instead he saw the handsome man guarding the door. Shiva instructed the man to open the door. The guard refused, saying that the owner was away. The guard shouted at Shiva, "If you want to save your life do not move any further." Shiva, annoyed, hit the guard with the sword, separating his head from his body. When Parvati returned she was saddened by the sight of her mind-born son in a pool of blood. Shiva told her what happened, and Parvati was angry. She went to her chamber and declared that she would not speak to Shiva until he found a head for her created son. Shiva was worried and sent his generals all over to find a head for the son of Parvati. Generals, having searched everywhere, saw an elephant sleeping near a pond. They stealthily approached the elephant, severed its head, and brought it to Shiva. Shiva was impressed and fixed it on the body of the guard. This is how Ganesh came to have an elephant's head. Ranmini, amused by the story, fell asleep on my lap, sucking her thumb.

Ganesh is worshipped by devotees as the god who provides knowledge to those who seek it, prosperity to those who ask, and spiritual elevation to all. Ganesh is associated with wisdom. Vows are made to Ganesh, and his blessings are evoked before sitting for exams. Devotees seek his blessings for every passage of life, birth, marriage, and business enterprises or even before leaving home on a daily journey. Ganesh is a remover of obstacles, and in general he rewards his devotees with blessings from material prosperity to spiritual enlightenment.

The Hindus, in the dry areas of Sri Lanka, also worship Ganesh in the *kovil* (temple). In these areas of the country people depend on rain, and its absence makes any type of cultivation difficult. Hindus make offerings in the *kovil* for rain and a good harvest. When the rain fails to come, in spite of the offerings, the angry and desperate villagers take the statute of Ganesh from the *kovil* and throw it in the reservoir. When the rain comes the statue is brought back bathed and is ceremonially reinstated.

A GOD WHO IS THE MONARCH OF ALL HE SURVEYS

Saman is a popular god worshipped by Sri Lankan Buddhists. His *adawiya* (territorial power) and blessings are most potent in the Sabaragamuwa province, an area in the southeastern part of Sri Lanka bordering the central highlands. Legend has it that the Saman *devale* was built in 1270 by a minister who came to this district to carry out a gem-mining project for the king. His first steps were fruitless, and he was advised by the villagers to make a vow to Saman where the present *devale* stands. Ratnapura, the city of gems, is the capital city in this province and famous for gem mining. Many who mine gems make vows and *pujas* to Saman. My mother had many relatives in this area, some of whom were engaged in the lucrative trade of mining and trading in gems. Many became wealthy by buying gems for a relatively small sum of money from miners and in turn selling them to merchants in the city who resold them for enormous profits. This was also done in the name of Saman and with his *pihita* (help). Saman helped and blessed all parties to make money.

SAI BABA IN SRI LANKA

Apart from traditional beliefs and worship systems, there are more recent phenomena, which have infiltrated into Buddhist extrareligious worship systems. One such belief is the faith in the Indian *sadu* Sai Baba. Many Sri Lankans worship Sai Baba. Sai Baba's popularity in Sri Lanka makes him a serious competitor to the god Kataragama. Sai Baba worship, essentially a middle-class phenomenon, has not yet spread to the lower classes or rural areas of Sri Lanka.

In some ways Sai Baba is different from the gods and deities to whom some Buddhists pray. Sai Baba is a living and breathing human being with supernatural powers. All the gods and goddesses to whom I have already referred are mythological characters not visible to the devotees, borrowed from the Hindu pantheon, and given local identity. The worship of Sai Baba is also quid pro quo in nature, with a difference. In exchange for devotion and prayer, miraculous favors are solicited. Sai Baba is worshipped on a regular basis for continuous help with weekly prayer meetings and devotional songs, along with regular visits to Puttapathi.

Sai Baba may well be among the most revered spiritual teachers in the world today. His followers come from all faiths and races and meet regularly for devotional singing and to study his teachings and engage in services in order to practice his teachings. His message to the world is love, peace, and unity.

Sai Baba, also known as Sathya Sai Baba, was born on 1926 in the village of Puttapathi in Andhra Pradesh, in South India. He was named Satyanarayana, and his family name was Raju. At fourteen he claimed to be the incarnation of an Indian saint and demonstrated extraordinary powers. He has exceptional qualities of wisdom, compassion, and generosity. At fourteen he changed his name to Sathya Sai Baba and proclaimed his mission: "To bring about the spiritual regeneration of humanity by demonstrating and teaching the highest principles of truth, right conduct, peace, love, and nonviolence." He left his childhood home and started work on his mission. He soon began to be known for miracles, materializing objects, and especially *vibuthi*, the holy ash endowed with magical powers that he causes to materialize out of nowhere. He assists people in distress and refers to his miracles as his "calling cards."

There are over 6 million devotees all over the world who revere him. In 1950, his devotees built a temple and residential quarters about a mile away from his birthplace. This *ashram* accommodates and feeds many thousands of devotees from all over the world. Under his patronage and care, the village has a well-equipped hospital, a high-quality school, and other facilities.

Sai Baba has his devoted worshippers in Sri Lanka, too. With political instability, lack of employment for the educated, and growing poverty, Sri Lankans seek the miraculous powers and healing ability of Sai Baba. Many in distress and ill health, having failed traditional means of help, make the pilgrimage to Bangalore for his help. Sai Baba devotees have immense faith in his ability to perform miraculous cures and assist them.

HOW SAI BABA HANDLED A HUMAN SITUATION

My first encounter with Sai Baba devotees was in 1975 when I was teaching in Kandy. Nanda, an elegant woman I knew, was married to a divorcee and had three children. Two of her children were born with deformities. She was a devoted mother and worried a great deal about the future of her deformed children and did everything to try to remedy their suffering, involving Bodhi *pujas* and regular trips to Kataragama. She did not realize that she was asking something that the gods were unable to grant. Other staff members blamed the misfortune on her bad karma for having married a man who had to leave his wife and children from the previous marriage.

She became a Sai Baba devotee and made a trip to Puttapathi. She was not someone important enough to get a special interview. *Darshan* is a special "seeing" of Sai Baba, where he calls the names of a few in the vast sea of his devotees each day, for a special blessing. *Darshan* gives the devotee a chance to get in close proximity to Sai Baba. This is what all devotees pray for in earnest and is generally reserved for politicians and influential delegations. On Nanda's visit to Sai Baba, she did all that was required of her and sat among the thousands of devotees waiting and praying to Sai Baba for recognition and assistance. She was awaiting a miracle.

She described her experience. An impressive and compassionate figure in yellow robes appeared before the crowd. The devotees were elated, cried out in devotion, breaking the absolute silence. Suddenly from nowhere he called out Nanda's name giving all the details of her hometown, her life, and the purpose of her visit. To Nanda, this was the miracle of which she had dreamed. She hurriedly, as in a dream, made her way to him. He made materialize some pendants and gave her holy ash (*vibhuti*). When he put his hand over her head and blessed her, she felt a surge of energy going through her entire body and felt suddenly empowered and relieved. She felt her pain was gone, and she was given strength.

However, Nanda did not get what she wanted. A cure for her children was something that was impossible. What she received from the blessed saint was inner peace, strength to deal with her predicament, and a feeling that she was never alone, that Sai Baba was with her all the time, looking over her. What she got from the saint was the power and ability to bear her cross with dignity and strength. This experience changed her life. She became composed and went about her daily routine with vigor and faith. She went to pay homage to Sai Baba every year and joined the local chanting groups.

Since then I have heard many stories of miracles performed by the great saint and his telepathic knowledge of his devotees' doings. I have heard stories from Sri Lankans about advice they received on professional matters and countless small objects and holy ash he made materialize for his devotees, along with instances of paranormal healings.

Some devotees of Sai Baba combined the daily Buddhist practices of worshipping the Buddha with the devotional practices of Sai Baba. After Buddha worship they sang hymns to Sai Baba, incorporating the view that Sai Baba was the Buddhist god Natha. Some urban Buddhists have private shrine rooms where they sing devotional hymns, the *bhajan*, to Sai Baba in praise of him. Some others conduct group prayer sessions in their homes regularly.

Well-known Buddhists have turned their shrine rooms into Sai Baba worship places. Ananda and I once visited the residence of the Sri Lankan ambassador in Washington, DC, whom we had known for many years. He was well known as a good Buddhist and a philanthropist. He took me to see his shrine room, which was different from many other Buddhist shrine rooms. The Buddha statute was on a lower level, and the entire room was filled with colorful pictures of Sai Baba and the many items he had acquired from his numerous visits to Puttapathi. The ambassador told me amazing stories and miracles he had witnessed.

I met a Sri Lankan cabinet minister at a social gathering. He was a practicing Christian but visited Sai Baba on a regular basis. Being a high-ranking government official, when he visited Puttaparti he got a special interview session. The minister had an exquisite diamond ring on his finger, which he said Sai Baba had made materialize on one of his visits, with specific instructions to wear it at all times for protection. When I met him at a party in summer 2005, he did not have the ring. I asked him what happened to the ring, and he said he threw it away. He added that he became a born again Christian and believed in only one God. Things do change.

SAI BABA: AN INSIDER PERSPECTIVE

I was traveling to Rockford, Illinois to a friend's place to dinner one evening with Dr. Asokan and his wife Mali. Dr. Asokan specializes in radiology; he and his wife were known in the community for their social work. They were devotees of Sai Baba, and Asokan volunteered in Sai Baba's hospital in Puttaparti on a regular basis for two to three weeks every year. I asked about Asokan's recent trip to Puttaparti. He told me that before breakfast, Sai Baba met with the doctors and discussed the news of the hospital and the condition of the patients. Sai Baba was well acquainted with the conditions of almost all patients in his hospital, although he did not frequent the place. In the course of discussion Sai Baba suggested medications and remedies for certain patients and changes in the prescribed medication for a more effective cure. Apparently, the patients responded well to Sai Baba's treatments. I asked Asokan if Sai Baba was a medical doctor and if not how he came to such medical decisions. Asokan replied that Sai Baba knew everything with his divine knowledge.

THE PARADOX OF IT ALL!

We were invited to a New Year's party in London to celebrate the millennium. I went with my brother and his English wife. Most of the guests were vegetarians because they were Sai Baba devotees, including the host. They were also Buddhists. The conversation always turned to Sai Baba. The guests were competing with each other to tell us convincing stories of how they had experienced miracles in their daily lives. These stories appeared more coincidental than miraculous. One person had lost his job as a computer programmer. It was not too difficult to get a new job in London with his qualifications, but he was waiting for a miracle to come from his faith. He related various instances of how he had missed job opportunities, and this time on his return from Puttaparti, he was sure he would get the position he wanted, with Sai Baba's help.

My brother, who was not a devotee, rather a pragmatic scientist, suggested that a systematic job search would be more productive than waiting for a miracle. The young man was offended by my brother's lack of faith. However, instead of waiting for the miracle, his life has changed to more profitable avenues, one of which is, with my brother Henry, initiating and actively engaging in a project to build Hampton Village in Sri Lanka for victims ravaged by the December 2004 tsunami. I believe Sai Baba directed his energies in this way. Each related their tales of what Sai Baba had done to help them. The other people at the party were all Buddhists but eagerly waited going to *bhajan* sessions on Wednesdays. The sessions were held in their homes in rotation. In the crowd of about twenty-five, only the three of us were not Sai Baba worshippers.

My glance fell by chance on a statue of the Buddha watching all the proceedings with serenity and (it seemed to me) with sadness. "Be lamps unto yourself" were practically his last words. But then who was listening? Soon the room was empty; the devotees were gone; the candle flickered and died. A thin wisp of smoke rose from here to eternity.

Many Gods, Many Altars

BUDDHISTS IN SRI LANKA take refuge in the Triple Gem and believe they are endowed with almost talismanic power. They also seek the protection of extraterrestrial beings they refer to as "gods" or "*devas.*" These are many faceted and take the form of gods, deities, demons, and spirits. There are legends and beliefs associated with these nonhuman entities. Among villagers in particular there are well-crafted rituals performed to secure protection and blessings from these entities. All these are not strictly part of Buddhist religion; nevertheless, they are practiced by Buddhists and exist side-by-side with Buddhist practice.

A SHADOWY WORLD OF PARADOXES

In crisis situations Buddhists seek the help of gods. We are stepping into an arcane shadowy world full of paradoxes reflecting our own paradoxical natures. Supplicants in distress make their *yajnawa* (appeal) to the gods or indulge in the human passion for *paligahima* (curse) or revenge for bad deeds. Fascinatingly, yesterday's friends become today's enemies, and vice versa. For example, I might go with a friend to make an impossible appeal on my behalf or on his account (metaphorically speaking). I might have a very good reason to visit the same deity to bring down divine prayer cursing (*paligahanawa*) on my friend who in the interim has done me harm. The curious shifts and turns keep the gods busy (privately amused, if you may) and of course enrich the officiating intermediary.

Simple ailments take simple rituals. A common headache or a stomachache is often attributed to a spirit influence and is cured by a *mantra* (sacred formulae) chanted by a *kattadiya* (magic master), who knows the science of spirits. The *kattadiya* is typically a man who uses spiritual, magical methods to heal. He communicates with spirits and conducts ceremonies. The *mantras* that the *kattadiya* resort to are like prayers endowed with esoteric elements, known only to him. If shared the mantras lose their efficacy. In instances of illness and misfortune of a graver nature, the villagers resort to complicated ceremonies to drive away the malefic spirits. Sometimes the appeals are to benevolent gods and at other times to powerful demonic spirits.

Sri Lankan Buddhists, especially in the villages, often attribute disease and ill luck to the influence of spirits, bad planetary positions, or a combination of these. Some are popularly referred to as *"dosas"* (bad influences), which could take many forms. The most common are those that come from the evil eye of a person, the *aswaha*, the poison of the eye or bad mouth (*katawaha*), the poison of the mouth. Once a *dosa* is detected it has to be ritually expelled.

Inexplicable occurrences in day-to-day life are often attributed to *dosas*. *Dosas* combined with the influences of bad spirits are believed to cause misfortune. Even those people with good intentions are believed to have the evil eye or an evil mouth, which can cause trouble to humans. These have no reasonable or scientific explanation and involve a spectrum of phenomena, both mythical and imaginary. The *aswaha* or *katawaha dosa* are expelled by performing a *puja* to the spirits and demons. A *kattadiya* or *yakadura* performs a chanting session, in which *mantras* (appeals to the spirits) and *pirit* blessings (from the Buddha) are combined, along with a special *puja* to please spirits. Spirits happy to receive the *pujas* make the parties free of *dosas*.

SO WHERE IS THE BUDDHA IN ALL THIS?

The title of the chapter may suggest that the worship of the Buddha (Buddhism) and the popular resort to gods and spirits through the intermediary of rituals are mutually exclusive. Interwoven into the rituals, the incantations and spells are the typical benedictions of Buddhism, which emphasize love and compassion and the power innate in Buddhist thought. In the litany of the *kattadiya* or virtuoso, its beginning, middle, and conclusion invoke Buddhist benedictions of the sort a monk would recite to laymen in chanting *pirit*, or more informally, when interacting with a layman who would come to consult the monk on a one-to-one basis. The demonic entities are cowed and subdued by the invocation of the power of the Buddha whose powers transcend all beings in the cosmos both benign and malefic. In the rituals, the gods are frequently invoked because they (the *devas*) predicate their own power on the greater cosmic spiritual energy of the Buddha.

NOVEL USES FOR THE COMMON LIME

The ritual to get rid of *aswaha, katawaha dosa*, is known as *dehikapima* (slicing limes), a ceremony done in combination with a special *puja* to the spirits. The number of limes cut varies according to the enormity of the *dosa* caused. The number 7 is magical in spirit offerings. Twenty-one and sometimes as many as one hundred limes are cut over the head, over the hands, knees, and feet of the affected person. Other items used in this *puja* are seven types of flowers, seven kinds of fruits, incense sticks, and fish or dried fish. Incense is used rather lavishly to ward off evil spirits throughout the ceremony. While the mantras are recited intermittently, incense powder (*sambrani*) is put over hot coals to create smoke. Limes cut using a nutcracker, an indispensable item used to cut arecanuts, chewed with betel. Some *dehikapima* rituals are complicated further by boiling a special oil using wood from seven different types of citrus trees, emphasizing the significance of limes to dispel *dosa*. While reciting *mantras* in a low voice very fast, the *kattadiya* places the limes and the nutcracker over the affected person's head, cuts the lime, and tosses the two halves into the sizzling oil. Along with this he blesses the sick person by dipping sprigs of margosa in a pot of water and sprinkling the sick person. In the final act of the ceremony he takes an egg, which he passes over the affected person's entire body from forehead to the toes, cracks it, and throws it into the pot. The *dosa* is now all drained and burnt, and the person is free of *dosa*. When the ceremony is over, the oil is applied on the head for healing. This is a gentler way of getting rid of the influence of bad spirits and is done even during normal times, to ward off evil influences and bring good luck.

Upul, our neighbor, got an appointment as the government agent of the district. The day before his party for his friends, he had a *dehikapima* to ward off the evil eye arising from the envy and jealousy of friends and neighbors. In a strictly private ritual, red-hot chilies were burnt over hot coals, and the smoke was let out at the entrance to the house to drive the evil influences away. Often lime cutting is done to nullify a spell. Villagers believe poor health may be caused by a malicious neighbor practicing black magic to bring the devil into the house. A *dehikapima* is done in secret to dispel such evil.

HE STALKS THE LAND WITH AN EVIL EYE

Mr. Janz, a Eurasian, was a well-known person in the neighborhood where I grew up. We had a large Jack tree in the garden. Poor people often used the fruit as a substitute for rice. Our Jack tree was abundantly laden with fruit throughout the year. Large fruit grew on the main trunk of the tree and on it branches, making it appear fecund and plentiful. Mr. Janz, a wealthy man, who did not have much to do in the way of work, went for walks in the neighborhood and observed everything and everyone. He was not an evil person, but his mouth was considered to be evil. Mr. Janz, who never ate jack fruit for a meal, saw our tree laden with fruit and exclaimed in surprise, "Oh what a lot of fruits on this tree! What a great crop!" He meant well and stated a fact. According to the villagers this was not a proper thing to say, as it would result in bad consequences. For some inexplicable reason there was no new fruit on this tree for a long time. Villagers attributed this to Mr. Janz's mouth. This was *katawaha dosa* the servants declared. Many who helped themselves to the fruit were disappointed and pointed an angry finger at Mr. Janz.

Women with young healthy children would hide their babies when Mr. Janz passed by, in case he might exclaim, "Oh what a beautiful baby!" The baby would invariably become ill. Mr. Janz, who loved children, was not aware he had *katawaha*. It is the custom in our culture not to say explicitly that a child is beautiful, healthy, or fat, because it could generate *katawaha*. Flattery is confined to thoughts and not uttered openly. It is not uncommon to see a beautiful baby with all its hair shaven to purposely make it ugly, wearing a black bead chain, or marked with a big black spot (*pottu*) on the forehead to ward off the evil eye of an onlooker. A popular welcome gift from relatives to a newborn is the *panchayudha* (five weapons), a pendant of gold, made from a gold coin with five weapons carved on it, worn for security at their most fragile and tender age for protection from evil influences. In the villages it is passed on from one generation to another as an heirloom. My friend Penny, who is Greek, hearing my story confirmed that Greeks too believe in mystical influences. She told me of a custom of giving the newborn children a gift of a gold pin with a blue stone in the form of an eye to ward off the influence of the evil eye. The eye-shaped pin is worn on the chest for protection.

A folk tale associated with *asvaha* known to the villagers concerns the spirit Balagiri, who visits newborn children. They believe that newborn children cry mostly when Balagiri casts an evil eye, *asvaha*, making them ill. In order to prevent Balagiri visiting the newborn, villagers resort to many tricks to keep him away. They write on the back door to the house a message to Balagiri, "Do not come today come tomorrow or another day." Balagiri reads this message and goes away to come another day. The message keeps him away indefinitely for a tomorrow that never comes.

There are other forms of *aswaha* and *katawaha* as well. While walking along the Rajapihilla Mawatha in Kandy, I saw many houses under construction that had a large scarecrow (a figure of a man) at their entrance well dressed in a coat and trousers, conspicuously hung in front of the construction site to detract attention from the house that was being built. Sarath, our patient itinerant companion, explained that this was done to avoid *aswaha dosa*. A large white melon, the *puhul gediya*, is also used for this purpose. In new houses it is common practice to hang an elaborately designed *ves muhuma* (a mask) in a prominent place to detract attention from the house to avoid *aswaha*. Sometimes these masks are large and look grossly demonic. There is the belief that the object is best served if the mask was not bought but was given as a gift by a close friend.

THE ETIOLOGY OF AN ILLNESS

Villagers attributing illness to the evil influence of bad spirits consult the *kattadiya* to get a thread or blessed oil, which acquires curative powers by being repeatedly chanted over by the recitation of sacred magic formulae (*maturanawa*). For more persistent ailments they resort to involved *pujas* for the spirits. The form and the content of these *pujas* are determined by custom and are strictly adhered to for best results.

Punchimanika worked in Ananda's household for many years. An educated woman in the Sinhala tradition, she married and lived with her family in the outside quarters built for the domestic staff. They came from a village near Kandy. When her daughter developed a high fever, she was taken to the doctor. Punchimanika believed that the disease had to be attacked on several fronts. She got the *kattadiya* from the village to get a thread charmed, a ritual called "*nool maturanawa*." With the help of her family and relatives she organized a *puja*. Flowers of several colors were laid on a chair, which was covered with banana leaves. Many types of fruit were used as an offering with oil lamps and betel leaves. The *kattadiya* spent hours chanting blessings and mantras in a language that appealed to the spirits. While chanting, he held onto the thread, ritually cleansed with lime and saffron water. The chanting was stopped at regular intervals to tie a knot in the thread, making it more powerful. Punchimanika and her family sat on a mat nearby attentively praying. At the end of the ceremony the thread was tied around her neck. This ceremony was not only to cure her illness but also to dispel bad spirit influences that might cause trouble in the future. Her daughter was instructed not to go out alone in the dark and refrain from eating meat, eggs, and fried food, referred to as *pulutu* in the *kattadiya* language.

When her son, Ruwan, got sick frequently, she consulted his horoscope and determined that he was going through a bad astrological phase. Mishaps in life are also blamed on bad times. Astrological readings of horoscopes are taken seriously. Punchimanika's relatives arrived with all the necessary ingredients along with the *kattadiya* from the village to perform a *telmatirima* (charming of oil). A *puja* platform was prepared with flowers of several colors and oil lamps. An offering to the spirits was performed in the late evening to coax them to leave Ruwan. The *kattadiya* in his usual style chanted many mantras combined with Buddhist sutras for blessings. Holding the oil on his palm, he blew on it at regular intervals to make it more potent. He used large amounts of incense powder on the hot coals to spread fumes in all directions to chase the bad spirits away. The entire ceremony took over an hour. Ruwan got better, and Punchimanika's faith in an arcane world of shadowy beings was confirmed. I was intrigued by these activities that went on at the back of the house. My mother-in-law paid little attention. Punchimanika, being part of the household, had the freedom to perform her rituals. It was like living in two worlds tolerant of each other. Punchimanika's world was so different from the world of "St. James," our main house.

It is widely believed, typically in villages, that evil spirits take possession of certain people. In common parlance such a person is *avesavela* (possessed). Sooner rather than later, the presence has to be exorcised. A person who comes to be possessed by a spirit is considered an unwell person. The villagers seek the assistance of an exorcist *kattadiya* to rid the person of this possession and make him or her well. In more involved cases they resort to complicated ceremonies such as *bali* and *thovil* and *kohoba kankariya*, which are also performed as exorcising ceremonies, entailing all night devil-dancing ceremonies. They are also social events, where people gather in large numbers to witness exotic dances and drumming performances.

In conventional Buddhism it is said that the purest Buddhist form of an exorcist ritual that has been practiced in Sri Lanka from very early times is the recital of the Atanatiya Sutta. There are many rituals connected with the chanting of this particular *pirit*. Monks who recite the *sutta* take precautions and observe certain rules. They abstain from eating meat and do not live in a cemetery, lest evil spirits harass them. Men carrying weapons and shields conduct the monks to the patient's house. The recitation is to be done within closed doors, guarded by men with arms, and thoughts of love should be foremost in the reciter's mind. If after all this the stubborn spirit refuses to leave the person, he or she is taken to the temple, and the ritual is performed in the temple premises. Flowers, incense, and alms are offered to the Buddha and merit transferred to the spirit. The spirit now appeased leaves the patient. If the spirit still refuses to leave, then the *devas* are invoked to deal with his obstinacy.

WHEN A SERVANT BECOMES SOMETHING ELSE

I was a young teen when our male servant Andiris (the Sinhalese version of Andre) became possessed. He had been visiting the Kali *kovila* (Hindu temple for Kali) with our neighbors. He lived in a room outside our house. Although we had been told not to peek into the servants' quarters, we did, as we were curious. Andiris would light a lamp to the goddess Kali and throw a red flower garland around the goddess' picture. All this frightened us. One Saturday he acted strangely. He had a bath in the well, in our garden, put on a white sarong, went into a violent trance, and spoke in a strange language. He swirled his head like a fast-turning windmill. In a few moments our neighbors proclaimed that he was possessed by Kali Maniyo (Mother Kali). He would call some of the neighbors by name, predicting their immediate future and recommending solutions to problems. He became a celebrity of sorts.

Shortly after, through the mouth of Andiris, the goddess Kali let it be known that she would like a shrine built for her near a Bo tree in one of my mother's properties. In a trance, Andiris located the place, some miles away from where we lived. My mother did not know how to deal with the situation. She was concerned that we were afraid. She also did not want to incur the displeasure of Kali by outright refusal. My father appeared on the scene and settled it all by forbidding Andiris to go into trances on the premises. My mother for her part realized that Andiris did not control the onset of the trances and built the little temple. We heard that he continued to go into states of *avesa* (trances) on Saturdays and Wednesdays in the new place, which was well attended and patronized by the neighbors and believers. Andiris continued to work in our house for several years after this. Exorcism became a lucrative, secure, part-time occupation. When we moved back to Colombo, we gradually lost contact with Andiris.

THE WILY WAYS OF NAUGHTY SPIRITS

Manika, who took care of us, had her share of strange beliefs and fascinating tales. There were seven young virgins in our family, and Manika felt that it was her duty to protect us from the eye of the bad spirits. She told a story of a *kalu kumaraya* (black prince), who eyed good-looking virgins. She believed virgins need special care before marriage and had to be kept away from his evil eye. She frightened us by saying that once you come under his influence, he will visit you in the night in your dreams to have sex. This she said must be prevented at any cost. There was also the folk lore involving naughty spirits eyeing young people, which she shared with us. To Manika sex and erotic dreams were taboo. We were not allowed to eat fried food or go out alone in the dark, even to the garden, for fear of the *kalu kumaraya* laying his eye on us. She made us keep an iron nail with us if we did go out and made it her job to follow us everywhere. We could not comprehend her thought process, but she made it her business to frighten us. Our young male cook, Dharmasdasa, was a good flute player. After work in the evenings he plaintively played his flute at the back of the house. I heard Manika gently warning him not to play it after dark for fear that the sex spirit Mohini (the female counterpart of the *kalu kumaraya*), attracted to the sound of the flute, would haunt him and would cast a spell on him.

AN ANCIENT ART IS
GENERATIONALLY TRANSMITTED

Sickness, misfortune, and other evil influences are believed to be due to unfavorable planetary placing or the displeasure of spirits. The actual cause is determined by the reading of the horoscope or by consulting a *sasthrakaraya* (fortuneteller), who would prescribe appropriate remedies to get rid of the evil influences. It may take many forms; sometimes a Bali ceremony is recommended. A *kattadiya* well versed in this ceremony is consulted.

In villages there are professional groups of exorcists *kattadiyas* who perform under a leader who teaches them. The science of exorcism is passed on from one generation to the next and is known as the *gurukula* system—a teacher-pupil relationship—involving a careful selection and training of students. (*Guru* simply means the "teacher," who is invariably a man.) Sometimes a particularly gifted student comes under the care of the teacher as a resident in his household and undergoes intense training for a number of years until satisfactory proficiency is attained. The student shares the chores of the household, takes care of the guru's needs, runs errands for him, and acts as his valet. There is constant interaction between the teacher and the pupil even after proficiency is achieved. It is a tradition for the best pupil to take the daughter of the guru in marriage so that he remains with the guru.

Kattadiya and *gunnnnase* are terms used within the culture to address the magic master. He is both feared, and in a way, respected by the villagers. He is feared because of his knowledge of the arcane sciences. He inspires a certain aura that he should not be trifled with. He is looked up to because he genuinely helps the villages to deal with sickness. A medical doctor is not freely available in the villages, and people use this resource for relief from minor ailments. At childbirth the *kattadiya* is sought after, to charm a young coconut as a drink for the woman in labor to facilitate easy delivery. Any phenomenon that cannot be explained is taken to the *kattadiya* for a charm or for blessings. In our partiality to modernization, we often fail to realize the completeness of the world of the village.

A YANKEE IN FAR FAR AWAY SRI LANKA

My old friend Sean, a white American graduate student, who had returned to Chicago from Sri Lanka in the mid nineties, had lived with a poor family in a remote village in the dry zone in the north central region of the country. He enjoyed his stay and had affection and respect for his village family. He referred to the host family in the village as his other family and the lady of the house as his other mother. The woman of the house firmly believed that Sean was her son from her previous birth, her *peraatmeputa* come back to take care of her. Sean seemed familiar and comfortable with the idea. He had learned

Sinhala and spoke it fluently, able to read and write the script, and was focused on his project. His empathic attitudes combined with his knowledge of the local language made it possible for him to communicate and fit into the village life. Villagers were excited that a white man could speak their language. Sean was kind, affectionate, and generous to the family, who were poor and their living conditions were primitive. Sean helped them to improve their living conditions. I had disagreements with him during this period about his views, attachments, and opinions of this family.

Sean showed me pictures of the one-room hut he had shared with the family and told many stories about them, which I found fascinating. In remote villages, the women sleep inside the house, and the men sleep in the outer verandah. They did not fear robbers, as they had nothing of value. The man of the house was a *gurunanse* (magical healer) in the village. He was well versed in a science that was handed down to him, transgenerationally by committing to memory the mantras, the magical healing stanzas. Some were preserved carefully written in *ola* leaves in the *gurunanse's* possession. Sean wanted to learn the lore and study according to accepted tradition. He was respectful of the *gurunanse* and performed *ava theva* (numerous sundry acts of service to the teacher), to win the confidence and affection of the teacher, an essential ingredient in learning his science. It is with the dedicated attention to detail that studying becomes a success. Another essential ingredient of this system of learning to ensure the best results was the teacher's love for the student and student's respect for the teacher. The *gurunanse* was fond of Sean and was keen to teach him. Sean was a good student.

Sean came from a fairly affluent middle-class, Christian home and was used to the comforts and conveniences of American living. In the village house there was no electricity, no water on tap, or proper outside toilet. He never complained but was grateful for the opportunity to learn the various mantras, the magic stanzas, from the *gurunanse* to heal minor ailments such as headaches and stomachaches. He said he learned the mantras to charm or win over the hearts of people. I suggested that he find the nicest girl on the campus and do a *mantra* to win her heart. I had a headache once and Sean willingly offered to say a mantra for me. It did not work, however, because I did not have the requisite faith, which was vital for healing. He had faith in the medicinal oils and herbs he had brought with him, which he was more than willing to share with his friends. He claimed that he was a Buddhist and had a picture of the Buddha in his apartment. It all seemed strange.

BALI: THE ANATOMY OF A GRAND CEREMONY

Jayalatha invited us to see a *bali* ceremony in her house. Her father was a traditional landed proprietor, and all around was evidence of affluence. We were amused to see her father wearing the traditional farmer's attire, the scanty *amude* exposing both his buttocks, barely covering his nudity, carrying a mammoty on his shoulder. There was nothing obscene as it was the traditional dress of the farmers working in the fields, but young adults from the city found this amusing. Jayalatha proudly introduced her father to us. He was cordial and quickly put us at ease. The *bali* ceremony was to bless his sick wife, appease evil spirits, and bring good health for his family and a good harvest. In Sri Lanka *bali* is an elaborate ceremony performed to achieve many ends. The neighbors, friends, and relatives brought large quantities of clay, made *bali* figures of deities, and colored them beautifully for the ritual. During the ceremony the figures were propped up against the wall near Jayalatha's mother.

Preparation for the ceremony had taken many days. Banana stems, young coconut leaves, flowers of different colors, oils, coconut and arecanut flowers, coconuts, betel leaves, and raw rice were some of the items used. Offerings were made to spirits and deities. Jayalatha's mother occupied a central place. The chief *kattadiya* began the ceremony by paying homage to the Buddha, the dharma, and the Sangha. Drumming and dancing went on, with the performers dressed in colorful outfits, all through the night. The majority of the stanzas recited in the ceremony glorified the virtues of the Triple Gem and referred to the previous lives of the Buddha. There was continuous reciting of magical stanzas and *pirit suttas*, calling for protection and blessings. Many pronouncements of invocations were recited—"By the power of the virtues of the Buddha, let the evil influence of the planets disappear or the evil spirit leave the possession of the person." The spiritual qualities of the Triple Gem, being superior to any other influence, could drive away the evil influences. Fire and the smoke of burning incense were used during the dancing; *sambrani* powder thrown over hot charcoal was lavishly used to drive away the spirits. *Kattadiyas* dressed in colorful costumes with oversized evil-looking masks looked like devils themselves. The main *kattadiya* went into a trance and danced in frenzied fashion for a long time possessed by the same spirit that had possessed the patient. He finally fell down in a state of exhaustion, presumably having got rid of the spirit who had made Jayalatha's mother sick. The *pujas* and images were carried out of the premises and left at a junction where four roads crossed, ending the ceremony.

Thovil is a devil-dancing ceremony of a primarily exorcist nature. Only men perform the role of *gurunanse* or *yakadura*, the devil's master. This ritual too uses devil masks and beards. Many Buddhist *gathas* and *pirit* elements are recited among the mantras in the ritual. It is also a healing ritual, to get rain at proper times and increase crop yields. *Thovil* requires an offering of banana sheath, immature coconut taken from the flower buds, banana, dried fish, fried deer or goat meat, and other items. The mention of the Buddha's virtues was sufficient to frighten these spirits. Offerings are made to please the spirits who leave the possessed person.

MYTHICAL ORIGINS OF A POPULAR RITE

I once accompanied a young woman anthropologist, who did research on the *kohoba kankariya* performance in a village near Kandy. The elaborate ritual was one of the most ancient folk ceremonies in Sri Lanka. The ceremony was held to cure a sick woman. We all sat on the ground on mats around the place where the ceremony was held. It was performed throughout the night with many dance forms and drumming to drive away the spirits influencing the sick.

There is a fascinating legend associated with this ritual. King Panduvesdeva (fifth century B.C.) was inflicted with an incurable disease, as a result of the previous king, Vijaya, not keeping his promise to Princess Kuveni. According to tradition Kuveni had helped Vijaya to establish his power, as the first king of Sri Lanka, and had every expectation that Vijaya would choose her as his queen. The god of gods, Sakka ruled that the only cure for King Panduvesdeva had to be done by a person who was born out of a flower, and not out of a woman. There indeed was such a person in India. Sakka suggested that the only way the king of the flower, who was in India, could be brought onto the island was by Rahu, the chief of the Asura tribe. He suggested that an Asura should take the form of a boar and lie in the garden of the flower king. The king of the flower, seeing the boar, would chase it as far as Sri Lanka and strike it with his golden sword. This is indeed what happened. While in Sri Lanka he heard of Panduvesdeva's illness and cured him of the affliction.

The story is acted periodically to ensure prosperity and freedom from disease. According to Dr. Ediriweera Sarachandra, who was my teacher in Peradeniya, the king born of the flower committed the people of Lanka, prior to his return to India, to the care of twelve deities. Kohoba Yakka was one of them. All these deities appear in the rituals of Kohoba Kankariya. Throughout the evening offerings of food and flowers are prepared ceremoniously. The dancers, having ritually purified themselves, dress in their red and white costumes, with demonic headgear, and dance all evening to the rhythm of the drum. They invoke the blessings of the gods on the owner of the premises and on the sick person. The sick person lies on a mat on an altar constructed for the ceremony. They solicit the blessings of the gods of the *kankariya*, the twelve deities. Far into the night the dancers continue singing verses honoring the gods and enacting the legendary tale of the king chasing the boar. Toward the early hours of the morning a flower is shot with a bow and arrow, ending the ceremony. It is an elaborate and costly ceremony, and its performance is rather rare.

THEY ALSO CURSE

There are other less elaborate practices in Sri Lanka, which the villagers resort to, cursing or *paligahanawa*, to get the help of evil spirits, to bring harm to

persons or families they consider their enemies. They pray that harm will
befall the evil doers, causing physical or mental disabilities. This can be
directed to families, neighbors, or relatives. The most common form is to
appeal to *huniyan deviyo* for help. Villages offer pujas to the gods and the
kapurala, on their behalf following hallowed tradition, appealing to the deities
and spirits to punish wrong doers.

Cursing is an old tradition in the village of Seenigama on the southern
coast. Help is sought from the god of the shrine, Devol Deviyo, for punishing
the wrong doer. Many visit the *devale* in normal times. The shrine is situated
off the sea coast a little distance from the village, and access to it is by a primitive raft operated by the villagers. Part of the shrine is on the main road, and
passing vehicles and buses never fail to stop to drop a coin to Devol Deviyo for
blessings for a safe journey. I passed this place recently on the way to Galle. I
was shown the shrine in the little island untouched by the tsunami waters and
winds. All around was massive devastation. Houses, buildings, and fishing
boats had been swept into the sea, but the little shrine of the Devol Deviyo was
left unharmed, marooned in the sea.

TIT FOR TAT IN THE BLACK ARTS

Another known form of black magic is *huniam*, done primarily for revenge.
Huniam is believed to cause harm and even death in certain instances to tar-
geted parties. The practice is clearly against the principles of Buddhism,
which teaches kindness and compassion, therefore, *huniam* is done in great
secrecy. If the person doing this malicious act is discovered, it can be counter-
acted by reversing the effects to the person who committed it. Once Edwin,
an old family retainer, related a gruesome story about a tenant who was angry
at the prospect of paying an increased rent on his house. The tenant resorted
to *huniam* to cast a spell on the landlord, who fell seriously ill. (Edwin, who
was good at exaggeration, would relate interesting stories to us after an
evening drink of arrack.) The well the landlord drank water from became
infested with worms. He also added that as a consequence the Jack tree, which
had once had an abundance of fruit, suddenly withered and died. Such was the
power of *huniam*.

Stories of this sort are common and reinforce the popular belief and fear
in its efficacy. *Huniam* is also done with somewhat more benevolent motives.
If a man wants to win the heart of a woman, the obstacles in his path are overcome by resorting to this form of black magic. It is a common practice for
young women in Sri Lanka to carefully dispose of their fallen hair, as this is
used in charming. I have heard the story of a man of a lower social status who
wanted to charm a pretty girl. He bribed her maid to get some hair from her
mistress to use in the charm. The maid being loyal to the mistress did not like

the idea of betraying her, but she was tempted. She gave a few hairs from the rug in the room. After the charm, the rug is said to have gone somehow to the man who did the charm instead of the woman he desired.

A rather strange story appeared in the November 2005 issue of the popular Sinhala newspaper *Sithumina*. A *kattadiya* in a village far away from Colombo fell in love with a pretty girl who rejected him. In anger he sent a charmed alligator to pursue her. The alligator followed her everywhere, the story read, and the desperate parents sent her to live with a relative a considerable distance from her home. The alligator reappeared and continued to pursue her. One is at a loss when it comes to stories of this nature, which are not too uncommon in our village culture. Typically they inspire a sense of conniving belief rather than outright skepticism.

Mothers often complain about families not of their standing charming their handsome sons, and warn them not to eat from unknown houses. With impassioned fervor, curiously combining vindictiveness with a religiously inspired righteousness, they resort to counter black magic to break off the spells, thereby saving their sons. It is a common belief that mothers, in order to get attractive partners for the children, charm prospective men and women. Food is believed to be the most common instrument used in charming.

Early in my career I was the librarian of the Theosophical Society in Wheaton, Illinois. The library had the most fascinating collection of material not found elsewhere on a wide variety of subjects. It attracted many different types of clients. One morning we had a visitor from Chicago, who told me that his neighbor in the apartment complex where he lived had performed voodoo to destroy him, and he had definite signs. Influenced by the American culture of which I was rapidly becoming a part, I did not want to ask too many questions. The man was looking for some material on how to perform counter black magic on the neighbor to make her mad. Taken aback at his anger, I showed him the section on black magic–related materials. This may not have been the most ethical thing to do, but as a librarian my job was to provide information.

Sri Lanka has its own forms of cursing and revenge. This can take the form of black magic called "*kodivina*." This is the most feared form of black magic, which is aimed at revenge, done primarily to harm or bring bad effects. I knew a woman whose husband ran away with a beautiful young girl. She did a *kodivina* to break up the relationship, destroy the bad woman, and bring back the husband. Even if such efforts fail to bring about the desired results, they serve as temporary relief mechanisms.

To recover her stolen money a servant woman went to appeal to Huniyan Deviyo for help. The *kapurala* resorted to an unusual method of cursing the robber. The curse suggested was *abaranawa* (grinding). On the grinding stone, a slab of stone, he made her grind seven hot items—hot chilies, black pepper, garlic, ginger, turmeric, and other ingredients—intoning at every turn of the

stone the crime with great maledictory intensity. The woman, well versed in
the practice of grinding condiments, ground the deadly items to her heart's
content. We found this amusing and intriguing. In the process an appeal was
made to Hunuyan Deviyo to make the person return the lost items and punish the robber in an appropriate manner. To my knowledge she did not recover
her lost property.

THE OMNISCIENT ENGLISHMAN

How indeed would one recover stolen property? The limits of playing the
detective are plain. Robert Knox (who never fails to rise to the occasion)
recalls a custom in the Kandyan villages in seventeenth-century Ceylon. I
quote him in *extenso*.

> When a robbery is committed to find the thief, they charm a Coker-nut,
> which is done by certain words, and any one can do it, that can but utter the
> charm words. Then they thrust a stick into it, and set it either at the door or
> hole the thief went out at. Then one holds the stick with the nut at the end
> of it, and the nut pursues and follows in the tract that the thief went. All the
> way it is going they still continue charming, and flinging the blossoms of the
> betel-nut-tree upon it. Nut at last it will lead to the house or place where the
> thief is, and run upon his feet. This nut will sometimes go winding hither
> and thither, and sometimes will stand still. Then they follow their charms,
> strewing on blossoms, and that sets it forward again. This is not enough to
> find the thief guilty; but if they intend to prosecute the man upon this dis-
> covery, the charmer must swear against him point blank: which he some-
> times will do upon the confidence of the truth of his charm: and the sup-
> posed thief must either swear or be condemned. (Knox 1958:179)

CHARMS AND COUNTERCHARMS

The art of protecting oneself from black magic is an involved science. Coun-
tercharms are made in secret to break a charm or a *huniam*. Complex chanting
and spirit *pujas* are done to overcome the evil effects of black magic. Many wear
amulets containing charmed oil or chanted *pirit* oil as a protection from the evil
effects of *huniam*. Monks chant as protective blessings certain *pirit suttas* several hundreds of times or even thousands of times to use as protective charms.
These are worn as *piritnulas* or chanted oils by Buddhists. Another kind of
amulet, the *yantara*—a metal or gold cylinder which holds charmed oil, a sheet
of paper, a palm leaf, or a gold sheet with figures or words on it—is worn by
people for protection from *huniam*. A *yantara* is worn also for general protec-

tion from bad planetary influences. Rich merchants wear heavy gold ones with gold chains to exhibit wealth and power. It is common to see men in villages with *yantaras* hanging round their necks. The sale of these magical amulets is a lucrative trade in Sri Lanka. I have seen large advertisements in local Sinhala newspapers, which sometimes occupy almost half a page, advertising amulets. The claims made in the advertisements are mind-boggling, bordering on fantasy. They extend from getting the most beautiful woman to destroying a marriage or a family business. Charmed threads or amulets are commonly used for protection: charmed snake oil is used for protection from various ailments or from evil spirits is familiar to the Sri Lankans. It is sold in various forms and containers in the streets and at bus stands.

There are a few Sinhala periodicals such as *Iranama* and *Sithumina*, which have interesting information related to extra Buddhist practices and beliefs. They have stories, advertisements, remedies, and health food columns. I was reading aloud to my mother-in-law from one of them an amusing story about a man who got a much desired, beautiful female partner by resorting to a powerful charm. She listened and in her gentle, refined way dissuaded me from reading these as literature of no value. She said that if you led a spiritual life, and practiced compassion, no one could harm you. The good dharma that you practice will keep harm away from you, and that alone is the best protection.

'Ithipiso' gatha (nine great qualities of the Buddha) is a short *gatha* recited by Buddhists in private for protection, known popularly as *Buduguna*. It's recited to dispel bad influences and unpleasant situations and bring about peace and calm. Sri Lankans believe in *holman* (ghosts), and when frightened by seeing one, the recitation of *'ithipiso' gatha* will keep the *holman* at bay. Buddhsits also believe that more powerful than all the yantra and mantras (apotropaic spells) is the recitation of a particular Pali *gatha*, the Buddha word, repeated many times. The verse is:

> *Sabbapapssa akaranam*
> *kusalssa upasampada*
> *Sacitta-pariyodapanam*
> *etam Buddanusasanam*

> To abstain from all evil,
> to do good,
> to purify one's mind,
> this is the teaching of the Buddha.

When Sri Lankan Buddhists write letters to each other they begin the letter with a saying Budusaranai (blessings of the Buddha) or *Teruvansarani* (blessings of the Triple Gem). When they part company they wish each other "Budusaranai" instead of a good bye.

Composing and reciting *seth kavi* (benedictory verses) is common practice among Sri Lankan Buddhists, to counter malefic planetary influences and bring good health and fortune. An astrologer or a Buddhist monk well versed in the science of combining words and sounds composes these verses. Choice, arrangement, and combination of vowels and consonants of the Sinhala alphabet are especially important. These verses often include the Buddhist stanzas to evoke blessings. These are recited in the Vishnu *devale* after the worship of the Buddha, for seven days morning and evening without a break, repeating the verse or verses, with the name of the person included in the text. People who have experience in the correct pronunciation and intonation of words are chosen to recite them. There are also *vas kavi*, verses made for cursing, which are recited to bring about evil directed to enemies. This is generally frowned upon and is resorted to in secrecy.

HOW RICE COMES TO BE RICE

Rice cultivation is the main occupation in rural Sri Lanka. Being the staple food, all activity connected with its cultivation is treated with honor and respect. The highest caste in Sri Lanka is that of the *goviya* (farmer). It is said that when the mud is washed off a farmer he is fit to be a king. There are many customs and ceremonies associated with the cultivation of paddy and its harvesting. Unforeseen contingencies such as floods, droughts, epidemics, crop failures, and sicknesses are attributed to the wrath of unseen gods. Farmers make offerings and rituals against these calamities.

There are also ancient customs connected with the threshing floor. Rice fields surrounded my aunt's house in Ratnapura. Threshing time was exciting. We learned the threshing songs the farmers sang as they went round the *kamatha* following the bulls. The songs are ancient and are handed down by word of mouth. They are in simple vernacular, easy to understand, easy to remember, and easy to sing. It was a joint activity, villagers joining with spirit and éclat. In some of these verses Gana Deviyo and other gods were evoked. Each *kavi* was chanted line by line by an elderly leader who was well versed in customs and repeated after him in chorus by the men and women at work, while the paddy was being trodden out. In the night with the moonlight the whole scene was breathtaking.

The *kamath hella* (threshing floor songs) began by evoking the Triple Gem. Songs evoking the blessings of the various gods followed this.

> The strength of refuge in Buddha, the strength of refuge in dharma.
> The strength of refuge in the Sangha, in these three is the strength
>   of the threshing floor.

Where the sun god appears, there will remain no dewdrops
Where the moon god appears, there will remain no darkness.

Where the great tuskers are tied up, there will remain no tree stumps
Where all the gods appear, there will be no mishaps.

Auspicious times for all activities are observed by consulting a regular astrologer or a farmer well versed in the knowledge of astrology. Newly harvested paddy is made into bundles and stacked in piles. Villagers believe that these stacks should not be left alone, and they take turns guarding them from evil spirits and there is an all night vigil and singing.

To prevent the young paddy plants from dying off, a charm is performed by a *kattadiya*. A banana tree is planted in the middle of the field and decorated with young coconut leaves and arecanut flowers with lighted torches on either side. The *kattadiya* enters the field from the east, performs the charm, and leaves to the west. He leaves the fields alone without speaking.

There is also a magical remedy to keep rats from eating the plants. A small, decorated platform or shelf is made up of banana stems and young coconut leaves and placed in the field. Five kinds of flowers are offered with a lamp lit with buffalo ghee. A thread spun by a virgin is knotted seven times, and the charm is repeated seven times for the seven knots. Finding a virgin in the village is not a problem as all young women before marriage are supposed to be virgins. Finally the thread is burned and left in the field. If ants eat the roots of the paddy plant, a different charm is done. A handful of sand from an untrodden place is charmed and thrown into the field.

Of course, villagers depend on rain for cultivation, and the crying of various types of birds is associated with the coming of drought and rain. The *awichchiya* bird makes a certain type of noise while flying over the fields and ponds. This bird supposedly announces near drought conditions. The *ukussa* or *wahilihine* birds flying over the fields indicate that rains are imminent. There is no scientific basis for such beliefs. But the immemorial faith of the villagers remains unshaken.

EMANATION TO KNOW THE FUTURE

Sri Lankans are enamored with the idea of knowing the future and resort to various means to know what is in store for them. Palm reading is very common. Apart from the professionals there are vendors in the streets and bus stands claiming to be masters in this science. There are those who regularly get horoscopes read by consulting an astrologer. There are others who go into a trance possessed by a good god who claims to read future events. Another science involves reading the future or specific events by looking into a plate with various herbs on it, *angananeli* (light reading). This is resorted to for more specific purposes, such as finding a lost or stolen item. This may, as some are quick to point out, be a form of mind reading, but it serves a need and is part of an elaborate and subtle *Weltanschauung* (worldview).

As discussed earlier, when a child is born the time is carefully noted, and the horoscope is cast. Synchronizing with the time of birth auspicious letters and sounds favorable to the newborn are determined, and the child is named accordingly. The idea was that the constant use of favorable sounds in a name confers good luck and helps to mitigate bad effects during times of adversity. From the readings of the horoscope, the first solid meal is given, the time to go to school is determined, as well as a host of other activities in a person's a life. In marriage it is considered important to consult the compatibility by means of reading and comparing the horoscopes of the parties. Astrologers therefore play an important part in our society. Our grandfather, with a good knowledge of astrology, did our horoscopes and had them written on papyrus leaves. The traditional horoscope is a thin, long strip of papyrus leaf, with information written on both sides, along with a chart of birth. It is rolled and preserved to be consulted when needed.

Horoscopes are not what they are widely assumed to be, that is, a means of telling what the future holds. In a more practical sense, horoscopes are consulted—with the help of professionals who are competent to interpret them—to explain the connection between planetary influences and misfortunes that happen to people. Nobody looks up a horoscope when things are going well. The practitioners believe that afflictions, disease, illness, and reversals of fortune happen for a reason, often a reason we are powerless to control. Contrary to what is told to Brutus in Shakespeare's Julius Caesar, the fault may well be with the stars. It is often said a person is under a bad star or having a bad period of time. The nature of the ritual to be performed to overcome the bad period is determined from horoscopes. Sometimes a simple *pahan puja* or a Bodhi *puja* or even a chanting of *pirit* suffices. In more adverse times other means of getting rid of the evil influences are needed.

Horoscopes, I feel, cannot be lightly dismissed as a classic example of "the brown man's magic." The following interesting stories, which Ananda shared with me, have baffled me. Periodically either when he wanted a lavish Sunday morning breakfast (at my father-in-law's house), or when someone's illness was the cause, the portly family astrologer, Dunuwila Mahatttmaya, would make a visit. The man, who wore gold-rimmed spectacles teetering precariously at the end of his nose and a gray coat, and was unusually fair, even for a Kandyan Sinhalese, looked very much like a Dickensian character. The cause of one particular visit was a lingering illness of Ananda's elder brother.

I must say in parenthetical vein, when we were growing up, a threefold attack was invariably made on a family illness. There was first the visit of a Western doctor, usually British trained, and unbeknown to him, the clandes-

tine visit of the native Ayrvedic physician who with an omniscient air prescribed a variety of decoctions (all equally unpalatable), and finally, the visit of
the astrologer whose prognosis was what really mattered. On this morning the
astrologer reading my brother-in-law's horoscope pronounced (scanning far
into the future into realms unborn) that he would become a banker working
for an English bank. In seconds my domineering father-in-law, throwing all
proprieties to the winds, was on his feet denouncing both the poor astrologer
and his ignoble profession. He thumped the table and roared, "My son will be
a doctor!" My mother-in-law, long used to such outbursts, calmly restored
order, discreetly sending a message to the kitchen for more egg hoppers.

In a year or so Ananda's brother cut the Gordian knot as it were. He
flunked the premedical high school classes, scoring poorly in zoology. On principle he refused to dissect frogs, clearly causing a problem for the Anglican
school authorities, who had for the first time to deal with a Buddhist boy with
a conscience. Strangely, almost a year later, my brother-in-law got an extraordinarily handsome offer from an English bank in Colombo, which dispatched
him (traveling first class in a PO liner) for a three-year training period.

ASTRO BOBBY IN OXFORD

Even educated and rational people believe in horoscope readings. Indeed education may have little to do with it. In Oxford we had a friend I will call
Bobby, a medical doctor studying for a D. Phil. degree in toxicology. It was
summer; he had successfully completed an experiment that was the basis of his
thesis. A more practical and rational person could hardly be imagined, yet he
firmly believed in horoscopes. Ananda called him "Astro-Bobby." He had to
do a laboratory experiment to confirm his theory one more time, before writing up his thesis, but something failed. After repeated attempts he was unable
to complete it successfully. He became despondent; he worked late into the
nights in the lab. There was something he was missing, and it would not fall
into place. He would come to our apartment in Ifley Road even at 1:00 A.M.
from the laboratory for a cup of coffee and for some consolation on his way
home, to talk to Ananda. We were concerned. He also believed in the folk
concept of 'bada' (obstruction). He firmly believed that when he came to visit
us if the traffic light turned red it was a sign of bada, and we would not be
home. He assured us that this happened too many times to be coincidental.
He had an old bicycle, which had no light at the back. Bobby bought a flash-
light, colored it red, and sat on it to serve as a back red light. In the dear city
of Oxford, with its dreaming spires, the local police did not bother him.

Somehow he believed that it would all turn out right after the 26th of
December, predicted by his astrologer. But he did not stop trying, continuing
ardently day after day. We went to London for Christmas. On December 28th

we got a call from Bobby. To our great joy he had found the clue he needed to complete his experiment conclusively, while reading a related magazine, which had been in his possession all the time. This had evidently happened on December 25th. He had run to the lab to retry his experiment, and it was successful. We celebrated with Bobby. He completed his thesis and returned to Sri Lanka to teach in the medical faculty at Peradeniya.

In Sri Lanka the wayside teller of fortune who reads one's palm is commonplace. We pass him by pitying the gullible client whose palm the seer reads. After summer vacation a young teacher in a school in Maharagama, my first job, walked into the staff room sporting a beard with an amused twinkle in his eye. Explanations followed. Gamini was interested in the sociological phenomena of people going to *sastarakaraya*. In order to find out why palm readers always had a steady clientele, Gamini decided to try it out. Much like a "wondering *sadhu*" he went to Anuradhapura, a particularly holy place in Sri Lanka, in the manner of a *sastarakaraya* and began to read palms. Gamini did not know anything about palmistry but skillfully picked up the jargon from his first run of clients. He gathered that mostly people with problems went to see the fortune teller. He reckoned that there were a number of common problems and predictable remedies. Most of the information he ferreted out from his clients. He gradually got better at the game and figured out why clients come to him, their anxieties, concerns, and forebodings. In a short time he began to develop a skill. He sadly commented on the angst of men and women seeking therapies wherever they could find them. The money he collected he donated to a Buddhist temple nearby. Our paths never crossed again.

THE LITTLE FELLOW IN THE CEILING WHO KNEW IT ALL!

Bada (obstructions) which unexpectedly get in your way, are a common belief among Sri Lankans. Certain omens are popularly considered as *bada*. Sights and sounds of birds, animals, and insects are believed to indicate the future and fortune. When one sets off on a journey or on some project, if a *huna* (gecko; a small lizardlike reptile that typically lives in ceilings and that every now and then emits an audible noise) calls, it is considered *bada*. Often a journey is put off for a few hours or so. The *huna* noise resembles someone clicking his tongue as if to say no. The little *huna* has a lot of decisive power over the villagers. There are pamphlets written about the household gecko. Certain things are predicted if a gecko falls as it often loses its balance, on the head, on the right hand, left hand, and so on. Some locations portend good and others bad. Villagers believe in the science of the gecko, which is known popularly as the *hunu sasthara*. In the local almanacs popularly used in Sri Lanka there is a column for ready reference on the *hunu sastharaya*. I am reminded here of a passage in Robert Knox's book in the chapter "Of the Inhabitants."

> They are very superstitious in making Observations of any little Accidents, as omens portending good to them or evil. . . . There is a little Creature much like a Lizzard, which they look upon altogether as a Prophet, whatsoever work or business they are going about; if he crys, they will cease for a space, reckoning that he tells them there is a bad Planet rules at that instant. They take great notice in a Morning at their first going out, who first appears in their sight: and if they see a White Man, or a big-bellied Woman, they hold it fortunate: and to see any decrepit or deformed People, as unfortunate. (Knox 1958:103)

There is also the science of the common black bird in Sri Lanka, the crow, *kaputu sastraya*. There is an involved science associated with the cry of this crow ranging from announcing out of town visitors, to the advent of good fortune, to misfortune. Appearance of the crow, the type of its cry, or with the side from which it appears portends different meanings—pleasure or displeasure, gain or loss, birth or death, and many other things.

A person carrying a pot full of water or a bunch of fresh cut flowers is a welcome sight, as they are considered good signs for prosperity. To see a beggar or a Buddhist monk is considered a bad omen. Paradoxically, much as monks are admired, they symbolically represent withdrawal from the world and its activities—not the best thought to have when you are stepping out to go to office. If one hears the cry of an owl at night, it is the harbinger of bad news or the death of a relative. There is no scientific explanation for all this; nevertheless, such beliefs are not uncommon in rural areas.

In the fourteenth-century poem "Salalihini sandesaya" which is about a message sent through the *salalihiniya* (a local bird in Sri Lanka), there is a stanza that specifies the good omens (*subhanimithi*) for the messenger to be aware of: soft and gentle fresh wind, pots full of water, luscious ripe mangoes, white lotus in bloom, beautiful happy words of young women, golden strands, waving of festive fans, powerful elephants. If you come across these on your journey, pay attention, for they are the best omens, more auspicious than the good astrological times.

A recent phenomenon in modern Sri Lanka is to visit the Indian *sadus* (saintly men) for much the same reasons. The horoscopes have already been written on *ola* leaves. Horoscopes of contemporary Asian and non-Asian people written on ancient palm (*ola*) leaves had been in South India for decades. These were believed to have been written by ancient *rishis* and include horoscopes of persons yet to be born in a series with dates and times. These were written for the guidance of the people. This is a costly process now, and only

the more affluent in Colombo and expatriates resort to this. Once I was passing the Galle road, the trunk route from Colombo to the south along the sea
coast, with a friend, Bill. I remarked that it would be a fun to get my *ola* leaf
read. He said he could get an appointment. (There is a great demand and a
long wait to get an appointment.) Through Bill's intervention I got a time. All
they requested was my date of birth and a thumb print (for a woman the left
thumb, and for a man the right thumb).

We were taken to a very modestly furnished, clean room overlooking the
beautiful Indian Ocean. Two men sat opposite us, one with a few *ola* leaf
books (the other was an interpreter). The *ola* leaf writings were read by the
Indian *sadu* in classical Tamil and translated into Sinhala or English depending on the preference of the client. All we had to do was to help him find the
correct reading. After a few attempts he stopped and read my full name. He
then went on to my father's name, which was an English name, and my
mother's full name, which was a conservative Sri Lankan name. He said I was
born in Sri Lanka but lived abroad, that I was a librarian and dealt with books,
and that I had master's degrees from well-known universities. He told my
husband's name and his profession and about my children. All this was the
genealogy chapter. All of it was accurate. One could choose the chapters one
would like to have read, and the reading of each chapter was charged for separately. I decided to get my family chapter, where he told me about my brothers and sisters and details about my children. I also got the last chapter read,
which told me the date and time of my death and my previous birth.

I am not sure what all this amounts to. Was it mind reading? But the
specificity and depth of detail was amazing. Was all this part of the mysteries
of the East, especially of India? If true (and I resist the conclusion) is our living merely an acting out of a script that was written long ago? Later I related
my interesting adventure to several of my friends in Chicago, and they too
later made their own pilgrimage to the place and found it very interesting.

When memory fails there are those precious moments that can never be
snuffed out. I remember my English teacher in Sri Lanka whose favorite lines
from Shakespeare were from Hamlet. I quote them as a postscript to my
sundry reflections on astrology: "There are more things in heaven and earth
Horatio than are dreamt of in your philosophy."

EIGHTEEN

God Kataragama

SOME CALLED HIM "MURUGAN." Others revered him as "Skanda." He was the son of Shiva. Sinhalese Buddhists, comparatively less knowledgeable about the pantheon of classical Hinduism, called him "Kataragama *deiyo*" (god) so named after the locality in which the jungle shrine is situated.

The Sinhala folk chronicle *Kanda Maala* has the story of the Sri Lankan legendary prince Dutugamunu, of the first century BC. When he was preparing for war with the Tamil king Elara, he was warned in a dream not to embark on the expedition, unless he secured the divine blessings and aid of the god Kataragama. Appearing in dreams is one way this god helped his devotees. The prince decided to make the trip to Kataragama to get the help of the god. He went through many penances in the god's territory, and one day while in meditation, he fainted. When he recovered the god appeared in front of the prince in the form of an ascetic, presented him with weapons, and assured him of victory. The prince made a vow that he would rebuild and endow the temple on his return. He ventured on the expedition, which ended in the defeat of Elara, and regained his crown.

Thousands of pious pilgrims from ancient times had made the traditional pilgrimage, the *pada yatra* (journey by foot), to the sacred place, from Jaffna to Kataragama, along the east coast of Sri Lanka. Everyone on pilgrimage sat in the open and slept in the open, in traditional resting places (*ambalamas*), or in temples. The *yatra* to Kataragama from Jaffna was a forty-five-day odyssey. Pilgrims being generally poor (none could carry adequate provisions to last forty-five days) depended on the sharing of food and hospitality of the villages they passed. They endured much hardship. They bore the heat of the scorching sun, rain, hunger and thirst, and encounters with wild animals and disease. At night the pilgrims under the golden stars (as they say in Sri Lanka) and in the glow of the campfire shared legendary stories and sang religious songs.

Kataragama is situated in the region of Ruhna in southeastern Sri Lanka and is about 130 miles from the metropolis of Colombo. Whatever the point of origin, all roads converge on Tissamaharama, which is about twelve miles from journey's end—the jungle shrine of Kataragama. The construction of modern highways and the amenities that go with them have made Kataragama easily accessible, but for much of its history Kataragama was virtually inaccessible. The proverbial hazards and dangers of the journey were part of the folklore and the mystique of the place.

THE LORE AND LURE OF KATARAGAMA

I have heard stories from my grandmother of a time when the only means of transport was by foot or by bullock carts. She had romantic, at times rather scary albeit devotional, stories to tell us. She talked of going through the jungle country teeming with herds of deer, sambur, wild boar, and even elephants. Among the stories were the terrifying ones of some who got sick and others who were killed or injured by herds of wild animals. She added that such people were punished for not being respectful to the god in his territory. In the endless journey of the night, a common bond arises from a sense of surrounding danger, makes friends of strangers. She talked of the overhospitality and kindness shown to each other by way of assistance in walking to elderly folk sharing of food and drink, and being kind and considerate. Under the canopy of golden stars against the muffled cries of jungle birds, often so plaintive and sad, men exchanged stories, wayfarers' tales of strange things that happened, mysterious incidents all to do with the great god and his powers. It was said that phantomlike *sadhus* looking like *rishis* of old suddenly appeared and melted into the night. Some others said that once in the surrounding jungle having strayed from the main party, they were lost. A stranger approached out of nowhere and pointed the way to Kataragama. When they turned around to thank him, he had disappeared. The only trace of his presence was a mound of sugar. So the night was fascinatingly enlivened.

Villagers on the way offered the pilgrims food, water, and sometimes a drink of young coconut and gave the pilgrims messages to the god in the way of *pandura* (*pandura* is a coin washed in saffron water for ritual purifying, tied in a clean white cloth, and offered to the god as a token of a promise when asking for a wish or sometimes as a token of goodwill). Dedicated pilgrims even today make the journey by foot. The pilgrimage begins when one leaves home. Traditional devotees undertake vows of self-denial, become vegetarians, refrain from smoking, and sometimes take vows of silence as ways of affirming their devotion.

Valliamma was a princess of sorts, a vedda princess, who lived in Ceylon many years ago and married the god of the mountain. Valli was only twelve years old when she had her heart set on the hunting god of the Kataragama mountain, whose power and wisdom was beyond human understanding. After many romantic escapades the two got married. The entire village took joy in the marriage of Valli and the god of Kataragama. Since that time they never left Kataragama and survive there in immortality. They say they are still like children; they have fun playing hide-and-seek with each other and with the devotees, who come in search of them from all over the island and from far away.

MANY SUPPLICANTS, MANY WOES

Devotees go to Kataragama with a specific reason or a specific agenda in mind. A variety of favors and blessings are asked of the god. The list is almost interminable—disease, physical afflictions of one sort or another, those whose medical conditions cannot be clinically cured, employment seekers, the hope of promotions, domestic strife, the birth of a child, a scholarship abroad, success in business ventures, and so on. The great god is believed to be endowed with infinite patience and compassion, to sort out all problems of all devotees. Repeated visits may be an indication of persistence in supplication or an index to success of prayers and imprecations. Presidents, prime ministers, and cabinet ministers have made their way to Kataragama. It all seems to work. One should not omit mention of litigation and legal issues, which in a society prone to litigiousness, becomes a genre in its own right. No Supreme Court judge or Solomon with all his wisdom could settle such complaints, yet there is indestructible faith that the great god can. Lavish gifts and bounties are offered to the god for favors. It would seem that the supplicants are very much aware of a quid pro quo principle in the gamut of spiritual transactions.

Many years ago much was made of a famous incident in Kataragama. It concerned the Ranjini taxi murder case, which involved a brutal murder and aroused national media attention. By coincidence when the family of the murder victim was exiting through a side entrance, after having asked the god for justice, the murderer was making an ostentatious entrance through the main entrance with its ornate, embossed brass portals leading to the sanctum. Such ironies, if one may call them such, were not unknown and added grist to the mill of the lore associated with the place and its mystique.

A VISITOR'S UNORTHODOX STYLE

It was the custom in Ananda' family to make an annual trip to Kataragama. It was fun to go with my father-in-law on trips because he relaxed in style. We could not ask him where we were going or the schedule. We knew that we were going to Kataragama via the central highlands, a particularly beautiful route. We broke journey at Ella in a fine bungalow in a tea estate. Our hosts were a wealthy Burgher family who had been close friends for many years of Ananda's family. Hubert and Connie Congreve were genial hosts. They too were invited to join the trip.

On the way, Father would stop near a little wayside tea kiosk speak to villagers about politics or their welfare and sometimes give them legal advice. He had been a socialist politician fighting for the rights of the working men and the underprivileged. Speaking to such people became his second nature. On our way back he would stop by the village vegetable stalls and buy local vegetables and fruit. Sometimes he bought the entire lot, feeling sorry for the villagers.

The tea kiosks (*thekades*) sold tea, local sweets, and *thambili* (young coconut, red in color) for thirsty travelers. I particularly remember how delicious the tea was brewed in a primitive way in locally invented utensils. The tea strainer was made with a cloth sewn around a circular wire, and the tea leaves in it were used many times over. Boiling hot water was poured into the funnel, and the tea came out hot and strong. Milk and a lot of sugar were added (milk was usually condensed milk) and then it was held high, poured over from one glass to another several times to make a hot foam on top. The final product was refreshing and tasty.

My father-in-law once decided to have a bath near a scenic waterfall. He loved water, and he was a forceful, determined personality. When he made up his mind, even the great Sakka could not change it. Everybody looked around, wondering how he was going to do this. We had not taken any change of clothes from the car, and we were quite a distance from it. Even my mother-in-law, who had some say in the decision making, could not talk him out of it. It was embarrassing to her because she was rather puritanical in her thinking, especially when her young daughter-in-law was in their company. For my part, I thought he was adventurous and admired him for his spontaneity. Father wore a large handkerchief for bathing trunks and got into the water. Even the largest handkerchief had its limitations. The handkerchief was not large enough to cover his essential body parts. My mother-in-law, embarrassed, showed her disapproval all the way. He had a good time and ignored the protests.

A SACRED GANGES IN SRI LANKA

When we arrived in Kataragama we stayed in a circuit bungalow, which had been given to Gamini, a friend of the family. He was the senior government official in charge of the entire district and had considerable clout. We enjoyed the privileges. Before going to the early morning *puja* we bathed in the Manik Ganga, the sacred river of the god as a purifying process. Although there was running water in which to bathe in the bun-

galow, in Kataragama one had to bathe in god's river. It was an important
ritual. Devotees bathed in the holy waters and wore clean white apparel for
the *puja*.

It was not appropriate to wear bathing suits in this part of the country.
Women wore the traditional *diyaredda* (the water cloth). It is piece of cloth
two meters long tied just above the swell of the breasts and reaching down to
the knees. This is traditional and considered by some as the sexiest bathing
costume. When wet it clings to the body, clearly outlining the contours of the
female figure and leaving little to the imagination of the observer. Women in
Sri Lanka wear the *diyaredda* when bathing outside at a river or at a hillside
water spout, at a well, or a community tap. We could not swim in this attire,
so we dipped in the cool murky brown water. Fish came in numbers and nib-
bled at our feet. Wriggling out of the wet *diyaredda* and into the white, dry
clothes with some kind of modesty was an accomplishment, given the large
number of spectators.

Manik Ganga is like the Ganges for the Hindus. The predominant factor being faith, it was not proper to talk about the cleanliness of the water,
although the water was muddy and unclean. One was reminded to guard one's
tongue at all times in the great god's country. It was the belief that the waters
of the river had miraculous healing powers.

Dressed in clean, white attire we went to rows of little shops, which sold
items for the *puja*. We needed a tray to offer to the god, with panduru (some
money to be placed on it) for the *kapurala*. The vendors had trays specially
arranged for this purpose, which differed in size and content. The more lavish ones commanded a higher price, as though all this mattered to the god. In
the trays were a variety of flowers, coconut, fruit, garlands of red flowers, and
items such as camphor. Red was the color for god Kataragama.

THE GOD'S INNER SANCTUM

Arriving at the *devale* the pilgrims really had nothing to see. The front room
of the *devale* was simple and bare. In the sanctum sanctorum hung a number
of curtains, one behind the other, thus separating the devotees from the god.
Only the *kapuralas* (officiating priests) were allowed inside these curtains,
which are never drawn apart. Inside the *devale* was a casket containing the
yantra (mystic diagram) representing the god, engraved on a golden tablet in
which his holy power and grace were believed to reside. There was no need to
have a statue or a pointer to reach god; it was the spirit that is important. The
presence of god was felt as an energy by the faithful while in his territory,
especially inside the *devale*.

The sounds of bells and conch blowing proclaimed the *puja* was in
progress. We joined the line of hundreds of other worshippers in front of the

devale. The devotees carried the *puja* trays, some on their heads, extending endlessly outside the temple. When it was our turn the *kapurala* took our trays into the inner shrine, and our hands were free to light the lamps. All offerings were done through the intermediary, the *kapurala*. On either side of the large room were rows of large brass lamps, and there was an empty passage all the way through the *devale* for those who officiated, serving the god. Men and women of all classes, high and low, rich and poor, freely moved about in the sacred space between the huge brass lamps in an air thick with perfumed smoke, lighting lamps, joss sticks, and camphor.

The god is worshipped for spiritual salvation and for deliverance of good fortune and curing of all human ills. We lit the lamps with the oil we had taken. Devotees took the sacred oil from the lamps, a family remedy for minor ailments such as headaches. There were brass bells of all shapes and sizes hung up from the ceiling inside the *devale*. We got hold of the strings and pulled the bells, which rang continuously with deafening raucousness throughout the service. The sound that the bells made, combined with drumming during the *puja* contributed to the ever-rising crescendo of noise. This was all a part of the *puja*, *sadda puja* (sound offering). Those who got their wishes granted offered brass bells and lamps or elaborately decorated cloth curtains with a picture of the god Skanda. There were many of these curtains at the entrance to the inner sanctum of the god. We stood there in reverence, each in silence asking for whatever we wished and promising to come again when it was granted.

In the great ritual there is at a certain point a lull, a sense of subsiding. The cacophonous clanging of bells has stopped. Everyone's eyes are directed to the *kapurala* dramatically extending his arms as if in an act of utter spiritual surrender over the hanging paintings of the great god. He repeatedly touches the entire expanse of the hanging picture, almost touching the body of the god, but not quite. Looking at him in silence, as intense as the din that would soon follow, are the devotees. One saw Sinhalese of all classes: Tamils, Indians, Westerners, Muslims, rich, poor, lords of the land, the lowly toiling proletariat, the sturdy, the crippled, the old, and exuberant youth all in subdued silence, humbled as equals under the god's canopy, all ritually cleansed, wearing white, with a common purpose to appeal to the god for help and his blessings. God would listen to them all, decipher their problems, and help each and every one. It seemed so beautifully symbolic, the near touching of a seemingly unhearing, unseeing god.

Here I saw conjoined a sense of unexpressed surreal unity, a poignant coming together of all of humanity, translocal, transregional, transracial, transgenerational, the peacock and the trident symbolized all. Then as a signal to spoil it all, the din of bells began to suggest that, nonetheless, we human beings will continue with our unremitting strife.

THE ELABORATE RITUALS OF OFFERINGS

The traditional service was complicated. There were a few women dedicated to the service dressed in colorful cloth and skimpy jackets and carried coconut oil clay lamps and other offerings to the god. A special offering of food was prepared daily in the *devale* kitchen (*muluthan*). It was rice cooked in *ghee* (milk), with raisins, jaggery, and nuts. This was done with care and reverence. *Muluthan* was brought at the *puja* time under a four-poled canopy by special attendants ceremoniously dressed for the occasion in red attire. When the *puja* was over, the drumming and the bells subsided. The priestly attendants emerged from the inner *devale* holding a brass tray of holy ash and sandal paste. Devotees clamored to receive a share of the sanctified ashes to smear on their foreheads. *Muluthan*, blessed by the god, was given in handfuls to all. The *kapuralas* returned part of the *puja* the devotees had offered to the god, divinely blessed. They ate what was given back for good luck, healing, and blessings.

Devale activity is a process of exchange. Worshippers offer *pujas* to the god through prayer, sacrifice, and offerings of food, fruit, flowers, coconut, and camphor. In turn the god blesses the worshippers with his divine presence. Pictures of Kataragama on screens inside the *devale* depicted him with six faces and twelve hands, riding a peacock. With the six heads he saw everything, and the peacock, his vehicle, is a sacred symbol. Peacock feathers were used in rituals and were considered symbols of good luck. Devotees chant devotional hymns to the god:

> *Muhunu sayaki ath dolasaki maurapita asane*
> *Kataragame pihiti kanda kadira deva rajane*
>
> The god of six faces and twelve hands who rides a peacock,
> the surrounding hills form the kingdom of this god of gods.

Devotees left the *devale* happy and contented. God had listened to each of their problems, all said in silence at the same time, with his divine presence and sorted out solutions and remedies to all it seemed. Pilgrims went about having the feeling of achievement to perform the next ritual, breaking a coconut at an assigned place in front of the *devale*. If the coconut broke in a certain way, it would indicate that wishes would be granted for a safe journey back home.

A GRAND RITUAL

What I have described is the *puja* activity of a normal day. In addition to this, the annual *devale* festivals are held in the month of Esala (July–August). This is of great importance to the Kataragama devotees, both Hindu and Buddhist. Every year on the full moon day of Vesak (May) or Poson (June) *kapuralas* at Kataragama perform the *kap hitawima* (vow-fixing) ceremony of planting a sapling tree in the vicinity of the temple. This is a promise to undertake the two-week-long festival in honor of the god. During the festival, every night a *perahera* (procession) is held to celebrate the god. The casket containing the mystic diagram or *yantra* is taken out of the *maha devale* by the *kapurala* on elephant back amidst the beating of drums, sounding of bells, wailing of conches, *kavadi* dances, and *haro-haras* (hosannas) of thousands of pilgrims. The procession goes to the Valli Amma *devale* where the *yantra* is left for thirty to forty-five minutes and then is brought back to the *maha devale* (main temple). This procedure is followed for two weeks. The *perahera* terminates with the water-cutting ceremony in the Manik Ganga when the *kapurala* bathes the *yantra* in the water, symbolizing the washing of the god polluted by sexual intercourse. During the fortnight of ceremony, mysticism and the supernatural reach their climax. Around the *devale* one would see pilgrims with their mouths gagged, some with silver arrows piercing lips and cheeks from end to end or the tongue pierced. Some pierce their back and hang from a beam or are dragged in a decorated cart in devotion to the great god. The mortification of the flesh and infliction of physical pain were to seek redemption from sins and favors from the god.

STRANGER THAN FICTION

I met Gillian, a cousin of Ananda's sister-in-law. She, a woman of Dutch extraction, was making a special trip to Sri Lanka to pay a *baraya* to the temple of Kataragama. She was not a Buddhist. I was told that her son was born deaf, and the available treatments in England at this time failed, so she made a vow to Kataragama that if the child was cured and if he got the ability to hear she would make the annual trip to Kataragama. I asked my sister-in-law, Pauline, how this was possible. She was surprised at my question. The simple explanation was that Gillian had faith in Kataragama, whose miraculous powers healed her son.

Once Henry's car got disabled in the middle of the jungle, and all they could do was pray to Kataragama for mercy. His wife, a Catholic, took out a rosary and prayed. There was no repair shop in sight, and it was dark with jungle all around. In the darkness of the night they switched off the light and prayed for mercy and forgiveness if they had inadvertently done anything wrong. From out in the woods a man approached with a traditional torch of fire offering help to fix the car. The car was fixed, and the visitor, who spoke little, literally vanished into the darkness. The party believed that he was a messenger from the god. Stories of this nature are plenty and much talked of.

KNOW ME WHEN YOU SEE ME

The lord appears in various human forms to sincere devotees in their unguarded moments to give them messages that heal the wounds of both body and mind, but just as they are brought to normal consciousness the divine messenger has already vanished, not to be seen again. I have read a story of a former British civil servant who was also a justice of peace. He was troubled by both stress and physical problems. His promotions were withheld, and he was superseded by local men from lower ranks. He had also been suffering from chronic skin ailments, which had not responded to treatment from physicians of the day in Ceylon. His own clerk suggested as a last resort a visit to Kataragama during the festival season when the power of the god is believed to be most potent. The civil servant made the pilgrimage to make a vow with his clerk while he was working in the Badulla Kachcheri. After the water-cutting ceremony, at the conclusion of the festivities, he was standing at the compound talking to his clerk when a mad man approached him and looking hard at his face exclaimed, "Go off to the north! You'll be all right." A few moments later when he searched for the mad man, he was nowhere to be found. When the festival was over the civil servant returned to Badulla with the clerk. A pleasant surprise awaited him, a telegram from the colonial secretary with instructions to assume duties as the government agent of the northern province. His stress was resolved. When he went to the northern province and was in his bungalow, his next-door neighbor, an old Ayurvedic physician visited him on his own accord, to treat his skin disease, and in a few days he was cured.

Many Sri Lankan Buddhists are not vegetarians, but for humanitarian and ethical reasons most Buddhists refrain from eating meat. The cow, per se is not a sacred animal in Buddhist culture. However, worshippers of Kataragama are generally required to abstain from consuming beef or any meat or fish and observe a strict vegetarian code. Vegetarian food is served, in rest houses and eating places that cater to the needs of pilgrims. Some devotees would observe a vegetarian regimen for many weeks or months prior to the visit to get better favors from the god.

POLLUTED WOMEN, KEEP AWAY FROM GOD

There are many do's and don'ts that one need be aware of both inside the *devale* and in the environs of the gods. During the period of menstruation women were considered unclean and would voluntarily refrain from entering the shrine. If there was a death or birth in the family one was not supposed to visit the *devale* for a period of time for reasons of *killi* (pollution). Whenever there was a death in the areas surrounding, the *devale* was closed. On that day there would be no *pujas* held until the body was removed and the place ritually cleaned. When we went to Kataragama with Ananda's friend Jerry and his wife, Yasa, it was considered not a good time for me to go inside the *devale*. I had a bath in the river, and while the others went inside I stayed outside. A senior lay priest came by and asked me why I was outside and gave me permission to go in. I was elated, after the long trip I too wanted to go inside, and I thought my monthly bleeding should not be a reason to stop me. I have heard many stories of bad happenings due to being disrespectful to the god. On our way out I sprained my ankle near the *devale*. It swelled and caused me great pain. I tend to talk a lot and I may have inadvertently said something disrespectful or may have been unclean, as Robert Knox records:

"Women having their natural infirmities upon them may not, neither dare they presume to come near the temples or houses of their gods. Nor the men, if they come out of houses where such women are" (Knox 1958:116).

I DANCED *KAVADI*

Over time I found myself going to Kataragama and observing the rituals even when Ananda was not with me. A visit with Bill and his wife, Anula, was memorable. Having participated in the *puja*, we were in the rest house. I always wanted to dance the *kavadi* and persuaded them to join me in the early hours of the morning. *Kavadi* is a sacred and special form of dance performed for the god. Devotees carry an arched shoulder pole, with lustrous tinsel and colored paper, adorned with peacock feathers, supported on their shoulders stepping and dancing to the drumbeat of popular music. A crowd of people danced *kavadi* to honor god Kataragama. It is a special *puja* for the god, often performed as a way of redeeming a vow, and was watched by large crowds. We danced for many hours. A popular song in the seventies about Kataragama was "Kanda suridinii" (god of the mountain). It was a song praising the power of the god sung by the Super Golden Chimes and especially suited for *kavadi* dances. It was played over and over again. Other music that suited the dance style of *kavadi* was *baila*. I was an oriental dancer in my young days, and I used the opportunity to dance to my heart's content. I wonder if I would have been able to do this if my conservative husband was with me. Women of my social background are not supposed to dance in public places, but I was dancing for a god and felt good. Besides, no one cared. We had a great time and came back vowing to go again.

WALKING ON FIRE

A more intense form of faith I have witnessed over the years was the fire walking at Kataragama in the name of god Skanda. This involved walking over a stretch of glowing embers. I was an inquisitive observer of a fascinating act. In Kataragama fire walking is done in devotion to the god. Extensive preparation is made for the ceremony. A four-foot-wide trench is dug extending to about thirty feet, and it is filled with wood and ignited. All throughout the ceremony it is kept alive and hot, by sweeping out the ashes to keep the fire burning. There were large crowds of spectators. The fire walkers were many and came from varied backgrounds. Some were veteran walkers who went from one ceremony to another, and they were the professionals. They walk the fire with ease without visible burns. Then there were the ones who were rather amateur and undertook it as penance to repay a *baraya* for a wish granted. I have heard stories such as that of a person who got an unexpected (probably undeserving position) in the government who walked the fire to show gratitude, and another after recovering from a serious illness also walked the fire. They prepared for this devotional act well ahead of time. They remained vegetarian for many months in preparation and followed a carefully regulated spiritual regimen. Some fire walkers spend a few days or weeks devoting their time to religious activities. Some Buddhists often perform elaborate Bodhi *pujas* to transfer merit to the god prior to their fire walking. It was an ultimate exercise in devotion and faith leading to power and renewed energy.

The fire walkers would attend the *puja* at the *devale* and pray to the god for courage and success in the venture. They bathed in the Manik Ganga, for ritual purification, and wore clean white or red clothes. They walked the fire one at a time at their own speed, some reciting devotional prayers to the god in faith.

GOD SAVED THE DAUGHTER

The story of my friend Sera and the vow her mother made when she was about four years old to go to Kataragama following a sickness is typical. It is a good illustration of faith Buddhists have in Kataragama. Sera was ill with double pneumonia. Her mother was desperate having lost her seven-year-old daughter to diphtheria. Being the youngest, Sera was precious to her. Her mother grieved and requested all the family to pray to save little Sera. They did not know to whom they could pray, as Buddha did not grant miracles. The whole house was sad, helpless, and miserable. The doctor was called in the night, and medicine was given to her. In her desperation the mother made a vow to visit Kataragama if Sera's life was saved. To Buddhists Kataragama is like Lourdes is to Catholics. She promised to do whatever the chief *kapurala* asked of her, to walk fire, or sweep the temple grounds, or dance *kavadi*.

With the break of dawn Sera's mother was up. The worst was over as she had signs of Sera's recovery. The whole household was delighted and relieved.

The family made the day-long trip to Kataragama to fulfill the promise. In the evening they came to the pilgrims' rest, and since it was not the season there was accommodation available. They spread mats and slept on the floor all huddled together. The following morning having bathed in the Manik Ganga, they went to the *puja*. The head priest of the *devale* had a strange appearance with a tiny knot of hair tied at the back of his head. He was stern and unapproachable. They took trays of fruit and flowers as offerings to god Kataragama. The head priest took them all in and returned the tray with cut fruit and smeared consecrated ashes from the inside of the temple on their foreheads as a blessing. The priest chanted many prayers. Through these prayers the gods have spoken to Sera's mother. The priestly attendant interpreted the desires of the gods for her mother. Sera's mother had to work in the temple grounds, sweeping all the courtyards surrounding the temple at dawn for three days. She was relieved that she did not have to walk fire or dance *kavadi*.

For three consecutive days Sera's mother woke up alone at dawn. She bathed and swept the temple courtyards. She swept the yard well, and the priest was pleased. She wanted to pay back the god for the great favor done to her, saving her beloved daughter. During these days she was quiet and peaceful, and the rest of the family followed suit. They were instructed to be careful in their speech in god's territory. Today Sera is a specialized doctor, a good Buddhist living an America, and she helps many people and engages in numerous religious activities.

In recent visits to Kataragama I noticed many changes. New access roads have been built and beggars spirited away from the sacred grounds. It is cleaner with modern conveniences. Pilgrim rests and hotels are provided for visitors, some in the nature of a four-star hotel. With political interest shown by successive governments, it has an aura of government sponsorship and support. It looks more like a place for a pleasure visit than a place of worship. Roadsides are made beautiful with flowering trees and bushes. Peacocks abound the place, proudly displaying their plumes. Many people visit Kataragama, unlike in the past, even if they do not have a particular request to make or a *baraya* to fulfill.

AN IMPISH ARTFUL DODGER

On my most recent visit to Sri Lanka, Ananda and I went to Kataragama. We bought *puja* trays from a vendor. I made a small tray of fruit to offer the god, the size that I could carry. A young boy appearing from nowhere persuaded me to let him carry it for me. I enjoyed talking to him. He had the character of the Artful Dodger in a gentler version. In conversation, I asked him if he went to school. He blurted out that the oil lamp, which he used to study by, fell, and his house burned. It sounded credible, but the ease with which he said it made me wonder. As we were walking towards the temple we saw a few Buddhist nuns. My young companion told me not to give them any donation as they smoked cigars and used ganja. He also told me they tell the sad story of how their houses got burned by a lamp. My companion and I were now friendly, and I turned to him and said, you too told me the same story. He then smiled impishly and told me that is the story they all say. I suggested to him that he should think of a different story next time. He laughed.

As we got to the entrance to the temple and there was a long line of people with *puja* trays, I had no intention of standing in line. He helped me to break the line and enter the temple; he knew all the tricks. We parted with my giving him a rather big tip. He flew away to carry another tray for another pilgrim with another story. I wondered how the good god would view these little cheatings of little people, in the powerful domain under his protection.

The actual temple however, remains the same in appearance in spite of the changes in the surrounding areas. I wondered why, with all the donations made by many pilgrims (some give lavishly for favors granted) and with all the political clout, there was little improvement to modernize the *devale*. It is the same structure I saw some forty years ago. Could it be that the god prefers to maintain its simpleå form, or is it unwillingness to change the god's sanctum? A modern housing for the god with elaborate décor, perhaps with air conditioning, would be impressive and convenient to pilgrims, or would the god worry about these external adornments knowing the pulchritude of celestial abodes?

Epilogue

Urged to write an epilogue, out of curiosity I randomly picked up a few books broadly within the genre and was struck by the absence at the end of the text. In older books it was de rigueur to write an epilogue. It made sense to do so. The epilogue serves the curiously psychological need to say one last thing, something in the grand manner before consigning one's manuscript to the vagaries and the perils of the book market where the best of books die young. In a pragmatic sense the epilogue enables the writer in the eleventh hour to attempt to rectify an omission in the text or to do some damage control.

For my part I have explained why I wrote this book, and I would like to add that the reader will be the best judge of whether I have succeeded. I consciously made it my purpose to let the subject speak for itself in unfolding the popular culture of Buddhism in Sri Lanka as it exists. I refrained from consciously structuring my narrative with prefabricated paradigms such as the current obsession with postmodern, and, more to the point, postcolonial interpretations. It seems to me that everything had to be structured to meet accommodation within a rigid mold. What in the process fades away or is obliterated is the spontaneity of the initial encounter between the author and its informant.

I count it a virtue in my book that I have made my informants the central characters in the unfolding drama. I was the narrator or more truly the faithful ancient scribe. Second, I believe I have brought out the volatility and protean nature of contemporary Buddhism in Sri Lanka that fascinatingly in a deeper sense reflects the very things about which Buddhist theory refers to. There are many Buddhisms in Sri Lanka, and it would be wrong to speak of Buddhism and Buddhist sociology in a rigidly normative sense. For example, in recent years, possibly arising out of the traumatized nature of the island there had been new developments in contemporary Buddhism in Sri Lanka such as neoritualistic forms of Buddhist worship and Buddhist-associated cults. It requires not merely a functional knowledge of the Sinhala language and its changing nuances but a deeper understanding of an idiom-related culture. In my book I have been sensitive to the new trends and changes that continue to transform Buddhism. And that is not the end of the story. Over a period of two years I visited the text on numerous occasions. It was not a functional exercise in crossing the Ts and dotting the Is. On each of these occasion I found that I was revising my subject with altered perspectives. It was a baffling experience whose depths I have not probed. I hope the reader has enjoyed my work and will make his or her own judgments.

Glossary of Religious Terms

akurukiyawima—first reading of letters

akusal—unwholesome actions

ambalama—resting places for travelers

ammavarunge dana—dana given to seven mothers in the name of goddess Pattini

arahat—enlightened person, one who has achieved transcendence

atapirikara—the basic eight requisites used by a monk and offered to monks by laymen

atasil—Eight Precepts

bali—a ceremony for exorcizing evil planetary influences

bana—Buddhist monk preaching a sermon

bana maduwa—preaching hall

bhavana—meditation

bhikkhu—Buddhist monk; a man who has given up the householder's life to live a life of heightened virtue

bhikkuni—Buddhist nun

Buddha puja—offerings to the Buddha

Buddha-sasana—Buddhist institutions and establishment in their totality

bodhi—Buddhist Enlightenment

Bodhi puja—ceremonies made under the Bo tree

Bodhisattva—one who aspires to become a Buddha

Bo tree—tree of the type (ficus religiosa) under which the Buddha attained Enlightenment

Buduge—place of worship, house of the Buddha

Buduguna—virtues of the Buddha

cetiya—stupa

dagaba—relic chamber, stupa

daham pasala—Buddhist Sunday school

dana—giving, the virtue of generosity

dayakaya—a person who gives to the sangha; a layperson

dasa sil—Ten Precepts

desana—teaching, preaching

deva—gods, deity

devatha—an inhabitant of the heavenly realms

dharma—Buddhist religious doctrine in its totality

dharma desana—Bana preaching by a monk

dharmaraja—righteous king

dharmarajjaya—righteous state

dharmasana—special seat used for preaching

dharmasala—place for preaching

devale—temple to a god of the Sinhala pantheon

divya loka—lay term for the celestial abode of the gods

diyaredda—cloth women wear in Sri Lanka to bathe in rivers, water falls etc.

dolosmaha pahana—lamp on temple premises which could be kept alight for twelve months

dosa—hatred, anger, ill-will

dukkha—stress; suffering; pain; distress; discontent

edanda—simple bridge, usually made of a tree trunk

Eight Fold Path—the path that leads to liberation

Enlightenment—complete elimination of all negative aspects of the mind

gathas—the technical term for verses or stanzas in the Buddhist canon.

gilampasa—beverage offered to the Buddha or a monks

golanama—novice monk who serve the senior monks

goyigama—the highest and the largest Sinhala caste

graha—planet-nine planets recognized by astrology

hamuduruwo—common term for a Buddhist monk

hevisi—drums; a particular kind of a cylindrical drum

indukatagema—ceremony for the first introduction of solid food, usually rice

Jataka—story of a former life of Buddha

kannalavva—invocation to god

kapruka—wish granting tree

kapurala—lay priest who serves in the temple of the gods

katina—a ceremony held in the fourth month of the rainy season when a monk receives a gift of cloth (robe) from a layperson

kattaduya—man who performs magic rituals to spirits

karuna—compassion

kendare—horoscope

killi—pollution

kiribath—rice cooked with milk for special occasions

kodivina—black magic

kotahalumagula—attaining puberty, or the coming of age for a young girl

kovil—Hindu temple

kusala—moral good

kuti—dwelling of meditation monks, or lay meditators

laukika—the mundane world

loba—greed

lokottara—above the world, supramundane

Loveda sagarava—15th century poem

magul bera—festive drums

mahakaruna—great compassion

maha pirit—three main suttas, Maha Mangala sutta, Ratana sutta and Karaneiya Metta sutta

malabatha—first meal cooked in the house after the funeral

manne—small axe

mantra—charm, spell

matakadane—a dana given in memory of the dead

mataka bana—homily of remembrance

matakavastra—twenty yards of white cloth presented to monk as part of a ritual in a funeral service

mara—the classic personification of evil and temptation in Buddhism often personified

margosa—Azadirachta indica also known as kohomba

metta—loving-kindness

nadegura—leader of the pilgrim party

naga—a kind of demi-god

nikaya—an organizational group of sangha in Sri Lanka belonging to a particular exclusive sect

nirvana—Buddhist Enlightenment leading to emancipation from the samsaric cycle of birth and death

pada yatra—pilgrimage by foot

Pali—a middle Indo-Aryan language. The language of the Theravada Buddhist canon

pahan puja—offering of lamps to the Buddha

paligahanawa—cursing

pandura—coin which accompanies a offering or request to a god

pansakula—12 yards of white cloth offered to a monk at a funeral

pansala—monastery, temple

pansil—Five Precepts

patimokkha—The basic code of monastic discipline, consisting of 277 rules for monks

patra—begging bowl or merit bowl

pau—sin

pavada—cloth traditionally spread on ground, as a mark of respect for people of distinction to walk on

perahera—procession, often religious

pin—moral good

pinannumodana—transfer of merit

pindapata—monks begging around for their daily meal

pinkama—act of merit

pin pettiya—merit box

pin potha—journal of meritorious deeds kept to be read at the time of death, recording of good deeds

pinsiddavewa—may you acquire good merit

pirikara—requisites for a monk

pirit—ceremony at which certain texts from the Pali canon are recited to avert evil

piritpota—book of protection

poya—quarter day of the lunar calendar; full moon or no moon

prathajjana—"worlding" or run-of-the-mill person. An ordinary person who has not yet realized any of the four stages of Awakening

prathana—an aspiration

preta—a "hungry shade" or "hungry ghost"—one of a class of beings in the lower realms, sometimes capable of appearing to human beings

puja—act of worship an offering before an object in a temple

Rodiya—lowest cast, gipsy-like people

sakra or *sakka*—the king of gods

samanera—Buddhist novice monk

samsara—the round of births

sangha—Buddhist monastic order

sasana—the totality of the institutions of Buddhism

sasara purudda—inclination of temperament and behavior coming from previous births as if by habit

Siddhartha—name of the Buddha before Enlightenment

sil, sila—precept, moral undertaking.

sima—boundary

stupa—large mound containing the relics of the Buddha

sutta—canonical scriptures that are regarded as records of the oral teachings of the Buddha.

tanha—craving

thathagatha—a Buddha, one who has thus come or arrived. A term of self reference used by the Buddha

Theravada—doctrine of the elders

tisarana—threefold refuge

tovil—bali ceremony

Uddana—the third book of the *Khunddaka Nikaya* collection of short suttas, a short verse by the Buddha

upasaka—the man who has taken the Ten Precepts

upasampada—higher ordination ceremony

uposatha—poya, observance day for monks

vandana—worshipping, act of worship

vas—rainy reason during which monks are to stay in one place

vihara—Buddhist temple
vinaya—Buddhist monastic discipline
vipaka—the fruition of a former deed (karma)
yakayadura—exorcist
yantra—amulet
yatikawa—invocation to a god

Bibliography

SOURCES CONSULTED

Abeysekara, Ananda. *Colors of the Robe*. Columbia: University of South Carolina Press, 2002.

Deegalle, Mahinda. *Bana: Buddhist Preaching in Sri Lanka: Special Focus on the Two-pulpit Tradition*. PhD. Dissertation, University of Chicago, 1995.

De Silva, Lynn. *Buddhism: Beliefs and Practices in Sri Lanka*. Colombo: Wesley Press, 1980.

Davids, Rhys J. W., trans. *The Questions of King Milinda*, 1894, vol. 1, reprint. Delhi: Motilal Banarsidass, 1969.

Disanayaka, J. B. *The Monk and the Peasant: A Study of the Traditional Sinhalese Village*. Colombo: State Printing Corporation, 1993.

Eck, Diana L. *A New Religious America*. New York: Harper San Francisco, 2002.

Gombrich, Richard F. *Buddhist Precept and Practice: Traditional Buddhism in the Rural Highlands of Kandy*. Oxford: Clarendon, 1971.

Gombrich Richard F., and Obeysekere, Gananath. *Buddhism Transformed: Religious Change in Sri Lanka*. Princeton, New Jersey: Princeton University Press, 1988.

Kariawasam, A .G. S. *Buddhist Ceremonies and Rituals of Sri Lanka*. Kandy, Sri Lanka: Buddhist Publication Society, 1995.

Knox, Robert. *An Historical Relation of Ceylon*. Maharagama, Ceylon: Saman, 1958.

Piyadassi, Thera. *The Buddha's Ancient Path*. London: Rider, [1964].

——— . *The Book of Protection*. Kuala Lumpur, Malaysia: Buddhist Missionary Society, 1992.

Saddhatissa, H. *Buddhists Ethics*. Boston: Wisdom, 1997.

Seneviratne, H. L., and Wickremeratne, Swarna. "*Bidhi-puja*: Collective Representation of Sri Lanka Youth." *American Ethnologist* 7, no. 4 (1980): 734–43.

Stevenson I. *Children Who Remember Previous Lives*. Charlottesville: University of Virginia, 1987.

Rahula, Walpola. *What the Buddha Taught*. Bedford: Gorden Fraser, 1959.

SUGGESTIONS FOR FURTHER READING

Amunugama, Sarath. "Buddhaputra or Bhumiputra? Dilemmas of Modern Sinhala Buddhist Monks in Relation to Ethnic and Political Conflict." *Religion* 21 (1990): 115–39.

Batholomeuez, Tessa. "In Defense of Dharma: Just-War Ideology in Buddhist Sri Lanka. *Journal of Buddhist Ethics* (1991).

Bond, George D. *The Buddhist Revival in Sri Lanka*. Columbia: University of South Carolina Press, 1988.

——. *Buddhism at Work: Community Development, Social Empowerment and the Sarvodaya Movement*. Bloomfield, CT: Kumarian, 2004.

Deegalle, Mahinda. *Popularizing Buddhism: Preaching as Performance in Sri Lanka*. Albany: State University of New York Press, 2006.

——. "Politics of the Jathika Hela Urumaya Monks: Buddhism and Ethnicity in Contemporary Sri Lanka." *Contemporary Buddhism* 5, no. 2 (2004):83–103.

De Silva, Lily. *The Cult of the Bodhi-Tree*. Ceylon Studies Seminar Paper no. 55, 1975. Cyclostyled.

Carrithers, Michael. "The Domestication of the Sangha." *Man* 19, no. 2 (1984): 321–22.

——. *The Forest Monks of Sri Lanka: An Anthropological and Historical Study*. New Delhi: Oxford University Press, 1983.

Holt, Clifford John, Kinnard, Jacob N., Walters, Jonathan S., eds. *Constituting Communities: Theravada Buddhism and the Religious Cultures of South and Southeast Asia*. Albany: State University of New York Press, 2003.

Kemper, Steven. "Buddhism without Bhikkhus: The Sri Lanka Vinaya Vardana Society." In Bardwell L. Smith, *Religion and Legitimation of Power in Sri Lanka*, pp. 212–35 Chambersburg, PA: Anima, 1978.

——. *The Presence of the Past: Chronicles, Politics and Culture in Sinhala Life*. Ithaca, NY: Cornell University Press, 1991.

Obeysekera, Gananath. "The Fire Walkers of Kataragama: The Rise of Bhakti Religiosity in Buddhist Sri Lanka." *Journal of Asian Studies*, 37, no. 3 (1978). 457–76.

Imagining Karma: Ethical Transformation in Amerindian Buddhist and Greek Rebirth. Berkeley: University of California Press, 2002.

Panabokke, Gunaratne. *History of the Buddhist Sangha in India and Sri Lanka*, Kelaniya: Post-Graduate Institute of Pali and Buddhist Studies, 1993.

Seneviratne, H. L. *Rituals of the Kandyan State*. Cambridge: Cambridge University Press, 1978.

——. *The Works of Kings: The New Buddhism in Sri Lanka*. Chicago: University of Chicago Press, 1999.

Smith, Bardwell, ed. *Religion and Legitimation of Power in Sri Lanka*. Chambersburg, PA: Anima, 1978.

Southwold, M. *Buddhism in Life: the Anthropological Study of Religion and the Sinhalese Practice of Buddhism*. Dover, NH: Manchester UI University Press, 1983.

Tambiah, S. J. *Buddhism Betrayed? Religion, Politics and Violence in Sri Lanka.* Chicago: University of Chicago Press, 1992.

Wickremeratne, Ananda. *Genesis of an Orientalist: Thomas William Rhys Davids and Buddhism in Sri Lanka.* Columbia, Missouri: South Asia Books, 1985.

———. *Buddhism and Ethnicity in Sri Lanka: A Historical Analysis.* New Delhi: Viakas, 1995.

———. *The Roots of Nationalism: Sri Lanka.* Colombo, Sri Lanka: Karunaratne and Sons, [1995].

Index